Religion, Media, and the Marketplace

Religion, Media, and the Marketplace

EDITED BY LYNN SCHOFIELD CLARK

RUTGERS UNIVERSITY PRESS

NEW BRUNSWICK, NEW JERSEY, AND LONDON

LIBRARY OF CONGRESS CATALOGING-IN-PUBLICATION DATA

Religion, media, and the marketplace / edited by Lynn Schofield Clark.
   p.   cm.
   Includes bibliographical references and index.
   ISBN-13: 978-0-8135-4017-7 (hardcover : alk. paper)
   ISBN-13: 978-0-8135-4018-4 (pbk. : alk. paper)
   1. United States—Religion.   2. Mass media—Influence.
   3. Sales promotion.   4. Religion and culture.   I. Clark, Lynn Schofield.
   BL2525.R46863 2007
   201.'7—dc22

                     2006019592

A British Cataloging-in-Publication record for this book is available
from the British Library.

Manufactured in the United States of America

For my family

CONTENTS

PART THREE
Representations of the Religious "Other" in Popular Media and in the Marketplace

PART FOUR
Media Courted, Media Resisted: Popular Rituals and Artifacts in the Crafting of New Public Religious Practices

PREFACE

As you read this book, take a moment to look around you. What brands are you wearing? What advertisements or promotional materials do you see on the walls nearby, or at the tables or desks around you? What sounds or music can you hear in the background? What's on your computer screen? If you're like most people, you will find that you are surrounded by both the popular media and evidence of the global marketplace.

Generally, people tend to think that the popular media and the global marketplace have little to do with the practices and beliefs of religion. Popular media and the stuff of the marketplace are contemporary and current, whereas religion is ancient and timeless. Popular media and especially things related to marketing are all about materialistic matters, whereas religion is about the spiritual and ethereal. Popular media and the marketplace can be crass and tasteless, whereas religion is something that elevates and inspires. But is that *really* the way we experience religion in our everyday lives: as something immaterial, ethereal, elevating? No, of course not. Religion is always experienced and practiced in a specific cultural context, and today's context is saturated by popular media and artifacts of the marketplace. So we experience and practice religion today in ways that reflect, draw upon, and sometimes even resist the media and the marketplace—but we never get away from that context. Religion, of course, is culturally bound, rather than out of time, and out of context.

It may be true that the world is more commercialized today and that people are more media-saturated than at any previous time in history. Yet it simply isn't the case that once there was a time when people were able to exist in everyday life and have no contact with the stories, sounds, images, and even persuasive techniques of those who wished to influence, sell, barter, or trade something. Religion has always taken place within cultural contexts largely shaped by both the culture's storytellers and the expectations of the marketplace of the day. And because the various religions of the world have had their own stake in the practices of storytelling and goods-selling, religion has always had some kind of interaction with the marketplace and the media of the day. Having a stake implies a struggle or a contest between differing cultural groups, and thus, as this volume will demonstrate, the media and the marketplace are important cultural locations in which struggles over ideas, economics, and cultural authority have played out.

This book is a collection of case studies of religion's relationship with forms of mass communication and the sale of commodities. It is organized to draw attention to the ways in which the logic of the market is transforming the meaning and experience of religions, and to explore the cultural and political conflicts that are at stake about what forms different religions are taking in and through these transformations. As you read through it, you will be invited to consider how religions have changed, or are changing, in relation to commercialism, consumerism, and economic development, as well as in relation to technological innovation, cultural diversity, and globalization. Yet throughout, attention is drawn not only to the power of the market or the media in influencing religion, but to the ways in which the market, the media, and religion as well are marshaled to reinforce and legitimize the organization of power as it exists in contemporary social relations. In other words, the marketplace and the media, as institutions of culture, are central locations for struggles over power and definition involving religion. It is in the marketplace and in the media that people and groups struggle over which form of religion is most important (and for whom), how religions relate to the identity of particular nations, and what the appropriate role of religion is within particular individual nations and in international relations.

The debates and protests surrounding the Muhammed cartoons published in a Danish right-wing newspaper in 2005 and republished worldwide in 2006 highlight this struggle. Many in the West ardently defended the publication of the cartoons under the notion of *freedom of expression* so central to democratic nations. Yet some in the Arab world pointed to the fact that Arab and Islamic societies want to enjoy *freedom from Western subjugation* and argued that the publication and reprinting of the cartoons were just illustrations of what they consider to be neo-colonial policies that favor the West at the expense of Arab-Asian regions of the world. Thus, the worldwide Muslim protests may have been as much about the right to be free from political and economic discrimination as the right to take a stand against what many considered to be insulting and blasphemous cartoons.[1] For those in the West, the cartoons and the furor they caused represent a cultural struggle, sometimes discussed as a "clash of civilizations" between a culture defined by individual freedoms and a culture under religious authority. In contrast, for those in the Arab-Islamic world, the cartoons and their publication represent a political struggle that has had serious economic and political repercussions for Muslim citizens around the globe. For the West, whether or not to publish the cartoons was a question of religion and its appearance in the media of a "free" nation; for the Arab-Islamic world, it was also a question of religious and political groups and their right to define their own political organization as well as their relationship to the global marketplace.

Religion, media, and the marketplace all play a role in how a culture's norms and values are defined and represented in specific contexts. They each contribute to shaping the ways in which a society's values and norms are conceptually or ideologically related both to the nation and to the market, and they also play a role in how some people will be identified as "insiders" who belong in a culture—and conversely, how others will be identified as the "others," or those at the margins. Ultimately, the struggle over access to the media and the marketplace is one of who will have access to the public imagination. How these issues play out in specific contexts of differing cultures and religions and the relations between them, and their struggles in media and in the marketplace, are at the heart of this volume.

The book is divided into four sections, and each chapter has a brief introduction designed to help you to understand the chapter's contribution to the overall approach of this book. The first section explores the negotiations between the aims of religious leaders and the prerogatives of capitalism, looking at how leaders in Christian and Jewish traditions have navigated the connections between the desire to have religious influence and the need to do so in the context of a commercial marketplace. The first chapter in this section is by David Nord, a historian who has traced the

ways in which Christian organizations negotiated their aims of evangelism
and teaching in the early publishing marketplace. By placing an emphasis
on giving away as well as selling books, these earlier purveyors of mass
media inadvertently paved the way for the development of a vibrant book
trade in the U.S. colonies. The second chapter, by Anne Borden, extends
the questions of this business/religion negotiation, looking at the case of
contemporary Christian booksellers. She explores how these business owners and their workers negotiate the inevitable tensions that emerge between
business acumen and the Christian goals of evangelism and teaching. The
final chapter in the section, by Hillary Warren, considers the development
of a small yet focused children's video market for Jewish children. These
videos are designed to provide material products for leisure time and for
religious socialization. Through the lens of a religious community that is in
the minority in the United States, this chapter explores the question of
how groups of little interest to the capitalist marketplace seek to carve out
a specific niche for the purposes not of evangelism, but of religious identification, belonging, and distinctiveness.

Chapters in the book's second section extend the themes of religious
identity as shaped in relation to media and the marketplace, exploring cases
in which intercultural conflict has figured in this interaction. Exploring the
tensions between Hindu nationalists and Christian missionaries in India,
Gauri Viswanathan looks at current struggles concerning economic development and India's place within a global market largely defined by Western
capitalist values. She considers how the question of literacy itself has come
under fire for its purported relation to a process of Westernization that
many in India would like to resist. How might one maintain a distinctive
Indian/Hindu identity, and what does that mean in the context of a postcolonial society with sizeable Christian and Muslim minorities, ambitions
of global economic development, and a satellite on nearly every back patio?
The question of distinctiveness in the midst of tension is elaborated in the
second chapter of this section, as Maryellen Davis explores the ways in
which Marian devotion was marshaled for political ends in the United
States during the First World War. Purchasing the media, medals, and other
memorabilia that carried the various Marian societies' politically charged
messages served the identity needs of those who wanted to embrace an
American and a distinctively Catholic identity in the context of a nation

largely defined as Protestant at the time. Expanding on the theme of U.S. Protestant hegemony and its relationship to intercultural politics and international relations, Erica Sheen's chapter examines how Hollywood professionals constructed Muslim identity in the film *The Prince of Egypt* and how various Muslim groups in the United States and elsewhere interpreted and responded to those representations. She concludes with reflections on Stephen Spielberg's film *Munich* and its expression of further ideas that play into political and economic international relations between the United States, Israel, and largely Muslim nations.

The book's third section continues to explore the representation of religious "others" in media, in the nation, and in religion itself. This section begins with a chapter by Phyllis Alsdurf. Alsdurf examines how evangelical Protestant leaders, who were on the rise in cultural authority in the 1950s, legitimated their claims about the relationship between evangelicalism and the "American way of life." She traces how these leaders saw in the presidential nomination of John F. Kennedy a threat to the very nation and, as a result, sought to marshal the public opinion of the evangelical Protestant troops through the pages of the then-nascent magazine *Christianity Today*. She argues that the 1960s were watershed years for the transformation of the American religious landscape, and *Christianity Today* played a role in defining evangelicalism's shift to a position of tolerance for, and eventually coalition with, American Catholics. Ferruh Yilmaz also focuses on the question of religious others, their relationship to the nation and its economics, and their representation in the media. Rather than finding increased tolerance, however, Yilmaz looks at how the lines of religious distinction and demarcation have hardened in the past few decades in Europe, exploring the ways in which Muslim identity is collapsed into immigration problems of Europe, as witnessed in the European press and politics. In the final chapter of this section, Kwabena Asamoah-Gyadu considers the ways in which African religious leaders are represented in opposition to one another in popular African cinema, including the traditional priest or diviner, who reveals peoples' destinies, and the Protestant pastor, who is depicted as at risk for falling under the influence of occult powers. Echoing the concerns of Viswanathan's earlier chapter, about the colonial other who has shaped and threatened traditional society, Asamoah-Gyadu considers how each religious leader becomes an other when contrasted with the other in popular culture and among religious groups vying for authority in West Africa.

The book's fourth and final section foregrounds the struggle over the power to define what religion or ritual looks like and how marketplace goods and beliefs are marshaled when certain religiously inflected rituals enter the public, mediated realm. In the first chapter, Lee Gilmore examines the media relations practices that are a part of the Burning Man festival, looking to how those involved in the festival seek to manage coverage of the event's spiritual, religious, anticapitalist, and countercultural dimensions while also providing interpretations of its spectacular visuals. This section concludes with a chapter by Regina Marchi. Building upon the interaction between media frameworks and expectations of religious practitioners, Marchi explores the ways in which various leaders in the Latino community have attempted to marshal the popularity of Day of the Dead rituals in efforts to build political solidarity among Latinos. She argues that such efforts often yield mixed results, in part because the material objects related to Day of the Dead have taken on a cultural cache through their association with art galleries and exhibits. Both of these chapters consider public events that have both religious and sociopolitical dimensions, and these events are highly mediated and include engagement with the marketplace in distinctive and interesting ways.

Together, these contributions will acquaint you with several concerns that are now at the forefront of how we can understand religion and its role in relation to contemporary culture, including issues of globalization and the growing influence of evangelicalism and Islam in key locations around the world; historic tensions over religious and political aims; struggles over the power to define and create distinctions between the religious, the cultural, the public, and the spectacular; and familial, organizational, and individual desires to maintain religious traditions in the face of contestation from other influences in culture. The volume includes contributions from sociologists, anthropologists, literary critics, historians, theologians, and scholars in mass media and in material culture, thus contributing to an emergent interdisciplinary conversation in creative and boundary-breaking ways.

An introductory essay begins the volume, setting the context for further examination of religion, media, and the marketplace and their relationships to the organization of social, political, and economic relations. This introduction explores relevant theories of religion and the nation, of religious material culture, studies in the sociology of religion, and studies in the development of the interrelated industries of marketing, advertising, and the media. It explores these theories through an examination of three cases of religious lifestyle branding at the intersection of religion, media, and the national and international marketplace: fashion Bibles, Hindu-inflected bhangra parties, and Muslim pop music.

NOTE

1. See the Point/Counterpoint Commentary, "Drawing a Line," featuring Daniel Pipes, "Will the West resist or give in to Islamic supremacists?" and Rami G. Khouri, "Europeans' arrogance the cause of Muslim anger," two editorials in the *Denver Post*, February 11, 2006, 10C, 11C.

ACKNOWLEDGMENTS

This book had its beginnings with a dissertation fellowship program in media, religion, and culture that was generously funded by the Lilly Endowment, Inc. The program, in existence from 2001 to 2007, was administered by the University of Colorado's School of Journalism and Mass Communication under the direction of Stewart M. Hoover and Lynn Schofield Clark. Several of the contributors to this volume were recipients of this fellowship and participated in joint activities during their final years of dissertation writing. Other contributors to this volume provided leadership and acted as resource persons to this gathering of dissertation fellows or served as reviewers of dissertation fellowship applications, and still others joined the conversation later upon invitation. Kristi Long, a former editor at Rutgers University Press, provided key direction in the development of this project, as did Diane Alters, former fellowship coordinator for the Media, Religion, and Culture Dissertation Fellowship Program and now assistant city editor at the *Denver Post*. Special thanks go to editor Adi Hovav, Beth Kressel, and Marilyn Campbell at Rutgers, who patiently ushered this project to publication; to Crystal Atkinson at the University of Colorado, who provided copyediting assistance; and to Morehshin Allahyari at Tehran University, who coordinated the photo for the book's cover.

"Free Grace, Free Books, Free Riders: The Economics of Religious Publishing in Early Nineteenth-Century America," by David Nord, was originally published as "Free Grace, Free Books, Free Riders: The Economics of Religious Publishing in Early Nineteenth-Century America," in *The James Russell Wiggins Lecture in the History of the Book in American Culture* (Worchester, MA: Proceedings of the American Antiquarian Society, 1997). Material from this chapter also appears in David Nord's book *Faith in*

Reading: Religious Publishing and the Birth of Mass Media (New York: Oxford University Press, 2004). It is reprinted with permission.

Parts of the "Introduction: Identity, Belonging, and Religious Lifestyle Branding (Fashion Bibles, Bhangra Parties, and Muslim Pop)," by Lynn Schofield Clark, were published as "The Emergence of Lifestyle Branding: Fashion Bibles, Bhangra Parties, and Muslim Pop," in *Papers from the Trans-Tasman Research Symposium, Emerging Research in Media, Religion, and Culture*, ed. Peter Horsfield, 22–39 (Mebourne: RMIT Publishing, 2005).

"*The Ten Commandments* and *The Prince of Egypt*: Biblical Adaptation and Global Politics in the 1990s," by Erica Sheen, here re-titled "Cartoon Wars: *The Prince of Egypt* in Retrospect," and "Literacy in the Eye of the Conversion Storm," by Gauri Viswanathan are reprinted with permission from *Polygraph: An International Journal of Culture and Politics* 12 (2000).

" 'Blowing the Cover': Imaging Religious Functionaries in Ghanaian/ Nigerian Films," by J. Kwabena Asamoah-Gyadu, is reprinted with permission from the *Legon Journal of Humanities* (2003).

Religion, Media, and the Marketplace

Introduction

Identity, Belonging, and Religious Lifestyle Branding
(Fashion Bibles, Bhangra Parties, and Muslim Pop)

LYNN SCHOFIELD CLARK

In the summer of 2003, ABC News interviewed Laurie Whaley, a spokeswoman for Thomas Nelson Bibles, about the new Bible her company was about to release. The Bible, called *Revolve,* had been designed to look more like a fashion magazine than the small-print, leather-bound, gilt-edged book that is familiar to most people. The magazine layout came about as a result of market research aimed at reaching the burgeoning Christian teen female market, Whaley said. "We asked teen girls how often they read the Bible," and "the response that came back was, 'Well, we don't read the Bible,'" Whaley said. She noted that in focus groups the teen girls told her, "'It's just too freaky, too intimidating. It doesn't make any sense.'" So, with the help of Hayley DiMarco, who had worked in teen marketing for Nike before coming to Thomas Nelson Bibles, the company created a complete New Testament for teen girls that freely drew its look from *Cosmo Girl, Seventeen,* and *Teen People.*[1]

According to the Christian Booksellers Association, *Revolve,* dubbed the "fashion Bible" by journalists, was the best-selling Bible of 2003.[2] Whereas normally about forty thousand Bibles are sold each year, *Revolve* was selling forty thousand copies a month shortly after its release.[3] Thomas Nelson quickly followed up its success with *Refuel,* the New Testament magazine designed specifically for boys, that borrowed its look from skateboard, soccer, and guitar magazines. In addition to the complete New Testament, it contained music reviews and lists of dos and don'ts such as "Don't pretend you don't know your family" and "Do wear clean underwear." Later, Thomas

1

BEAUTY SECRET

TIME WITH GOD

As you apply your sunscreen, use that time to talk to God. Tell him how grateful you are for how he made you. Soon, you'll be so used to talking to him, it might become as regular and familiar as shrinking your pores.

FIGURE I-1 "Beauty Secret: As you apply your sunscreen, use that time to talk to God," from *Revolve: The Complete New Testament* for teens, © 2003.

Nelson released *Becoming,* a *Good Housekeeping* look-alike designed to appeal to young twenty-something women, and *Magnify,* a "Biblezine for kids" that resembled *Highlights* and *Jack and Jill.* They also returned to the lucrative teen market, releasing *Revolve #2* and *Revolve: Psalms and Proverbs* in 2004, *Refuel: The Epic Battles* in 2005, and a new *Revolve* in 2006.

The complete New Testament is offered on the pages of these magazines, framed by a number of colorful sidebars and photo illustrations. On one page, from the first *Revolve,* you can read, "Beauty Secret: Time with God: As you apply your sunscreen, use that time to talk to God. Tell him how grateful you are for how he made you. Soon, you'll be so used to talking to him, it might become as regular and familiar as shrinking your pores."[4]

Perhaps for some, there is no problem with this linking of consumerism, Christianity, and skin care. Yet it does raise the question, What *is* this phenomenon, exactly? Is this "fashion Bible" an item of religion or of popular culture? Is it timeless reading material or a disposable consumer product? Is it something that is superficial and transitory or something that expresses ideas about what it means to be a certain kind of U.S. citizen and Christian at this point in history? It is all of these things and more, of course. The aim of this chapter—indeed, of this entire volume—is to explore the kinds of products and practices, like the fashion Bible, that are emerging today and have emerged in the past at the intersection of religion, media, and the marketplace. These products and practices are not found only in the United States, nor are they unique to Christianity. As a result of an expanding global marketplace, such phenomena are present in ways that cross all kinds of religious beliefs and practices, in all kinds of locations.[5] They intersect with and represent issues of religious identification, and they mediate struggles over religious and national identity in ways that are both interesting and "epic," to quote the title of one Thomas Nelson Biblezine. The goal of this book, then, is to consider these questions: How do the things that we pay for—the consumer goods, leisure activities, artifacts of popular culture, and news publications—become imbued with meaning within the context of religious cultures? How are these paid-for items related to and expressive of larger concerns of an emergent global economy in a culturally and religiously diverse world? How do different social groups marshal these and other products in the media and the marketplace to maintain or challenge bonds between religions and nations, between religions and economies, between religions and cultures? And what role do the media and the global marketplace play in these struggles? What are the inevitable contradictions that arise in this nexus of religion, media, and the marketplace? And how are these resolved—if, indeed, they are?

To set the context for the chapters that follow, this introduction explores these questions by considering three case studies, at the intersection of religion, media, and the marketplace, that are meant to highlight some of the issues that are woven throughout the rest of the book. First, however, these issues are briefly framed in relation to three different sets of scholarship: studies of religious material culture, studies in the sociology of religion, and studies on developments in the interrelated marketing, advertising, and media industries. I will then propose that we consider these phenomena and their appeal in relation to what I will label the emergence of "religious lifestyle branding," as I will explain below.

Religious Material Culture Studies

Where did all of this consumerism in religion come from, one might ask? Isn't religion about asceticism, ritual, and even self-denial? The answer to this latter question seems to be yes and no. Religion in the United States, in particular its Protestant variant, has had strong ties to asceticism and self-denial. Most people would relate this connection to Calvinism's emphasis on the need for restraint when it comes to earthly pleasures. Calvinism tends to applaud hard work and self-discipline as practices consistent with the Christian faith and its place in the world. Yet the Protestant work ethic, as Max Weber first pointed out, can lead to monetary as well as spiritual rewards, thus giving rise to the question, What does one do with the financial benefits that are assumed to be the results of one's faithful submission?[6] If they are spent on such things as artwork that glorifies God or readings that encourage greater faithfulness, would that not also be considered an aspect of faithful practice? Such negotiations of faith and finance resonate throughout the intertwined histories of religion, modernity, and capitalism.

In the United States, Christianity has been a majority religion since the country's beginnings, and as such it should not be too surprising to see an intersection between Christianity and the development of the consumer marketplace. This interrelated history has been of interest to a number of U.S. historians who deal with religion and media. David Nord, whose chapter follows this one, has traced the sale and free distribution of Bibles as material cultural products, noting that while Bibles were expressions of faith and vehicles for literacy in eighteenth-century U.S. culture, they were also products that served to establish expectations in the realm of publishing and book sales.[7] Historians Lawrence Moore and Charles Lippy have similarly considered how religious leaders in the United States have interacted with the marketplace, paying particular attention to those religious leaders and organizations that sought out the commercial realm more actively. Such leaders have looked upon commercial goods, as well as publicity through the press or (later) visual media, as useful means by which to promote their viewpoints and garner support for their claims to authoritative power.[8]

Looking less at the interests of leaders and more at what has been happening for those in the pews, David Morgan and Sally Promey have focused on the visual cultures of American religion, considering why certain "middlebrow" art and artists have found a place in homes and churches throughout the United States in the twentieth century and earlier. Morgan has proposed that such products have promoted practices of what he has termed "visual piety," or ways of employing images for religious reflection, meditation, moral instruction, and ritual use.[9] Robert Orsi, the Harvard religious historian who is concerned with religious "stuff" and its role in private and public practices, also centers his studies on both material objects and the rituals and practices that give them meaning. He has explored how material artifacts have been employed in popular religious rituals, such as that of the Madonna of 115th Street in the early twentieth century to the present.[10] Tracing the stuff of U.S. Protestant evangelicalism and Catholicism in the nineteenth and twentieth centuries, Colleen McDannell coined a phrase that was also the title of her book: *Material Christianity*.[11] Together, these works opened up a way to rethink Protestantism's and Catholicism's purported claims to otherworldliness and antimaterialism, bringing attention to the fact that there is a long tradition of the selling of Christian goods. Such goods have ranged from the high-culture art of Marc Chagall to such low-culture fare as cherubic refrigerator magnets, encompassing all manner of popular cultural objects in between.

Whereas material culture studies of religion began in the exploration of Christianity's intersection with the marketplace, scholars have begun looking at the materiality of majority religions outside the United States. Such studies have explored Japanese Zen gardens, Eastern Orthodox icons, architecture and Jewish memory, the images of the railroad in African American spirituality, the proliferation of Sufi saints in artistic depictions, the relation of word and image in Islamic calligraphy, and the role of divine images in India, among other topics.[12]

All of these religious popular cultural artifacts have a close relation to what has been called the "lived" or "vernacular" religion, or the "religion of the streets."[13] Religion, the scholars in religious material cultural studies have pointed out, is about much more than what happens during services or prayer times and is much more than a set of beliefs or ideological commitments. Religion is lived out in everyday life, and, as such, there are objects and practices that have become a part of religious practices both formally and informally conceived. Faith practices have arisen in the context of a marketplace in which goods are for sale, and thus enterprising individuals and industries have arisen to satisfy the needs for these goods. The consumerist marketplace of capitalism has been an important context that has made religious material culture possible and profitable.

The Marketplace of Religion

Perhaps it is not surprising, then, that in recent years sociologists of religion have become intrigued with the use of the "marketplace" as a metaphor for how people come to understand themselves and their relationships to religious identifications. From "spiritual marketplaces" to religion's value as a source of "spiritual capital," the marketplace has come to be seen as central to how religion operates, especially in the U.S. context. Catherine Albanese, for example, uses this metaphor when she explains the structure of religion in U.S. society. Pointing to the disestablishment of religion, or separation of church and state, Albanese argues that in the United States, people feel they can pick and choose their faith, much like consumers pick and choose products from a plethora of choices in the marketplace.[14] Books such as Wade Clark Roof's *Spiritual Marketplace* and Richard Cimino and Don Lattin's *Shopping for Faith* also capitalize (so to speak) on this metaphorical connection between religious choice and a consumer orientation.[15] All of these offer good insights into the ways in which some in the United States tend to see religious identification as something we *choose* rather than something into which we're born. Some scholars have even suggested that the more religious choices there are in a given context, the more religious competition will ensue, thus contributing to the creation of a stronger felt need to identify with one particular tradition over and against another competing one.[16] Most of these theories explore how economic theory can be applied to help us understand individual and group behaviors related to religion around the world.[17]

Interestingly, far greater attention is paid in these studies to what people report about their beliefs and practices concerning the religious or spiritual "marketplace" than what they do with the "stuff" of the *actual* marketplace. Sociologists have been interested in why individuals buy certain products or seek out certain media, but less analysis has been devoted to how and why the marketplace itself has provided certain products and how and why the media have participated in the naturalization of certain religious beliefs over others.[18] This book is one of several current efforts that aims to contribute to the conversation on the relationship between religion, media, and the marketplace in what has come to be known as the "new paradigm" studies of the sociology of religion.[19]

In what is probably closer to the popularly accepted concerns of the relationship of religion, media, and the marketplace, scholars following in the wake of Robert Putnam's *Bowling Alone* thesis (which argued that participation in public life is on the decline) have argued that the media and commercial marketplace undermine traditional values such as those of religion.[20] Practices related to these realms are viewed more or less as a distraction from the real or "authentic" practices of faith.[21] Yet buying things like fashion Bibles or attending events like bhangra parties or Muslim pop concerts can help people to solidify an identification with a religious group and foster a sense of belonging.[22] Thus, in some cases the commercial realm may facilitate, rather than undermine, authentic practices of faith. But such items also may be marshaled for political ends in ways that the original producers never intended, thus making them less a distraction from faith than an accomplice in a larger political project.

One of the main contributions of this volume, then, is to encourage us to consider the dominance of the consumer marketplace itself and its relationship to both religion and the political or economic organization of society. The marketplace—both where people consume and where people labor—is the meeting point between religion, the nation-state, and popular culture and is supported by its relation with the media industries. Thus, we begin with the assumption that the marketplace is an important site for religious expression, religious understanding, and sometimes religious and national conflict.

The Birth of Advertising and the Rise of the Consumer

Historians tracing the rise of the current consumer-oriented marketplace often begin their stories with the Industrial Revolution at the turn of the late eighteenth and early nineteenth century. As many have noted, the Industrial Revolution coincided with the development of the nation-state and the emergence of an economy based not on feudal, craft, or agrarian systems, but on a capitalist marketplace.[23]

David Harvey, author of *The Condition of Postmodernity*, argued that by the end of the nineteenth century the economy had undergone a change in emphasis from labor to consumption.[24] By that point in the industrial revolutions of the United States and Europe, he argued, the forces of supply were in place and the workplace was becoming increasingly productive and streamlined. There needed to be not only mechanisms for producing, but mechanisms of desire for those mass-produced commodities. Thus, this time marked the birth of advertising and marketing, industries that were born out of the need for a greater expansion of the consumer marketplace.

In its early years, advertising drew upon the practices and traditions of the peddlers and carnival barkers who, before them, had sought to draw attention to goods and services for sale.[25] Yet advertising also quickly came to play a role in relation to the important myths and utopian hopes of society, as Jackson Lears has argued. Advertising, with its focus on the production and management of desire, borrowed from the tropes and themes of Christianity's emphasis upon the transformation of the self as well as the promises of a brighter future. Advertising therefore existed in the tensions "between dreams of magical transformation and moralistic or managerial strategies of control."[26] Advertisements reflected popular fantasies rather than social realities; they dramatized the American dream through what Michael Schudson has termed the style of "Capitalist Realism."[27]

The early decades of the twentieth century saw these developments in advertising along with the evolution of the modern print and broadcast media. These media, along with new service institutions such as department stores and mail-order catalogs, and the development of the fashion and transportation industries made it possible for industries to develop promotional campaigns, trademarked goods, sales techniques, and distribution plans that further centralized and organized the consumer marketplace in terms of both goods and desires. James R. Beniger has likened the development of these media and service-oriented industries to the hardware and software of the consumer society, noting that they instigated "a trend toward integration of informational goods and services, media and content, that has continued unabated to this day."[28]

Yet it is important to note that such a centralized system of the control of production was rather widely resisted throughout the world in the 1920s and 1930s. In part, the resistance grew out of tense class relations, based in the expectation that workers would labor for long hours in repetitive, routinized labor and that supervisors would maintain their productivity through careful observation and control. This form of labor was quite a contrast

from the agrarian life and the small shops and slow development of traditional craft skills that had dominated the economy in the decades before.
Yet the mass-production assembly-line work of the early twentieth century
in the United States drew largely on a labor pool comprised of new immigrants, former slaves, and the children of these workers, all of whom were
in need of labor—and all of whom increasingly organized and resisted the
dehumanizing effects of factory labor.[29]

In somewhat interesting ways, advertisers of the 1920s and 1930s capitalized on these cultural tensions and individual needs by promoting "the
modern" as an era that was full of excitement and possibility. Focusing on
technological developments and new fashion, Roland Marchand argued,
enabled advertisers to turn their appeals from attention to the product to
the concerns of the consumer: "Advertisers, then as now, recognized a much
larger stake in reflecting people's needs and anxieties than in depicting
their actual circumstances and behavior. It was in their efforts to promote
the mystique of modernity in styles and technology, while simultaneously
assuaging the anxieties of consumers about losses of community and individual control, that they most closely mirrored historical reality—the reality of cultural dilemma."[30]

This cultural dilemma of loss of individual control in the face of heightened corporate control was an area of innovation for Henry Ford. Ford, like
several other major industrialists of the era, sought to rationalize the labor
system to bring about greater profits through greater efficiency. Ford's
innovations in workplace management extended to a philosophy about
life outside of the workplace. He believed that in order to maintain a vibrant
economy, his workers needed to have the leisure and the income necessary
to participate in the marketplace not only as laborers, but as consumers.
Historian Martyn Lee has argued that when the rationalized and hierarchi-
cal management style known as Fordism reached its peak in the two decades
following World War II, there came to be what he described as a kind of
a postwar consensus: workers would go along with management and, in
exchange, they would be able to afford to purchase the trappings of middle-
class life.[31]

In the affluence of the decades following World War II, then, consumption, rather than production, became the driving force of the economy. Jean Baudrillard has termed this shift as one of "consummativity,"

which he defined as "an indefinite calculus of growth rooted in the abstraction of [human] needs."[32] The very key or foundation to this process, Baudrillard argued, is that the consumer needs to *believe* that he is making his consumption decisions as a result of his own self-expression.[33] Consumers came to see themselves as active and willing participants in the postwar consensus, then, as they focused on their ability to meet what they perceived as their needs—rather than questioning how those needs were often manufactured in the interests of the corporations creating the goods they wished to consume.

Baudrillard noted that it was not until the industrial system was almost in crisis, with over-production and falling profits, that the idea of the "individual qua consumer" took hold. At that point, the consumer "was no longer simply the slave as labor power," destined to work in the factories, but rather "a new kind of serf: the individual as consumption power," subjected to advertising and its related industries of fashion.[34] Consumption, rather than labor, Baudrillard claimed, had become a powerful mechanism of social integration by the 1970s, and it remains so today.

From the perspective of the present, the choices of consumption as self-expression in the decades immediately following World War II appear curiously conformist. Part of the reason for this is that we need to remember the sheer limitations of the availability of goods in the marketplace at the time—which, while expanding at an unprecedented rate, offered much less consumer choice than what we are familiar with now. Advertisers at the time, however, also took note of the contradiction between conformity and the desire for self-expression and viewed it as an opportunity. Thomas Frank, a historian of advertising, has noted that the concept of "market segmentation" arose on the wave of a desire to dissent from conformity in the late 1950s and early 1960s. This desire, he argued, was an important theme both in the counterculture and in business circles of the time.[35] Businesses were learning that it was more profitable to target slightly different products to specific groups than to try to create one uniform product for everyone.

With this shift to consumption as an organizing principle, as David Harvey has observed, marketers began responding to the shifting needs and desires of consumers with increasing speed.[36] Market segments became more and more specialized, requiring ever-greater product differentiation and relying upon the development of more and more sophisticated marketing research techniques. Harvey has related this increase in the speed of marketplace responsiveness to the rise of postmodernism, in that we have seen an increase in emphasis on difference, fashion, and spectacle and on image in our various media—all of which are meant to provide the consumer with the means by which to express herself or himself with ever-increasing distinctiveness, yet always within the realm of consumer goods.[37]

This emphasis on image and spectacle has reshaped the very organization of the marketplace itself, as Robert Goldman and Stephen Papson have argued in *Nike Culture: The Sign of the Swoosh.* Goldman and Papson have noted that Nike is a company built almost entirely upon symbols and narratives.[38] Nike does very little in the more traditional realm of manufacturing; and, in fact, the company has largely become synonymous with "outsourcing" of labor so as to achieve flexibility of production, which keeps costs down for the company—and also restructures the marketplace as one that is global, interconnected, and exploitative. Nike has fought charges of its exploitive practices, but one could argue that their continued success rests less on changes in their manufacturing practices than on their ability to marshal symbols in ways that are meaningful throughout the Western world. Nike, like many other multinational corporations, is a company that is defined not by what they manufacture, but by the brand they build.

Branding is not so much about linking products with certain attributes that we then select when we are looking for means of self-expression. Branding is about how companies like Nike identify things that are already a part of us, letting those of us in the Western world make the connection between what they're selling and who we see ourselves as being. To use the language of hegemony, branding hails us: it creates a space for us to occupy, one that we actually see ourselves already occupying. The company is just claiming that space as its own. In the case of Nike, what they lay claim to is our sense of achievement, our love of sports, our high self-expectations, our desire to see ourselves as unique individuals. They then sell all of this back to us through running shoes and apparel. We like to believe those things about ourselves, and branding works when it speaks to what we think we already are. It also works when we are willing to pay more for a product or service because it better speaks to who we are than other products or services do.

Operating simultaneously within the economy of capital and the economy of signs and symbols, Nike and other global brands have taught us all about how to see ourselves in relation to symbols. As those of us in the West identify with specific subcultures, we find that there are certain symbols and stories that go along with that identification, in terms of products, services, and even mediated stories and images. We also recognize, perhaps even more clearly, that there are many symbols in the economy of signs that do not appeal to us. Our processes of identity construction within the media and the marketplace therefore mirror the ways in which companies construct a market segment for a brand. Or to put it another way, corporations have learned about our processes of identity construction and have marshaled this knowledge in a way that makes it possible for them to encourage us to participate in consumption practices even if we prefer to think of ourselves as reluctant consumers.

Branding has become a technique employed not only by companies seeking to sell things, but also by nation-states that seek to strengthen a sense of cultural identity and community among a diverse group of citizens, as Nadia Kaneva has pointed out. She writes, "Creating emotional associations and identities is central to the process of nation branding."[39] If, as Benedict Anderson has argued, the nation is an "imagined community," united not by force but by an agreed-upon definition of what "the nation" is, then a project like branding may be an effective way to use the media to organize and promote such symbols of the nation for political and economic benefits.[40] This assumes that nation-states exist in a realm of finite resources and must compete to ensure that they are afforded the greatest possible access to such resources. But it also rests on the assumptions that the marketplace metaphor is an appropriate way to conceptualize relationships between social groups and nation-states and that branding, which works primarily in the realm of symbols and ideas, can overcome material problems and inequities that exist in the "real world." This approach, as Kaneva has argued, can mask the serious material inequities that have long shaped the ways in which the marketplace is structured and the ways in which various groups can (and cannot) participate in it and in other aspects of global political and economic relations.

Branding has its limits, therefore, but there is little doubt that it has come to play a role in how we conceive of ourselves and how nations and other political groups work to employ products, images, and symbols in ways that benefit their interests over those of competing groups. Thus, as this chapter highlights the emergence of religious lifestyle branding, it must take into consideration not only those who produce certain religiously oriented goods or services and those who consume them, but also those groups that seek to lay claim to the identification that emerges, marshaling that identification for the interests of certain political or economic projects related to the nation-state.

Globalization, Media, and the Religious Marketplace

Religious historians have pointed out that the spread of religion has long been related to trade routes and that immigration routes follow economic opportunity. Thus, at this point we turn briefly to two specific examples of the intersection of religion, media, and marketplace in relation to labor and economic shifts, highlighting additional issues to be explored in this volume. The first example enables us to consider what happens when people relocate to the United States and bring cultural and religious practices from elsewhere into a new context—in this case, from South Asia to the United States. This example highlights how certain transported and reshaped cultural and religious practices can serve indirectly to reinforce religious understanding while also being marshaled in the interest of certain political and economic commitments. The second example explores a phenomenon that has emerged as a minority religious tradition in the United States—Islam—has come into dialogue with media available in the United States in a way that directly aims to reinforce religious understanding and, in the process, inadvertently contributes to political aims as well. Both of these cases therefore point to how mediated popular culture related to religion and circulated in relation to the marketplace can inadvertently provide support for certain nationalist ideologies.

Bhangra Parties and Hindu Nationalism

In the book *Desis in the House: Indian American Youth Culture in New York City*, Sunaina Marr Maira studied second-generation Indians or children of immigrants who were born in the United States or moved to the United States from India or Pakistan by age seven or eight.[41] She noticed in her interviews that these young people associated "true" Indianness not with concern about the politics in India or Pakistan, but with social and cultural criteria: how "Indian" they judged someone to be depended on how familiar they were with Hindi films, whether or not they could speak Indian languages, whether they attended Hindu cultural festivals, and whether they participated in student groups and Indian parties.

While she was doing her research on college-age children of South Asian immigrants, Maira was also noticing that in the United States in the late 1990s there was a surge of interest in Asian culture: suddenly martial arts films, Japanese anime, bhangra music, and henna tattoos had entered mainstream U.S. popular culture. Even more recently we could add to that list the popularity of films like *Bend It like Beckham* and *Monsoon Wedding.* Maira, who herself was raised in India and moved to the United States when she was seventeen, started attending bhangra parties in the mid-1990s to get a sense of what she called the "ethno-chic" of the "Indian scene."

While the bhangra party scene is certainly not about religion, there are interesting linkages to religion that should not be overlooked. First of all, traditional bhangra music has long been a form of popular or vernacular religion associated with Sikh traditions. It grew out of a celebration of the harvest, although over time it was also linked with music that celebrated romance, and thus became a central feature of soundtracks in popular Bollywood films. Sikh leaders tend to see popular bhangra and the bhangra dance party scene as an affront to their religious traditional music. At the same time, because traditional bhangra music is Sikh and Punjabi and not Hindi, even traditional bhangra has been considered outside formal religious traditions for the elite Hindus of India, or too "popular" to "count" as anything having to do with religion.[42] Clearly, there are layers of claims to legitimacy here that can be somewhat puzzling for the Western newcomer to bhangra. And although bhangra is dominated by popular romantic and festive bhangra songs by artists such as Daler Mehndi and Bally Sagoo, songs such as "Ik Onkar," a soothing Punjabi prayer sung by Harshdeep Kaur and written by Bollywood music legend A. R. Rahman for the film *Rang de Basanti,* remind the listener of bhangra's historic connections to religious practices.

While the bhangra of dance parties and clubs is played for entertainment rather than for worship, participation in bhangra parties and other more formal celebrations of Indian culture have an aspect to them that is nostalgic, often for an imagined, traditionally Hindu India where the current generation of young people has never lived. Sunaina Maira has argued that this nostalgia can work to the benefit of Hindu nationalist movements in India. To illustrate the case in the instance of bhangra parties, we turn to an example from the bhangra party scene.

One of the first breakout songs to achieve popularity beyond the bhangra party scene was that of the group Apache Indian, whose lead singer is Steven Kapur. Apache Indian has since scored seven top-ten songs on the U.K. charts—more than any other Asian performer. Kapur is a musician born and raised in Birmingham, England, in a large community of both Indian and Jamaican immigrants. In the music of Apache Indian, one hears influences from India as well as British-inflected reggae, ragamuffin, and U.S. hip-hop music. Songs range from the dance hit "Boom Shack-a-lak" to the social and religious commentary of "I Pray," "Shackle and Chain," and "All Religions," three tracks, featured on the 2005 collection, *Time for Change,* that speak of the need for justice and increased understanding across differences. The song "Arranged Marriage" was Apache Indian's first breakout song to feature social commentary, however. The song, released in 1993 on the album *No Reservation,* is about a bachelor living in Britain who is ready for his parents to help him select an appropriately traditional wife in an arranged marriage. But, as he sings, "about me arranged marriage, me have a problem: when is the right time to tell my girl friend?" The lyrics note his preference for a wife who is from Jalandhar City, the oldest city of Punjab in northwest India and home to several women's colleges. He wants a wife who is "sweet like jalebi," a reference to the syrup-soaked, deep-fried treat eaten at social events and sold on city streets in India and Pakistan. Continuing with his request, the lyrics note that he wants his future wife to wear a sari (a traditional Indian dress) and make him *roti* (a traditional Indian bread).

The words offer a tongue-in-cheek, very traditional view of femininity in Indian culture. This is certainly not an image most Western feminists would embrace. But for young South Asians, their interpretation of the song isn't quite so simple. They note that it can be heard ironically, as if the singer is making fun of the bachelor's dilemma.[43] Some South Asians have commented that in the song, arranged marriage may come to symbolize

FIGURE I-2 Steven Kapur of Apache Indian performs in Singapore, 2005.

Photo by Susan Bulkin for Urban Photographers. Courtesy of Steven Kapur and BHX Management.

the tension they feel between parents' expectations and Western ideas of allure and mystery of romance.[44] This may be why the song got so popular: that tension of being pulled in two directions feels familiar to children of South Asian immigrants. The young fans of the song aren't necessarily interested in making fun of arranged marriage or in accepting it, even in the less restrictive forms it often occurs in Indian families today. But the song reflects the larger issue of articulating the tension of having a critical look at one's parent's traditions that most people associate with religion, even as one embraces some of the nostalgia embedded in that tradition in a way that is far from progressive.

Certainly, in a song like "Arranged Marriage," there is some nostalgia, even as that nostalgia forms the basis for the song's humor. Yet nostalgia appears in numerous songs that have become popular within bhangra music more generally. This is consistent with what Arjun Appadurai has observed about popular culture in the diaspora: "one of the central ironies of global cultural flows, especially in the arena of entertainment and leisure," is that they are often marked, in the diaspora, by a "nostalgia without memory."[45]

Similarly, Sunaina Maira points out that second-generation young people draw upon a collective memory forged through their parents' experiences as they imagine their parents' experiences in relation to the Hindi films and other elements of popular South Asian culture to which they've been exposed.[46]

But such nostalgia is not always purely innocent. Maira notes that transnational Hindu right-wing organizations are interested in defining India as a Hindu nation. She writes: "Traditional Hindu right-wing organizations have attempted to draw on local articulations of ethnic ideologies in immigrant communities in the United States and to fulfill the desires of second-generation youth to be 'truly' Indian. This is accomplished by producing a packaged version of Indian diasporic nationalism that has no room for non-Hindus and keeps its political truths hidden from most second-generation youth." [47] Religion is thus politicized; and nostalgia, through its appeal in such things as bhangra music, can become harnessed to a political platform.

For the most part, however, criticism of bhangra's popularity has come not from those concerned about its usage by political groups, but from those who see it as an affront to religious traditions. Sikh leaders in Toronto, who were interviewed about traditional bhangra music in a documentary titled *Bhangra Wrap,* objected to the fact that they believed bhangra music in its popular "club" form indirectly supported drinking, smoking, and mixed-gender situations, all of which, as one leader noted, are against the Sikh religion. A number of South Asian young people interviewed in the same film seemed to enjoy the fact that the popular bhangra scene incites the religious elders. That, as one young man said, should be the role of Punjabi youth: to shock the elders.[48]

This kind of exchange recalls the role of irreverence that often emerges among children raised in and expected to continue in their parents' religious traditions. The challenge of young people born into a religious tradition is that in some way they need to make the tradition their own. Usually, this happens as they find things to rebel against, to change, and to adapt. Whereas some end up rejecting their tradition, many retain an affiliation, particularly in the case of Hinduism, with its connections to national identification and class standing as well as religious practices.

Thus, as this example of bhangra music illustrates, studies of religion's role in relation to media and the marketplace need to consider three aspects in relation to the maintenance of religious and cultural identity over time. First, through cultural creativity like the creation of bhangra music, younger generations reshape understandings of religion and culture in ways that reflect the needs and conditions of the time, and they do this by drawing upon older traditions in unexpected ways that are often troubling to those who have seen themselves as maintainers of those traditions. Second, these new practices and cultural artifacts, which may have little to do with religion as understood by older generations, may play an inadvertent role in maintaining religions as well as, in some cases, the national ideologies that go along with them. And third, these artifacts, which may or may not have been part of an intentional effort to "brand" a religious lifestyle, may be approached by consumers as part of a certain identity—in the case of bhangra music, a reinforcement for Indian identity—and hence part of a process that mirrors the branding process. Once cultural artifacts become part of the realm of possibilities for identification, they also become available for the branding efforts of others—specifically, in this case, they can be marshaled for the political project of garnering support for Hindu nationalism and its conservative policies regarding the nation-state. They are therefore not part of a branding project for a religious group, but a branding project of the nation-state that utilizes the religious and cultural dimensions of the artifact for political purposes.

In the case of bhangra music, which developed over hundreds of years, the maintenance of religion in and through its cultural products has, in most cases, been inadvertent and a product of a broader sense of cultural identity. Although there is no doubt that the products of bhangra and Bollywood reinforce identity projects for many South Asians now living in the United Kingdom, the United States, Canada, and other places in the Western world, there has been no centralized, intentional effort to brand the "ethno-chic" experience for the purposes of religious socialization. In other instances, however, music has been a source of inspiration for those who seek to underscore religious identity projects with greater intentionality. Perhaps the most influential example of this kind of intentionality is visible in contemporary Christian music. Taking a page from those efforts, however, is another emergent form of religious music: American Muslim pop.

Muslim Pop and U.S. Nationalism

Islam is the second-largest and the fast-growing religion in the world. In the United States, there are between 5 and 8 million Muslims. The largest group of Muslims in the world and in the United States is of South Asian heritage, although fully 85 percent of new converts to Islam in the United States are African American, so now nearly one-third of all Muslims in the United States are African American. Many but not all of these African American converts to Islam identify with the Nation of Islam, a religious and sociopolitical organization founded in the United States in 1930 and now associated with its leader, Louis Farrakhan.[49]

The Nation of Islam has had a visible influence in hip-hop and rap music and in all aspects of black urban culture. Rap artists who are members or sympathizers of the Nation of Islam include Lauren Hill, Talib Kweli, Mos Def, K-Solo, and Ice Cube. Others with ties to the Nation of Islam, or splinter groups such as the Five Percent Nation, have included Public Enemy, Brand Nubian, Lakim Shabazz, Queen Latifah, Sister Souljah, Big Daddy Kane, and others. Whereas many of these artists incorporate their beliefs into their lyrics and view themselves as role models for the Islamic community, fewer see themselves as ambassadors of Islam with a particular role to play in the socialization of young people into this religious identification.

But one particularly North American phenomenon that seeks to participate in the Muslim socialization of young people has emerged in the development of Muslim pop, or Muslim rap, as the group Native Deen refers to themselves. Native Deen is a group of three African Americans, named Joshua, Naeer, and Abdul-Malik, who live in the D.C. area and perform their music at Islamic conferences, fund-raisers, and even weddings. Unlike other Muslim rappers, they are not members of the Nation of Islam. And unlike in the bhangra scene, the young men who comprise Native Deen stay away from bars and clubs because they say that those places encourage activities that are against their religion. The group also eschews the use of turntables and sampling, traditional tools of the hip-hop trade. They play only traditional drums, so as to remain consistent and acceptable to the branches of conservative Islam that believe Mohamed forbade the use of wind and other instruments.

Although they describe themselves as hip-hop, their music, they admit, is designed to appeal to parents who want to encourage their children as

FIGURE I-3 Joshua Salaam, Naeem Muhammad, and Abdul-Malik of Native Deen perform onstage.

Photo by Susan Bulkin for Urban Photographers. Courtesy of Native Deen.

they grow up Muslim. The lyrics and music, therefore, are easy to recall and are designed to encourage young people to sing along. One popular selection is titled "Muslim," and its lyrics include the chorus: "M-U-S-L-I-M, I'm so glad to be with them" (repeated four times).

With Native Deen, Muslims in the United States can, in the words of one of its members, "feel like they have something of their own."[50] One member says that people who attend their events say, "Now we can have entertainment at our events, and it doesn't have to be in Arabic." He continues, "Our music is American, it's hip, and it's something everybody can be comfortable with."[51] They record on the label of Yusef Islam—the artist formerly known as Cat Stevens.

At this point, Native Deen is still a rather small phenomenon with a focused, but growing, following. One can definitely observe some parallels to the early days of contemporary Christian music, in that sometimes the music can sound a little more focused on the lesson than on the musical qualities itself. A Native Deen song called "Ramadan," for instance, has come in for criticism on the alt.Muslim newsgroup site and in several blogs. As one blogger writes—in echoes of critiques of contemporary Christian music—"Why does every Muslim effort at contemporary music turn into regressive childish nonsense? All the subtlety of a sledgehammer. 'Waking up in the morning, gotta make my prayer' . . . give me a break! The cheeziest of Western boy-band fare isn't even remotely as blunt and trite."[52]

But others have blogged about the fact that Native Deen appeals to families with children. After a Native Deen show in California, one blogger wrote, "I have never been more convinced that music and Islam can have a beautiful relationship that unites Muslims around the world. Those who open their hearts and minds to this new phenomenon will feel the power that these artists convey. This event was proof that more and more Muslims are catching on to the idea of halal entertainment. May Allah strengthen and further the movement to break down the barriers among us and unite us all. Amen."[53]

Native Deen is therefore also part of a longer-standing effort to confront the strict understanding of Islam that forbids all kinds of popular music. In this effort, a notable leader is Sahlman Ahmad, leader of Junoon, the most successful Pakistani rock group of all time, that has received recognition throughout the Asian world and beyond. Ahmad, who has been named the U.N. Goodwill Ambassador for his peace efforts between Pakistan and India, infuses his lyrics with traditional Sufi prayers and has been compared with U2's lead singer, Bono. Ahmad was featured in an award-winning BBC documentary, *The Rockstar and the Mullah*, in which he interviewed right-wing Islamic leaders about the prohibition on music that has come to symbolize larger issues of ethnic oppression in northwestern Pakistan.

Certainly, the music of Junoon and Sahlman Ahmad, as well as that of the emergent group Native Deen, has been important to members of the Muslim community in the United States, especially after the tensions of September 11, 2001, and the battles in Afghanistan and Iraq. As Junoon has grown in worldwide popularity, so too Native Deen concerts are increasingly drawing not only African American Muslims, but Muslims of Arab descent in the United States and elsewhere in the world as well. Native

Deen, in particular, has been very involved in Islamic relief efforts and benefits around the world.

Native Deen did not intentionally set out to brand the black Muslim subculture, even though some in that subculture may identify with this music as something that speaks to experiences that are already a part of their lives. Interestingly, the fact that their music resonates with a felt need and a set of narratives and symbols in the U.S. Muslim community seems to have led Native Deen and their music to be mobilized in the branding efforts of others: namely, in the efforts of the U.S. State Department, which includes a very positive description of Native Deen on its Web site (there was no similar treatment of Junoon or Sahlman Ahmad at the time of this writing).[54] The U.S. State Department is now home to what used to be known as the U.S. Office of War Information, which was set up during World War II as the propaganda arm of the U.S. government. The U.S. State Department is the source of news for international outlets and was designed to (and remains committed to) win the hearts and minds of those outside the United States. Native Deen is highlighted by the Bush administration as part of its "Shared Values" initiative. This claiming of Native Deen for U.S. State Department purposes helps to brand the United States as a tolerant and humane society toward Muslims, certainly a contested claim in light of the Guantanamo Bay and Abu Ghraib prison scandals, but a belief that many in the world, especially those in the United States, like to hold.

As one Native Deen member explained to a reporter, "The State Department called us again, and they have somebody who's interested in taking us overseas to someplace where there's an American Ambassador, because . . . they think this would be a good presentation of Muslims in America, to show that—well, maybe it's a little political—Muslims are living well in America."[55] Thus, in interesting ways, this music, created for such different purposes from popular bhangra music and with no intentional political efforts on the part of Native Deen, can end up supporting a particular ideology and a nationalist political agenda: in this case, that of the United States and its foreign policies.

In some ways, examples like these help those who are from the United States to reconsider how the dominant religious tradition in the United States, Christianity, might be related to conservative nationalist agendas as well, and how some artifacts of religious culture might be marshaled for the benefit of certain political agendas. In the years of the Bush administration, words like "crusade" and battles against "evil" made it easier to consider how religious rhetoric could be employed in support of political agendas. This book therefore helps us to think about how artifacts of the marketplace and the media may play a reinforcing role in relationship to messages heard in rhetoric. Thus, we return to the cultural artifact, at the intersection of religion, media, and the marketplace, that was mentioned at the beginning of this chapter: *Revolve,* the fashion Bible. Bhangra parties and Muslim pop do the same work as that of the fashion Bible, as they all enable younger persons to identify with a set of cultural and religious practices in ways that are different from their parents—and are hip to the popular and the commercial.

What the young people who buy fashion Bibles, go to bhangra parties, and buy Muslim pop are therefore participating in is what I would like to suggest we call "religious lifestyle branding." Religious lifestyle branding is a process that occurs as commercial industries provide materials meant to appeal to those seeking articles designed to express religious distinctiveness and as individuals locate, purchase, and claim those commercial items as their own. The industries of the contemporary marketplace make lifestyle branding possible, and individuals living in today's mediated society find it appealing to employ these materials—which may include elements of fashion, music, body art, film, books, accessories, home decorative items, and more—in their quest for self-expression. As those producing items such as "Jesus is my homeboy" T-shirts and the "Buddha box" kit or cell-phone entrepreneurs producing accessories that issue audible Islamic calls to prayer have found, there are people for whom such goods constitute an appealing alternative to that which is already available in the saturated marketplace. It seems that such entrepreneurs have discovered that perhaps for those who want to figure out how to not eschew but embrace at least part of a religious tradition, the hipper the forms of expression available through religious lifestyle branding, the better.

Moreover, religious lifestyle branding is something that we are likely to be observing as an area of growth in the coming years. For evidence of this possibility, we can look to the marketplace and its trends toward consolidation.

The Religious Marketplace and Media Consolidation

Within the field of media studies, the increasing consolidation of the entertainment and news industries is a growing concern. There are five companies that now own more than 85 percent of the media and entertainment
companies in the world. This includes newspapers, magazines, fiction and
nonfiction publishers, record labels and music studios, Internet service
providers, television and radio production facilities and stations, Hollywood
production studios, advertising agencies, and more. Those five companies,
as of late 2006, are Time Warner, Bertelsmann, Viacom, Disney, and
the News Corporation. These companies are increasingly vertically integrated, meaning that the ownership of various complementary media outlets makes it possible for effective and profitable cross-promotion. An
example is the case of Howard Stern. Stern's talk-radio program was syndicated on fifty of Viacom's Infinity radio stations, and his TV program was
broadcast on Viacom's CBS. Simon and Schuster, another Viacom property,
published his best-selling autobiography, which was then released as a
major motion picture by Viacom's Paramount Pictures, after which Viacom
has continued to profit from the movie's availability at the Viacom-owned
Blockbuster video stores.[56] Stern has since established Howard 100, a Sirius
Satellite radio station, to benefit more directly from the vertical integration of
his interests.

The potential for profit making is not related only to the business syn-
ergies inherent to vertically integrated businesses; in the media industries,
it is related directly to the rise of the lifestyle marketing and branding
atmosphere of today's society, as Robert McChesney has suggested: "The
pressure to become a conglomerate is also due to something perhaps even
more profound than the need for vertical integration. It was and is stimu-
lated by the desire to increase market power by cross-promoting and cross-
selling media properties or 'brands' across numerous, different sectors of
the media that are not linked in the manner suggested by vertical integration." McChesney has quoted Viacom's president Sumner Redstone, who
stated, " 'When you make a movie for an average cost of $10 million and
then cross promote and sell it off of magazines, books, products, television
shows out of your own company, the profit potential is enormous.' "[57]

The increase in horizontal and vertical integration within these international media conglomerates goes a long way in explaining how it came to

be in the interests of large corporations to approach the marketplace with not just media entertainment, but with tie-ins and products that reinforce an association with a certain lifestyle and with cross-promotions that can cut across various media outlets and products. Companies now approach audiences with increased sophistication, thus facilitating the shift in emphasis toward lifestyle marketing, branding, and niche marketing.

Industries within these mega-companies are constantly searching for new, lucrative market segments. Over the past decade in the United States and now beyond its borders, the evangelical Christian market has emerged as just such a profitable subculture. With *Veggie Tales* videotapes and tie-ins available at Target and Wal-Mart and contemporary Christian music as the fastest-growing genre in the otherwise-moribund music industry, it is no wonder that Christianity suddenly seems much more available in commercial form than has been the case in the past.

There are three reasons why evangelicalism has been the largest "new market" segment for mediated, marketed religion: the size, or the number of people who claim to be evangelical (somewhere between 30 and 40 percent of the U.S. population), the emphasis in that tradition on expression, and the disposable income of the group. Combined, these things make evangelicalism an ideal marketing niche. Once conservative Christian religion was identified as capable of producing and selling goods and services as part of what marketers would call a hot lifestyle brand, companies serving other religions have followed suit in the United States, such as in the case of Jewish "kewlju" and "Hot 4 Hebrew" T-shirts, the Celtic tarot card and handbook set, or the chakra kit that "shows you how to locate the seven energy centers and achieve balance."[58]

While entrepreneurs continue to discover the possibilities in religious lifestyle branding, corporations continue to seek out new ways for profit maximization. In the past few years, there has been a consolidation of certain evangelical Christian industries within one of the big five media conglomerates: News Corporation, or Rupert Murdoch's company. In addition to owning Fox Broadcasting, 20th Century Fox, the *New York Post*, UK News International, and several sports arenas and teams, News Corporation also owns HarperMorrow Publishers, which, in turn, owns Zondervan, one of the world's largest producers of evangelical published materials. They published Rick Warren's *The Purpose-Driven Life,* which was on the *New York*

Times best-seller list for more than one hundred weeks from 2002 to 2004 and has sold more than 21 million books. Also under this umbrella are the books by Billy Graham, Bill Hybels of Willow Creek Megachurch in Chicago, Brian McLaren of the best-selling "emerging church" literature, and Tim and Beverly LaHaye (Tim LaHaye is a coauthor of the best-selling *Left Behind* series, and Beverly LaHaye is the head of a right-wing lobbying organization, Concerned Women of America, and author of numerous books on traditional gender roles).

The News Corporation also holds exclusive publishing rights to the NIV—the New International Version of the Bible—the best-selling version among evangelicals. Additionally, Zondervan owns more than eight thousand independent and chain Christian and general bookstores in the United States. This means that in many ways the evangelical Christian marketplace has become vertically and horizontally integrated: one company now owns the means to both create and distribute a large amount of the media materials that are made, and are made available, for consumers.

And this is where we return, again, to our story of the fashion Bible. Thomas Nelson, the company that publishes *Revolve* and its newer Biblezine versions, has been in the publishing business for more than a hundred years. It owns the copyrights to several lucrative versions of the Bible, including the American Standard Version, the Revised Standard, the New Revised Standard, the New King James, and the New Century Version. Yet Zondervan's increasingly powerful competition in the realm of Bible creation, sales, and distribution led Thomas Nelson to look for ways to integrate its own business horizontally and vertically. In 1992, Thomas Nelson purchased Word Inc., publisher of many Christian fiction and nonfiction best-sellers and owner of the largest Christian music record label. Thus, like the News Corporation but on a much smaller scale, Thomas Nelson is now a part of the horizontally and vertically integrated landscape, profiting from their ability to segment the marketplace by age for the sale of their lucrative Biblezines. Such consolidation may be necessary in order to compete with products emerging from the vertical integrated behemoth of the News Corporation.

As has been made evident in the examples of bhangra parties and Muslim pop, not all that becomes popular emerges from the mega-corporations of the marketplace, and Christianity is not the only religious lifestyle to be increasingly branded. There will always be a profit motive that helps to determine which products or events might be made available for a fee, but the other side of the equation is that such products require a willing marketplace or a collection of people who are willing to pay their money to participate in popular cultural and popular religious activities. Not all of the items available for sale—even those heavily promoted by the mega-corporations of Time Warner and its parallel industries—are going to achieve unmitigated success. Think of all of the marketing and tie-ins that surrounded the 2003 Vivendi box-office bomb, *The Cat in the Hat,* or the 2005 Dreamworks flop, *The Island,* for example.

Yet even to discuss these profit losses in the context of consolidation is to buy into the framework of society as one of consummativity. It is to the benefit of such large-scale and efficient operations to construct and support religious lifestyle branding that can occur nowhere other than the commercial marketplace—a prospect that is sure to have an influence on how religion, and its role in relation to public and personal life, will be understood and enacted in the future.

Conclusion

The strategy of seeking alternative forms of self-expression through commercialized media works well for those in religious groups as they want to distinguish themselves from others, perhaps especially from what they believe are the conspicuous consumption and "amoral" values of other consumers. No one, including a religious person, wants to be seen as "fake"; thus, through the commercial marketplace, people can buy things that demonstrate their true faith and their unique authenticity as persons while remaining firmly within middle-class norms. When religious people want to be hip in the U.S. context, perhaps it is not surprising that we choose to turn to consumer goods that are advertised, or that get "good buzz," for clues as to what to embrace so as to express ourselves as persons who are unique, interesting, intelligent, and whatever else we care to express.

The phrase "religious lifestyle branding" is thus meant to build upon terms like "spiritual marketplace" or "material religion" to combine the ways in which sociologists have explored the felt sense of choice among those choosing to be religious (or not) in contemporary society and the ways in which historians have pointed to the role of consumer goods that have long been part of such forms of expression and practice. The phrase reflects the fact that corporations cannot dictate which aspects of religious material culture people will accept and claim as an aspect of their own religious identification. It highlights the sense that individuals do have choices in the marketplace and in media consumption, yet it also suggests that those choices are made within the range of what has been made available in the commercial realm and are in the interests of those who stand to gain the most from a streamlined, commercialized marketplace. As the examples of bhangra parties and Muslim pop have suggested, however, once artifacts achieve popularity in the marketplace, those in positions of power may look for ways to profit from association with those artifacts by incorporating them into their own branding efforts, thus profiting politically rather than through the direct sale of goods or services. In a world in which resources are scarce and political decisions have grave economic consequences, the way in which artifacts associated with religion can be marshaled for political purposes is an important area for exploration and understanding.

Each of the examples noted in this chapter highlighted what Peter Beyer has identified as a seeming paradox concerning globalization: in globalization, all religions become more particularistic, and yet all religions also must be understood as operating under the influence of a common global culture, in this case, a culture increasingly organized around consumption, media spectacle, and a marketplace of cross-promotion, speed, and efficiency.[59] It is important that we understand more about individual religious traditions while also understanding how they all relate to common influences of this mediated marketplace. This is a challenge for all of us choosing to study something about religion in contemporary times, and it is the challenge taken up in the chapters that follow.

As a concluding thought, it is important to comment on the fact that each of the examples highlighted turned out to have a strong conservative element. Certainly, conservatism is not the only way in which religions can be practiced, nor is religious conservatism automatically linked with conservative social or political agendas. There are also progressive religious traditions that keep alive a commitment to human rights and work hard to eradicate poverty and injustices around the world. Yet it is always going to be easier to mobilize people against change, in the name of "traditional values," than to mobilize people for change. Perhaps, then, it is not surprising that there seems to be an element of the traditional, even the retrogressive, in each of these examples of where popular culture meets popular religion. Scholars, thinkers, and leaders of the community need to carefully analyze and understand these ideological connections between marketplace and religion, exploring how such connections are reinforced and circulated in the media. Such work is especially critical now, when international policy seems to embody an inherent and volatile contradiction: a tendency to think of globalization as the need to "open" markets, and hence increase the appreciation for differing religious traditions; and yet a tendency to also view difference from a perspective of fear and, in the worst case, to allow our fears to guide foreign and military policies. We need to better understand the emotional, religious, and ideological appeal of everything that people do in popular culture and popular religion so that those of us interested in human rights can assist in figuring out better ways to engage those sentiments toward the betterment of the human condition for all. It is for these purposes that this volume is dedicated.

NOTES

1. Available online at http://abcnews.com. Retrieved November 1, 2003. See Deborah Solomon, "The Way We Live Now: Questions for Laurie Whaley," *New York Times*, September 14, 2003, 6(1)17.

2. Christian Booksellers Association Best-Seller Lists: http://cbaonline.org/TrackingLists/BSLHome.jsp. See also Jim Remsen, "A New Spin on the Bible," *Philadelphia Inquirer*, August 28, 2003, C2.

3. Paul Gutjahr, "*Revolve*-ing Notions of the Culturally Relevant Bible," paper presented at the History of the Printed Word Conference, Madison, Wisconsin, September 2004. See also A. Tennant, "Ten Things You Should Know about the New Girls' Biblezine," *Christianity Today*, September 16, 2003. Available online: http://www.christianitytoday.com/ct/2003/137/21.0.html. Retrieved June 20, 2005.

4. *Revolve: The Complete New Testament* (Nashville: TransitBooks, a Division of Thomas Nelson Bibles, 2003), 5.

5. See the journal *Material Religion;* see also Brent Plate, ed., *Religion, Art, and Visual Culture* (New York: Palgrave Macmillan, 2002).

6. Max Weber, *The Protestant Ethic and Spirit of Capitalism* (New York: Penguin, 2002).

7. Paul Gutjahr, *An American Bible: A History of the Good Book in the United States, 1777–1880* (Sanford, CA: Stanford University Press, 2001); David Nord, *Faith in Reading: Religious Publishing and the Birth of Mass Media in America* (New York: Oxford University Press, 2004).

8. Laurence Moore, *Selling God: American Religion in the Marketplace of Culture* (New York: Oxford University Press, 1994); Charles Lippy, *Being Religious, American Style: A History of Popular Religiosity in the United States* (Westport, CT: Greenwood Press, 1994).

9. David Morgan, *Protestants and Pictures: Religion, Visual Culture, and the Age of Mass Production* (New York: Oxford University Press, 1999); David Morgan, *Visual Piety: A History and Theory of Popular Religious Images* (Berkeley: University of California Press, 1998); David Morgan and Sally Promey, eds., *The Visual Culture of American Religion* (Berkeley: University of California Press, 2001). See also Gail Husch, *Something Coming: Apocalyptic Expectation and Mid-Nineteenth-Century American Painting* (Hanover, NH: University Press of New England, 2000).

10. Robert Orsi, *The Madonna of 115th Street: Faith and Community in Italian Harlem, 1880–1950* (New Haven: Yale University Press, 1985); Robert Orsi, *Gods of the City: Religion and the American Urban Landscape* (Bloomington: Indiana University Press, 1999). See also Thomas A. Tweed, *Our Lady of the Exile: Diasporic Religion at a Cuban Catholic Shrine in Miami* (New York: Oxford University Press, 2002).

11. Colleen McDannell, *Material Christianity: Religion and Popular Culture in America* (New Haven: Yale University Press, 1995). See also David Bjelajac, *American Art: A Cultural History* (Upper Saddle River, NJ: Prentice Hall, 2000/2005); Gretchen Townsend Buggeln, *Temples of Grace: The Material Transformation of Connecticut's Churches, 1790–1840* (Hanover, NH: University Press of New England, 2003).

12. See S. Brent Plate, ed., *Religion, Art, and Visual Culture: A Cross-Cultural Reader* (New York: Palgrave Macmillan, 2002); Morgan and Promey, *The Visual Culture of American Religions;* and the introductory issue of the journal *Material Religion* 1(1).

13. David D. Hall, ed., *Lived Religion in America* (Princeton, NJ: Princeton University Press, 1997); Leonard Primiano, "Vernacular Religion and the Search for Method in Religious Folklife," *Western Folklore* 54 (January 1995): 37–56; Orsi, *Gods of the City.*

14. Catherine Albanese, *America: Religion and Religions* (Belmont, CA: Wadsworth Publishing, 1998).

15. W. Clark Roof, *Spiritual Marketplace* (Princeton, NJ: Princeton University Press, 1999); Richard Cimino and Don Lattin, *Shopping for Faith: American Religion in the New Millennium* (San Francisco: Jossey-Bass, 2002).

16. Roger Finke and Rodney Stark, *The Churching of America, 1776–2005: Winners and Losers in Our Religious Economy,* 2d ed. (New Brunswick, NJ: Rutgers University Press, 2005).

17. Philip Gorski, "Historicizing the Secularization Debate: Church, State, and Society in Late Medieval and Early Modern Europe, ca. 1300 to 1700," *American*

Sociological Review 65 (February 2000): 138–167; Stephen R. Warner, "Work in Progress toward a New Paradigm for the Sociological Study of Religion in the United States," *American Journal of Sociology* 98 (1993): 1044–1093; Nancy Ammerman, ed., *Religion in Modern Lives* (New York: Oxford University Press, 2006).

18. Anthony Giddens, *Modernity and Self-Identity: Self and Society in the Late Modern Age* (Stanford, CA: Stanford University Press, 1991); Raymond Williams, *The Long Revolution* (London: Penguin, 1975); Raymond Williams, *Culture and Society 1780–1950* (London: Penguin, 1966).

19. Roof suggests this direction in his book *Spiritual Marketplace*. One good example is Barbara Wheeler's look at "Bible cozies" and the cultural stuff of evangelicalism as contrasted to the lack of "stuff" in mainline/liberal denominations. Another promising direction is Monica Emerich's work on the appeal of Eastern philosophies and attendant stark aesthetics among high-culture religious practitioners. She argues that despite the claims to a "simple" lifestyle, such homes nevertheless include such products as indoor fountains and high-end art that attest to the materiality of this form of spirituality. Monica Emerich, "The Spirituality of Sustainability" (PhD diss., University of Colorado, 2006).

20. Robert Putnam, *Bowling Alone: The Collapse and Revival of American Community* (New York: Simon and Schuster, 2001).

21. Artifacts of popular culture and, in particular, television programs have been viewed as a distraction to social good for a long time. See Joli Jensen, *Redeeming Modernity: Contradictions in Media Criticism* (Thousand Oaks, CA: Sage, 1990).

22. Pierre Bourdieu, *Distinction: A Social Critique of the Judgement of Taste* (Cambridge, MA: Harvard University Press, 1987).

23. Jürgen Habermas, *The Structural Transformation of the Public Sphere* (Cambridge, MA: MIT Press, 1991).

24. David Harvey, *The Condition of Postmodernity* (Cambridge: Blackwell, 1990).

25. Jackson Lears, *Fables of Abundance: A Cultural History of Advertising in America* (New York: Basic Books, 1994).

26. Ibid., 41–42.

27. Michael Schudson, *Advertising, the Uneasy Persuasion: Its Dubious Impact on American Society* (New York: Basic Books, 1986).

28. James R. Beniger, *The Control Revolution: Technological and Economic Origins of the Information Society* (Cambridge: Harvard University Press, 1986), 28. Critiqued in Rob Latham, *Consuming Youth* (Chicago: University of Chicago Press, 2002), 280.

29. Roger Streitmatter, *Voices of Revolution* (New York: Columbia University Press, 2001).

30. Roland Marchand, *Advertising the American Dream: Making Way for Modernity, 1920–1940* (Berkeley: University of California Press, 1985), xxi.

31. Martyn J. Lee, *Consumer Culture Reborn: The Cultural Politics of Consumption* (New York: Routledge, 1993).

32. Jean Baudrillard, *For a Critique of the Political Economy of the Sign*, trans. Charles Levin (St. Louis: Telos Press, 1981), 83.

33. Ibid., 85.

34. Ibid.

35. Thomas Frank, *The Conquest of Cool: Business Culture, Counterculture, and the Rise of Hip Consumerism* (Chicago: University of Chicago Press, 1998).

36. Harvey, *The Condition of Postmodernity.*

37. Ibid.

38. Robert Goldman and Stephen Papson, *Nike Culture: The Sign of the Swoosh* (London: Sage, 1999).

39. Nadia Kaneva, "Reimagining Nations as Brands: Identity, Commercialization, and Globalization," paper presented to the International Communication Association, New York City, 2005.

40. Benedict Anderson, *Imagined Communities: Reflection on the Origin and Spread of Nationalism* (London: Verso, 1991).

41. Sunaina Marr Maira, *Desis in the House: Indian American Youth Culture in New York City* (Philadelphia: Temple University Press, 2002).

42. Http://sihkamerican.org. See also "What Is Bhangra?" at http://www.punjabonline. com/servlet/community.theme?Action=Category&Param=4. Retrieved June 20, 2005.

43. Http://www.mybindi.com/arts-entertainment/music/feature-apacheindian.cfm; http://www.desitunes4u.com/Reality_2K3_Bhangra_In_The_Mainstream_Part_I. htm. Retrieved June 20, 2005.

44. Priya Lal, "Beyond the Horse and Carriage: Arranged Marriage," Bollywood from Beyond column, PopMatters Web site, August 12, 2004. http://www.popmatters. com/columns/lal/040812.shtml. Retrieved June 20, 2005.

45. Arjun Appadurai, *Modernity at Large: Cultural Dimensions of Globalization* (Minneapolis: University of Minnesota Press, 1996).

46. Maira, *Desis in the House.*

47. Ibid., 137.

48. *The Bhangra Wrap* (documentary), Nandini Sikand, director, National Asian American Telecommunications Association Distribution, 1995.

49. Http://www.religioustolerance.org/islam.htm. Retrieved on June 20, 2005.

50. Http://www.nativedeen.com. Retrieved on March 23, 2005.

51. Ibid.

52. Http://www.altmuslim.com/perm.php?id=870_0_26_0_C27. Retrieved May 9, 2005.

53. Http://muslimhiphop.com/forum/index.php?showtopic=1228.   Retrieved   on May 9, 2005.

54. Http://usinfo.state.gov/products/pubs/muslimlife/rap.htm. Retrieved on May 9, 2005.

55. Beth McGraw, "Propaganda Cross-Cultural Rap," *New Yorker,* December 23, 2002. Available online at http://www.newyorker.com/printables/talk/021223ta_talk_mcgrath.

56. This example comes from the PBS Frontline Web page describing the popular classroom-use documentary *Merchants of Cool.* See http://www.pbs.org/wgbh/pages/frontline/shows/cool/tour/.

57. Robert W. McChesney, *Rich Media, Poor Democracy; Communication Politics in Dubious Times* (Urbana: University of Illinois Press, 1999), 22.

58. http://www.wildeagle.com.au/products/display_category.asp?DID=60&CID=49&iCP=16; www.kewlju.com.

59. Peter Beyer, *Religion and Globalization* (Thousand Oaks, CA: Sage, 1996).

PART ONE

Selling, Influencing, Publishing, Purchasing

Establishing and Participating in the Mediated Religious Marketplace

At the beginning of the nineteenth century, what we might call the "mass media" were largely limited to newspapers, tracts, pamphlets, novels, and sheet music. In general, these publications were made available through local sales within a rather small region, were sent by ship, or were transported through the services of the nascent post office. Much of what was circulated was religious or political in nature, echoing the concerns related to the political and economic revolutions in America, France, and Britain and the enduring role of religious life throughout the developed and colonized world.

As David Nord describes in the first chapter of this section, the first Bible Society of the United States had its beginnings in 1808, when religious leaders sought a way to distribute Bibles to poor immigrants in the Philadelphia area. Because they wanted to increase the circulation of their materials, they both gave away and sold books, a balancing act that required careful management, according to Nord. As the Bible Society became not only a distributor but a publisher of religious materials, they were confronted with many issues that publishers still grapple with today, including the need to find a combination of low cost and high volume to satisfy consumer expectations and the need to centralize operations for greater efficiency and quality control.

In this chapter, Nord discusses the religious motivation that led publishers to offer free books to those they considered to be nonbelievers. Such a practice was consistent with the belief that salvation was related to knowledge of the scriptures and thus justified the practice of giving books to "free riders," or people who received books for which they had not paid. As economic logic prevailed in the development of a business that could support both the sale and giving away of books, the religious publishing industry was birthed. The two chapters that follow Nord's explore tensions and opportunities in the religious publishing industry as it exists today. In Anne Borden's chapter, we follow the rise of Christian booksellers and their current struggle to negotiate ministry and marketplace needs. In Hillary Warren's chapter, we consider how Jewish media producers engage in a similar struggle as they attempt to provide distinctive materials to a subculture that is of little interest to the mass market due to its size, yet remains important within the scope of those who wish to socialize young people into a nondominant religious and cultural tradition in the United States. Nord's opening chapter offers a foundational understanding for these two explorations, as it considers one important starting point for what we now understand to be the intersection of media, religion, and the marketplace.

1

○○○

Free Grace, Free Books, Free Riders

The Economics of Religious Publishing in Early Nineteenth-Century America

DAVID NORD

A few years ago I gave a lecture that opened with what I hoped would be a helpfully dichotomous proposition: selling books is one thing; giving them away is quite another. My subject was religious publishing in antebellum America, especially the work of the American Tract Society. I argued that because the leaders of the Tract Society hoped to extend their message to everyone in America, regardless of ability to pay, they were unable to depend upon a market/price system to deliver their wares. To move their product outside the commercial market, even against that market, the American Tract Society gradually built a national organization that relied on management—that is, organization, communication, and supervision—rather than upon the invisible hand of the marketplace—that is, prices, discounts, and commissions. The mission to *give* rather than to *sell* drove the American Tract Society to become an innovator in the methods of modern business management, what the economic historian Alfred Chandler has called "the visible hand" of administration.[1]

Dichotomies, of course, radically simplify the messy complexity of history. That is why they are good for thinking (and good for lectures). But because they inevitably *over*simplify, they offer easy access to critics—so easy, in fact, that I can't resist playing the critic myself and questioning my own dichotomy, giving versus selling. Why focus so much on *giving* away tracts and books? I hear my inner critic ask. After all, most religious publishers gave away only some of their books; they sold most of them. Even when they worked against the commercial market, even when they sought to reach everyone regardless of ability to pay, they still sold more books than they gave away. Is this not important for understanding the business practices of religious publishers in the early nineteenth century? What do you say to that, Professor Nord?

Tough critic. Good questions, too. And my reply is yes, selling is important and so is giving. It was not pure giving or pure selling, but the mixture of giving and selling in the same operation that characterized the practice of the large religious publishing organizations in early nineteenth-century America. And this is important, indeed, for it is in the management of that mixture that the economics of religious publishing is revealed.

Some organizations did not mix the two very much. Some small tract societies were givers only, while some denominational book publishers were sellers only, wholesaling their wares to their own preachers, churches, and schools. With some exceptions, they left the distribution of their material—whether via giving or selling—to others. But the largest religious publishers imagined universal circulation of their materials (genuine *mass* media), and for those publishers distribution could not be left to others or to chance. It required management, including a managed mixture of giving and selling. This could mean a simple distinction between what was given (small tracts) and what was sold (books). Or it could mean that books ordinarily were sold but were sometimes given away through special programs. It also could mean a more sophisticated marketing strategy, a strategy that economists call *differential pricing*. This was the strategy that several of the national publishing societies pursued in early nineteenth-century America. The idea was neither to sell books at a fixed price nor to give them away, but to sell them at a variable price, a price that each individual buyer was able and willing to pay *all the way down to zero*. That last phrase is crucial, for, on the one hand, setting a price at any level above zero would exclude some buyers: those who would be willing to pay less or to receive the product for free. And any number excluded is too many, if the goal is universal circulation. On the other hand, setting the price at zero, though splendid for universal circulation, would be unnecessarily inefficient, for it would subsidize those buyers who could pay and would be willing to pay. For a commercial business to produce and sell at a price of zero or at any price below the marginal cost (the cost of the last unit produced and sold) would be irrational. But for a religious publisher whose goal is not profit but universal circulation, selling at a price that falls to zero is not irrational; it is simply charity.

I hasten to add that the money men who managed the religious publishing societies were at least as rational as they were charitable. Like all sharp businessmen, they aimed to stretch their resources to the limit. The goal was universal circulation, but within the constraints of that goal they strived for production at the lowest possible cost and distribution at the highest possible revenue. Clearly, differential pricing, if it can be done, will produce universal circulation with maximum revenue and, therefore, least net loss. If most prices are at cost or below, all the way down to zero, there will be losses, and losses must be covered by subsidies, or, to use the philanthropic term, charitable donations. But the smaller the losses, the smaller the subsidy, and thus the larger the circulation. That is the goal of differential pricing in charity book publishing.

In practice, low cost via high volume turned out to be a manageable task. It is this cost/production side of the business that led the large societies to adopt centralized, highly capitalized, high-tech printing operations early in the century. This is the story that has often been told by historians, including me.[2] On the other hand, the achievement of maximum revenue in a way consistent with universal circulation turned out to be more difficult. It is this revenue/distribution side that kept the societies so long wedded to a fragmented and frustrating localism that seems to us (and often seemed to them) inconsistent with their efforts to build modern national business enterprises. Some historians—including me—have portrayed the national/local schizophrenia of these societies as a story of historical change, as a movement from localism to nationalism over time.[3] In a sense, that is true. The national societies did gradually extend the visible hand of administration down to the local level. But local decision making had its economic virtue, and its long retention was not a matter of mere organizational inertia. I would now argue that nationalized production and localized distribution were two sides of the same economic coin, two simultaneous strategies within a single enterprise driven by the logic of differential pricing.

It is this two-tiered economic structure in large-scale religious publishing that I would like to discuss in this chapter. I will concentrate on the charity Bible business in the early nineteenth century, with a few comparisons at the end to other large religious publishing societies.

Popping up from time to time in my story will be the role-playing character that economists and sociologists call the "free rider." A free rider is simply a consumer of something who gets more than he pays for. The free rider problem is a central concern in the sociology of organizations. Voluntary organizations, including churches, produce "collective goods," but these goods benefit members as individuals. The sociologist Laurence Iannaccone explains what can and often does go wrong: "The problem arises whenever the members of a group receive benefits in proportion to their collective, rather than individual, efforts. Because each member benefits whether or not he contributes to the common cause, each has a strong incentive to minimize his own efforts and "free ride" off those of others. If enough members yield to this temptation, the collective activity will surely fail." [4] The free rider plays a role, however, not just as a member of organizations, but as a consumer of mass media, especially religious publishing. In most ordinary commercial businesses, the free rider is excluded automatically by price. If he doesn't pay, he doesn't get. But in a business based on differential pricing the free-rider problem is endemic, because no one ordinarily wants to pay a high price for something that someone else is getting for less or even for free. Furthermore, in *religious* publishing, free ridership is not necessarily a problem at all, for the free rider may be the chief target of the publishing mission. The person who does not value the message enough to buy it because he has never heard it is just the sort of free rider the evangelical publisher would like to reach, with a free book if necessary.

The cost structure of religious publishing also complicates the free rider concept. Some components of the publishers' product have no marginal cost; and if a commodity has no marginal cost, then there may be no economic incentive to expend resources to exclude free riders. The message (the word) is such a commodity. The vessel that carries the word, the book, has a marginal cost, but the word itself does not. Consumption (reading) of a message does not use it up. So, is it good business to exclude free riding *readers?* It may be, if that is the only way to force anyone to pay. But sometimes it may not be worth the effort. The fact that publishers allow libraries to exist or that some computer applications are distributed as shareware suggests as much. Furthermore, the chief product of evangelical religion, the grace of God, has no cost at all. It is, as the apostle Paul liked to put it, abundant and free. (Even the strictest Calvinist in the early nineteenth century did not suppose that grace was a scarce commodity in the economic sense.) These products are what economists call "public goods," goods that have no cost at the margin because they are not used up when consumed. With such goods, if free riders don't add to costs or diminish revenues, then there is no economic incentive to exclude them.

Indeed, there may be compelling reasons to include free riders, even if they don't want to be included. This is dramatically true in religion and religious publishing, for the distributors of these goods reckon their utility (their use to the consumer) to be valuable beyond price. That utility is nothing less than salvation and eternal life. Yet the consumer may not recognize that value at all. He or she may even scorn it. Such a striking difference in the valuation of utility means that the consumer will surely buy far less of the product than someone else thinks is good for him. This is the prescription for subsidy. And subsidy, in this sense, is what religious evangelism—including religious publishing—is all about.

So, we have differential pricing, free riders, cost and utility, and subsidy: religious publishing generates such a fascinating collection of economic themes because it involves both the economics of religion and the economics of media, two of the most interesting subjects of contemporary economic analysis.[5] But I've floated enough abstractions here at the outset. It is time for some historical substance to draw these ethereal themes down to earth. It is in the actual work of religious publishing that these themes are revealed and made flesh.

Let us consider the evolution of charity Bible work in the United States. In the decades after the end of the War of 1812, the distribution of Bibles as a form of evangelism came to be dominated by the American Bible Society. This national organization was founded in 1816 in New York City, and it grew into one of the largest publishing houses in the country by the 1830s. But the American Bible Society was not something new under the sun. It was patterned after the British and Foreign Bible Society, founded in 1804. More important, the American Bible Society (ABS) was born into an America that already had more than one hundred local and state Bible societies.[6] Though the ABS styled itself the "parent society" in American Bible work, it was really as much child as parent. The relationship between the national society and the regional societies that became its auxiliaries shaped much of the history of the ABS in the nineteenth century, and the work of these local societies before 1816 laid a foundation for the economic arrangements that continued to undergird Bible work through the middle decades of the nineteenth century.

The earliest Bible societies in America were book-giving charities. They acquired books from commercial publishers to give to the "destitute," a term they used to mean lack of scripture and usually lack of money as well. The first Bible society in America was organized in Philadelphia in 1808. The opening sentence of its constitution made its charitable mission clear. That mission was "the distribution of [the Bible] among persons who are unable or not disposed to purchase it." In an address to the public in 1809, the organizers of the Philadelphia Bible Society declared that "it is the intention of the Society to offer the Bibles which they disperse, as the sacred treasure which they contain is offered, 'without money and without price.'"[7] This phrase, from Isaiah (55:1), is one of the many wonderful passages in the Bible that use commercial metaphors, in this case a metaphor of price to suggest pricelessness. It became a favorite of the American Bible movement: "Ho, every one that thirsteth, come ye to the waters, and he that hath no money; come ye, buy, and eat; yea, come, buy wine and milk without money and without price."

The efforts of the Philadelphia Bible Society to carry out its charitable mission were at first simple and unsystematic. They raised money through local membership subscriptions; they bought Bibles and New Testaments (mainly from Mathew Carey, the leading publisher of Bibles in the United States at that time); and then they gave them to the poor folk of Philadelphia and vicinity. They also sent copies off to distant lands with missionaries, travelers, and pious sea captains. This was standard charity. But in their first door-to-door canvasses the managers of the society were stunned by the magnitude of the problem they faced: "The deficiency of Bibles has been found to be much greater than was expected; and it is believed to be as great in many other places. The number of families and individuals, who are destitute of a copy of the Scriptures is so great, that the whole of the funds in the possession of the Society, could be profitably expended in supplying the wants of this city alone; and the opportunities of distributing them in other places are so numerous, that if their funds were tenfold as great as they are, they would still be inadequate to satisfy the demand."[8]

With this grim scene looming before them, the managers of the Philadelphia Bible Society made a fateful decision. They would become publishers as well as distributors of the Bible. And they would become capitalists, sinking all of their meager resources into one of the newest and most capital-intensive of printing technologies: stereotype plates.

In Philadelphia in 1809 this was a daring and visionary plan. Stereotype printing was a new process even in England, where Cambridge University Press had just a few years before begun to adapt it to Bible printing. In stereotypography, a plaster-of-paris mold was made of a page form of movable type, and in that mold a solid metal plate was cast. After each mold was made, the types could be redistributed and used again. In this way, a set of printing plates for an entire book could be made and then used, stored, and used again without the expense of keeping moveable type "standing" or of resetting type for each new edition. Stereotype plates were especially well suited to the printing of steady-selling books in many editions over time—books such as the Bible.[9]

But stereotype plates were expensive. The first set of plates that the Philadelphia Bible Society ordered from England cost about $3,500, an enormous sum for the fledgling publishers. The managers of the society were wary but resolute:

> When they considered that the possession of a set of such plates would enable them to multiply copies of the Bible at the lowest expense, and thus render their funds more extensively useful; and still more when they reflected that it would put it in their power to give greater effect to the operations of other Bible Societies, which are springing up daily in every part of the country, the Managers did not hesitate to order the plates to be procured and forwarded from London as soon as possible. The expense is indeed great, when compared with the fund at their disposal; but they were willing to believe, that the obvious and high importance of the measure could not fail to draw from the public liberality a sum sufficient to counterbalance the heavy draught.[10]

This statement suggests the economic implications of stereotype printing. Even though the society would continue to contract out its printing, it would henceforth be a publisher of Bibles as well as a buyer and distributor of them. And to derive the full economies of scale from its heavy capital investment in plates, the society would have to become a *large* publisher, serving other societies' needs as well as its own.[11]

In other words, the Philadelphia Bible Society would have to *sell* Bibles. This was a problem, for the constitution of the society seemed to contemplate only free distribution. One way of solving the problem was to deny that it existed, at least at the wholesale level. The managers took for granted that they could sell at cost to other Bible societies. They were less certain that they could sell to outsiders at a profit. After some creative soul searching, they decided that they could, as long as profits were plowed back into the charitable enterprise. Their reasoning was ingenious, and it nicely reveals the seductive power of economies of scale in stereotype printing:

> The copies of the sacred scriptures, from your press, it is expected, from the excellence and beauty of the type, will be much superior to those which are generally in our market; and the managers have, at several meetings, deliberated on the question, Whether it be their duty to use the means which Providence has put in their hands for increasing your funds (all of which must be expended in a gratuitous distribution of the sacred volume) by selling, at a moderate gain, to other persons, as well as to Bible societies, who may prefer their copies, and send orders. After mature consideration of this question, they have resolved, that . . . it is both their duty and their interest, to supply any orders that may be sent to them for Bibles.

From the start of stereotype printing, then, economic logic prevailed over constitutional scruple and over the traditions of charity. Indeed, of the very first stereotype edition of the Bible in America in 1812, 250 copies of 1,250 printed "were on finer paper and for sale."[12] Happily, duty and interest could be made to coincide.

Still, most of the new stereotyped Bibles were intended for *free* distribution. But here, too, the economies of scale in stereotype printing encouraged (even forced) the managers to expand their own work dramatically. How they planned to do this was outlined in a pamphlet widely circulated in 1810, shortly after they had decided to invest in stereotype plates. To raise money to pay for the plates and to set up a delivery system for the flood of Bibles that would soon flow from them, the society announced a plan to establish "a little Bible Society in every congregation of Pennsylvania." These congregational groups would collect donations and seek members for the Philadelphia Bible Society. In return, they would "be allowed to demand Bibles from the managers of the Society, at first cost, and to the full amount of the contributions made;—the Bibles to be distributed as a free gift, by the congregations, or by their agents, to the poor of their own neighborhood, or to whomsoever else they may choose." Though the Philadelphia Bible Society would become a publisher and wholesale bookseller, the work of the auxiliary societies must remain pure charity. "Let it be remembered," the managers declared, "that the sole object to which this money is to be applied—the sole object to which by our charter we can apply it—is the purchase and printing of the Bible, to be ultimately bestowed as a free gift." [13]

Thus, as the production side of Bible work became more centralized, the distribution side became more localized. The central society increasingly needed local auxiliaries, for two reasons. First, their large capital requirements now forced them to seek funds far beyond the city of Philadelphia, where they were beginning to tap out local largess. As the managers admitted, "Those individuals among ourselves who could reasonably be expected to make donations of important sums, have mostly made them; and the contribution of five dollars, paid by each individual who becomes a regular member of the Society, and which can be demanded but once, has likewise been received." [14] They needed new money and therefore new people to get it. Second, they needed local organization in the hinterland to do the distribution. Lacking the invisible hand of a price system to allocate the books, a conscious human choice—to give or not to give—had to be made. Only local people knew the local scene well enough to distinguish between the pious poor and the "impostor"—or what I have called the free rider.

As distribution moved beyond their own participation and control, the managers in Philadelphia became more concerned about free riders. They directed the little Bible societies to make "the most particular inquiries . . . into the character of those who should apply for bibles. . . . The best endeavours should be used, before a book was bestowed, to ascertain that it was likely to be applied to its proper use. . . . All proper means should certainly be devised and employed, to prevent impositions and to detect impostors." At the same time, the Philadelphia managers cautioned Bible distributors not to exclude worthy free riders (the pious poor) or even to worry too much about seemingly unworthy free riders (impostors), for even they might benefit mightily in the end. As the managers put it, "Care, indeed, must be taken not to discourage, but rather to invite applications, from those who need, and who will duly prize the gift of a bible; . . . though the guilt of the frauds contemplated admits of no palliation, yet the favorers of this charity ought to be less influenced by the apprehension of them, than perhaps in any other concern; for though a bible may be improperly obtained, yet 'wherever it shall be found, it will be a bible still; and it may teach the knave to be honest, the drunkard to be sober, and the profane to be pious.' " [15]

By 1816, then, on the eve of the founding of the American Bible Society, the economic arrangements of charity Bible work were largely in place in Philadelphia.[16] In less than a decade, the Philadelphia Bible Society had evolved from a local charity, passing out free books, to a substantial publisher and high-tech printer. At the same time, it had become the "parent society" of a far-flung network of local societies. These two developments were inseparable. The Philadelphia Bible Society required a multitude of local organizations precisely because it had become centralized and highly capitalized. After 1812, when it launched its stereotype printing enterprise, the society needed to *sell* Bibles as well as *give* them; indeed, it needed to sell them in order to give them. Large revenues were needed to achieve the economies of scale required to lower the costs sufficiently to give Bibles away. That, of course, was the ultimate goal. The stereotype plates *and* the little societies made it possible.

As the Philadelphia Bible Society experimented with ways to achieve both economy in production and efficiency in charity distribution they gradually adopted the rudiments of differential pricing. Essentially, they had four prices: (1) a premium price for trade Bibles on fine paper; (2) a price modestly above cost for regular Bibles sold to outsiders; (3) a "first cost" price for Bibles sold to other societies and auxiliaries; and (4) a zero price for Bibles given to the destitute, through the Philadelphia headquarters directly or through the little societies. Though the economic pressures to sell were great, the Philadelphia Bible Society remained true to the traditional belief that charity meant ultimately giving, not selling. This fundamental principle, however, was already gradually eroding. It would erode still further in the era of the American Bible Society, which came upon the scene in 1816.

The founders of the American Bible Society hoped to adapt the techniques pioneered by the Philadelphia Bible Society to a new scale of enterprise: the nation. Some Bible men doubted that it could be done, and chief among the doubters were the managers of the Philadelphia Bible Society. The Philadelphians—and others, too—believed that the new society would be too large, too centralized, and that it would sap the vitality of the state and local organizations.[17] The ABS founders believed otherwise. They professed a simple organizational faith: "Concentrated action is powerful action." And they proposed to concentrate everything: capital, technology, information, and organization. The headquarters would be in "the London of America," as one founder called it: New York City.[18]

The concentration of capital and technology worked out well, even better than the founders had imagined. By 1816, it was already obvious that large-scale stereotype printing was the key to low-cost Bible production; and the first order of business for the new board of managers was not to acquire Bibles, but to acquire stereotype plates. In August 1816 the managers contracted to buy six sets of plates, three in octavo and three in duodecimo. But even these ardent centralizers did not propose to concentrate all these plates in New York. They feared the country was too large for that. Instead, they imagined a network of several regional printing centers. In late 1816, the managers voted to send plates to Lexington, Kentucky, to serve the trans-Appalachian west. By 1819, the Kentucky Bible Society was printing Bibles for the ABS.[19]

Very quickly, however, the Kentucky experiment proved to the New York board that branch printing was a mistake. Western paper was expensive and poorly made; press work was sloppy; bindings were inferior. An ABS committee reported that suitable materials and skilled workmen were not available in Lexington, and, in any case, the society there had neither the funds nor the demand to keep the plates efficiently employed. "The Committee ... feel confident," they wrote in 1819, "that the Auxiliary Societies in the Western Country would be more satisfactorily supplied with Bibles from the Depository in New York, notwithstanding the expenses of freight and transportation." The New York board decided to keep the

Kentucky plant going for a few more years, because of the currency crisis that had followed the Panic of 1819. (For several years, western money was virtually worthless in New York, and western Bible societies begged to be allowed to spend their bouncing banknotes in Lexington.) But, except for currency exchange, regional printing had few advantages, and the first branch was the last.[20] Moreover, with the advent of steam-powered printing presses and machine-made paper in the 1820s, the concentration of *all* Bible manufacturing in one place, New York, seemed ever more efficient, even providential. By the end of the 1820s, the American Bible Society's New York operation was one of the largest publishing houses in the country, virtually monopolizing the production of inexpensive Bibles in the United States.[21]

To power this enormous, centralized publishing operation, the American Bible Society, like the Philadelphia Bible Society before it, needed a decentralized network of local societies. As one of the founders of the society, James Milnor, put it in the late 1820s, "The machinery of a mill may be mechanically perfect in all its parts, but not a wheel will move without the impetus of water. And so those stereotype plates, giving so much facility to the art of printing, and those power-presses, multiplying with such unexampled rapidity impressions of the sacred pages, to produce their expected results, must be supplied, and for these means, the occupants of these plates and presses must be dependent on their Auxiliaries."[22]

The American Bible Society was dependent upon its auxiliaries because it was a charity publisher. Like the Philadelphia Bible Society, the ABS needed to sell books in order to give books away. Eventually, the ABS traveled farther down the road to selling than the Philadelphia Bible Society had dared to go. To achieve real efficiency in charity publishing on a grand scale, the American Bible Society needed to develop a full-blown system of differential pricing. And the managers believed that only local societies could make that happen.

In the beginning, the mission of the ABS was the traditional one in Bible work: "gratuitous distribution," to give Bibles away for free. Like the Philadelphia Bible Society, they sold books at cost or even below cost to their auxiliaries, and the auxiliaries distributed them for free to the poor. In 1819, however, the society changed policy and began to urge auxiliaries to move more into selling, but on a differential price basis. The charitable purpose and economic implications of the new plan are nicely summarized in the society's annual report for 1821:

> The plan recommended by the Managers, of selling Bibles and Testaments at cost or at reduced prices, where persons are able and willing to pay, has been highly approved by all the Auxiliaries from whom accounts have been received; and has been carried into effect, in many instances, with unexpected and very pleasing success. Those who needed Bibles have usually preferred to give something for them; and the process of distribution has not been impeded, if it has not been accelerated, by the measure referred to. The Auxiliaries have found their ability enlarged by it; and they have been enabled to supply more fully the necessity of those who were not possessors of the Sacred Volume, and yet could not, or would not, purchase it. For it should be distinctly understood, that the Managers were very far from designing, by the plan, to diminish the circulation of the Scriptures: they designed rather to add to it. They were satisfied that many persons would gladly become possessors of a Bible by paying the full, or a reduced price, whose feelings of independence revolted from receiving it as the gift of charity. On the plan which the Managers have recommended, the Scriptures are still given freely to the destitute who are without means, or without disposition to pay for them; while receiving the whole, or a part of the cost from such as are willing to pay, the funds are rendered more availing, and a degree of security is obtained, that the volume which has been purchased will be prized, preserved, and used.[23]

This policy of differential pricing was mainly a revenue enhancer. But it also suggests a psychological insight into pricing and utility, especially with a product as spiritual as religion. It is an economic truism that people will pay more for something they value more; but the reverse is often true as well: They will value something more if they have paid more for it. It is a twist on the old saying, "You get what you pay for." It may be that in religion that is automatically so.[24]

The society's new policy to sell, rather than to give, struck some critics of the American Bible Society as confirmation of widespread Jacksonian suspicions—that the society was a conspiracy of meddlesome and self-aggrandizing elitists whose aim was "wealth and power" and "political privilege," not charity, as one writer put it in an 1830 pamphlet titled *An Expose of the Rise and Proceedings of the American Bible Society*. This anonymous pamphleteer, probably a disgruntled printer or bookseller, mocked the society's embrace of the traditional motto of Bible work: "without money and without price." The reverse was true, he declared:

> The Managers of the Parent Institution, in their Fourth Report [1820], mention the fact of their having sent a Circular to their Auxiliaries, urging them to use their influence and endeavours to *sell*, not to *give*, the "bread of life." This they have iterated and reiterated, year after year, with a pertinacity worthy of a better cause. The effect of this has been to make almost every pulpit in our churches a stall for the sale of their books, or clerical bookstores of temples of worship; and our pious young men have become travelling peddlers and hawkers, forcing their entrance into families which they had never before seen, and urging them to buy, at reduced prices, the books issued by this "National Institution." They district cities, towns, and villages, and scour them, either singly or in squads, seeking purchasers with money, not the indigent without it.

Furthermore, the writer continued, "the Managers . . . would render nugatory all competition." By subsidizing the price of Bibles through charitable contributions, they were able to undersell and ruin all commercial competitors.[25]

This latter judgment is fair enough. The American Bible Society did hope to dominate—even to monopolize—the market for cheap Bibles. In that way only could they achieve maximum economies of scale in printing and thus the most efficient use of capital. But it does not follow automatically from this that they were interested in selling *only*. That judgment is unfair. The writer of *An Expose* assumed a false dichotomy between giving and selling: The former was charity; the latter, commerce. The ABS managers believed, on the contrary, that efficient charity required *both* selling and giving. That is, it required differential pricing, with the price falling to zero. And such a price system is what they tried to achieve, as they lectured, nagged, and cajoled their auxiliaries throughout the 1820s.

On the one hand, they regularly pressed the auxiliaries to sell books. (The writer of *An Expose* was certainly right about iteration and reiteration.)

In a typical exhortation, they wrote: "The Managers deem it expedient to renew their recommendation to the Auxiliaries to sell the Scriptures at cost or at reduced prices, in preference to distributing them gratuitously. There are some, and even many, cases in which it may be advisable to give a Bible or a Testament without receiving any amount as the price of its purchase; but in general this is found in our country and in other countries not to be the wisest course. Whatever sum may be obtained for a Bible or a Testament, is so much preserved to the funds whence the really needy are to be supplied." And free riders must be closely scrutinized: "Those who are really unable to pay any thing, should be supplied gratuitously without hesitation: but this is by no means the condition of all who are not possessors of the Scriptures. And as to such as can pay, and will not pay any part of the price of a Bible or a Testament, there certainly is very little reason even to hope that they would use and improve the sacred Book, were it placed into their hands." [26] On the other hand, when some overly parsimonious auxiliaries took this as a mandate to grant *no* free books at all, the managers chastised them for being too strict with free riders. "The principle of the Parent Society seems to have been misapprehended," they wrote to one offending auxiliary. "It is designed that the Scriptures shall be furnished gratuitously to those who are truly poor, and will faithfully use them. We would cheerfully *give* in such cases, and trust Providence to furnish means for the future." [27]

If the auxiliaries were good, the wide circulation of books through differential pricing seems to have worked. By the late 1820s, ten state societies had launched "general supplies"—that is, distributions of Bibles, through both selling and giving, to everyone in their states.[28] For universal circulation to succeed, the little societies at the local level had to make differential pricing work. And throughout the 1820s ABS annual reports and *Extracts* were filled with correspondence from auxiliaries describing their efforts to follow company policy, to sell *and* give simultaneously. In a typical report, the officers of the Nassau-Hall Bible Society of New Jersey wrote: "To some we sold Bibles at reduced prices; and before we gave gratuitously, we were careful to ascertain the inability of the persons to purchase, and their desire to use the Bible aright." Meanwhile, they resisted the pressures of greedy free riders who "were displeased because we did not give Bibles to them as well as to their neighbors, who, in their opinion, were not more worthy than themselves." [29] Sorting the good free riders from the bad—the sheep from the goats—was not an easy task, but the energetic auxiliaries struggled to do it.

Not all auxiliaries were energetic, however. Indeed, the most troubling free riders turned out to be neither the unworthy nor the worthy poor, but the third kind, the kind the sociologists worry about, the organizational free rider—in this case, the lax and self-serving members of the auxiliaries themselves. Local societies often used Bibles as lures to membership, and many people, it seems, joined the local societies just to get cheap Bibles for themselves and their families. They paid little attention to the destitute. Some members were selflessly diligent for a while, but only a while. The managers in New York wrote constantly of auxiliaries "languishing." In 1824, in a typical lament, they complained that "some of the auxiliaries were as if in a deep slumber, or slowly wasting away, or in the last feeble struggles of existence, or actually dead and existing only in name." To boost morale, the New York office sometimes gave struggling auxiliaries free books. But, as with individual grants, this could have an effect opposite of the one intended, inducing "a spirit of dependence" that seemed further to drain away their zeal.[30] Especially troubling, from a business point of view, many auxiliaries failed to pay for the books they had ordered on credit. By 1829, auxiliaries had run up some thirty-six thousand dollars in unpaid bills, and the exasperated managers in New York seriously considered dunning them for interest.[31] Worst of all, in many newly settled parts of the country there were no auxiliaries of any kind, languishing or otherwise.

To stir up languishing auxiliaries and to spark the creation of new ones, the American Bible Society in the 1820s began to extend its managerial influence down to the local level. They did this through the use of paid agents. The first was Richard D. Hall, appointed in 1821 to work in the South and West. By 1828, the society had twelve agents in the field. These agents were employees of the central office, and they brought the New York system to the hinterland—i.e., careful organization and record-keeping, financial accounting, communication with the central headquarters, and attention to the policy of differential pricing of Bibles. Certainly, their work had a centralizing tendency to it. That was the point. Yet the New York office made it clear in the agents' instructions that their mission was not to do the distribution work of the society; it was to prod the auxiliaries to do it.[32]

At the end of the 1820s, then, the American Bible Society had in place a system for conducting a charity through both selling and giving. Parts of the system were working well. Production of Bibles was prodigious—in both meanings of that term. With sixteen power presses and twenty hand presses on line at the New York Bible House by 1829, the managers were confident that they could produce enough Bibles to supply everyone in the country. Meanwhile, many state and local auxiliaries were running efficiently and were bubbling with enthusiasm. To many Bible men and women, the times seemed propitious for a great national commitment: the "general supply" of the entire United States within two years. The New York managers were skeptical. They knew that many auxiliaries were neither efficient nor enthusiastic. They knew that money and Bible workers were scarce in the West. And they knew that everything would depend on the auxiliaries. Without water, the great mill in New York could not turn. But they agreed to try, and in the summer of 1829 the first great general supply of Bibles to the United States was launched.[33]

On the production side, the general supply was a triumph. In three years, 1829–1831, the society's presses churned out more than one million volumes. In a country of fewer than three million households, this was an impressive and unprecedented publication performance.[34]

But by the spring of 1833 the managers were disappointed. After four years, many remote areas remained entirely unsupplied. Even in areas fully canvassed, the managers said that "the work was often imperfectly done—many families were overlooked." Many auxiliaries defaulted on their special pledges for the general supply, and so the national society was plunged even more deeply into debt to banks and paper suppliers. During the general supply, to help achieve the goal of universal circulation quickly, the society allowed more free grants than usual, but this relaxed policy led many people who could afford to pay to demand free Bibles (free riders again). This, of course, drove up the cost of the enterprise. Most serious of all, even some of the stronger auxiliaries, which did conduct systematic surveys and careful distributions, could not sustain the effort for long, and "apathy . . . followed the season of high excitement and great exertion." In their 1833 report, the managers complained that "many Auxiliaries which supplied their destitute families two or three years ago have not ordered a Bible since." All in all, the managers of the American Bible Society judged the general supply a failure and the auxiliaries largely to blame.[35]

Not surprisingly, after 1829 the society experimented with strategies for improving the auxiliaries and for distributing Bibles outside the auxiliary system. They added more agents and new schemes for selling Bibles and raising revenue in ways more directly under the control of the New York office. In 1847, for example, the managers greatly enlarged their agents' authority to stockpile books and to sell them for cash to all comers. In many ways, paid agents became increasingly important to the work of the national organization. By the mid-1850s, the American Bible Society had county agents as well as general agents. These men were employed by auxiliaries but directed by New York. The *Bible Agent's Manual* of 1856 laid out a system vastly more centralized and businesslike than the system of 1829. Even the lowly county agent had fifteen different kinds of official documents and forms to juggle and, in many cases, to fill out and post to New York. When the society decided to mount a second general supply in 1856, agents would play a much larger role than they had played in 1829, including a role in organizing distribution. The society was determined not to repeat the failures of 1829. The managers admonished their agents and their auxiliaries that "by whatever means the intended result must be reached." If that meant that men must be hired and paid to distribute Bibles, so be it.[36]

And yet the managers still stuck with the auxiliary system. They remained devoted to the local voluntary association. Only local societies were equipped to sell and to give efficiently, they believed. The agent's main task was still to serve the auxiliaries, not to supplant them. And the more local, the better, the *Agent's Manual* declared: "The people feel that these local Societies, organized in their own neighborhoods, with their officers selected from among them, their annual meetings held in their midst, and of which all are invited to become members, are their *own*, and hence manifest much more interest in sustaining them than they would a mere county organization, having its head quarters at a distance, controlled by men with whom they are unacquainted, and the annual meetings of which they seldom or never attend." [37]

The American Bible Society was the model for other national associations that defined their mission as the universal circulation of religious publications. The two most prominent were the American Sunday School Union (founded in 1824) and the American Tract Society (founded in 1825). Like the ABS, both of these societies became major publishers through investment in stereotype printing. The mission of the American Sunday School Union was to found Sunday schools, but also to supply them with children's books and periodicals. The mission of the American Tract Society was to distribute small tracts and religious books. Both concentrated their printing work (ASSU in Philadelphia and ATS in New York), and in the 1820s and 1830s both followed the pattern of the American Bible Society in distributing their books through local auxiliaries.[38]

Like the ABS, the American Sunday School Union and the American Tract Society believed that the most efficient strategy for universal circulation was differential pricing. In its own version of a general supply in 1830, the ASSU launched the Mississippi Valley Project, an effort to start Sunday schools (with libraries) in every community in the West in two years. To accomplish this great work, they proposed to sell books at cost and to provide them at reduced rates or for free where needed.[39] In 1834, the ATS launched a similar effort in the South and West, called the Volume Enterprise, whose aim was to place at least one religious book into every household. Here, too, the strategy was differential pricing:

> It is most clear, that the tremendous influence of the public press in our country *may not be left* solely to the operation and influence of sales for the purposes of gain. The most valuable books must be *prepared in an attractive style,* and *furnished at cost, or less than cost,* and Christian efforts must be put forth all over the land to *place them in the hands of people*—by sale, if it can be done—gratuitously, if it cannot. . . . To every donor to the Society there is also this encouragement, that as the volumes are chiefly *sold*, the amount of each donation returns with every sale; is sent out again, and again returns; and thus continues to revolve, and may, and probably will revolve long after the benevolent donor shall be sleeping in dust.[40]

Also like the ABS, these societies grew frustrated with their auxiliaries. Though it had an extensive network of auxiliaries by 1830, the American Sunday School Union turned increasingly to the employment of paid agents and missionaries during the Mississippi Valley Project.[41] The American

Tract Society moved dramatically in 1841 to sidestep its auxiliaries and to distribute tracts and books through its own paid agents. This was the beginning of a system for which the ATS became famous: colportage.[42] "Colporteur" was a term applied to a book distributor who was not a local volunteer but an itinerant who earned his living in the work. For religious publishers in the 1840s and 1850s, colportage was a seductive panacea, a way to centralize control of distribution, and the apparent solution to the nagging problems of languishing local auxiliaries.

In the weak form of colportage, a religious colporteur was little more than a traveling bookseller, working on commission. Colporteurs for the Baptist Publishing Society and the Methodist Tract Society worked largely on commission, though they sometimes received a modest stipend from the central office. Giving away books was only a minuscule part of their mission.[43] And as commission agents, their economic, if not their evangelical, incentive was always to sell, not give, and thus to go where the money was. In the strong form of colportage, on the other hand, the colporteur was a salaried employee, not dependent on sales commissions for income, and therefore free to go to any house, every house, regardless of the potential for sales. The American Tract Society pioneered this form of colportage. By 1851, the ATS had more than five hundred colporteurs in the field, all hired, paid, and supervised through the New York headquarters. This was the most centralized, most nationalized effort by any American religious publisher before the Civil War.[44]

The American Tract Society quickly fell in love with colportage. In the first ten years of the program, ATS colporteurs distributed more than 3 million books, along with many millions of small tracts. Most of the books were sold, but some 650,000 were given away—about 21 percent of the total.[45] Impressed by the success of the ATS, other societies took up colportage as well. Only a handful, however, such as the Presbyterian Board of Publication, employed fully salaried colporteurs on the ATS model, and no one before the Civil War fielded as many colporteurs as the American Tract Society.[46]

The strong colportage system—the ATS model—seemed to solve or sidestep several of the free rider problems that faced religious publishers. Salaried colporteurs who called on everyone, including the destitute, and who had authority to give away books were able to reach the obviously good free rider, the pious poor who merely lacked the money to buy. If giving away books had been the only task, the traveling colporteur, who knocked on every door, would have been the best person to do it. Strong colportage also sidestepped the problem of organizational free riders in the auxiliaries. Colporteurs were employees, not volunteers, and their morale and conduct were dependent upon compensation and supervision flowing from New York. They had their own morale problems, of course, but those problems were different from the free rider problems of voluntary organizations. The colporteur was not equipped, however, to solve the problem of the bad free rider, the person who sought a free book but who could afford to pay or who received a free book but may have made poor use of it. As an itinerant outsider just passing through the neighborhood, the colporteur was in no position to sort the good free riders from the bad—that is, to administer a full-fledged differential pricing system.

Most denominational book and tract societies dealt with this problem by drawing a distinction between what was to be given and what was to be sold. Tracts were to be given; books were to be sold, always. The colporteur had no price decision to make. ATS and Presbyterian Board colporteurs had authority to give away books, but the subtlety of differential pricing was gradually replaced by a dichotomous sell/give decision. Even so, the question of when to sell and when to give, the crucial economic decision, was not easily made. To simplify the decision process, ATS colporteurs were permitted to give away only certain small, cheap volumes (often Richard Baxter's *Call to the Unconverted*). These were the give-away books; the others were to be sold.[47] ATS colporteurs were supposed to judge the recipients of their books, but it was an impossible assignment. And this system really looked ahead to a simpler style of religious book distribution in which some books are given, some sold, but no attempt is made to sort the good free riders from the bad. Everyone gets a cheap book, no questions asked. That, of course, is the modern style of print-media evangelism, the style that we all routinely run into on the sidewalks of American cities and college campuses.

The American Bible Society, willing to try most anything to get the Bibles distributed to everyone, also adopted colportage. Indeed, after 1869, colporteurs—supervised and paid by New York—became an important part of the ABS system.[48] But for the American Bible Society this change came slowly and reluctantly. Long after the American Tract Society had largely given up on its auxiliaries, the ABS managers remained steadfast in the belief that an itinerant colporteur could never do what a local society could do. For more than fifty years, despite deep frustration and incessant complaint, the American Bible Society retained, even sometimes celebrated, the auxiliary system. As late as 1860, the managers declared: "The Board have by no means lost confidence in the auxiliary system. We believe it to be the only effectual one for carrying the Word of God to every door and every individual in the land. In no other way, we believe, could the Bible be so generally and so effectually distributed. . . . This is not mere theory. It is well sustained by facts." [49]

My point here has been nearly the opposite. The "facts" weighed heavily against the auxiliary system. Time and time again, the managers of the American Bible Society (and other societies that depended on auxiliaries) were disappointed in practice. But the theory was a good one. From an economic perspective, the American Bible Society's strategy was clearly the least-cost route to universal circulation. National concentration of capital and production coupled with distribution through differential pricing was the most efficient way to go. And only local decision-makers could administer a differential price system effectively. Only they could size up a customer's ability and desire to pay; only they could exclude bad free riders while including the good ones; only they could sell and give simultaneously. Of course, the managers recognized the problems that could bedevil the local societies, and they searched for ways to punch up the morale of languishing auxiliaries. But for decades they believed that the economic advantages of the local auxiliary system outweighed these internal organizational problems. It may not have worked out in fact, but the theory was irresistible. In a sense, it might be said that the managers of the American Bible Society were better students of the economics of media and evangelism than of the economics of organizations.

Current sociologists of religion, on the other hand, are better students of the economics of organizations than of media or evangelism. In their provocative study *The Churching of America*, Roger Finke and Rodney Stark make much of the free rider problem in church organizations. They develop what they call a "rational choice" model of religious participation, arguing that "religion is a *collectively produced* commodity," that individuals gain religious rewards within a shared, communal experience. Free riders consume the group's resources—both material and psychic—without contributing their fair share. This saps the vitality of the church. Since the early nineteenth century, they argue, strict churches in America have been more successful than lax churches because they have devised ways to exclude these organizational free riders. By requiring more sacrifice of their members, strict churches raise the cost of membership, which screens out free riders and thereby raises the average level of participation. Paradoxically, in an organization such as a church, raising the cost of participation can produce *more* participation, and therefore more individual satisfaction.[50]

But what about the other kinds of free riders that I have discussed, the free riders in the realms of religious evangelism and religious media? These are not savvy consumers seeking religious utility. They are not seekers at all. They won't buy because they do not value the product. These are the free riders *sought* by evangelism. They are lost sheep, whom the things of this world have led astray; "rational choice" will not bring them into the fold. Though I am using biblical imagery here, the religious publishers of the early nineteenth century were just as adept as Finke and Stark at putting the matter into economic terms. In the words of the Presbyterian Board of Publication, "Religious knowledge is a benefit, of which men less feel the need the less they possess of it. Here the demand does not create a supply, for the demand may not exist, however extreme the necessity. The gospel provides for its own dissemination. It was never contemplated that men would 'seek,' and hence the command is 'to send,' 'to go,' and 'to preach.'"[51]

And, I would add, to print. Religious evangelism and religious publishing merged easily because their economic natures are the same. Once produced, the word (whether the Gospel or any media message) is free. Like its subject, the grace of God, the word has no cost at the margin. These are "public goods," goods that are not used up when consumed. "One taper kindles many without diminishing its own light."[52] The common mission of the evangelist and the publisher in early nineteenth-century America was to deliver the free word as freely as possible. The free rider could be carried at little cost and that cost could be subsidized (indeed, in a latter day, the age of broadcasting, one could be carried at no cost at all). In organizations—including churches and little Bible societies—the exclusion of free riders through strictness, discipline, and sacrifice may well be needed to achieve strength and vitality. And that is important. But evangelism and mass media move in another economic realm, a realm of infinite abundance. The Bible has passages aplenty to vindicate the purveyors (and the economists) of religious strictness and discipline. But the religious publishers sang a different economic song: "Freely ye have received, freely give." "The Word of the Lord has free course, and is glorified." "Yea, come, buy wine and milk without money and without price." [53]

NOTES

1. David Paul Nord, "Systematic Benevolence: Religious Publishing and the Marketplace in Early Nineteenth-Century America," in *Communications and Change in American Religious History,* ed. Leonard I. Sweet (Grand Rapids, MI: William B. Eerdmans, 1993), 239–269. See also Alfred D. Chandler Jr., *The Visible Hand: The Managerial Revolution in American Business* (Cambridge: Belknap Press of Harvard University Press, 1977).

2. David Paul Nord, "The Evangelical Origins of Mass Media in America, 1815–1835," *Journalism Monographs* 88 (May 1984); R. Laurence Moore, *Selling God: American Religion in the Marketplace of Culture* (New York: Oxford University Press, 1994), 17–18; Nathan O. Hatch, *The Democratization of American Christianity* (New Haven, CT: Yale University Press, 1989), 41–45; Jon Butler, *Awash in a Sea of Faith: Christianizing the American People* (Cambridge: Harvard University Press, 1990), 277–278; and Paul Charles Gutjahr, "Battling for the Book: The Americanization of the Bible in the Publishing Marketplace, 1777–1860" (PhD diss., University of Iowa, 1996), chapter 2.

3. Nord, "Systematic Benevolence," 254–255; Peter J. Wosh, *Spreading the Word: The Bible Business in Nineteenth-Century America* (Ithaca, NY: Cornell University Press, 1994), 62–63, 71. See also Daniel Feller, *The Jacksonian Promise: America, 1815–1840* (Baltimore: Johns Hopkins University Press, 1995), chapter 6.

4. Laurence R. Iannaccone, "Why Strict Churches Are Strong," *American Journal of Sociology* 99 (March 1994): 1184.

5. On media economics, see Alison Alexander, James Owers, and Rod Carveth, eds., *Media Economics: Theory and Practice* (Hillsdale, NJ: Lawrence Erlbaum Associates, 1993); Robert G. Picard, *Media Economics: Concepts and Issues* (Newbury Park, CA: Sage Publications, 1989); and John H. McManus, *Market-Driven Journalism: Let the Citizen Beware* (Thousand Oaks, CA: Sage Publications, 1994). On religion economics, see R. Stephen Warner, "Work in Progress toward a New Paradigm for the Sociological Study of Religion in the United States," *American Journal of Sociology* 98 (March 1993): 1044–1093; Laurence R. Iannaccone, "Voodoo Economics? Reviewing the Rational Choice Approach to Religion," *Journal for the Scientific Study of Religion* 34 (1995): 76–89; Steve Bruce, "Religion

and Rational Choice: A Critique of Economic Explanations of Religious Behavior," *Sociology of Religion* 54 (1993): 193–205; Roger Finke and Rodney Stark, *The Churching of America, 1776–1990: Winners and Losers in our Religious Economy* (New Brunswick, NJ: Rutgers University Press, 1992), chapter 7.

6. [William Jay], *A Memoir on the Subject of a General Bible Society for the United States of America* (New Jersey: n.p., 1816), 6. For overviews of the pre-1816 Bible societies, see Eric M. North, "The Bible Society Movement Reaches America," ABS Historical Essay, No. 7, Part 1 (New York: American Bible Society, 1963); Eric M. North, "The Bible Societies Founded in 1809 in the United States," ABS Historical Essay, No. 7, Part 2 (New York: American Bible Society, 1963); and Rebecca Bromley, "The Spread of the Bible Societies, 1810–1816," ABS Historical Essay, No. 8, Parts 1 & 2 (New York: American Bible Society, 1963). On the context of charity Bible work, see Conrad Edick Wright, *The Transformation of Charity in Postrevolutionary New England* (Boston: Northeastern University Press, 1992). On the British and Foreign Bible Society, see Leslie Howsam, *Cheap Bibles: Nineteenth-Century Publishing and the British and Foreign Bible Society* (Cambridge: Cambridge University Press, 1991).

7. Bible Society of Philadelphia, *An Address of the Bible Society Established at Philadelphia to the Public: To Which Is Subjoined the Constitution of Said Society and the Names of the Managers* (Philadelphia: Fry and Kammerer, 1809), 10, 22. On a similar effort elsewhere, see "Address to the Public, the Massachusetts Bible Society," in *The Panoplist* (June 1809).

8. Bible Society of Philadelphia, *First Annual Report* (1809), 4, 8–9.

9. Howsam, *Cheap Bibles*, 77–79. On the stereotype process, see George A. Kubler, *A New History of Stereotyping* (New York: Little & Ives, 1941); and George A. Kubler, *Historical Treatises, Abstracts, and Papers on Stereotyping* (New York: Brooklyn Eagle Press, 1936). Two very early pamphlets on the process have been reprinted. See Charles Brightly, *The Method of Founding Stereotype* (New York: Garland, 1982); and Thomas Hodgson, *An Essay on the Origin and Progress of Stereotype Printing* (New York: Garland, 1982). Brightly's pamphlet was originally published in 1809; Hodgson's in 1822.

10. Bible Society of Philadelphia, *Second Annual Report* (1810), 10–11; Bible Society of Philadelphia, *Third Annual Report* (1811), 7. The plates arrived in October 1812 and were turned over to the Philadelphia printer William Fry, who immediately struck off an edition of 1,250 copies, the first stereotyped Bible in America. By 1816, the Philadelphia Society had printed more than 55,000 Bibles and New Testaments from several sets of plates. See Bible Society of Philadelphia, *Fifth Annual Report* (1813), 9; Bible Society of Philadelphia, *Eighth Annual Report* (1816), 3–4. See also Margaret T. Hills, *The English Bible in America: A Bibliography of Editions of the Bible and the New Testament Published in America, 1777–1957* (New York: American Bible Society and New York Public Library, 1961), 37.

11. In the Philadelphia book trade in this era, the role of the publisher was splitting away from the role of the printer. See Rosalind Remer, *Printers and Men of*

Capital: Philadelphia Book Publishers in the New Republic (Philadelphia: University of Pennsylvania Press, 1996). In Bible work, this distinction existed as well, but the long-term trend was in the opposite direction; printer and publisher were coming together. From the beginning, Bible societies owned their own plates. Later they owned their own presses, even though their printers worked as independent contractors. In 1845, the American Bible Society took over its own printing; in 1848, its own binding; and in 1851, its own stereotype plate founding.

12. Bible Society of Philadelphia, *Fifth Annual Report* (1813), 11–12; Bible Society of Philadelphia, *Sixth Annual Report* (1814), 13; Bible Society of Philadelphia, *Fourth Annual Report* (1812), 7.

13. *An Address of the Bible Society of Philadelphia to the Friends of Revealed Truth in the State of Pennsylvania* (Philadelphia: Fry and Kammerer, 1810), 6, 8–9. This system was different from the one developed by the British and Foreign Bible Society. In England, auxiliaries were expected to sell Bibles, not to give them away; and they received Bibles in exchange for only one-half of their contributions to the parent society. The rest of the money was used by the parent society to fund translation and foreign work. From the beginning, the Bible society movement in England was much more commercial and centrally controlled than it was in the United States. See Howsam, *Cheap Bibles,* 42–43, 50–51.

14. *Address of the Bible Society of Philadelphia to the Friends of Revealed Truth,* 4.

15. Bible Society of Philadelphia, *Third Annual Report* (1811), 4.

16. A similar story might be told about the New York Bible Society, the only other state society that took up stereotype printing before 1816. On the New York society, see David J. Fant, *The Bible in New York: The Romance of Scripture Distribution in a World Metropolis from 1809 to 1948* (New York: American Bible Society, 1948); and Margaret M. McGuinness, "The Relationship between the American Bible Society and the New York Bible Society, 1816–1987," ABS Historical Working Paper Series, No. 1990–3 (New York: American Bible Society, 1990).

17. The debate within the Bible movement over the founding of the ABS is described in Eric M. North, "The Pressure toward a National Bible Society, 1808–1816," ABS Historical Essay, No. 9 (New York: American Bible Society, 1963), 46–76.

18. *Constitution of the American Bible Society . . . Together with Their Address to the People of the United States* (New York: G. F. Hopkins, 1816), 16. See also Elias Boudinot, *An Answer to the Objections of the Managers of the Philadelphia Bible-Society, Against a Meeting of Delegates from the Bible Societies in the Union* (Burlington, NJ: David Allinson, [1815]); [Samuel Mills], "Plan of a General Bible Society," *The Panoplist* (October 1813); and [Jay], *Memoir.*

19. American Bible Society, Minutes of the Board of Managers, Aug. 7, 1816, and Dec. 4, 1816, in American Bible Society archives, New York; American Bible Society, *First Annual Report* (1817), 10, 21; American Bible Society, *Second Annual Report* (1818), 11–12; American Bible Society, *Third Annual Report* (1819), 10. See also Hills, *The English Bible in America,* 60.

20. American Bible Society, Minutes of the Board of Managers, July 15, 1819, Nov. 18, 1819, and Feb. 1, 1821; American Bible Society, *Fourth Annual Report* (1820), 8.

21. Nord, "Evangelical Origins," 10–14, 18; Gutjahr, "Battling for the Book," chapter 2.

22. James Milnor, speech text, in *Monthly Extracts of the American Bible Society* 17 (May 1829): 239.

23. "Circular Letter of the Committee on Auxiliary Societies," in American Bible Society, *Third Annual Report* (1819), 74; American Bible Society, *Fifth Annual Report* (1821), 30; American Bible Society, *Sixth Annual Report* (1822), 32–33. Though the managers sometimes cited the sales policy of the British and Foreign Bible Society as a precedent for their own, it was in fact different. Within Great Britain, the BFBS policy was to sell only, never to give. And the poor who received Bibles were, in a sense, members of centrally administered Bible associations who received their books through small weekly subscriptions. See Howsam, *Cheap Bibles*, chapter 2.

24. This idea, put more subtly, is a theme in the recent literature in the economics of religion. The argument is that strict churches do better than lax churches because members value highly what they and other church members have paid a high price to obtain. See Iannaccone, "Why Strict Churches Are Strong," 1182–1183; Finke and Stark, *Churching of America*, 249–250.

25. *An Expose of the Rise and Proceedings of the American Bible Society, during the Thirteen Years of Its Existence, by a Member* (New York: n.p., 1830), 13–14, 17–18. For a similar critique, focusing mainly on the American Tract Society, see [Herman Hooker], *An Appeal to the Christian Public, on the Evil and Impolicy of the Church Engaging in Merchandise; Setting Forth the Wrong Done to Booksellers, and the Extravagance, Inutility, and Evil-Working, of Charity Publication Societies* (Philadelphia: King & Baird, 1849).

26. American Bible Society, *Seventh Annual Report* (1823), 24; American Bible Society, *Eighth Annual Report* (1824), 28–29.

27. American Bible Society, *Eleventh Annual Report* (1827), 37.

28. American Bible Society, *Thirteenth Annual Report* (1829), 25, 41–42; American Bible Society, *Fourteenth Annual Report* (1830), 89–90.

29. American Bible Society, *Ninth Annual Report* (1825), 63.

30. American Bible Society, *Fifth Annual Report* (1821), 28; American Bible Society, *Seventh Annual Report* (1823), 11; American Bible Society, *Eighth Annual Report* (1824), 27; American Bible Society, *Thirteenth Annual Report* (1829), 43–44.

31. American Bible Society, Minutes of the Board of Managers, June 18, 1829, and July 3, 1829.

32. American Bible Society, Minutes of the Board of Managers, Nov. 8, 1821; American Bible Society, *Seventh Annual Report* (1823), 20–21, 74; American Bible Society, *Twelfth Annual Report* (1828), 30–31; *An Abstract of the American Bible Society, Containing an Account of Its Principles and Operations* (New York: Daniel Fanshaw, 1830), 18–19, 38; *A Brief Analysis of the System of the American Bible*

Society, Containing a Full Account of Its Principles and Operations (New York: Daniel Fanshaw, 1830), 27–30.

33. *Address of the Board of Managers of the American Bible Society to the Friends of the Bible of Every Religious Denomination, on the Subject of the Resolution for Supplying All the Destitute Families in the United States with the Bible in the Course of Two Years* (New York: J. Seymour, 1829). For narrative overviews of the general supply, see Creighton Lacy, *The Word Carrying Giant: The Growth of the American Bible Society* (South Pasadena, CA: William Carey Library, 1977), chapter 4; and Henry Otis Dwight, *The Centennial History of the American Bible Society* (New York: Macmillan, 1916), chapter 12.

34. American Bible Society, *Seventeenth Annual Report* (1833), 14. On production data, see Nord, "Evangelical Origins," 19.

35. *Monthly Extracts of the American Bible Society* 26 (March 1830): 325; American Bible Society, *Fifteenth Annual Report* (1831), 6–7, 17–18; American Bible Society, *Seventeenth Annual Report* (1833), 16–17; American Bible Society, Minutes of the Board of Managers, June 18, 1829, and July 3, 1829; American Bible Society, *Twenty-fourth Annual Report* (1840), 25–26.

36. American Bible Society, *Thirty-first Annual Report* (1847), 37; American Bible Society, *Forty-third Annual Report* (1859), 33–35; *Address of the Managers of the American Bible Society, to Its Auxiliaries, Members, and Friends, in Regard to a General Supply of the United States with the Sacred Scriptures* (New York: American Bible Society, 1856), 8–10; *The Bible Agent's Manual* (New York: American Bible Society, 1856), 4–8. See also Wosh, *Spreading the Word*, 70–71, 176–177; and Mary F. Cordato, "The Relationship of the American Bible Society to Its Auxiliaries: A Historical Timeline Study," ABS Historical Working Paper Series, No. 1991–1 (New York: American Bible Society, 1991).

37. *Bible Agent's Manual*, 1.

38. For general overviews of the work of these societies, see Anne M. Boylan, *Sunday School: The Formation of an American Institution, 1790–1880* (New Haven, CT: Yale University Press, 1988); Nord, "Evangelical Origins"; and Nord, "Systematic Benevolence."

39. American Sunday School Union, *Sixth Annual Report* (1830), 3, 18–19; American Sunday School Union, *Seventh Annual Report* (1831), 30–36; American Sunday School Union, *Eighth Annual Report* (1832), 36–38.

40. American Tract Society, *Eleventh Annual Report* (1836), 41–44. See also *Proposed Circulation of the Standard Evangelical Volumes of the American Tract Society to the Southern Atlantic States* (New York: American Tract Society, 1834).

41. American Sunday School Union, *Seventh Annual Report* (1831), 9, 30–34. See also Boylan, *Sunday School*, 75.

42. For contemporary overviews of ATS colportage, see the special report "Ten Years of Colportage in America," in American Tract Society, *Twenty-Sixth Annual Report* (1851), 45–72; *The American Colporteur System* (New York: American Tract

Society, [1843]), reprinted in facsimile in *The American Tract Society Documents, 1824–1925* (New York: Arno Press, 1972); [R. S. Cook], *Home Evangelization: View of the Wants and Prospects of Our Country, Based on the Facts and Relations of Colportage* (New York: American Tract Society, [1849]); R. S. Cook, "The Colporteur System," in *Proceedings of a Public Deliberative Meeting of the Board and Friends of the American Tract Society, Held in Broadway Tabernacle, New-York, October 25, 26, and 27, 1842* (New York: American Tract Society, 1843); [Jonathan Cross], *Five Years in the Alleghenies* (New York: American Tract Society, 1863); and *Toils and Triumphs of Union Missionary Colportage for Twenty-five Years, by one of the Secretaries of the American Tract Society* (New York: American Tract Society, [1866]).

43. J. Newton Brown, *History of the American Baptist Publication Society, from Its Origin in 1824, to Its Thirty-second Anniversary in 1856* (Philadelphia: American Baptist Publication Society, [1856]), 156–157, 170–171; American Baptist Publication Society, *Sixth Annual Report* (1845), 38–39; American Baptist Publication Society, *Seventh Annual Report* (1846), 17–18; Abel Stevens, comp., *Documents of the Tract Society of the Methodist Episcopal Church* (New York: Carlton & Phillips, 1853), 22; Methodist Episcopal Church, *Journal of the General Conference* (1852), 120, 123; Methodist Episcopal Church, *Journal of the General Conference* (1856), 229.

44. The story of the centralizing mission of colportage is told in Nord, "Systematic Benevolence." See also David Paul Nord, "Religious Reading and Readers in Antebellum America," *Journal of the Early Republic* 15 (summer 1995): 241–272.

45. "Ten Years of Colportage in America," 64–65.

46. On the colportage program of the Presbyterians, see *Instructions for Colporteurs of the Presbyterian Board of Publication* (Philadelphia: Presbyterian Board of Publication, n.d.); *Presbyterian Board of Publication, Its Present Operations and Plans* (Philadelphia: Presbyterian Board of Publication, [1848]).

47. *Instructions of the Executive Committee of the American Tract Society, to Colporteurs and Agents, with Statements of the History, Character, and Object of the Society* (New York: American Tract Society, 1868), reprinted in *American Tract Society Documents*, 38–41. Nearly identical editions of this handbook were published from the early 1840s into the late nineteenth century. See also [Cook], *Home Evangelization*, 86–87. On the use of Richard Baxter's *Call to the Unconverted* by colporteurs, see *Colporteur Reports to the American Tract Society, 1841–1846* (Newark, NJ: Historical Records Survey Project, Work Projects Administration, 1940), passim.

48. Lacy, *Word Carrying Giant*, 96–100; Dwight, *Centennial History of the American Bible Society*, 180.

49. American Bible Society, *Forty-fourth Annual Report* (1860), 21–22.

50. Finke and Stark, *Churching of America*, 252–255. See also Iannaccone, "Why Strict Churches Are Strong," 1182–1183.

51. *Principles and Plans of the Board of Publication of the Presbyterian Church in the United States of America* (Philadelphia: Presbyterian Board of Publication, [1854]), 19–20.

52.   *Utility of Religious Tracts* (New York: J. Emory and B. Waugh [1826]), 1.

53.   These passages—from Matt. 10:8, II Thes. 3:1, and Is. 55:1—appear from time to time in Bible societies' reports. See, for example, American Bible Society, *Fifth Annual Report* (1821), 13; American Bible Society, *Third Annual Report* (1819), 15; and Bible Society of Philadelphia, *Address of the Bible Society Established at Philadelphia*, 10.

2

∞∞

Making Money, Saving Souls

Christian Bookstores and the
Commodification of Christianity

ANNE L. BORDEN

As noted in the previous chapter, those who seek to influence religious life through the marketplace are forced to contend with the tensions that emerge in the conflicting desires for ministry and for business survival. In this chapter, Anne Borden looks at the Christian retailing and bookselling industry. She analyzes interview materials from people directly involved in the management of Christian bookstores, theorizing that there are different ways in which these businesspeople negotiate the tension between business and ministry. She notes that whereas some in the business feel forced to make accommodations within the capitalist environment, others position themselves as cultural arbiters of Christianity and thus resist the pressures of the marketplace, sometimes with direct negative results on their business. In between these two positions, Borden argues, are those who seek to find a negotiation between business and ministry. These individuals sacralize the process of selling; and, in so doing, Borden argues, they may in some cases be better situated to meet the increasing demands of the consolidating Christian marketplace.

This chapter, therefore, introduces ideas of secularization into the discussion of media, religion, and the marketplace. It also makes a contribution through its analysis of those who are most directly involved in the negotiations between ministry and sales: those who have a stake in the survival of the Christian bookstore and retail industries.

If the ministry is doing well, the money will come in. It's a testimony to run a professional business, and profit is one of the surest gauges of success.

—Bill Moore, *Twenty-five Years of Sterling Rewards in God's Service*

Our members measure success in terms of both business and ministry. The two are integrated. Your business is a ministry; your ministry is a business. Retailing requires mastery of key business disciplines. Without a healthy store, your ministry will go out of business; but if we lose ministry perspective, we've simply become another retailer capitalizing on the popularity of Christian products.

—Bill Anderson, Christian Booksellers Association president,
"President's Column"

A recent newspaper article, playing on the popular Christian slogan "What would Jesus do?" asks the apt question: "What would Jesus buy?"[1] Christian books and products currently comprise a $4.2 billion-dollar industry.[2] Protestant Christian stores carry a variety of merchandise such as music, apparel, jewelry, videos, and toys. The Christian Bookseller's Association, the national trade association for Christian retail, recently changed their name to simply CBA, no longer calling themselves a bookseller's association in an effort to recognize that their members include suppliers and distributors and that their retail members sell much more than books.[3] Figures from CBA indicate that sales in Christian stores are distributed as follows: II percent of total Christian store sales are for Bibles, 25 percent for books, 16 percent for music, 3 percent for church supplies, and the remaining 45 percent for gift merchandise, cards, videos, and other items such as jewelry.[4] One scholarly observer, drawing our attention to the capitalistic nature of many contemporary Christian bookstores, refers to Christian retailers as "for-profit prophets"[5] Christian retailers fuse both their religious beliefs and their pursuit of profit into what CBA president Bill Anderson refers to as a "business ministry."

Christian bookstores and the sale of Christian commercialized material culture survive against a background of secularization. Secularization theorists contend that religion is declining in the face of rationalization,[6] that religion is competing in a pluralistic society,[7] and that religion is becoming privatized.[8] The core of the secularization paradigm, however, is that religious and nonreligious institutions have become increasingly differentiated over time (e.g., separation of church and state).[9] That is, religion no longer plays the same role that it once did in the economy, the government, and other arenas of public life.[10]

In this chapter, I explore the question of secularization in relation to how Christian bookselling evolved and how those who work in and manage such stores today negotiate secularization.[11] I begin by considering precursors to the Christian Booksellers Association's (CBA) stores and the early years of the CBA through an analysis of trade documents. This establishes the foundation for my analysis of the contemporary industry and the tensions of secularization faced by those who own, manage, and work in these stores. Employing qualitative analysis of interviews conducted with these individuals, I explore the possibility that tensions arise from running a for-profit business with a sacred mission in a secular society, examining the ways in which Christian ministry and modern business practices intersect. Christian booksellers juggle the institutional logics of both their religion and the capitalist market.[12] This intersection is particularly interesting in relation to issues of media, religion, and marketplace because this case demonstrates how for-profit businesses operate in relation to the media desires of their consumers.

As they change their merchandise from the traditional media of books to material products that supplement book sales (and, indeed, for some consumers these products become the reason to frequent Christian stores over other possibilities), booksellers are able to follow the lead of "lifestyle branding" that now characterizes the media marketplace and also extends beyond it to related products and services. Lifestyle branding refers to products and services that allow consumers to purchase an emotional attachment to an identity. Products with identical uses may be branded with various lifestyles. For instance, an Apple iPod functions in the same way as other mp3 players (e.g., it allows one to store and transport music), but it connotes an "urban hipster" lifestyle, unlike similar products by other brands, such as Sony and SanDisk. In a similar manner, a key chain with WWJD on it functions as much more than a key chain. It functions as an identity marker for contemporary Christians. It allows for what Clark referred to in this volume's introduction as "Christian lifestyle branding." Hip Christian products allow for self-expression and identity. As I will note, whereas some Christian booksellers see this shift as an important business move that retains the vibrance and viability of the Christian bookselling industry itself, others see a problem in this shift in emphasis from books to products. How booksellers negotiate these tensions sheds light on the role of Protestantism in relation to commerce and secularization in contemporary society.

A Brief History of Christian Retail

Contemporary Christian bookstores with their fusion of religion and capitalism have deep historical roots, as noted in the previous chapter by David Nord. Nonprofit organizations, such as the American Tract Society, the American Sunday School Union and the American Bible Society, have all been publishing and dispersing Christian reading materials since the early 1800s. These organizations began as charities but ended up with a mix of benevolence and retail sales. In his chapter, David Nord described how the increased costs of equipment, especially new printing technologies such as stereotyped printing, pushed the leaders of the Bible Society of Philadelphia to turn to retail sales as a source of revenue as early as 1812.[13] This move was not made without concerns regarding both theology and the founding principles of the organization. It was one thing to sell Bibles at cost to a local society whose mission was to provide the product to individuals for free. It was quite another to sell Bibles directly to individuals. The idea of requiring people to *pay* for the Word of God was new and required justification. The managers of the Bible Society of Philadelphia defended the practice in several ways. They argued that people would value the Bible more if they had paid for it. They also argued that the increased flow of money from *sold* Bibles would allow them to *give away* more Bibles to those who could not afford them. The ultimate goal was to reach as many readers as possible, and selling Bibles to those who could afford to buy was argued as a way to achieve this goal. The practice of organizing a charity around "differential pricing"—selling at a variable rate, depending on what the buyer can afford to pay—was imitated by the American Bible

Society and diffused to other similar organizations. These organizations paved the way for contemporary retail sales of Christian wares.[14]

This Christian bookstore boom started years later, after World War II. Due to social and cultural factors such as a growing middle class, population shifts, and increased transportation and technology, "mom and pop" Christian bookstores emerged as one of the primary ways of distributing Christian reading materials.[15] People started many of these shops with a commitment to Christian faith but with very little business experience. In 1950, the Christian Bookseller's Association (CBA) was formed with these goals: (1) encouraging wide distribution of Bibles and church supplies; (2) supplying members with merchandising suggestions and assistance; and (3) providing a liaison between bookstore owners, publishers, and suppliers. The founders of the CBA, Ken Taylor and Bill Moore, both of Moody Press, and John Fish, manager of Scripture Press Store in Chicago, were concerned about the lack of capital and lack of management skills among booksellers.[16] They started the organization in an attempt to help struggling bookstore owners who were rich in faith but lacking in capital and business know-how.

The first CBA convention took place in September of 1950. Forty-eight publishers and distributors attended, along with representatives from 102 bookstores. At this first convention, there was some debate over how to structure the organization. Debates centered on fusing both religion and business. Founding members searched for an organizational model.[17] Questions arose regarding what a Christian industry should look like. Should the convention be organized like trade meetings of similar organizations, such as the American Booksellers Association? Or should it be organized more like a Christian revival? As Jenkins wrote in his story of the Christian Booksellers Association's beginnings, "There was a problem early of what to do spiritually at the first convention and conventions to follow. If this were to be an annual affair, some uniform activities would have to be developed and followed. Since CBA was a Christian organization, most members would come for instruction and motivation. It would be a working business convention. But, on the other hand, since those early founders *were* such men of prayer, they insisted on putting their God and spiritual matters first." [18] Thus, from its earliest days, the Christian Booksellers Association struggled with the tensions between the commercial and spiritual dimensions of their work.

The first convention also dealt with the issue of profit and the fusing of business practices and religious callings. In an address given at the first convention, the speaker said, "It is to their [Christian bookstore owners'] credit that most of them are motivated by a desire to spread Christian literature more than to make a profit, although that too is absolutely necessary." [19]

From the beginning, leaders in the Christian bookstore field stressed the importance of combining both ministry and business. A 1968 guide to starting a Christian bookstore advised potential retailers to have both a religious calling to this type of work and the financial backing necessary for success. The guide provides the reader with a detailed minimum operating budget in order to open a Christian store. The authors advise: "First, you must be certain that God has called you into this field of service. To expect his blessing in the future you must be certain that this is His present will for you. A second factor is adequate financing. We have already noted that lack of financing has been the prime cause for many Christian bookseller 'drop outs' when other things were favorable. In the previous chapter a basic minimum has been suggested and anything less than this would be defying business logic." [20]

Adopting contemporary business practices led eventually to an expansion in the product lines carried in Christian stores. Until the late 1960s, Christian bookstores were, for the most part, simply bookstores. The transformation into "Christian department stores" that carry a variety of merchandise began in the late 1960s. [21] In 1967, there were no ads in the trade journal of the Christian Bookseller's Association for items other than Bibles, books, and print educational materials, such as curricula for Sunday school and vacation Bible school. The first ads for nonprint sidelines appeared in 1968. These were largely for church supplies, such as communion ware, choir robes, and candles. By 1970, 40 percent of all advertisements in the *Bookstore Journal* (the name of the CBA trade journal from 1968 to 1996) were for sidelines. Items for sale included cards, jewelry, and gifts.

Handicrafts were also one of the first sideline items sold in CBA stores. Bookstore owners and managers were taught how to display and sell handicrafts at a 1968 CBA convention workshop. A 1969 article in the *Bookstore Journal* asks the question, "What about Handicrafts?" The article suggests holding a craft workshop in your store and inviting customers to learn crafting techniques. Once customers, such as Sunday school teachers, became skilled in making and teaching crafts, stores were advised to keep supplies available for purchase.[22] Craft kits were geared largely for children and sold in bulk to church youth workers. An advertisement from 1970 shows "Craft Packs for Groups" with complete kits for projects such as a seed mosaic of a cornucopia, a leatherette wallet, and a mosaic tile trivet. The ad boasts to bookstore owners, "Watch your browsers turn into buyers." [23] It is interesting to note that many of these early items of Christian material culture did not portray explicitly religious symbolism. The kit for making a leatherette wallet is a simple wallet, unadorned with scripture, a cross, or a likeness of Jesus.

Eventually, manufacturers developed products specifically for the Christian marketplace. Christian bookstores began to expand their sales of sidelines to the general customer, rather than only to church personnel. The types of sidelines available grew dramatically, and many adapted contemporary fashions and styles by putting a Christian label on them.[24] Christian lifestyle branding emerged as hip retail products came on the market. Coffee mugs, pencils, patches, and bumper stickers promoted sayings such as "God Is Alive" and "Jesus Loves You." Some manufacturers borrowed directly from contemporary culture, producing products such as bumper stickers with the slogan "Jesus Christ, He's the real thing" in a style imitative of advertisements for Coca-Cola.[25]

Christian bric-a-brac emerged as a vital part of contemporary Christian bookstores. For example, a 1971 advertisement for "Gifts of Distinction" includes items with a Christian emphasis, such as a Bible bank, a Bible flashlight, a "musical praying boy and girl," and Bible story snowglobes.[26] Trade journal articles instructed retailers on the details of purchasing, displaying, and promoting this new merchandise. Articles such as "Why Not a Children's Department?" [27] and "We Pay Our Rent with Greeting Card Sales" [28] provided readers with inspiration and guidance.

It has been argued that the "Jesus Movement" played a role in the emergence of sidelines in Christian bookstores.[29] One advertisement from 1971 shows stickers and embroidered emblems with mottos such as "One Way Jesus" and "Try Jesus." The ad claims, "Although this 'Jesus Movement' has not come through the traditional church it does touch some traditional Christian institutions. . . . The tracts and stickers on this page have received the enthusiastic approval of high school and college young people." [30]

The new youth market paved the way for the apparel and music that are present in contemporary Christian bookstores. Below, I outline my methods for researching contemporary stores from the perspectives of bookstore owners and managers.

Research Methods

This chapter is based primarily on in-depth interviews with four Christian booksellers.[31] These four cases were chosen for this chapter, from a larger project, because of their typicality. They exemplify the strategies that booksellers use when negotiating their spiritual mission and the profit-oriented marketplace. The interviewees are all white males and range from forty-seven to seventy-five years old. They are all lay people who own or manage independent bookstores. The interviews lasted from forty-five minutes to two hours. I focused my interview questions on key arenas in which the tensions between ministry and business potentially arise. Fruitful questions include the following: Is your store successful? How do you define success? Do you have guidelines for the type of books and merchandise that you carry? Who do you see as your store's competition?

Interviews were transcribed, and I coded and analyzed the resulting documents. I initially developed a deductive coding scheme, drawing on the work of others exploring tensions between the sacred and the secular. Through re-reading the documents and creating memos, I found that new themes, or codes, emerged inductively from the data. Through my analysis, I found that the responses of booksellers clustered around three themes: resistance, accommodation, and sacralization, which I discuss below.[32]

The Contemporary Christian Industry and Responses to Secularization

The rise of commodified Christian culture posed a challenge for some in the Christian retail industry. For others, these items became sacred and accepted as part of a ministry. These two differing responses to secularization are consistent with the classic works of Peter Berger and James Hunter, who have argued that there are two main responses to secularization: resistance and accommodation.[33] "Resistance" refers to situations in which religious groups and individuals shelter themselves from the modern world and avoid secular activities. This may include acquiring a specific manner of dress, speech, or food rituals and avoiding activities including dancing and consuming alcohol.[34] In the case of Christian bookstores, resistance involves avoiding some contemporary business practices, such as refusing to sell low-quality Christian bric-a-brac and not worrying about competition. "Accommodation," on the other hand, refers to situations where religious groups change to fit the modern world and sacrifice some of their belief system in the process.[35] Christian booksellers may engage in this strategy by carrying books or items that are profit-generating yet conflict with their beliefs systems.

A recent strand of research expands the academic discussion to explore a third possible response to secularization, which, following Christian Smith, I label "sacralization." This refers to the practices of "reinvigorating lost sacred traditions and practices, generating new religious goods, and using modern tools to promote traditional worldviews and ways of life."[36] The key difference between accommodation and sacralization is that accommodation implies "selling out" or making concessions to secular society, whereas sacralization envisions reinvigorating religious traditions. The addition of the sacralization concept (along with those of resistance and accommodation) allows researchers to address adequately the exchange and contact between religion and contemporary society. It acknowledges that there exists a middle ground where religious and secular cultures coexist, inform each other, and even garner strength from each other.[37] Religious groups and individuals may both successfully incorporate aspects of modern secular culture and remain loyal to traditional belief systems. Members of the Christian retail industry who engage in sacralization fuse Christianity and capitalism in their "business ministry."

I examine these three responses to secularization in the context of the Christian bookstore field. According to Paul DiMaggio and Walter Powell, an organizational field includes "those organizations that, in the aggregate, constitute a recognized area of institutional life: key suppliers, resource and product consumers, regulatory agencies, and other organizations that produce similar services or products."[38] Key organizations in the Christian bookstore field include publishers, churches, the Christian Booksellers Association, and Christian bookstores themselves, while key individuals include the Christians who shop at the stores and those who own or manage bookstores. This chapter focuses on the latter. I now turn to an example of a Christian bookseller who negotiates the organizational field through a strategy of resistance.

Resistance

Those who adopted a strategy of resistance emphasized the ministry aspects of their work, resisting what they claimed were secular business practices that, they believed, could lead to a compromising of their religious principles. These individuals were critical of books and products that did not clearly meet their understandings regarding ways to live a Christian life. They put their religious convictions before making money.

This approach to running a Christian bookstore is exemplified in the type of language that they use. This became obvious when I was conducting interviews and two respondents who own independent stores corrected me in my choice of words. In one case, I asked the interviewee if he was the owner of his store. He responded, "I'm the manager, and the Lord is the owner." [39] He explained that it was important to him theologically to consider his work in this manner. I asked another retailer about his experiences in the Christian bookstore "industry." He immediately corrected me and informed me that he did not work in an "industry" but in a "ministry." [40] These interviews draw our attention to the ways in which these Christian booksellers prioritize their religious convictions.

The Christian retailer mentioned above who prefers to be referred to as the "manager" is a white man in his seventies who has been operating his store in California for thirty-four years. When I asked him about the success of his business, he responded by talking about his faith and trust in God to sustain the business.

> You know, we trust in the Lord to keep us going. We don't trust in the financial aspects, although they are important. [We] trust the Lord to provide all of our needs and that's the promise He's made us and I don't know what else to say. I don't worry about the financial aspects of it. I, my, my philosophy is, I don't look at the bottom line. I couldn't tell you what the bottom line is here. I don't know. I look at it: Are our bills paid and our people being blessed? And that's the

only thing that we go by. As long as we keep our bills paid and our staff paid, things like that, well, I'm perfectly happy, even if we get smaller and smaller. But, the Lord has sustained us all these years and He'll sustain us as long as He wants us around here.[41]

Unlike other booksellers who openly discuss struggling for a piece of the market where stores like Wal-Mart, Borders, and Amazon.com make it hard for independent Christian bookstores to survive, this retailer talks of trust and faith, rather than business strategies for survival. He describes the survival of his store not as something dependent on his business strategies, but as dependent on God's will to sustain the store.

This Christian retailer does not sell any gift items such as music or jewelry and sticks exclusively to books. He is careful about what books he will carry in his store and refuses to carry books that do not follow his theological position. He is open about how his strategy of resistance sets him apart from many of the other members of CBA. He has been vocal at trade association meetings regarding the need for CBA members to be selective about the materials they sell. This bookseller arranged a meeting with Bill Anderson, president of CBA, where he discussed strategies to educate other Christian retailers in theology so that they will avoid what he sees as heretical books. When I interviewed him, he elaborated on his position of resistance: "My philosophy of literature is quite different than most of the Christian bookstores. My philosophy has always been to provide the very best literature available to the people that's consistent with the Word of God. And we don't carry things that I don't feel are consistent with the Word of God. . . . A person who had been our customer for many years was in here on Friday and he said, 'You know Mark, I send a lot of people over here because I have confidence that we could come in here blindfolded and just reach up and grab a book and be sure it's a good book.'"[42]

This bookstore owner went on to explain that he does not carry self-help books that rely on psychology rather than biblical principles and biblical counseling. Nor does he carry the best-selling *Left Behind* series, which focuses on dispensationalism, which goes against the owner's theological beliefs.[43] By choosing to place his religious values before the possibility of making money on best-sellers that potentially conflict with his belief system, this owner articulated a strategy of resistance.

This bookstore owner had also approached publishers with his concerns about the appropriate distribution of certain books. At a recent trade convention, he reported, he entered the elaborate booth of a large publisher and observed the revolving sign above the booth that stated, "A name you can trust." He pulled two books from the shelf that he believed contained conflicting messages and approached the publisher with them. "Which book should I trust?" he asked, illustrating his concern with the lack of consistency and reliability of the materials offered for sale by the publisher.[44] This bookstore owner framed his approach to the work of selling Christian books in terms of issues of trust in relationships, or integrity. He wanted to be viewed by customers as consistent, a reliable arbiter of Christian goods. Moreover, he held a similar skepticism regarding the ability of consumer goods to support one's faith, preferring instead to sell only books.

Accommodation

I hypothesized, based on previous research, that some booksellers—in contrast to those who resist books and gifts that conflict with their belief systems—would engage in the strategy of accommodation by engaging in practices that prioritize business over Christianity. I did not find anyone in my sample who clearly prioritized business. Rather, I saw that some booksellers are reluctant, hesitant, and uncertain as they struggle with the fact that they must conform to market pressures (e.g., sell contemporary Christian music) in order to make enough money to stay in business.

I asked a bookseller who has been in the business for forty years about changes over time in the merchandise he carries. He described the transformation he experienced from running a small store centering around books to owning several larger stores that sell many gift items and music: "I had very, very few gift items. They were really, really minor. Music was not that much; of course we had, I think; I think eight tracks were coming in at that time. Most everything was on the, on the LP's, the disks. It was mainly, mainly books. And I think most Christian bookstores at that time were the same way. We've kind of all grown with the development of more and more product. As annual product was developing, the industry grew and, of course, the space to [hold merchandise] grew along with it. I'm not sure it was anything conscious at the time, that I'm aware of."[45] When I asked him how he felt about the changes in his stores, he spoke about market pressures. It was not a conscious decision. Rather, the industry grew, new products became available, and booksellers followed the trend. He went into detail about his uncertainty about contemporary Christian music. Not only does he dislike the music itself, he is also concerned about the personal lives of musicians, including popular performer Amy Grant's divorce, and describes some as having "lost their halos." For a while he quit carrying the music of what he considers disreputable artists, but he carries them again now. "I do know that the pressure to pay your bills and the pressure to, to make a profit and a pressure, pressure to compete with others who may be carrying things or doing things that you wouldn't normally do otherwise has, has changed us all. I think it's the nature of human nature to do that. We're socialized or inculturated, or whatever you want to call it, kind of unconsciously. And until we get together and talk about the good old days, we're really not aware of how things are changed." [46] This bookseller recognizes the pressure to compete and the sacrifices that one must make to stay in business.

Some booksellers point out the ways in which they observe accommodation in others in the industry. For this case, I focus on a white male bookseller in his forties who has been in the industry for fifteen years. He manages an independent store in the Atlanta area. He described compromise in the form of opening a Christian store on Sunday, traditionally the day of rest. He told me the story of another store owner: "There was a retailer, an independent retailer, who felt in order to compete she had to open her store on Sunday, just to keep up. She was very conflicted about it. [She] didn't feel it was the right thing to do, but she made the change. She went that way, and that's, you know, that's an example of how the pressure, whether it's internal or external, you feel in order to be respected, financially or economically, or to have any sort of business success, that you have to follow certain trends that aren't necessarily, you know, connected with your ministry philosophy." [47] He is explicit about the conflict between business pressures and ministry. In this case, for business success, the retailer he describes sacrificed part of her religious beliefs and chose to open her store on Sundays. He articulates a struggle in following trends that may lead to "business success" but may conflict with a "ministry philosophy." He is careful to describe her reluctant attitude toward this accommodation. It appears that accommodation for some happens with some hesitancy and through a process of thoughtful consideration.

However, much of the accommodation in the Christian products industry occurs not at the level of the individual bookstore owner or manager but with the suppliers. The same retailer quoted above talked about the accommodation in the industry at large:

> The larger you get, the greater your market share, the greater the temptation to make compromises. And the more attractive you become to secular interests who really aren't interested in your ministry at all. Now, they may be in the sense that that's what you do well as a company, and they want you to continue doing whatever it is that you do well. But you have most all the major music distributors wholly owned by secular enterprises now; a lot of the Christian publishers are as well. One of the things that I've been following closely, and I think a lot of people have, particularly, is Zondervan Publishers and their association with Harper Collins and Rupert Murdock's empire, and what pressures are brought to bear upon Zondervan, as a publisher, to conform to more worldly pursuits.[48]

In general, the Christian booksellers I interviewed agree that publishers are accommodating to a secular world. Consolidation, in which secular entities buy out small Christian publishers, is resulting in fewer and fewer publishers that booksellers can trust to share their goal of ministry rather than worldly pursuits. Christian booksellers talk in terms of which publishers they can "trust" and which cannot be trusted.

Sacralization

Christian retailers adopting a strategy of sacralization fuse their business training and their religious calling in a way that is much more direct and clearly articulated than the previous examples of accommodation. I interviewed a bookseller who owns four stores in the Midwest. We spoke at the CBA convention in Atlanta. He explained that he carried what he referred to as "Jesus junk" because his customers asked for it and his store profited from it. Music alone made up 20 percent of this retailer's sales. Yet he explained his decisions to sell items such as Christian music and gifts in reference to his desire not only to provide products to a religiously diverse marketplace, but to "minister" to his customers while also generating a profit: "I got in the business and most people here [CBA International 2004] my age [in his fifties] got into the business to sell books. That's what we got in it for. But once you are in it, you realize that there are other Christian products that people want. . . . I'm a book and Bible man, but I sell all this other stuff because people want it." [49] Not only do people want these items, he explained, but these items have the potential to strengthen religious conviction and to serve as a means of evangelizing. With regard to Christian music he noted, "I know it blesses people and has a big ministry in people's lives." [50] This latter statement is important because he sees the power of the items he sells to *both* generate profit for his stores and serve as ministry. He also mentioned that 50 percent of items sold in his stores are given away as gifts. Books and gifts may or may not be a way of spreading Christian faith, but clearly it is a win-win situation for Christian retailers when products are both profit-generating and, in his words, "Christ-honoring." For this retailer and others like him, selling Christian goods has become both a business venture and a sacred mission.

The president of CBA, Bill Anderson, engages in sacralizing discourse when writing and speaking to the members of the CBA. In a recent "President's Column" in *CBA Marketplace*, he wrote: "Our members measure success in terms of both business and ministry. The two are integrated. Your business is a ministry; your ministry is a business. Retailing requires mastery of key business disciplines. Without a healthy store, your ministry will go out of business; but if we lose ministry perspective, we've simply become another retailer capitalizing on the popularity of Christian products." [51] For Bill Anderson, Christianity and ministry are tightly linked for the Christian retailer. The column quoted above was especially aimed at motivating Christian retailers who are currently facing competition. This is an especially pertinent point, as many retailers fear they may face the demise of their niche market due to increased competition. The need for a workable strategy for survival is paramount, and Anderson sees ministry as an important aspect that differentiates Christian booksellers from an otherwise crowded marketplace.

The Future of Christian Retailing

A number of changes in the industry are currently challenging Christian bookstores. One of the biggest challenges comes from the availability of Christian books in both discount department stores such as Wal-Mart and secular bookstores such as Barnes and Noble. Another competitor comes in the form of Internet stores such as Amazon.com. These stores are able to offer deeply discounted Christian books in a way that few small Christian booksellers can. The registration page for the CBA International 2004 convention poses the problem of the competition: "[Christian retailers face] formidable competitors— 'big box' global retailers as well as 'small box' personal computers and e-commerce. These Goliaths are employing the most sophisticated and powerful marketing and merchandising machines to claim as much of this market as possible." [52] CBA reminds booksellers to draw on their unique strengths, including building relationships with customers, creating warm store environments, and carrying products that go beyond the best-sellers sold in mainstream stores,

FIGURE 2-1 A Christian bookstore in Georgia.
Photo by the author.

offering the opportunity to rely on the CBA for information and ministry opportunities.[53]

There are several strategies which Christian retailers are using to address competition. One strategy is the attempt to compete through discounting book prices. For example, one mall-based store in Missouri is located within a five-mile radius of five Wal-Mart stores, in addition to other nearby competitors such as Books-A-Million and Target. The manager interviewed said, "I finally started listening to customers. They were saying, 'Don't buy this book here—you can get it cheaper at Wal-Mart.'" With this knowledge, he established a "Wal-Mart watch" in which his employees regularly monitor the price of Christian titles at retail giants. He dropped the price of best-seller *The Purpose Driven Life* from $16.97 to $10.97. In three months they sold 1,700 copies. The most the store had sold up until that point was 40 copies a month. By placing higher-priced titles and other items related to the book near the display for *The Purpose Driven Life,* they were able to sell multiple items to customers and therefore increase their profits. In his interview, the store manager expressed his belief that Christian bookstores must work to be competitive in order to survive the current market: "I vehemently disagree that CBA retailers can't be competitive on price points. I believe we have to be very aggressive. It's how we can recapture customers we've lost. If we keep doing business the way we were, it's just a matter of time and CBA stores will cease to be relevant. The old ways aren't working."[54] Thus, this retailer decided to adopt a business strategy that mimics that of big-box retailers, betting that the added benefits of a Christian store would outweigh the appeal of competitors. Note that in this exchange the retailer justified his decisions based not on ministry goals but rather on profit motives, thus illustrating a strategy of accommodation.

Another strategy retailers have adopted is the development of relationships with churches, generating income through direct sales made to church personnel such as pastors and Christian education directors. This is a niche market that Christian booksellers can meet without competition from big-box stores like Wal-Mart. In the spring of 2004, the Church Ministry Industry Task Force was formed by several publishers and met for the first time at the CBA headquarters in Colorado Springs, Colorado. The focus of this group is to encourage Christian stores to serve churches and benefit from increased revenue from church buyers by providing Christian education resources such as Sunday school materials. Task force chairman Bill Corte has said that churches can generate high volume sales, arguing that retailers have not been able to serve them effectively in recent years. The task force provided training sessions and materials at the CBA 2004 annual convention, including a session titled "Growing Your Church-Ministry Revenue." [55] This position seems to embrace a position of sacralization by emphasizing both generating high volume sales and serving church members in need of quality Christian reading material.

Along the same lines, Lemstone, currently the only Christian bookstore franchise,[56] has begun to encourage franchisees to open satellite church stores in order to reach more customers. There are presently four Lemstone church stores. The management and inventory are operated through the main store and the church stores are open only twenty hours a week, making them less expensive to run.[57] Stores located in churches have direct access to those interested in buying Christian books and gifts, thereby both generating profit and serving their niche market.

In spite of the concerns raised by CBA, some Christian retailers are not worried about the future of the industry. One interviewee who engages in a strategy of resistance told me that he would have no problem with Amazon.com putting his store out of business. He said, "It's fine as long as the good stuff is getting out. I don't have a problem with it. That's our ministry. It's getting good books out, and if someone else can do it better, that's fine." [58] Rather than focusing on the future of the Christian retail industry, therefore, he was concerned with the distribution of Christian books and their power to change lives, regardless of where they would be purchased.[59]

Conclusion

The tensions that arise when profit and ministry are combined in the distribution of Christian books and merchandise are not unique to contemporary times. As shown in Nord's work, Bible societies have struggled with the appropriate way in which to finance their mission since at least 1812. Contemporary Christian retailers operating in contemporary secular society face similar challenges. The organizational field of Christian bookselling exists in two institutional environments: American Protestantism and the capitalist market. This chapter poses the question of how those at the center of this organizational field—Christian booksellers—negotiate these environments. I explore the different ideological strategies that Christian booksellers utilize. Some, which I label resistors and accommodators, struggle with potential incongruencies within the institutional logics. Resistors attempt to avoid modern business practices (e.g., carrying sidelines) that go against their religious beliefs. Accommodators seem to struggle with the challenges faced by the pressures of the market. I find that accommodation in this setting—unlike the more rigid concept of accommodation previously theorized by Hunter—refers to those who are reluctant, hesitant, and uncertain as they struggle with the fact that they must conform to market pressures (e.g., to be open on Sunday) in order to make enough money to stay in business. They are not simply selling out without forethought. Rather, they are carefully juggling and negotiating both market demands and their mission of ministry.

On the other hand, some Christian booksellers seamlessly fuse the institutional logics of a Christian ministry and a capitalistic market. For these booksellers, there is no tension between potentially contradictory institutional logics. These booksellers survive within capitalism as well as fully embrace their faith. The sacralization strategy dominates the writings and speeches of Bill Anderson, president of the CBA, and it is the stance advocated in the discourse of the CBA trade journal. Sacralizers align themselves with the ideology of the trade association, fully embrace a fusion of ministry and market demands, and refer to their work as a "business ministry." They look to the accommodators and resisters as examples of what is wrong with Christian bookstores today. From their perspective, accommodators are selling out and sacrificing important religious principles for the sake of earning a profit. Resistors, on the other hand, may be regarded as old-fashioned from a business perspective and often too narrow theologically (e.g., refusing to carry the best-selling *Left Behind* series because of the theology it espouses).

The Christian bookstore field is facing several challenges, including increasing consolidation in both the publishing and the music industry, the growth of Christian chain stores, and competition from secular chain bookstores. In order for Christian bookstores to survive in this environment, they must develop strategies to face these challenges. Historically, Protestants have been masters at figuring out how to survive in a secular world. Christian Smith describes American evangelicals as "embattled and thriving." There is little doubt that Christian booksellers will devise strategic plans for their survival.[60] The Christian retail industry depends on adapting features of the modern world, including contemporary media products (e.g., books, videos, magazines, and music) and infusing these products with religious messages. Thus, we have popular Christian book series such as *Left Behind*, Christian children's entertainment in the form of the animated videos *Veggie Tales*, and teen magazines such as *Campus Life*, all products available in Christian bookstores.[61] This chapter challenges readers to see the selling of these products that fuse secular media and religious culture as a potentially sacralizing act. Previous research would have us believe that Christian retailers have two options. They may make concessions to a modern world (i.e., accommodation) and survive, or they may set themselves apart from the world (i.e., resistance) and risk going out of business. In the current competitive marketplace, the strategy that is most likely to be successful is the one embraced by booksellers who are sacralizers. This third strategy allows booksellers to fuse the institutional logics of Christianity and capitalism. Booksellers draw on contemporary business practices and media products to strengthen and share their faith. Sacralization allows them to be successful in both their business and their ministry.

NOTES

1. Gwen Florio, "Christian Merchandise Wades into Culture's Secular Waters," *Denver Post*, December 23, 2003, A-1. This chapter is concerned only with Protestant bookstores. Catholic bookstores will be explored in a future project.

2. Http://cbaonline.org/MarketPlace/Convo3Rel.jsp.

3. Lynn Vincent, "Trinkets or Truth?" *World Magazine*, June 1, 2000.

4. Cbaonline.org/General_Research.jsp.

5. Heather Hendershot, *Shaking the World for Jesus: Media and Conservative Evangelical Culture* (Chicago: University of Chicago Press, 2004).

6. Max Weber, *The Sociology of Religion* (Boston: Beacon Press, 1964).

7. Peter Berger, *The Sacred Canopy* (New York: Doubleday, 1967).

8. Thomas Luckmann, *The Invisible Religion* (London: Collier-Macmillan, 1967).

9. Philip S. Gorski, "Historicizing the Secularization Debate: Church, State, and Society in Late Medieval and Early Modern Europe, ca. 1300 to 1700," *American Sociological Review* 65 (2000): 138–167.

10. Frank Lechner, "The Case against Secularization: A Rebuttal." *Social Forces* 69 (1991): 1103–1119. For the purposes of this chapter I will set aside the current "secularization debate" and regard secularization as a given.

11. I use the expression "Christian bookstores" when "Protestant bookstores" would be more accurate. I do so to be consistent with the manner in which those in the industry refer to themselves. Whereas the Christian Booksellers Association (CBA) is primarily comprised of Protestant stores, the Association of Catholic Bookstores in the United States and Canada is the Catholic equivalent. Nonetheless, the boundaries between Protestant and Catholic retail are not always clear. Some CBA member stores carry Catholic merchandise; articles in the CBA trade journal advise its members on how to reach the Catholic market; meanwhile, some Catholic suppliers are also CBA members. Likewise, Protestant bookstores are often, but not always, evangelical in nature.

12. Roger Friedland and Robert R. Alford, "Bringing Society Back In: Symbols, Practices, and Institutional Contradictions," in *The New Institutionalism in Organizational Analysis,* ed. Walter W. Powell and Paul J. DiMaggio (Chicago: University of Chicago Press, 1991), 232–263.

13. David Nord, "Benevolent Capital: Financing Evangelical Book Publishing in Early Nineteenth-Century America," in *God and Mammon: Protestants, Money, and the Market, 1790–1860,* ed. Mark A. Knoll, 147–170 (New York: Oxford University Press, 2001).

14. Ibid.

15. Colleen McDannell, *Material Christianity: Religion and Popular Culture in America* (New Haven: Yale University Press, 1995), 246–247.

16. Bickel and Jantz, *His Time, His Way: The CBA Story, 1950–1999* (Colorado Springs: CBA Press, 1999), 31.

17. Paul J. DiMaggio and Walter W. Powell, "The Iron Cage Revisited: Institutional Isomorphism and Collective Rationality in Organizational Fields," *American Sociological Review* 48 (1983): 147–160.

18. Jerry Jenkins, *Twenty-five Years of Sterling Rewards in God's Service: The Story of Christian Booksellers Association* (Nashville: Thomas Nelson Publishers in conjunction with Christian Booksellers Association, 1974), 21–22.

19. Quoted in Jenkins, *Twenty-five Years of Sterling Rewards in God's Service,* 19.

20. John Bass and Robert DeVries, *The Christian Bookstore* (Colorado Springs: Christian Booksellers Association, 1968).

21. Stephen R. Clark, *Selling Sidelines* (Wheaton, IL: Christian Bookseller Magazine, 1981).

22. Dorothy Fish, "What about Handcrafts?" *Bookstore Journal* 2 (January 1969): 12–13.

23. Advertisement, *Bookstore Journal* (April 1971): 35.

24. McDannell, *Material Christianity.*

25. Advertisement, *Bookstore Journal* (June 1973): 43.

26. Advertisement, *Bookstore Journal* (October 1971): 37.

27. Dolores Rainey, "Why Not a Children's Department?" *Bookstore Journal* (June 1970): 32–33.

28. Mike Farrell, "We Pay Our Rent with Greeting Card Sales," *Bookstore Journal* (April 1972): 86.

29. McDannell, *Material Christianity*. The Jesus movement was a counterculture youth movement in the late 1960s and early 1970s that incorporated fashion (e.g., long hair for men) and music as well as spirituality.

30. Advertisement, *Bookstore Journal* (September 1971): 19.

31. This project was approved by the Emory University Institutional Review Board for the protection of human subjects. The larger project includes interviews with fifteen booksellers, both owners of independent stores and managers of chain stores.

32. I used the qualitative software package NVivo to assist in the storage, coding, and analysis of data. NVivo allows you to efficiently search the data and identify themes. Coding is done in a manner similar to the old-fashioned technique of using a highlighter, in that the researcher develops a coding scheme and coding rules and applies the codes to passages of text. Searches allow the researcher to examine hunches and explore patterns in the data. For instance, NVivo allows me to pull up all of the text coded as a discussion of "success." A Boolean search allows me to look at passages including the intersection of the codes "success" and "profit" as well as the intersection of the codes "success" and "ministry."

33. Berger, *The Sacred Canopy;* James Hunter, *American Evangelicalism: Conservative Religion and the Quandary of Modernity* (New Brunswick, NJ: Rutgers University Press, 1983).

34. See Nancy T. Ammerman, *Congregation and Community* (New Brunswick, NJ: Rutgers University Press, 1997); and Lynn Davidman, *Tradition in a Rootless World: Women Turn to Orthodox Judaism* (Berkeley: University of California Press, 1991).

35. Mark Shibley, *Resurgent Evangelicalism in the United States* (Columbia: University of South Carolina Press, 1996).

36. Christian Smith, *American Evangelicalism* (Chicago: University of Chicago Press, 1998).

37. See Bruce David Forbes and Jeffrey Mahan, *Religion and Popular Culture in America* (Berkeley: University of California Press, 2000); Stewart M. Hoover and Lynn Schofield Clark, eds., *Practicing Religion in the Age of the Media: Explorations in Media, Religion, and Culture* (New York: Columbia University Press, 2002); R. Laurence Moore, *Selling God: Religion in the Marketplace of Culture* (New York: Oxford University Press, 1994); Diane Winston, *Red-Hot and Righteous: The Urban Religion of the Salvation Army* (Cambridge, MA: Harvard University Press, 1999).

38. Powell and DiMaggio, *The New Institutionalism in Organizational Analysis*.

39. Interview #2, July 3, 2004.

40. Interview #5, November 3, 2004.

41. Interview #2, July 3, 2004.

42. Ibid. All names have been changed for the protection of human subjects.

43. The *Left Behind* book series is based on a particular understanding and interpretation of the Bible chapter Revelation. The series focuses on what is commonly referred to as "end times" or the "rapture" in which those who are "saved" will suddenly be swept up from Earth to join Jesus Christ in Heaven. The rapture is just one tenet of the complex theology of dispensationalism.

44. Interview #2, July 3, 2004.

45. Interview #3, August 2, 2004.

46. Ibid.

47. Interview #4, August 5, 2004.

48. Ibid.

49. Interview #1, June 28, 2004.

50. Ibid.

51. Bill Anderson, "President's Column," *CBA Marketplace* (July 2004): 9.

52. Http://www.cbainternationaI2004.com/.

53. Ibid.

54. "Pricing Strategies Work: Aggressive Pricing Strategy Drives Customers Back into For-All Bible & Music Center," *CBA Marketplace* (June 2004), 23, 28.

55. "Curriculum Supplier Task Force: Publishers Form Task Force to Help Independent Stores," *CBA Marketplace* (June 2004), 25.

56. The Parable Group, an association of independent Christian retailers, announced in a press conference at CBA International on June 27, 2004, that Parable franchising opportunities will become available beginning August 2004, making them the second Christian retail franchise after Lemstone. Lemstone stores are located in eighteen states. In addition to franchises, there are a number of chain stores, the largest chains being Family Christian Stores (320 stores) and Lifeway Christian Stores (123 stores).

57. "Ahead of the Curve: Lessons from Lemstone, America's only Christian-Retail Franchising Company," *CBA Marketplace* (July 2004), 54–57.

58. Interview #1, June 28, 2004

59. Interview #2, July 3, 2004.

60. See Laurence Moore, *Selling God: American Religion in the Marketplace of Culture* (New York: Oxford University Press, 1994); Smith, *American Evangelicalism*.

61. See Hillary Warren, *There's Never Been a Show like* Veggie Tales: *Sacred Messages in a Secular Market* (Walnut Creek, CA: Altamira Press, 2005) for more on the *Veggie Tales.*

3

"Jewish Space Aliens Are Lucky to Be Free!"

Religious Distinctiveness, Media, and Markets in Jewish Children's Culture

HILLARY WARREN

Christianity is not the only religion to look to the marketplace for clues as to how to offer cultural resources for those concerned with socializing others into the religious faith. In this chapter, Hillary Warren looks at a relatively recent phenomenon—that of Jewish video, magazine, and Web-based creative products that aim to provide Jewish young people with a greater understanding of their faith and traditions. She introduces the importance of providing distinctiveness for Jewish youth, a desire that has become key to the expansion of religious lifestyle branding beyond Christianity. She argues that these videos and other media products are designed to help young people understand the Jewish traditions, reinforcing what is unique about being Jewish while also conveying the sense that identifying with Judaism is "hip." Importantly, she notes, many of these products do not place many demands on those who watch, nor do they suggest to their young viewers that they should encourage their parents to be more observant. Contrasting the Jewish with the Christian marketplace, Warren observes the ways in which media presentations differ in part due to the minority position of Judaism in the United States, which in turn explains its smaller market share and hence its need for evaluation beyond that of sales numbers—or conversion numbers, to take the evangelical standard. "They are using media to respond to a need that does not fit well with the requirements of mass media retail sales," she notes. Such a position introduces new ways of thinking about the interconnections between religion, media, and the marketplace.

On the Planet Matzah Ball, the Jewish space aliens were learning about Passover and preparing to host their first Seder. After learning the story of the Exodus, they looked at one another and declared, "Jewish space aliens are lucky to be free!" The aliens of *Planet Matzah Ball* also looked forward to learning how to use a menorah for Chanukah—possibilities included using it as a vase and hot-dog holder—and, in the process, teaching Jewish viewers about the holidays.[1] The aliens aren't alone in this desire to teach. The Rugrats of Nickelodeon fame have been eating latkes,[2] and Muppet-style puppets are searching for the Afikoman.[3]

Older children can learn about Israeli culture with the Shalom Sesame series and some Orthodox kids have become fans of Agent Emes.[4] In the Agent Emes series, a yeshiva student employs Talmudic study to foil the evil Dr. Lo Tov at every turn in Lo Tov's quest to thwart the efforts of the Jewish people. Teens are being courted by a variety of activities and media intended to keep them in the Jewish community after their bar/bat mitzvahs, including youth groups, Maccabi games, and glossy magazines.

To some extent, this explosion in Jewish youth media mirrors the number of products available for Christian kids. *Veggie Tales, Jay Jay the Jet Plane,* and the *Last Chance Detectives* demonstrated that there is a willing market of parents eager to purchase quality media with a religious message for their kids. But unlike the Christian products, the likelihood that *Planet Matzah Ball* aliens will be featured at the local Target or Wal-Mart is pretty slim both because the market just doesn't justify the shelf space and because a high Amazon ranking doesn't appear to be the goal for Jewish media producers. That's not to say that some producers aren't hoping to turn a profit, but mostly they just want to survive economically and get their message out. In fact, many of the products are produced with money from foundations and nonprofits in a model along closer lines to Focus on the Family than Zondervan. This is media with a message, and that message is more about preservation and cultural survival than evangelicalism or expanding market share.

Judaism: Cool New Trend?

"From Britney's Hebrew tattoo and JEWCY sportswear to Phish singing 'Avinu Malkeinu,' Judaism is all the rage right now. Is Judaism gaining

FIGURE 3-1 *JVibe*, the Jewish lifestyle magazine.

Courtesy of *JVibe: The Magazine for Jewish Teens.*

mainstream acceptance or is it just a pop trend?"[5] From the pages of *JVibe: The Magazine for Jewish Teens*, the writers and editors seek to tell Jewish teens that not only are they fine as they are but they are better than fine—they are hip. Madonna, Britney, and Demi Moore are just red-string-wearing wannabes. The readers of *JVibe* not only understand the Hebrew reference in the pop song, but also can place those references in context—they really get it. *JVibe* started as a Web site and mailing list, but with the support of the United Synagogue of Conservative Judaism, the Union of Reform Judaism and Jewish Family & Life! they've expanded their efforts with a bimonthly glossy magazine to reach Jewish teens—particularly teens who are post–bar/bat mitzvah.

That is because Jewish teens have assimilated rapidly into an American culture that no longer tells them not to intermarry, many of them come from intermarried households, and those who go to Hebrew school often drift away after bar or bat mitzvah. The same typical teen phenomenon of not going to church on Sunday or shul on the Sabbath and then going to a non-sectarian college has led to levels of assimilation that are striking.[6] According to the National Jewish Population Survey, 2000–2001, updated in January 2004, the American Jewish population is aging at a faster rate than the U.S. population and has lower fertility rates than the U.S. population.[7] Both of these measures are below population replacement levels. In addition, intermarriage has stabilized at just below half of all marriages over the past ten years and most children in intermarried households are not being raised Jewish.

However, the same survey has shown that more Jewish children are attending Jewish day school or yeshiva than in earlier surveys and that an interest in Jewish education for those children tends to continue for some into the college years. While this is encouraging to those interested in the maintenance of the Jewish community, other studies have found that up to 70 percent of teens after bar/bat mitzvah are detached from the Jewish community. Since intermarried families are less likely to participate in the Jewish community and unaffiliated Jews are less likely to seek out other Jews to marry, multiple factors may contribute to the likelihood of population decline in the American Jewish community.

A follow-up study, released in July 2004, considered the impact of Jewish education in fostering Jewish identity among adults. The study looked at the role of day school/yeshiva, travel to Israel, and other experiences on the likelihood that adults would fast on Yom Kippur, light candles on Shabbos, and/or keep kosher at home.[8] That study found that while Jewish education enhances identity, once-a-week Sunday school programs do not, and that all forms of informal Jewish education, particularly trips to Israel, enhance Jewish identity in adulthood. In the context of these studies and the wide attention they received at the national and local level from Jewish Federations and individual foundations, multiple initiatives have attempted to increase opportunities for Jewish youth to have the kinds of educational and cultural experiences that would lead to increased identity later in life. These initiatives have included teen social clubs, all-expenses-paid trips to Israel, increased scholarship opportunities, and a proliferating Jewish media landscape. The growth in media is, of course, also tied to the new and relative ease in creating glossy, professional-quality media and the limited expense now involved in creating Web content and video programs, but these media are qualitatively different from the Christian media that have been so intensively studied.

One indicator considered to be significant in building cohesion among faith communities is the degree of distinctiveness offered by the culture, faith system, or other requirements of that faith community. Within Christian denominations or other entities, that distinctiveness may include avoidance of dancing or alcohol, attendance at more than one church service per week, modest dress, or other means by which adherents can demonstrate that they are different from members of the larger culture. Of course, Jews may demonstrate distinctiveness through keeping kosher, Shabbos observance, modest dress, or covering their heads; but while Christians attempt to use distinctiveness in part to lure new adherents, Jews articulate it as a means of demonstrating faith by the already Jewish. The embrace of Judaism and, in particular, Kabbalah by celebrities devoid of an actual conversion is not cause for celebration, it is just odd.

There's No Such Thing as a Chanukah Bush, Sandy Goldstein

There are two points of comparison that are theoretically fruitful in examination of Jewish youth media. The first draws a distinction between media intended to build identity through daily practice as opposed to identity through major Jewish holidays. The second demonstrates the differences between youth media intended for Jewish children and youth media intended for Christian children. The first comparison allows one to consider the points of tension within the Jewish community and the different ways in which the producers have chosen to attempt to combat assimilation. The second comparison traces how core values in each religious tradition are manifest in each religious tradition's youth media and the ways in which these manifestations determine the ability of the media to find a market.

Keeping Kosher or Spinning the Dreidel

Religious identity is built through large and small actions. Some are as public as the lighting of a menorah in a prominent window of your home and inviting friends to the Passover Seder, and others are as private as avoiding the telephone on the Sabbath and ritual hand washing.[9] Both offer opportunities through which to build and demonstrate one's identity, and different movements of Judaism would debate which are more important in maintaining a Jewish life.

The choices offered by Jewish youth media are similarly divided. On one side are the videos and books intended to explain the Jewish holidays to children (perhaps in hopes that they will get their parents to be more observant?). On the other side are videos and magazines that seek to immerse youth in Jewish culture as a part of daily life. On Planet Matzah Ball, the primary concern of the Jewish space aliens is learning about the history and the observation the holidays of Passover and Chanukah. The focus is on the meal, the ritual, the story, but there is no mention of keeping a kosher home or keeping the Sabbath. There is also no discussion or video associated with observing the High Holy Days of Yom Kippur or Rosh Hashanah, which makes sense because fasting all day and going to synagogue don't make for great video. There is also no potentially competing Christian holiday such as exists with Easter or Christmas's proximity to Passover and Chanukah.

One series, *Alef bet Blastoff!* has two Muppet-type children and Mitzvah Mouse to guide viewers through Bible stories that provide the foundation for modern celebrations.[10] Most of the videos in the series center on celebrations and encourage viewers to identify with what is good about being Jewish. One video on Hanukkah has clips of children saying what they like best about the holiday, with the eight days of gifts prominently featured. An older video that more obviously addresses the challenge posed by the holiday's proximity to Christmas features young Sandy Goldstein, who tries to reconcile her parents willingness to allow her to attend a Christmas party but refusal to put up a Chanukah Bush (aka Christmas tree).[11] *Rugrats* covers all of the holiday bases with videos for Christmas, Kwanzaa, and Chanukah.

The focus on holidays seems to stem from a couple of issues. First, as with the proliferation of televised Christmas programs that start at Thanksgiving, producers are aware that there is a market for media associated with particular holidays. These videos are useful as gifts and are particularly popular at libraries as holiday time approaches. Second, the videos provide a parallel for Jewish children growing up in a predominantly Christian society; the plotlines seek to encourage viewers to realize what is special about being Jewish. Third, the videos in no way challenge the viewer to become an observant Jew beyond knowing about the holiday or participating in a festive meal. These videos won't challenge children to get their parents to observe the *mitzvot*, avoid work on the Sabbath, or wear tefillin. Judaism in this incarnation is fun, it is special, but it isn't work, and it doesn't make demands that can only be justified as being commanded by God.

The other strain of media, primarily targeted at older children and teens, attempts to present some tension between Jewish faith and culture and mainstream society. Most notable in this is *Agent Emes*, the series about a yeshiva student with a secret identity as an agent intent on thwarting evil.

By day, Agent Emes looks just as bored listening to his teacher as any kid would be, and he lives in a world that exists separately from one infused with MTV, navel piercing, and girls other than his sister and mother. He wears side-locks, covers his head, and speaks earnestly about doing what he can to do what HaShem wants. The view of daily life presented here is unapologetically orthodox and, depending on the upbringing of the viewer, is comforting in its familiarity or is interesting or challenging to those from a more secular background. Within the overall plotline of defeating evil, Agent Emes and his community demonstrate daily Jewish life, from morning hand-washing to *tzedakah*.

Certainly more approachable is the soft-sell of *JVibe*, which weaves embracing Jewish culture with advice on friendships and dealing with parents. Supported by sources including the Richard and Rhonda Goldman Fund, the advice column offers help for teens who have a different standard of observance from their friends, deal with anti-Semitic "jokes," and make friends with people from a variety of religious backgrounds. Daily or even weekly practice isn't the issue; although there is little mention of holiday observance, identifying with the Jewish community is the core message. *JVibe* seems to be seeking to demonstrate that being Jewish isn't so out of the mainstream that one can't make choices, but it is something worth honoring as an overall identity. Judaism is a tool "whether it's helping you recover from getting dumped or inspiring you to take action against life's injustices." [12]

Join Us or Join In?

While there certainly are Christian parallels with Jewish video in that the Christmas movie genre morphs and proliferates with every holiday season and no Thanksgiving aftermath is complete without a screening of *It's a*

Wonderful Life, overtly Christian media for kids, such as the series by Focus on the Family or the *Veggie Tales* series, are distinct from their Jewish partners. Christian video, even without a direct salvation message, offers itself to the outsider. *Veggie Tales* assumes no knowledge on the part of the viewer, and it and *Adventures in Odyssey* (Focus on the Family's product) attempt to guide the viewer to embrace Christian faith and values—regardless of the viewer's current belief system.

Agent Emes and *Alef bet Blastoff!* on the other hand, are primarily interested in the Jewish viewer. There is no call to be like the characters in the show to anyone but someone who already "gets it," to use a phrase from *JVibe*. There is no acknowledgment that a viewer who wasn't Jewish would be watching the videos (a good bet), and if someone who wasn't Jewish happened by, well, that's nice, but they aren't the target. This "preaching to the choir" is most evident in *Agent Emes*, which uses Hebrew word play and references to texts such as the Gemara as part of the plotline. There is no effort to educate on the basics; the viewers is fully expected to know some basic Hebrew and Talmudic teachings. Those who are "in the know" are treated to a number of subtle jokes about Jewish mothers, Orthodox family life, and other stereotypes, but most references will be missed by those outside the community.

Similarly, the Muppet children of *Alef bet Blastoff!* are proxies for the viewer in that they are educated by Mitzvah Mouse about Jewish history and customs, but this knowledge is intended for Jewish viewers primarily. The series explains what a mezuzah is, but it doesn't encourage non-Jews to put one up. In neither series is the viewer addressed. In contrast, Christian video talks directly to the viewer repeatedly, engages the viewer with letters and situations that depict the lives that viewers might lead, and encourages kids to adopt the beliefs—not just the customs—depicted on the videos. The Jewish videos make no mention of beliefs—the viewer is assumed to be past all that.

Belief, Media, and Market

Of course, it is easy to point to the significant differences in attitudes on proselytizing between Judaism and Christianity. Christianity is more interested in statements of faith and issues of belief than practice. Judaism, as a minority religion, relies on continuity and growth through family lineage, and while Jewish history honors prominent converts, conversion is not identified as a means of growth. Christianity, on the other hand, actively seeks conversion. Further, the very attributes and behaviors that support the growth of Christianity support the marketing of media in a capitalistic society. No one got on the best-seller list by relying on sales to family alone.

The Christian model of seeking converts and building a faith community by welcoming outsiders positions media from that tradition to do particularly well in a system that rewards increasing sales. The Jewish model of seeking increased identity and practice doesn't grow in the same terms, and the Jewish model of growth doesn't fit on a profit-and-loss statement. That difference in how Jewish stories are told via media combined with the minority position of the Jewish community in the United States goes a long way toward explaining why *Veggie Tales* is at Wal-Mart and *Shalom Sesame* is found on library shelves instead.

Of course, the dramatic difference in market size and the limited potential of Jewish media producers to support themselves producing media hasn't discouraged all market entries. Instead, these entrants are funded along the same lines as Focus on the Family media, albeit with quite different goals. Focus on the Family is a conservative Christian ministry and political organization that uses media as a means of disseminating its cultural message; Dr. James Dobson's radio program is its best-known product. Focus is supported by donations, large and small, and is diverse in the ways it seeks to achieve its political and social ends. While being quite mindful of the profound differences between Focus on the Family and Jewish philanthropic and cultural organizations, they are similar in that they are using media to respond to an identified need that doesn't fit well in the requirements of mass retail sales.

Supported by a combination of personal donations, major family foundations, individuals, Hadassah and Hebrew Union College funds, Jewish Family & Life! (or JFLmedia.com) produces media products for a range of Jewish audiences with a particular focus on the youth market.[13] Its *JVibe* magazine recently moved from an online existence to print and joins *Babaganewz* as a source of information and cultural teaching about Jewish issues and values. While JFLmedia.com uses the term *market*, it doesn't do so with the sense of sales, but instead as a market to reach with information, with the goal "to spark and nurture Jewish identity." [14] Other media products include MyJewishLearning.com and JewishFamily.com. Rather than articulating a goal of sales or even profit, JFLmedia.com uses the language of capitalism as a way of explaining how the organization works, but not the organization's goals. Words like *partnering, entrepreneurship,* and *market* seem to be a way to make its operations understandable and attractive to donors even though the end goal is education and rejuvenation as a response to the demographic pressures highlighted by recent studies.

In contrast, however, Focus on the Family's materials related to marketing and media are firmly couched in the language of Christian evangelism, with frequent use of the words *blessing, salvation, ministry,* and *discernment.* Despite the organization's clear embrace of American capitalism and its increasing use of partnerships with mass retail and media conglomerates, the language remains that of ministry. What both Jewish media and Christian media have in common, though, is an overall message about separating oneself from the mainstream culture at some level to allow for a connection to a faith community. This call to separation, to distinctiveness, highlights the key commonality that ties together disparate media products, producing organizations, and levels of practice and identity.

Fitting in While Set Apart

Distinctiveness is a critical means by which a faith system and community lures adherents by telling them how that faith and community makes the adherent different, special, distinctive from the overall mainstream culture. Whether that be through a savvy understanding of *Seinfeld* (as noted by *JVibe*) or a sense that one must, in large and small ways, adhere to the commands of the Torah, religious youth media encourages kids to find their identity outside that of the masses. Christian media has the luxury of operating within a Christian-dominant culture in which schools are closed for Christmas and Easter egg rolls happen on the White House lawn, but it, too, must make its bid for outsider status as a way of reinforcing a distinctive identity.

But Jewish youth media has a special challenge. It has to encourage kids and particularly teens to identify with a culture that can look very foreign to mainstream American society and to even encourage their parents to be more observant. It also has to reassure teens that being Jewish is cool and hip and won't make them an outcast among their friends. For youth who are already active in Maccabi games in the summer and youth groups, that is probably not too hard, but the goal is reaching those in unaffiliated families. In that challenge, the mainstream language of markets and media spurs Jewish media producers to create products that are parallel to those found at the local mass retailer, and the level of identification chosen is in the eyes of the reader.

Distinctiveness is a key element of religious adherence and growth; it provides followers with a clear identity and a means of separating from the dominant culture. Within a dominant Christian culture, however, embracing distinctive elements within a Christian denomination is measured in shades of gray. But distinctiveness can be much more challenging for Jewish kids growing up in a dominant Christian culture, and media that allows kids to choose their own level of identification can keep them in the fold without pushing too hard.

Echoing this emphasis on choosing one's level of identification, the December 2006 Web edition of *JVibe* featured an essay on how, when, and where teens wear religious jewelry such as a Star of David or a *chai* pendant.[15] The essay's author, Abby Hoicowitz, talked to teens about how and where one would wear such a symbol (inside or outside a shirt, at home or at school) and how important the style of pendant was in those decisions. Hoicowitz's essay illustrates the diversity of Jewish identification and the challenges for those seeking to reach the Jewish youth market. Do they follow the lead of Christian media producers and focus on holidays? Do they focus on culture over religion? Or do producers seek readers at whatever level of identification they are ready for, whether that means a working knowledge of Hebrew and the Torah or just wearing a Star of David inside the shirt? Such questions go to the heart of what those in nondominant religious subcultures must consider as they encounter the marketplace's newest entries and decide how their own faith will be displayed and lived out within that marketplace.

NOTES

1. Sisu, *Seder on Planet Matzah Ball*, videocassette (New York: Sisu [media publisher], 2004).

2. A. Klasky, G. Csupo, and P. Germain, *A Rugrats Chanukah*, in Jewish Heritage Video Collection, videocassette (New York: Nickelodeon, 1997).

3. Sisu, *Seder on Planet Matzah Ball.*

4. Reel Jewish Entertainment and L. Cohen, *The Adventures of Agent Emes*, videocassette (Pittsburgh: Reel Jewish Entertainment, 2003).

5. D. Fine, "Judaism: Cool New Trend?" *JVibe* (December 2004): 14–16.

6. A. Keysar and B. A. Kosmin, *Eight Up: The College Years* (New York: Jewish Theological Seminary, 2004).

7. *The National Jewish Population Survey, 2000–01: Strength, Challenge, and Diversity in the American Jewish Population* (New York: United Jewish Communities, 2005), 3.

8. S. M. Cohen and L. Kotler-Berkowitz, *The Impact of Childhood Jewish Education on Adult's Jewish Identity: Schooling, Israel Travel, Camping and Youth Groups*, Report no. 3 (New York: United Jewish Communities, 2004).

9. Reel Jewish Entertainment and L. Cohen, *The Adventures of Agent Emes.*

10. M. Baron, a Chanukah Mitzvah, in *Alef bet Blastoff!* videocassette (Brooklyn, N.Y.: Jewish Educational Toys, 1995).

11. A. P. Goldberg, *There's No Such Thing as a Chanukah Bush, Sandy Goldstein*, videocassette (Santa Monica, CA: Loxley Hall Productions, 1994).

12. M. Cove, "Letter from the Editor, " *JVibe* (December 2004): 30.

13. Jewish Family & Life! *Annual Report* (Newton, MA: Jewish Family & Life! 2002).

14. Mission Statement, www.jflmedia.com. Accessed March 15, 2006.

15. A. Hoicowitz, "Chai'd and Sleek," *JVibe* (December 2005) www.jvibe.com/realife/chaid_sleek.shtml. Accessed December 28, 2005.

PART TWO

∞∞

Religion and Politics in Tension

Mobilization and Mission through Media and Material Artifacts

In this section, we turn to an exploration of conflicts that emerge at the intersection of religion, media, and marketplace. These chapters explore political tensions that become encoded in media and media-related products or practices that then further contribute to misunderstandings and strife between religious and national loyalties. The last chapter in this section, by Erica Sheen, analyzes the differences between two big-budget Hollywood spectaculars focused on the story of Moses: the Cecil B. DeMille classic *The Ten Commandments* and Dreamworks' family film *The Prince of Egypt*. The chapter considers the ways in which these films work in concert with nationalist agendas even as the latter film, in particular, was promoted as cross-cultural and unifying in appeal. The middle chapter in the section, by Maryellen Davis, explores how Marian devotion has been marshaled in specific instances in relation to nationalist as well as religious agendas. The first chapter in this section considers the connection between the desire to influence through media materials and the need to ensure that potential observers are literate and able to interpret those materials in ways that those wishing to influence so desire. In this sense, literacy becomes crucial in the ways in which religion, media, and the marketplace can interrelate within and between particular cultures.

4

∞∞∞

Literacy in the Eye
of the Conversion Storm

GAURI VISWANATHAN

This chapter looks at how religion, and specifically Christian mission work and its emphasis on literacy, has operated in relation to the social and economic development of the Indian marketplace and political system. Beginning from the standpoint that literacy is a key aspect of development and modernization, Gauri Viswanathan explores how literacy, and its historic ties to Christian proselytizing, is currently at the center of debates about the future of India. To fully grasp the argument of this chapter, it is necessary to begin by considering India's relationship to its colonial past.

In the middle of the twentieth century, India became an independent state, freed from the political, economic, and cultural control of the British colonial empire. When under colonial power, it was believed by those in Britain that India's prospects for development were directly linked to the country's ability to model itself after its Western colonial rulers. Yet in the postcolonial era, many people, including leaders such as Gandhi and intellectuals like Edward Said, have criticized that viewpoint as imperialistic. India needed to free itself from the chains of colonialism, such leaders insisted, and that meant exposing the ways in which such colonial-inspired development efforts tended to suppress Indian and Hindu culture and tradition in favor of Christianity and Western cultural approaches.

One of the issues that has come under discussion in India, therefore, is the issue of Christian missionary organizations and the role these groups have played in relation to social programs. Prior to colonial rule, for example, there was no funding or much general support for an educational system that would

educate those in the lower castes of Indian society; government-sponsored education was for those in the privileged castes. Christian missionaries then stepped
in to fill this need of the lower castes. Yet whereas missionaries at first claimed
to be about closing the gaps between the castes, an emphasis on conversion
turned their attention toward specific pedagogies. These pedagogies favored
introducing young people to Christianity through catechism and the interpretation of scripture as well as through a linking of Christianity's concept of the
"newly made self" with what might be termed the popular media of the day: the
English literature of romanticism.

The emphasis on conversion in missionary schools resulted in hostility
among some Indians who perceive missionaries as targeting poor persons and
offering conversion as an avenue of escape from poverty. Such a strong sentiment against conversion even led to an effort to include in the Indian constitution a provision that would outlaw conversion. The language was softened,
however, in part because religious and other non-governmental organizations
have long played an important role in the social programs of India due to the
failure of the state to fund such programs.

In this chapter, Viswanathan analyzes why it is that a Nobel prize–winning
economist of Indian descent, Amartya Sen, came under attack from Hindu
nationalists who purportedly wanted to protect India from further colonial influence. She argues that Hindu nationalists, in their inability to address the country's
overwhelming problems of illiteracy, poverty, and discrimination, have turned
to attacking religious groups that, unlike Hinduism, support proselytization. Yet
in doing so, she argues, they conflate issues of religion and development. She
suggests instead that what India needs to do is to de-link literacy and conversion
and note the way in which literacy is linked to development and to modernity.
Literacy, she argues, not only has been a means of introducing people to
Christianity, but also has introduced people to the value of critical thought.
Thus, people in modern India are well positioned to accept *or* reject Christianity—
or Islam, Hinduism, or even secular modernism, for that matter. Thus, literacy
can be seen as something foundational for economic development and social
change—a goal, she argues, that all in India should embrace.

In an otherwise cheerless and desultory year, euphoria seized India as it celebrated the award of the 1998 Nobel prize to economics professor Amartya Sen for his work on welfare economics. On hearing the news, even those on both the left and the right who had long questioned the pragmatic usefulness of Sen's work suspended their skepticism and joined the rest of the country in lauding his achievement. There was, however, a lone voice of dissent and disapproval. It came from the Vishwa Hindu Parishad (VHP), the right-wing Hindu religious organization that backed the socially conservative Bharatiya Janata Party (BJP) government, which ruled India from 1998 to 2004. VHP president Ashok Singhal gave a sinister turn to Sen's economic program, darkly interpreting his Nobel award as a Western conspiracy to promote literacy in developing societies in order to bring them within the ultimate pale of a global Christian order and thus "wipe out Hinduism from this country." [1] "Despite the accuracy of Professor Amartya Sen's conclusions," he charged, "the same could prove harmful to Hindu society as Christians would be bringing in more money ostensibly for promoting education, but actually proselytization would increase and everything in India would be undermined." [2]

Incidentally, this was the same Ashok Singhal who launched a scathing attack on Mother Teresa's Nobel prize. Then, too, he accused the Nobel committee of rewarding only those who promoted the work of Christian charity. Dismissing the humanitarian goals of Mother Teresa's work, he insisted that the driving aim behind all the activities of the Missionaries of Charity was to convert poor and ignorant Hindus to Christianity. At that time, unlike the present, Singhal's voice was joined by others, though admittedly not in huge numbers. Publicly at least, this time around, there were no other takers to his bizarre and twisted view. Even the prime minister of the BJP-led government, Atal Behari Vajpayee, denounced such provocations as churlish, intemperate, and irresponsible. [3]

Yet even as he refused to participate in Singhal's derision of Sen's award, Prime Minister Vajpayee simultaneously urged that there be a "national debate on conversion" following the attacks on Christians and their places of worship in 1998 and in subsequent years. These attacks seemed to echo the horrendous violence of December 6, 1992, which had resulted in the destruction of the Babri Masjid in Ayodhya by Hindu extremists. Christian churches were razed to the ground and, in one particularly gruesome event, a Christian missionary and his sons were burned alive. Ostensibly a response to Christian proselytization, the violence began in the western state of Gujarat but spread to other states as well, including the eastern state of Orissa. In this context, Prime Minister Vajpayee's appeal sounded innocuous enough, outwardly a sincere attempt to engage in serious dialogue and discussion about the motive and force behind the violence.

However, the call for a debate was clearly intended to reopen the discussions that took place when the Indian constitution was framed at the time of independence. In the Constituent Assembly discussions that were held between 1946 and 1950, there was a strong move by powerful Hindu lobbies to ban conversions altogether. The call for constitutional provisions against conversion was made in response to the widespread fear that Hinduism, typically described as a non-proselytizing religion, would be under threat and its numerical strength diminished if conversions to other religions were allowed. While all religious groups may theoretically disseminate their beliefs, it has been a long-standing belief among Hindus that only Christians and Muslims actively proselytize. This conviction lay behind their attempt to bar conversions altogether. Furthermore, Gandhi's famous distrust of Christian missionaries and Christian conversions offered a screen behind which the anti-Christian lobby could conveniently hide, as they continue to do today. The fear of conversion produced a strange marriage between Gandhi and the Hindu nationalists, who in all other instances denounced him for making concessions to Muslims but heralded him as the voice of reason when he opposed Christian proselytization. Of course, the vital difference between Gandhi's position and theirs was that while he believed Christian conversions were the instrument of British colonialism and therefore must be resisted as vigorously as British rule, Hindu groups had no such larger aim and remained trapped within their own self-interests.

The final draft of the Indian constitution effectively resisted all such attempts to outlaw conversions and, instead, made the propagation of religion permissible under the law. Article 25 (1) of the constitution gives everyone the fundamental right to "profess, practice, or propagate religion," a right that is only circumscribed by considerations of "public order, morality, and health."[4] Whereas the constitutional freedom of conscience is described as a mental process, the right to propagate religion externalizes the mental freedom of conscience, rendering active propagation a field of open and lawful endeavor.[5] Freedom of conscience was interpreted to mean the right not only to choose one's religious views but also to disseminate them. Not until 1977 was this provision modified, influenced in part by a commission, headed by Justice Bhawani Shankar Niyogi in 1954, which concluded that the right to propagate religion did not necessarily extend to the right to convert. Noting that the term was originally intended to refer to freedom of expression and conscience, the commission implied that conversion militates against such freedom and therefore cannot be regarded as a disinterested dissemination of religious knowledge.

The ambiguity in the semantic distinctions between "propagation" and "conversion" went a long way in creating a charged environment culminating in such incidents as the recent Gujarat violence. "Conversion" has been taken to imply force, a radical takeover of people's will, whereas "propagation" has a more intransitive connotation, a middle term between force and instruction. Slipping from one meaning to another, Praveen Togadia, the general secretary of the conservative Hindu nationalist VHP party, invoked comparative history (in balefully incorrect ways) to argue that no other society gave a free rein to conversion, so why should India be an exception? Seeking a universalist point of reference, he linked economic well-being with free will to argue that "if these are the views of even the developed countries, how can we allow conversion in India where a large section of the society is poor and illiterate?"[6] In rehearsing the earlier constitutional debates on conversion, he failed to mention that the constitutional framers invoked Western precedent, particularly that of American freedom of conscience, when they decided to include provisions to permit propagation of religion. Togadia's comparative perspective evidently broke down in its inability to deal with the multiple genealogies of religious freedom comprising the constitutional debates. Selectively calling up the West as a reference point for India's position on conversion was not only incomprehensible but perhaps even disingenuous.

At any rate, then Prime Minister Vajpayee's call for a national debate on conversion insisted on revisiting the role of missionary institutions in India: to ask, in other words, whether their aim was to propagate religion—which could also broadly include morality, civic virtue, and character—or to convert people to Christianity. Without attacking the constitution itself,

Vajpayee asserted that, while the right of religious propagation was consti-
tutionally guaranteed, "the country must ensure that it is not misused."
A dire warning, indeed, to those who would use constitutional provisions
as a license to apply force. "Poverty cannot be a reason for conversion,"
concluded Vajpayee, firmly dissociating economic circumstances from the
imperatives of religious change.[7] Regardless of his own disapproval of the
Hindu nationalist leader Singhal's attack on Nobel laureate Sen, Prime
Minister Vajpayee kept the two issues of Christianization and welfare economics squarely within the same frame of reference, however much he may
have denied that there was any connection between the two. It is thus no
coincidence that Amartya Sen is denounced for advocating basic education—
and religious conversion by extension—at the same time that Christianity
is under siege in south Gujarat for promoting tribal conversions. In being
forcibly linked with conversion, literacy is disengaged from development
issues and relocated as an exclusively religious issue. In an effort to reclaim
literacy from Christian uses, Singhal pointed to what is now a consistent
thematic of anti-missionary resistance: literacy has legitimacy only when it
is a marker of indigenous cultural identity. Either way, the development
issue drops out of the picture.

The public repudiation of his viewpoint, however, does not mean that
the Hindu nationalist leader's view is an aberrant one, the voice of the
lunatic fringe unable to make a dent on mainstream opinion. On the contrary, India's history of colonial education provided a real context for the
deep suspicion cast upon the Nobel prize committee's recommendations
(howsoever irrational it undoubtedly was). That this context was exploited
to detach literacy from issues of social reform is perhaps one of the dimensions of the conversion controversy that needs analysis and clarification.
Views such as those held by Ashok Singhal have been articulated over time
and buttressed by references to India's colonial history. The deep distrust
of missionary institutions has a colonial past providing Hindu nationalists
a much-needed moral stance to defend Indian religion and culture. (The
collapsing of "Hinduism" and "India" is not the least of the rhetorical slippages.) It is well known that Christian missionaries were attacked long before
the VHP and the BJP came on the scene in the 1960s and 1980s, respectively.
Hinduism put up a stiff resistance to Christianity on both an organizational
and a theological level. Richard Fox Young has meticulously documented the

development of a whole tradition of anti-Christian polemics in nineteenth-century India, focused on a refutation of Christian doctrine, point by point.[8]

There is nothing new in the Hindu antagonism to missionary schools as hotbeds of conversion activity ("wolf in sheep's clothing," as they were often called).[9] Opposition to literacy reform has long been motivated by fear that its ultimate intent is religious change. On the other hand, why Sen's economic development research would benefit Christians more than any other group is never clear in the Hindu nationalist attacks on him. But it is telling that VHP general secretary Ashok Singhal complained that the Nobel prize was never given to social activists like Gandhi or Baba Ante, who had both worked tirelessly for the uplift of the poor and other marginalized sections of society.[10] Despite this argument, it is important to note that social activism in India, even that practiced by a Gandhi or an Ante, has never been totally removed from a related compulsive desire to contest the reach of Christian missionaries, particularly in tribal and outlying areas. In regions where lower castes and outcastes were denied the educational facilities open to higher caste groups, missionaries often stepped in to fill a social vacuum. In the light of caste tensions, it is easy to see why social reform has been as contested as conversion itself. Neither can be separated from a colonial history that continues to inform attitudes to an ethics of improvement, which to many today is still indistinguishable from the mission of civilization. This is by no means to justify the crudest premises of cultural nationalism, but we are obliged to acknowledge the complex historical formations driving nationalists to the depths of paranoia and suspicion.

Historically, missionary schools opened their doors to socially excluded groups, while the schools run by the colonial government had as their main clientele students from the upper castes. This division so heavily reinforced the caste structure that it appeared as if the very form and spirit of colonial education were driven by caste feeling. There was more complacency than truth in colonial administrators' belief that English studies altered attitudes to caste. As the Serampore missionary John Marshman wryly observed, "I am not certain that a man's being able to read Milton and Shakespeare, or understand Dr. Johnson, would make him less susceptible of the honour of being a Brahmin." [11] The association of missionary schools with vernacular education and the government schools with English education marked

the differential development of languages and literary instruction.[12] Yet
precisely because missionary schools were so closely identified with lower-
caste education, missionaries found their aims compromised by their
desire to lure the upper castes to their schools, if only to extend the range
of Christian influence. Partly this was motivated by their fear that, by
attracting only "the most despised and least numerous of society," they
were creating a new virulent strain in Indian society, "a new class superior
to the rest in useful knowledge, but hated and despised by the castes to
whom their new attainments would always induce us to prefer them."[13]
Caste lines being as implacable as they were, missionaries dreaded that the
huge efforts they expended on the education of the lower castes would
remain confined to these groups and not spread farther. Recognizing that
the reform of Hindu society was impossible without involving all castes,
they modified their instructional objectives, expanding their curricular
offerings to include English literature alongside the vernaculars. In time,
the lines between missionary and government schools blurred as both
types of institutions competed for students from the upper castes.

Interestingly, the work of vernacular education started by missionaries
was taken up by Hindu reformist organizations, such as the Ramakrishna
Mission and the Arya Samaj. The linguistic stratification was so rigid that
the vernacular schools produced a militant brand of youth who pledged
themselves to the preservation of Hindu culture, religion, and language
against the encroachments of an English-educated, Westernized elite. So it
is somewhat ironic that this form of cultural nationalism occurred largely
because the vernacular missionary schools and the so-called government
schools switched their linguistic orientation, with surprising if not unman-
ageable results. It has also inspired the defenders of Hinduism to view the
English press, which has extensively covered the atrocities against Christians
in the past years, as a key player in the drama of linguistic, religious, and
caste stratification, its corps of writers having themselves been educated
primarily in Christian mission schools.

In seeking to break out of narrow caste identification, the missionary
schools set in motion a number of significant developments. The original
objectives of imparting basic literacy skills were considerably qualified by
the new infusion of literary content. If missionary schools initially sought
to remedy the exclusionary effects of caste prejudice by offering educational

opportunities denied to lower castes, their turn to an English course of studies took them in a markedly different direction. That conversion, rather than caste or poverty relief, more often engaged their interest is evident from the perfection of certain pedagogical techniques to produce belief. Catechism and hermeneutics are prominent among these. The Word offered access to the world, but it also opened up access to faith through the power of imagination. Education in imagery supplemented, and in time surpassed, instruction in the fundamentals of literacy. In all its clarity and brilliance, imagery pointed the way to the Bible, to the power of arguments, reasons, and demonstrations vividly impressing themselves on the mind, to an experience of truth that could only be known when seen and felt. To missionaries aware of the hostility that direct Christian instruction might produce, there was no better way to convey the deep swell of religious feeling than through the rich tapestry of images, sensations, and impressions found in the best of English Romantic writers like Wordsworth, Cowper, and Young.

These alternating instructional objectives in missionary institutions kept the pendulum swinging between poverty and caste relief, on the one hand, and conversion, on the other. Remember former Prime Minister Vajpayee's admonition that "poverty cannot be a reason for conversion." He was far closer to the course of the colonial state than he may have realized, for institutional developments suggest a complex evolution of conversion motives not always directly related to economic circumstances. The violence against Christians in Gujarat and elsewhere was caused by the perception that missionaries were targeting poor tribal members to convert them to Christianity, often by imparting literacy skills to them. Radical Hindu groups interpret Christian conversion as an inducement, an enticing avenue of escape from grinding poverty. But conversion is just as importantly involved in the constructions of new selves, and it is this shift from the ground of economics to that of culture that continues to alarm Hindu opponents, perhaps even more than the threat of religious change. Their will is steeled, therefore, to reclaim culture and make it the ultimate goal of all future attempts at literacy reform.

Religions assign different functions for reading and writing religions of revelation: the word is the Word. Hinduism's self-description as a non-proselytizing religion has also meant that it conceives of reading and writing in different ways. One point of difference is the affirmation of community.

This does not necessarily mean relative community, however, but a community marked by systems of inclusion and exclusion, which are in turn determined by rules of purity and pollution. Verbal acts are modes of community stratification as much as they are forms of communication. But where the use of language signals the expression of faith in a supreme being, religions that employ such language open up the new possibility that language can cause changes in one's conceptions of divinity. Are these then proselytizing religions? It can be argued that Hinduism establishes a relation between literacy and faith different from that of Christianity and Islam. If, as is maintained about Hinduism, faith does not lie in words, then a Hindu can have access to the world without the mediation of language. Language, however, is threatening when it is tied to faith. Literacy arouses suspicion because it can alter faith by providing a different form of access to the world. Access to language is essential for economic betterment, yet it also contains the potential to introduce worldviews at variance with those affirmed by the community. The conflicting perspectives on literacy throw open the divide between economics and culture, which further translates into artificial distinctions between religions on the basis of whether they proselytize or not.

Surprisingly, the Hindu nationalist VHP leaders who attacked the Christian conversion of illiterate tribal members do not accept that literacy can also be a defense against forcible conversions of any kind, Christian, Hindu, Muslim, or any other religion. Their unquestioned assumption is that illiteracy is gullibility. But if its opposite is also true—that literacy is skepticism and critical judgment—then the threat posed by the lure of other faiths should be diminished. The Word may be the source of faith, but it is also the maker of selfhood and independent judgment. However, the rhetoric of the VHP suppresses this fundamental understanding of literacy's role, which, in offering the tools of knowledge, discrimination, and evaluation, shapes the modern self. We are led to inquire whether literacy as self-making, independence, and private judgment poses the real threat, an unnamed one perhaps, acknowledged only as a tool of Christianization but not of Hindu modernity.

At this point I want to return to Amartya Sen and his Nobel prize for economics. We may now place Ashok Singhal's diatribe as the work of a perceived shift in literacy's address from economics to culture. That is why no matter how much of a non sequitur his comments may appear, his view that Sen's mass literacy would benefit Christians reflects how definitively culture, not economics, has become the contested ground for discussions of development issues. In part, this shift had strategic uses for a government seeking to deflect attention from the dismal failure of *swadeshi* (self-sufficient) economics, despite the BJP's campaigning for power on this issue. And as its economic policies met with one disaster after another, the BJP needed to keep economics out of public discussion. Religion has always been its surrogate theme, and it is not surprising that turning even literacy into a conversion issue worked to offset the government's dismal showing on the economic front. But apart from turning the focus away from a string of economic failures, the perception that mass literacy is a tool of cultural imperialism undermines the developmental rhetoric of secular progress that literacy reform also tends to generate. Singhal's denunciation of Amartya Sen reflected attitudes toward literacy that are part of an ongoing tension between development priorities and cultural purity.

By objecting to literacy as a missionary-inspired practice, do Hindus really want to say they object to the introduction of social benefits to the people? Most would probably say no, but the ethics of social reform has been challenged in the mounting anti-Christian rhetoric since the BJP assumed power in early 1998. It can, and should, be argued that if missionaries give people services they would otherwise not have, no one has a right to restrict their activities, particularly when there are no other state-supported or private initiatives. After all, missionaries do not have a monopoly on the opening of new schools and hospitals, and there is nothing to stop Hindus or any other group from doing likewise. But the cumulative effect of the attack on Christianity has been a fierce questioning of whether social benefits can ensue at the cost of religious and cultural integrity. This is nothing less than an anti-Orientalist response to a condition sewn into Indian history through the reformist ideology of British colonialism. But its corollary is that social reform always has been, and always will be, politicized in postcolonial India. The view that social service has a national or a religious identity is among the shocking revelations of this history. It seems that no act of reform or service can take place in postcolonial India without it being measured against a corresponding degradation of Hindu customs and rituals in the process.

But I think there is something fundamentally more worrying in the anti-literacy, anti-conversion posture of the VHP. The numbers of Hindus who actually converted to Christianity are far less than the numbers of those who detached themselves from Hinduism over time and affiliated themselves to more secular conceptions of modernity. Today we call the latter group "secular Indians," though that term has its own problems. The main difference between these two groups of Hindus is that the former have converted to Christianity and the latter to modernity. The mechanism is the same, even though the characterization may be different. Critics will argue this was the effect of mission-school education on the middle classes. But I think there are deeper issues involved. Hinduism is once again at the crossroads of change. Instead of attending to the problems of overwhelming illiteracy, caste and gender discrimination, and poverty, the most extreme among the Hindu nationalists have narrowed their agenda to attack other groups—notably Muslims and Christians—for the erosion of cultural traditions. India's struggle to keep pace with a changing world is most pronounced in a stagnant educational system which, while professing secularism, is still caught up in the forms and practices of a religious culture. Is the desire to interrogate mass literacy ultimately a desire to renounce the modern world altogether? Is the quest for cultural integrity so supreme that it creates a longing in Hindus to supplant modernity with a more reassuring past in which their traditions are uncorrupted? These are difficult questions, but they go to the heart of the resistance to literacy as a development issue.

Significantly, even as some Hindus recoil from the demands of modernity, at another level they are reclaiming literacy as a hallmark of Hinduism's cultural past. Indeed, when literacy performs the work of culture in Hinduism, it is assigned an economic role denied in the work of missionary schools. In the context of an ancient past, literacy extends beyond reading and writing to encompass a range of technical and vocational skills. On a trip to the southern city of Mysore, former Prime Minister Vajpayee lauded the work of Basaveshwara, a social reformer who made significant efforts in educating the masses while also promoting women's education. Vajpayee pointed to the Veerashaiva *mutts* as ideal service institutions providing training for literacy training that the government ought to provide but did not. The Veerashaiva mutts, he further added, were the only institutions serving society for a long period of time with the same missionary zeal as that of Christian educational institutions.[14] As if on cue in a musical duet, the state chief minister who hosted him glorified the work of institutions like the JSS Mahavidhyapeetha, saying they were providing opportunities for the disabled and the disenfranchised to become useful citizens. Significantly, both political figures consider the indigenous schools important because they are first and foremost technical training institutes. The vocational training offered in these indigenous institutions becomes that site of difference, turning basic literacy into a colonized space, a zone of foreign domination.

Conflicting approaches to developmentalism underscore a deep ambivalence about literacy that has remained unresolved since the framing of the Indian constitution. Amartya Sen reopened the old debates about rights versus directives when he released the Public Report on Basic Education (PROBE) on January 1, 1999. The PROBE report is described as "a people's report" on school education. Prepared by a team of independent academics and social activists, it set out to counter the prevalent official myths about Indian schooling. The report claims to be the first attempt of its kind to examine the condition of India's elementary education from the standpoint of the underprivileged. It demolishes a set of ruling myths that have guided Indian education since the country's independence, among which are, first, that poor parents are not interested in sending their children to school, as is conventionally believed; second, that most of the schoolchildren do not attend school because they have to work; and third, that elementary education is free. Most important, the report established that there was no direct link between child labor and lack of interest in schooling.[15] Amartya Sen had argued this point for a long time, noting with chagrin that "child labour is considered perfectly acceptable for the boys and girls of poor families, while the privileged classes enjoy a massively subsidized system of higher education."[16]

Encouraged by the report's conclusion that education remains sought after even by the most economically disadvantaged sections of society, Sen declared that the time for demanding elementary education as a fundamental right had arrived. Simultaneously, he unveiled his plans to set up a charity trust with the Nobel money for development of education and health in India and Bangladesh.[17] Stressing the West's economic progress as a function of its planned development of human resources, Sen persuasively spoke of how the general availability of elementary education would

enhance a sense of citizens' participation in India's overall economic
expansion. He sounded a theme that placed the economic imperatives of
educational growth in the perspective of social choice theory. Economic
advantages, he appeared to suggest, were the fruit of a participatory democracy whose foundations rested on basic literacy.[18]

It is therefore all the more scandalous that, if literacy is the chief basis of
economic development and social change, education as a fundamental right
has still remained largely undefined in the Indian constitution. On the other
hand, articles 25 and 26 of the constitution, comprising the section on
fundamental rights, were careful to give "every religious denomination" the
right to propagate religion and maintain religious institutions. Constituent
Assembly discussions struggled to untangle the contradiction between the
secular goals of Indian democracy and the permission granted to religious
groups to practice (and preach) their religious philosophies in their own
institutions. Article 30 addresses educational rights, but it is less interested
in universalizing education than in providing for the rights of minorities to
maintain their own educational institutions and have full control over curricular content. Even after fifty years of independence, the Indian government has been unable to respond satisfactorily to the right-to-education
needs of its citizens. Vajpayee acknowledged the continued failure of his own
government to address educational needs, uttering, in a moment of utter
candor, "We pray to Saraswati (the Hindu goddess of learning) but make no
arrangements to educate our children." [19] Hence we see his admiration for
the efforts of nongovernmental institutions like the Veerashaiva mutts or the
Mahavidhyapeetha for doing what the government was obliged to do, but
failed to do. Unable to invest adequately in education, the Indian government has appeared to be resigned to the possibility of nongovernmental
organizations taking the initiative. Yet social strife results when religious
groups (operating as parallel nongovernmental organizations) undertake the
work of education, often work that is considered disruptive of another religious tradition. And in order to resolve conflicts of such a nature, the state is
required to intervene, even though it prefers to leave educational initiatives
to nongovernmental organizations. This contradiction remains at the core of
the state's fraught relation with the education of its citizens.

By proposing universal education as a fundamental right, Amartya Sen
called for alternative ways to rethink "inconsistencies of means and ends," by

which he meant the present arbitrary distribution of resources and the uncertain division of labor between government and nongovernmental (minority) agencies.[20] To be sure, he was less forthcoming about the sources of investment in education, for it is never entirely clear whether he would be willing to settle for an education funded by nongovernmental agencies to supplement government funding. To some extent, this uncertainty has augmented the deep anxiety of his opponents that groups seeking to propagate their own beliefs—such as Christian missionaries—would seize the momentum for educational change. But Sen's most important intervention is in shifting freedom away from a concept that denotes a community's right to practice and propagate its beliefs. Rather, freedom for him is the creation of conditions for the wholesome participation of citizens in the democratic process. Universal literacy is the key to this process. As the instrument for securing the representation of people belonging to the unorganized sector, universal primary education is more than an entree into people's participation in their economic advancement. By enacting democracy, it confers a reality on participatory processes that Indian democracy still lacks, despite its adult suffrage.

At the same time Amartya Sen has been careful not to make freedom an all-encompassing category overriding goals of equality, such that one person's freedom becomes another's un-freedom. For instance, he argued that the freedom accruing from a market economy is accompanied by far too many dangers of inequality and poverty stemming from the market.[21] Instead, he proposed five kinds of freedom: (1) enabling freedom, which signifies that each individual is able to participate in social and economic activities and that the quality of life is improved through education and health facilities; (2) political freedom, which invariably involves democracy and civil rights; (3) economic freedom, which involves transactions and the market and could thus promote efficiency and equity; (4) transparency freedom, which encompasses a person's right to know that he or she is not being cheated in a transaction; and (5) protective freedom, which is freedom from droughts, floods, famine. These freedoms are important insofar as they constitute the legitimate end of development.[22]

Thus, for Sen literacy is not exclusively an economic issue, as some commentators believe. His notion of freedom encompasses culture—the kind of life we would like to lead—as an essential goal of development.[23]

What his critic Ashok Singhal evidently feared was that culture would be made synonymous with social choice, and to that extent Amartya Sen's notion of freedom confirmed his anxiety that development had a Christian trajectory. Singhal obviously got the story wrong in most of the particulars. But on the subject of choice Sen offered a new set of questions that could potentially have more bearing on how individuals construe selfhood, as opposed to being affirmed by their community. Instead of asking the old question, "Is it possible to have socially rational decisions based on the interests and preferences of the members of the society?" he proposed asking, "Which of the various ways of equity and justice are most relevant?" The choice, he suggests, is between different ways of evaluation whose ultimate validity is that they draw upon foundational notions of justice and fairness. Even the apparently scientific subject of choosing a suitable measure of poverty for a nation or a state can be approached in terms of the competing values reflected in different ways by distinct statistical measures. Because welfare economics and social choice theory link knowledge with practice, their operative premise is that self-construction is national construction. So even though economic development has merged into an issue of culture in the rhetoric of the postcolonial state, driven by its own sense of cultural nationalism, the question of choice is deliberately suspended. Where it does appear, it is turned into proof of forcible conversion.

NOTES

An earlier version at this paper was delivered as a keynote lecture at a symposium, "The Future and Past of Education in India," held at Syracuse University on February 26, 1999.

1. "Sangh Parivar Comes under Fire," *The Hindu,* December 28, 1998, 13.

2. "Singhal Statement on Amartya Sen Misquoted," *The Hindu,* January 3, 1999, 15.

3. "Vajpayee Criticises VHP Remarks on Christians," *The Hindu,* December 31, 1998, 1.

4. Ministry of Law, Justice and Company Affairs, Government of India, *The Constitution of India (as modified up to the 1st August 1977),* 14.

5. M. M. Singh, *The Constitution of India: Studies in Perspective* (Calcutta: World Press, 1975), 480.

6. "VHP Charge against Sonia Gandhi," *The Hindu,* January 9, 1999, 6.

7. "PM Calls for National Debate on Conversion," *The Hindu,* January 11, 1999, 6.

8. Richard Fox Young, *Resistant Hinduism: Sanskrit Sources of Anti-Christian Apologetics in Early Nineteenth-Century India* (Vienna: Roberto de Nobili Research Library, 1981).

9. See Antony Copley, *Religions in Conflict: Ideology, Cultural Contact, and Conversion in Late Colonial India* (Delhi: Oxford University Press, 1997). See also my *Outside the Fold: Conversion, Modernity, and Belief* (Princeton, NJ: Princeton University Press, 1998), particularly chapter 3, "Rights of Passage," for a discussion of the antagonism felt by Hindu parents toward Christian missionaries, whom they blamed for the Christian conversions of their young children. Deprived of their rights to inheritance on conversion, converts were often assisted by missionaries in bringing their cases to court so that their rights would be restored.

10. "Singhal Statement on Amartya Sen Misquoted," *The Hindu*, January 3, 1999, 15.

11. Great Britain, *Parliamentary Papers*, 1852–53, Evidence of J. C. Marshman, 32:119.

12. See my *Masks of Conquest: Literary Study and British Rule in India* (New York: Columbia University Press, 1989), 151–152.

13. *Great Britain, Parliamentary Papers* 1831–32. Minute by M. Elphinstone, December 13, 1823, 9:519.

14. "Poverty Hindering Spread of Literacy: PM," *The Hindu*, January 4, 1999, 10.

15. "People's Report Explodes 'Myths,'" *The Hindu*, December 31, 1999, 5.

16. Amartya Sen, "Basic Education as a Political Issue," in *Amartya Sen and Jean Dreze Omnibus* (Delhi: Oxford University Press, 1999), 120.

17. "Sen to Set Up Charity with Prize Money," *The Hindu*, December 28, 1998, 13.

18. Sen's research in Indian villages consistently pointed to the special value of basic education as a tool of social affirmation. As the PROBE report later confirmed, even among the most socially and economically disadvantaged groups, education was strongly valued for enabling upward mobility. Sen punctured the myth propagated by upper castes that the lower castes did not place much importance on literacy and rejected education as an instrument of upper-caste domination.

19. "Poverty Hindering Spread of Literacy: PM," *The Hindu*, January 4, 1999, 10.

20. Sen, "Basic Education as a Political Issue," 117.

21. See Amartya Sen, *Inequality Examined* (Delhi: Oxford University Press, 1992), in which he trenchantly shifts the question economists typically ask ("Should there be equality?") to the more important one: "Equality of what?" Sen forces the discussion to concentrate on the diversity of human populations, which inevitably involves different standards of equality; in other words, what is equality to one group of people might be deemed inequality to another. The heterogeneity of social groups requires one to constantly rethink how a range of human capabilities might be harnessed to achieve specific goals, from which standpoint questions of rights and equality can be raised more profitably.

22. See Amartya Sen, "Well beyond Liberalization," in *Amartya Sen and Jean Dreze Omnibus*, for an exploration of these themes as well as an assessment of India's

recent economic reforms. His conclusion that the "'uncaging of the tiger' has not—at least not yet—led to any dynamic animal springing out and sprinting ahead" (180) draws attention to the still unfulfilled promises of participatory growth, evident in the alarming illiteracy rates and social deprivations.

23. See particularly Sen's essay "Freedom, Agency, and Well-Being," in *Inequality Reexamined,* which describes freedom as our right to set goals for ourselves and our ability to get what we value and want; in short, to lead a life we would choose to live.

5

<hr>

Mary as Media Icon

Gender and Militancy in Twentieth-Century U.S. Roman Catholic Devotional Media

MARYELLEN DAVIS

The previous chapter suggested that the historical role of Protestant missionaries in India can be viewed as directly related to the resistance contemporary development efforts encounter among various leaders and groups in India. Yet equating mission with conversion is not limited to the Protestant impulse alone. In this chapter, we consider the ways in which Marian devotion, and in particular the mass-produced products that have circulated in an effort to promote that devotion, has at certain key points in history constructed Mary as the model missionary. In the Cold War years immediately following World War II, Marian devotees viewed purported miracles attributed to Mary, along with her role as intercessor between ordinary individuals and the divine beings of God and Jesus Christ, as a means for conversion—specifically from communism. Such a focus on anticommunism, combined with the Cold War's apocalyptic anxiety, enabled Catholic publishers of religious materials promoting Marian devotion to provide a meaningful interpretation of Mary as protectress of the United States. With its attention to the details in the construction of Marian publications and material artifacts, this chapter speaks to the need for those in the field of historical studies to consider how religion can be mobilized through material artifacts for politico-religious ends.

Sensing Media, Sensing Religion

Close your eyes and imagine a life without mediation. You are blind, deaf, dumb, and unable to touch or smell anything in your environment. The majority of us would find it difficult to cope with the loss of even just one of these senses. Now pause and consider a religious life without mediation. Even the least overtly sacramental faiths depend on visual, oral, and material culture in everyday life. Imagine religion without art, without architecture, without the faces, both human and divine, that define religious communities. This is a daunting proposition. Is religion, at its core, constituted by multiple forms of media? Today, new forms of technology that extend our definition of media culture are transforming the way many human beings experience religion. The study of religion is invigorated by contemporary scholarship that pays serious attention to the multiple forms of media that shape our world. The emerging field of media, religion, and culture illuminates the dynamism and complexity of mediated interactions in both contemporary and historical settings.

Scholars of religion and media study the senses: the construction of religious senses and sensibilities through processes of mediation. This chapter examines representations of the Virgin Mary created and disseminated by particular groups of people in America's religious past. I investigate traditions of seeing, showing, and using Mary as a *media icon*—a popular image saturated with religious significance—within the print culture of the Militia of the Immaculata and the Central Association of the Miraculous Medal, two prominent Roman Catholic devotional organizations in the United States.[1] These print culture sources, rich in visual images, demonstrate explicit ties to other forms of material culture (such as religious medals and other sacramentals), and also to Catholic ritual action.

As my research led me to the study of Roman Catholic cultures in the United States, I found my mailbox filling—week after week—with medals, holy cards, scapulars, and pamphlets. The material culture of haphazard mailing-list memberships began to infiltrate my home. Overwhelmed by the richness and diversity of these cultural artifacts at my door, a single image on a holy card stopped me in my tracks. A crowned woman in blue tilts her head quietly to one side, her hands gently clasped. Seven swords pierce her torso, as golden rays emanate from her head, mirroring the pattern of the firmly anchored daggers. Some of these daggers pierce her heart. Yet her eyes remain downcast, her mouth serene, her robes un-bloodied by the violence at her breast. This is not a new image. This is the classic image of the "sorrowful mother" (*mater dolorosa*)—the Virgin Mary pierced by seven sorrows that mark the sufferings of her son. I flipped the card over to see an outline of a particular devotion to "Our Lady of Sorrows." At the bottom was a name and place: "Scapular Guild, Philadelphia, PA." I read on to the smaller print: "reprinted with permission of the Servants of Mary, Berwyn, IL." My knowledge of Marian devotional organizations in the United States was minimal at the time: I couldn't recall having read any major books or articles on the topic during my exploration of Catholicism in America. I was curious, but put the card aside. Still, the mail kept arriving. The images and invocations of Mary started to fill the largest portion of my file. As I continued to read the small print on the mass-produced images and texts, a few organizations emerged as prominent promoters of Marian material culture: the Militia of the Immaculata; The Blue Army of Our Lady of Fatima, U.S.A.; and the Central Association of the Miraculous Medal. I knew about the history of Roman Catholic popular piety, but I began to wonder why I knew so little about these organizations, why their dissemination of Catholic material culture is so prolific, and why Mary seems to occupy the center of their media representations and their devotional practices.[2] Behind the shiny medals and the glossy guides, I sensed an important phenomenon, something worthy of sustained and systematic scholarship.

Soon after I started my research, I happened upon a memorable Web page that has served as a focus for my work. "Come home to Marytown!" exclaims the Web site for the Militia of the Immaculata National Center and National Shrine of St. Maximilian Kolbe. The Militia of the Immaculata makes the same invitation to potential devotees in a color pamphlet: "Can't make a pilgrimage to Rome? Then consider a visit to Marytown!" Devotees who respond to the online or print invitations learn that Marytown is a shrine and retreat center within the township of Libertyville, Illinois. Yet, for the purposes of this study, Marytown, U.S.A., is much more than a place—it is a metaphor, a lens that illumines a great deal about the history of American Roman Catholic devotions.

For Roman Catholics, Mary is famous for her use of publicity: countless apparitions offering messages of hope, comfort, warning, and despair to her children around the world. American Catholic devotional organizations have adopted and adapted Mary's public persona in pursuit of evangelization. In a 2003 issue of *Immaculata* magazine, Ada Locatelli, a member of the Missionaries of the Immaculata, links the group's evangelistic focus with Mary as exemplar: "Our work of evangelization, according to the needs of our contemporary world, requires the ability to use the extraordinary possibilities of modern communication. After Fr. Kolbe's example,[3] the Institute's apostolic choices include the use of mass media, especially by publishing and spreading periodicals and books in various languages. The intention to be 'in the world,' for the salvation of the world, following *the example of Mary*, 'the star of evangelization.' And the path traced out by Fr. Kolbe, have led our Institute to boundless missionary outreach."[4]

The Militia of the Immaculata is not alone. Other groups—including the Association of the Miraculous Medal and the Blue Army—also turn to Mary as a model for their evangelization. They disseminate representations of Mary in multiple forms of media: magazines, direct mail, Web sites, books, pamphlets, audiotapes, videos, and medals. These organizations also run shrines, retreat centers, and pilgrimage programs based on Marian spirituality. The Militia of the Immaculata Web site asserts that "through God's grace, Marytown is becoming one of the most vibrant centers of Catholic renewal in the United States."[5]

The Iconology of Marian Media

Mary, as a media icon,[6] offers an evocative symbol and effective signpost for the intersection of religion and culture, medium and message. Mariologists have traced the multiple nesting and overlapping roles and representations of the Madonna, from the post-biblical era through the Middle Ages and the Renaissance, in their historical and cultural contexts. These images persist in present-day images and practices of Marian devotion, but to what extent can we assume that these traditional images have maintained coherence and consistency in their historical trajectories? When classic images become unhinged from their points of origin and circulate freely, even within the "same" religious system, how are they disseminated, transformed, and interpreted in new contexts?

In his sweeping work, *Mary through the Centuries: Her Place in the History of Culture*, Jaroslav Pelikan sets out "to show historically what Mary *has meant*, by following a roughly chronological order to box the compass of some of the provinces of life and realms of reality in which she has been a prominent force at various periods in history."[7] Pelikan introduces us to multiple Marys, with multiple images, roles, and contexts, both religious and cultural, yet his work is infused with the *telos* of Mariology (and/or history). Mary's multiplicity emerges as a religious problem (and perhaps a historical problem, too): one woman, many roles. How does the one contain the many and remain coherent? How does Mary *mean*? John Gatta's *American Madonna: Images of the Divine Woman in Literary Culture* and Sarah Jane Boss's *Empress and Handmaid: On Nature and Gender in the Cult of the Virgin Mary* offer more focused (but still typological) studies of Marian representations in particular historical and cultural contexts.

Similarly, my work attempts to capture the proliferation of particular Marian representations at specific cultural and historical moments. This cultural history entails a practice of excavation that attempts to unearth what lies beneath the diverse and striking range of Marian images among American devotees. My approach draws on pioneering scholarship in print, material, and visual culture, such as that of Colleen McDannell, David Morgan, Sally Promey, and Jenna Joselit.[8] My research also relies on material objects and devotional imagination as sources for cultural history. Representations of Mary in devotional publications both structure and symbolize the beliefs and practices of adherents and serve as points of departure for my own analysis and narration of Marianism in the United States.

How does Marian devotion shape the American landscape? How do we find Mary in America? Where and when do we look? For Marian devotional organizations in the United States, the construction of the Virgin Mary as a media icon is an ongoing, complex, and reciprocal process. The appropriation, alteration, and dissemination of Marian images by these groups transformed traditional religious images into popular ones, mass-produced and mediated by visual and textual representations in magazines and print media. Images of Mary come alive as symbols of religious, political, and social positions. The Virgin Marys depicted in magazines, such as *Immaculata,* not only reference a religious person, but also a religious persona.

Where does Mary wax iconic? The contested body of artist Alma Lopez's bikini-clad virgin ("Our Lady," 1999). The nationalistic symbols of Our Lady of Guadalupe and the Virgin of Charity. A billboard for the controversial animal rights organization PETA (People for the Ethical Treatment of Animals): a Renaissance Mary cradles a dead chicken in her arms instead of baby Jesus, with the message, "Go Vegetarian: It's an Immaculate Conception" (2003). The ongoing stream of reported apparitions and their associated miracles, both sanctioned and not sanctioned by the Roman Catholic Church. Mary at pro-life demonstrations. Mary as goddess force for feminist theologians. Pop icon Madonna. Mary's face pressed into a grilled cheese sandwich, auctioned for thousands on Ebay (2004).

Why does Mary matter for scholars of religion and media in the twenty-first century? Mary is one of the most widely recognized religious and cultural personages in the world and wields a megaton of symbolic capital.[9] In many religious circles, she stands for THE WOMAN. For me, Mary raises the important question of how we recognize and interpret religious images. We typically recognize images based on their form and context. However, the range of presentations and uses of Marian images is so incredibly diverse, what makes Mary recognizable? Works by controversial artists, such as Alma Lopez ("Our Lady," 1999) or Robert Gober ("Untitled Installation," 1995–97), that reference the Virgin Mary spark controversy because they gesture to a norm, while subverting it.[10] But "sacrilege" requires a uniform standard for what "counts" as sacred.

There is a stillness there in the frozen moment of the icon that is mediated through image and word, color and texture, and teetering between passivity and activity, silence and responsiveness. The media icon scintillates with possibility, occupying a space between material humanity and the ephemeral sacrality, both realms shaped by the context of belief and the enactment of practice.

My use of the phrase "media icon" is multilayered. The history of Christianity involves a long-standing tradition of use of visual representations. The term "icon" (from the Greek for "image" or "portrait") refers to a "visual representation of Jesus Christ, the Virgin Mary, angels, individual saints, or events of sacred history." Typically "frontal, flat, laconic, and shadowless, the icon was a visual window to the meaning of the event or holy person depicted, not a realistic presentation sacred in and of itself (and, thus, idolatrous)." [11] The use of icons was widely debated among early Christians, as iconoclasts sought to blot out their potential for idolatry, and those in the Byzantine and Orthodox Churches vehemently argued for their importance. The issue was formally settled when the Second Nicean Council (787) approved the use of icons in Christian practice. Iconoclasm resurfaced during the sixteenth-century rise of Protestantism, as reformers tried to strip away what they saw as the visual decadence of the Roman Catholic Church. However, new traditions in Protestant iconography developed that would contribute a lasting chapter to the history of Christian art.

In Christian devotional practice, however, icons, images, and material objects are often tied to a notion of divine presence and the possibility for communication. In some cases this represents a literal means of communion between human and divine agents, as the divine power fills the material image or object with its presence. Scholar Margaret Miles explores the significance of the visual encounter with the Eucharist in medieval Catholic liturgy: "Vision was . . . the strongest possible access to an object of devotion. Viewing the consecrated bread with concentrated attention was considered of equal or superior value to ingesting it, and medieval congregations were often urged by their priests to communicate 'spiritually,' that is, visually, rather than physically." [12] In this way, the visual, in the context of Catholic devotion, designates a dynamic interface of devotee and object of adoration.

"Icon" also suggests the captive and captivating natural visual image. The icon preserves an essence, a frozen moment in time. The implications of visual capture were certainly troubling to the iconoclasts, who believed that any attempt to fix the divine or saintly essence was tantamount to blasphemy.

The term "icon" invokes the contemporary discourses of celebrity and pop culture. Mary is a *popular* image, one intimately engaged in the everyday lives and practices of devotees around the world. She is a religious celebrity, a pop icon in her own right, a personality whom many believers assign as their primary communicator and mediator with their God.

"Media" references both the explicit religious roles of the Virgin Mary as a mediator in Roman Catholic tradition and the formal ways that these roles are expressed in various media (image, text, sound, etc.). Scholars of religion and media studies suggest that "practice" is "the most logical scholarly interpretive standpoint" for evaluating the intersection of these fields. [13] Stewart Hoover argues that the goal of this emerging discipline "is to describe in some detail moments and locations where we can see active the kind of religious, spiritual, transcendent, or meaning-centered practice that seems to be evolving with reference to, and in the context of, media culture." [14] What distinguishes media studies from other approaches (for example, a literary critical approach that "reads" culture and image as text) is an emphasis on operation: "the task becomes a collective enterprise which examines the way media texts are operating to reproduce the common, mediated culture. . . . [I]t is no longer a question of learning *from* the text, but rather *how* the text actually works." [15] Studying representations of the Madonna offers a rich opportunity for examining the mediated operations of a religious symbol and the deployment of Marian media within a particular tradition of religious representational practices.

Developing a theory for understanding Marian representations among devotees requires careful attention to uses and practices surrounding religious media. In their introduction to *The Visual Culture of American Religions,* editors David Morgan and Salley Promey suggest four ways that "images participate in religious practice": "First, images are understood to communicate between human and divine realms in an economy of ritualized exchange [Communication]. Second, they help establish the social basis of communion by consolidating and reinforcing a range of alliances, large and small [Communion]. Third, images help create and organize memory [Commemoration]. And fourth, they fuel constructive, synthetic acts of imagination in the kind of meaning-making practices that form a basic aspect of religious experience [Imagination (Meaning-Making)]." [16] The Marian representations produced and reproduced by the Militia of the Immaculata and the Central Association of the Miraculous Medal circulate in webs of engaged practices that demonstrate these four functions. For Marian devotees in these groups, Mary, as a media icon, communicates by intervening between human and divine realms, creates communion by consolidating and symbolizing religious and cultural identities, commemorates pasts, presents, and futures (real and imagined), and acts as a central catalyst for meaning-making endeavors and source of religious creativity. My use of the term "media icon" in this context follows David Morgan's logic. Morgan writes: "I use the term icon not in a merely metaphorical sense but to designate the devotional image or object of civil religion. Just as icons among the Eastern Orthodox Christians operate as apertures or windows to the sacred, so Bibles and flags in particular have acted as sacred evocations of the divinely ordained republic, the nation that is invested in these symbols to such a degree that the cherishing (or abuse) of them conveys the devotees' veneration of the nation itself." [17] In my work, I am interested in reuniting icon with its religious context, by tracing the way in which a symbol like the Virgin Mary enters the public space and returns to the religious context, bearing the trappings of media, celebrity, and publicity in the profane sense and mediation in the religious sense.

Understanding Mary in America: The Theological Backdrop

Any study of the Virgin Mary, no matter how localized, must account for the theological basis for Mariology and Marian devotion in the Roman Catholic tradition. Some theologians attempt to define Mary's unique and essential nature as "Mother of God" and determine her position relevant to God and believers based on that role. Other scholars go further to posit the constituent and consequent special privileges and powers of Mary's essential nature.[18] Mary's actual and spiritual motherhood of God in the incarnation of Jesus and the expansion of that motherhood to all human beings are typically understood to be the primary components of her essence. Mediation, on multiple levels, defines her role. Mary's special privileges and powers include her immaculate conception and absence of sin, her holiness and "fullness of grace," her virginity, her assumption into heaven, and her intervention via apparitions.

Most relevant to this study are the nineteenth- and twentieth-century dogmatic pronouncements asserted by the Roman Catholic hierarchy about the Virgin Mary.[19] These official proclamations solidified Mary's theological status within the church and put her squarely in conversation with the issues of modernity. Where dogma was paired with miraculous appearances, the question of Mary's modern relevance came to the forefront. Barbara Corrado Pope gives an overview of Marian devotion during the nineteenth century, highlighting the importance of French apparitions, including Our Lady of the Miraculous Medal (Paris, 1830), Our Lady of La Salette (1846), and Our Lady of Lourdes (1858). Pope skillfully analyzes the political, social, and cultural context for the apparition-based revival in Marian devotion. She characterizes the proclamation of the Dogma of the Immaculate Conception in 1854 as a deliberately nonscientific and antimodern tactic by Pius IX. Pope also couches the entire phenomenon of Marian devotion in terms of antimodernism.[20]

Since World War I, Marian media sources in the United States demonstrate an ongoing narrative of resistance and incorporation of "modern" themes. The self-definition of American Catholics was necessarily shaped by the broader religious and social context, including traditions of anti-Catholicism and Protestant dialogues about modernity and evangelization.

The Cultural Context

In his comprehensive work *The American Catholic Experience: A History from 1850 to the Present,* Jay Dolan offers a helpful periodization of Catholic history and the formation of Catholic identity. From colonial times up until the election of John F. Kennedy in 1960, anti-Catholicism was a widespread and systemic phenomenon. From nineteenth-century convent burnings to sordid convent tales and to the rise of the Know-Nothing Party, Catholics were ostracized as dangerous "others" even as they served as a source of Protestant desire.[21] At every step of the way, Catholics resisted the attacks upon them by asserting their own Americanness in public settings.

From 1920 to 1960, Dolan identifies the "end of an era" in Catholic history. Catholics increased in social mobility due to widespread prosperity, many moved from the cities to the suburbs, brick-and-mortar Catholicism took over, the laity increased in power, and the trappings of the immigrant church and ethnic distinctiveness began to dissolve.[22] However, Catholics were actively involved in defining their own "Americanization." They maintained extensive publications, belonged to devotional organizations, and developed community institutions. This was an era of Catholic pride, when to be Catholic was to be intensely American.

Assertions of American Catholic identities also emerged against a backdrop of increasing Protestant evangelicalism, beginning with the First Great Awakening in the mid-eighteenth century and infusing the Protestant-dominated culture of the nineteenth and twentieth centuries. This brand of Protestantism emphasized emotion, individual conversion, and the call to evangelize one's neighbors at home and abroad. Scholars have typically deemphasized the role of evangelization among American Catholics. However, devotional organizations such as the Militia of the Immaculata and the Central Association of the Miraculous Medal developed their own brands of evangelization, certainly influenced by the broader religious and cultural milieu.

Two Devotional Organizations

The Militia of the Immaculata and the Central Association of the Miraculous Medal promote different but related forms of Marian devotion in the United States. The Roman Catholic Church officially approves both organizations. Each group advocates its own methods of evangelization and renewal. The Militia of the Immaculata in the United States is tied to an international movement founded in 1917 by the Polish-born Conventual Franciscan, Maximilian Kolbe (who was canonized in 1982). The main emphasis of this movement is the concept of "Total Consecration" to Mary (as developed by Kolbe). This is the primary mission pursued by the Militia of the Immaculata, and the ritual act of consecration defines its membership. Members become "dedicated to the conversion and sanctification of the world and share in the maternal mission of Mary." [23] Consecration.com (the Web site of the American Militia of the Immaculata movement) tells potential members that they will join "with Mary in the work of building up and renewing the Church of the third millennium." [24] Members gain spiritual support in the form of prayers and media support through "access to Militia conferences and resource materials, . . . its national magazine, *Immaculata,* and to regular mailings from the national office on how to better live out your consecration." [25] The Militia of the Immaculata movement is founded on the premise of "continual conversion," evangelization, and renewal. The message of "Total Consecration" is spread primarily through mass media, and Marytown functions as the geographic and metaphorical center of this movement in the United States.

The Central Association of the Miraculous Medal in the United States is connected to an international movement based on Mary's appearances to a Parisian nun in 1830. Sister Catherine Labouré reported Mary's instructions to strike a medal according to a special design in her honor. This medal would provide protection and "special graces" to its wearers.[26] The Association of the Miraculous Medal in the United States, founded in 1918 as an "apostolate of the Vincentian priests and brothers," promotes devotion to "Our Lady of the Miraculous Medal," distributes miraculous medals, and advocates a Marian spirituality centered on prayer. The group clearly sees their efforts as a form of evangelization that depends on lay membership: "We are convinced of the important role and mission of the laity in the Church in the future of evangelization. As it has been said, 'The third millennium will be the age of the laity.' " [27] The organization estimates that it has 1,000,000 members, 65,000 "Promoters," and 350,000 current contributors.[28]

Overview of Media Sources

My research focuses on periodicals published by the Militia of the Immaculata and the Central Association of the Miraculous Medal. I examined issues of *Immaculata* magazine (published by the Militia of the Immaculata from 1949 to the present) and the *Miraculous Medal* magazine (published by the Central Association of the Miraculous Medal from 1928 to the present) in depth. These magazines share a self-consciously articulated awareness of editorial purpose. They constantly invoke the notion of a "Catholic press" as a source of authority, moral responsibility, and public pride. The editors are often explicit about the intentions behind the representations of Mary they put forth.

Immaculata magazine began in 1949 as the primary publication of the Militia of the Immaculata in the United States, run by the Conventual Franciscan Friars and the Franciscan Marytown Press. Marytown was originally located in Kenosha, Wisconsin, an area rich in Catholic immigrant diversity. The first volume of the magazine (1949) was a bilingual French and German publication titled *Immaculata: Revue Missionaire des Pères Oblats de M. I. (Marie Immaculée) de l'est.* The magazine offered readers articles, stories, illustrations, and photographs, often of an exotic nature, based on mission life. Missions documented in the first year include such distant locales as Japan, the North Pole (Eskimos), Africa, Ceylon, and Chile. Early cover designs paired photographs from the mission field with traditional images of Mary, metaphorically overseeing the evangelistic work.

By the end of 1949, the magazine invited readers to participate in the mission movement. An ad for L'AMMI (Assoc. Missionaire de Marie Immaculée) figures prominently on page 3 of the November/December issue and reminds readers of their religious obligations: "All Christians must help save their brothers. All Christians must be missionaries. All Christians must be apostles of Christ. By Prayer—By Sacrifice—By Action. All oblates love their congregation. All members of L'AMMI will become zealots for winning new adherents." [29] Membership in the association promotes zealous evangelization, with Mary as model for the movement.

In 1950, the magazine changed to an English-language monthly (bimonthly June/July issue). *Immaculata* developed a new glossy style with sensational headlines and numerous photographs. The cover art was now exclusively devoted to Marian images, both new and old. An ad from the June/July 1950 issue reveals the editors' intended goals for the magazine: "Immaculata is the only modern monthly Marian magazine for $2.00 per year. Is there really any better way to spread the most vital message for our time than by spreading this Voice of Our Lady and Herald of Perpetual Adoration in your homes, schools and societies?" [30] The editors were clearly concerned with "modernity" and evangelization under the auspices of Marian devotion.

Early on, articles about the Militia of the Immaculata itself comprise a central feature of the magazine. Columns like "The Militia Explained," "The Militia Mission," "Why the Militia?" "The Knight of the Immaculate," and "MI Roundtable" take off in 1951 and sustain organizational publicity. The magazine was published by the Franciscan Marytown Press, but lay people wrote many of the articles and editorial pieces and remained popular and continuous contributors.

Although the critical issues changed with the times, and the magazine became slightly less sensational, *Immaculata*'s format remained fairly consistent until 1984. In 1977, the subtitle *Voice of Our Lady* was briefly appended to the magazine title. In 1979, Marytown relocated permanently to Libertyville, Illinois. In 1984, the magazine stopped publication due to financial problems. It resumed nearly ten years later in 1994 in what the editors termed a "more modest" form, on a bimonthly basis. In 1999, the magazine adopted another new title: *Militia of the Immaculata: National Voice of the MI*.

The *Miraculous Medal* magazine, "The National Organ of The Central Association of the Miraculous Medal," began publication much earlier, in 1928. A comparison of style, tone, and features with *Immaculata* magazine shows the striking differences between the two organizations. The *Miraculous Medal* never engaged in sensational reporting, although it remained heavily invested in the miraculous from its inception. Although, the magazine addressed a national audience, it was firmly grounded in the activity of the organization's Philadelphia shrine and remained under tight clerical control.[31] Each issue begins with a lengthy editorial, "With the Director." The *Miraculous Medal* reads like a family digest, filled with shrine and mission news, true and fictional stories, and games. The publication's stated mission remains consistent with its earliest articulations and emphasizes devotion to the miraculous medal, support of the priesthood, assistance to the poor, and foreign missions. Fund-raising pleas are frequent and unabashed. In general, the magazine portrays Mary as a powerful force behind the scenes of the organization. The centerpiece of the magazine (and central to this study) is the column "Rays from the Hands of Mary," which has appeared in every issue of the magazine since its beginning. This column reflects the association's status as a prayer network of members bound by their commitment to the miraculous medal. The subtitle under the logo of Mary, hands extended and projecting rays, reads: "These rays are the symbols of the favors which I shed on those who ask for them."[32] The substance of the column is selected letters of thanks and praise from those who believe in the Madonna's intercession. The short letters are always accompanied by a longer "medal story" that shows her miraculous intervention in depth. Other notable and continuous features include: "Mary's Shrine" and "Mary in the News." The *Miraculous Medal* was published on a monthly basis until the 1990s, when it became a quarterly.

"Marylike" Women and "Marylike" Men:
Marian Models of Gendered Performance

In her introduction to the 2001 documentary volume *Gender Identities in American Catholicism,* Paula Kane issues an invitation to scholars of American Catholicism to "consider how the concept of gender can powerfully reshape traditional master narratives about the past. Just as deploying the categories of race, ethnicity, and nationalism has led historians to reconsider the way they narrate American history, so the category of gender should enable historians of religion to rethink their conceptualization of American Catholicism."[33] Emerging from the social critiques posed by the women's movement of the 1960s and 1970s, gender studies, and the widely accepted definition of gender as a performance within a social context,[34] have expanded in importance in all academic disciplines, including religious studies. However, scholars like Kane suggest that there is much more work to be done to attend to the complex and significant issue of gender, especially within Catholic studies. This issue continues to be important as a new papacy comes to power and the issue of women's roles within the church has come to the forefront. I accept Kane's call to participate in a process of "rethinking" by examining the dominant gendered symbol in the American Catholic landscape.

Enter Mary: What religious figure is more gendered than the woman titled both "virgin" and "mother"—a woman whose gender performance is rooted in paradox? The turn to Marian imagery when investigating gender in American Catholicism is obvious, but the conclusions of such an investigation challenge stereotypical assumptions about Mary's symbolic role, especially in the realm of modern devotional media. Marian representations are ubiquitous in the Catholic landscape, already codified by the doctrinal and institutional apparatus of the church. Even as scholars, we are tempted to assume we already know what Mary *means*. However, as Ludwig Wittgenstein once argued, "meaning is use."[35] The *uses* of Mary as a gendered *media icon*—a popular image saturated with religious significance—illustrate the *creativity* of Marian devotional organizations like the Militia of the Immaculata and the Association of the Miraculous Medal as they grapple with cultural and religious ideas about gender identity and relations.

As part of my broader consideration of Marian representations in U.S. Catholic devotional media, this chapter explores the reconfiguration of gender roles along Marian lines represented in *Immaculata* and the *Miraculous Medal* magazines from the 1950s to the 1970s.[36] The models of gendered behavior promoted by these print culture sources provide rich insights into public assertions of religious and social identity for particular (and understudied) groups of American Catholics.

Marylike Models

"Be Marylike! Buy Marilyke Gowns!" exclaims an article from an early 1950s issue of *Immaculata* magazine (see fig. 5.1).[37] This article reveals more than a creative exercise in mid-century Catholic branding. An exploration of

FIGURE 5-1 "Marylike" fashions offer models of gendered behavior for Catholic women, from *Immaculata*, October 1953, 7.

Courtesy of Militia Immaculata National Center.

the adjective "Marylike" and its associated beliefs and practices illuminates an intricate system of gendered values within the Marian devotional tradition in the United States. For groups of Mary-oriented American Catholics, such as the Militia of the Immaculata and the Association of the Miraculous Medal, images of Mary function as Geertzian *models of* and *models for* gendered performance enacted on a complex socioreligious stage.[38] This sphere of action encompasses public and private, home and church, individual and community and reflects the increasing entanglement of culture and consumerism as religion is mediated by the marketplace.

In the wider context of devotional media, "Marylike" has multiple imperatives: first, to *like* Mary and demonstrate appropriate devotion to her; second, to *be like* Mary and model one's self after her virtuous example; third, to see one's own likeness reflected in the "mirror of Mary" (Mary *is like* us). Marian organizations accept the basic premise that the Virgin Mary is a person worthy of devotion and praise. The notions of emulation and reflection define Mary's iconic content in a particular devotional context, where the call to be Marylike is an essentially gendered command. Gender distinctions remain significant, even as the Madonna serves as a perfect model of and for virtue for both genders. Marylike conduct becomes both women and men, but we discover that such virtue is often defined differently for each.

As for most devotional organizations centered on the Virgin Mary, gender issues emerged at the inception of the Militia of the Immaculata (M.I.) and the Central Association of the Miraculous Medal. Both groups were founded by male clerics, steeped in the institutional authority of the Catholic Church. The devotion these groups espoused, however, praised the paradigm of Catholic motherhood and femininity. At the same time, through their media, these groups also emphasized Mary's regal qualities. Mary was domestic, but not domesticated. Her supernatural qualities remained at the forefront.

The M.I. relies heavily on the devotional writings of St. Louis Grignon de Montfort and quotes him extensively throughout *Immaculata*'s tenure. An excerpt appearing in the October 1950 issue shows how significant Marian models were for M.I. members: " 'Mary Forms Jesus in Us—A Living Mold of God': St. Augustine calls Mary the living 'mold of God,' and that indeed she is; for it was in her alone that man can be truly formed into God, in so far as that is possible for human nature, by the grace of Jesus Christ. . . . In that mold none of the features of the Godhead is wanting. Whoever is cast in it and allows himself to be molded, receives all the features of Jesus Christ, true God. The work is done gently, in a manner proportioned to human weakness, without much pain or labor." [39] Here, Mary is represented as a tender and compassionate and spiritual sculptor, shaping each human being in her mold, just as she perfectly cast God as Christ in her womb.

Who Can Find a Virtuous (Marylike) Woman?

From the 1950s to the 1970s, Catholic magazines such as *Immaculata* and the *Miraculous Medal* put forth powerful and often conflicting Marian models for women. Embracing the of/for dichotomy, Mary represents both every woman (as the primary symbol of feminine sacrality, defined by the capacity for birth and the act of motherhood) and no woman (as the exceptional woman whose fundamental gender identity is confused by an immaculate revision of the motherly role). The Virgin Mary resembles Eve enough to be recognized as woman, but undercuts this womanhood as her theological foil.

Mary as "Model of" Gendered Performance

In "Catholic Domesticity, 1860–1960," Colleen McDannell describes the ways in which American Catholics entered the twentieth century reflecting broader cultural trends in the domestic sphere: "By the end of the nineteenth century, middle-class American Catholics possessed a domestic ideology as colorful and sentimental as any proper Victorian. . . . Cloistered in their home, the domestic ideology explained, mothers devoted their energies to their little ones and modeled their homes on the Holy Family." [40] She goes on to describe a transformation of American Catholic thinking about Mary during the period 1860–1920 in light of the newly framed norms of domesticity:

> The activities of the Catholic mother were also compared to the role the Virgin Mary played within the Holy Family. The association of women with Mary presented certain problems for domestic writers. The Virgin Mary enjoyed in Catholic tradition a long history that emphasized her powerful and royal characteristics. Mary was the queen of heaven who was often portrayed in medieval and Renaissance art as the "fourth member of the Trinity." Her connection to Christ was more direct than that of her husband Joseph. In order to reduce the feminine power of the Virgin Mary, writers placed her within the domestic structure of life in Nazareth. No longer the queen of the universe, Mary became a Hebrew housewife who looked after the needs of husband and child. Advice book writers stripped Mary of her supernatural powers and presented her in the peaceful house of Nazareth industriously pursuing the vocation of a poor artisan's wife. Mary, seen from this perspective, was the ideal model for women—an ever-virgin mother, obedient, suffering, unselfish, and pious. [41]

While this shift in representations of Mary had real effects on perceived and promulgated roles for American Catholic women, its impact on the Virgin Mary as a *religious* symbol was much less. In fact, such assertions about Mary and domestic life enhanced tensions in her iconic nature during the post–World War I period.

Organizations like the Association of the Miraculous Medal and the Militia of the Immaculata reclaimed Mary's power as warrior queen and universal mother. Mary could not be fully domesticated. The apparitions at Fatima (1917) and the universal church's response to them reaffirmed Mary's supernaturalism and her role as protectress of human beings and prophetess of doom. Devotional organizations and the wider media culture seized onto images of Mary as "immaculate and powerful," and her special place was designated both *because of* and *despite* her womanhood. For these groups, the post-Fatima Mary was not the submissive "handmaiden of the Lord"; rather, her affirmation of God's will gave her radical power as messenger, mediator, and crusader. M.I. members, by consecrating themselves to Mary, give her personal and direct power over their lives. They use the language of slavery, ownership, and property to describe their relationships with Mary: "We imitate good, virtuous, holy people, but none of these is without imperfection. Only *She, immaculate* from the first moment of her existence, knows no fault, not even the least. It is she whom one should imitate and come close to. It is she who is put up as an example of imitation for all Militia members and all Christian souls. We, particularly, who have consecrated ourselves to her, should become more and more her property, become more and more like unto her. Behold the peak of perfection in man. O Immaculate, O Great Mother of God, pray for us and attract us to thyself!" [42] To become like Mary is to be possessed by her, in the literal sense of the term. She is not a passive agent, but rather an active and interactive role model, with a firm grasp on the vicissitudes of human lives. Mary, for the M.I., is director, owner, model, and reward. Her motherly love is more like fire from heaven than a cup of warm milk.

Mary as "Model for" Gendered Performance

Despite Mary's significant religious power, as woman elevated beyond humanity by her lack of original sin, her image was also deployed to define the terms of human femininity. Of course, many Roman Catholic women experienced Marian perfection as an impossible standard for womanhood. Was the domestication of Mary suggested by McDannell an institutionalization of reproach, the putting of women in their place? Were the Virgin's eyes on the household wall plaque piercing the souls of Catholic women with a panoptic gaze, while she bore her rent but immaculate heart as her outer garment? Or was it an elevation of the domestic to the supernatural realm?

Certainly, female readers of *Immaculata* may have received mixed messages about womanhood through images of Mary. Representations of Mary often served as double-edged swords: venerating saintly femininity while apparently denigrating ordinary women. Yet, the Militia of the Immaculata offered many important spiritual opportunities for flesh-and-blood females. As members, they were called to imitate Mary's power by serving as members of her spiritual armed forces. As I will discuss later, military representations of Mary offered more unisex and nontraditional models of gendered performance for both women and men.

As model for women in the temple of the home, Mary reigns as domestic goddess and paragon of motherly love, traits to be reproduced in daily life. The marketing and popularity of "Kitchen Madonna" plaques and prayers among other household statues and images reflects this trend in American Catholic consumerism: Mary, as icon, pervades domestic space through religious material culture. Marylike women are modest, self-sacrificing, obedient, and nurturing. Relevant columns from the 1950s and 1960s that present this domestic model include "Modesty Is the Best Policy," "A Lady's Apron Pocket," "From Mother to Child," "Rosary Meditations by a Housewife," "Our Marionette," and "At Forty . . . Look in the Mirror of Mary."

As noted in the campaign for Marylike attire, modesty becomes a central part of Mary's model for young women, often linked to particular consumer practices in the religious and secular marketplaces. Modest and tasteful dress demonstrates feminine purity and devotion to Mary but does not exclude beauty: "Wherever Our Lady has appeared she has been well dressed. If Fatima has meant nothing else in some cases, people have collected pictures of how Mary looked because she was so beautiful." [43] The magazine recounted the efforts of a group of girls at Seton High School in Cincinnati, Ohio, organized as S.D.S. (Supply the Demand for the Supply), whose response to Mary's appeals for modesty included a boycott of immodest dress: "To be like Our Lady in the sense of being more beautiful than ever and to share none of the moral ugliness of certain modern dresses, has become the rage of the girls of 'S.D.S.'—thousands of them." [44] The girls received the highest form of praise for their efforts by the article's author: "Finally the girls paid another of their great tributes to Mary. At a formal, they discredited the idea of taking off Scapulars and miraculous medals for the sake of showing bare backs and shoulders. 'If you can't wear the Scapular, don't wear the gown.' Sounded like hard medicine for lively youth—but the girls went this difficulty one better. They wore their Scapular *over* their gowns! Of course they don't do it at every formal, but it showed the way they felt about hiding their devotion under a bushel and leaving off the Scapular for the sake of looking like daredevils." [45] For members of S.D.S., displaying religious convictions became a fashion statement in line with Mary's example. The girls' consumer choices reflected their commitment to a cause that was, in many ways, countercultural.

The authors and editors of *Immaculata* strove to keep the ancient model of the Virgin Mary relevant to contemporary life (see fig. 5.2). In the

FIGURE 5-2 *Our Lady of the United States,* from *Immaculata,* December 1954, front cover.

Courtesy of Militia Immaculata National Center.

June/July 1955 issue, Sister M. Deborah, O.P., considered what would happen in her article "If Mary Lived Today":

> Are you one of those who feel that Our Lady is much too perfect and too holy for you to imitate? Have you ever secretly thought, "Could Mary be as good and holy if she lived today?" . . . In our social life with its many problems, how would Mary solve them? We are practically submerged in temptations of every kind. Suggestive advertising abounds, widespread atheism is current; divorce, birth control and drink are accepted practices in ordinary living. . . . What would Mary do beset by all these problems? We know she would not be overcome by their false teaching or suggestive flattery, believing every commercial she heard or "ad" she read. For some people life's most important principles are using Smiro Soap, Snowfluf Shampoo, Pearly Dental Cream and driving the latest Dreamboat. These are modern, worldly standards. Mary would rise above such emptiness and mockery.[46]

Sister Deborah urges her readers to resist the enticements of secular culture, while attempting to reduce the distance between the Virgin Mother and modern women. Marylike conduct is achievable, even in a rapidly changing society full of challenges to traditional gender roles: " 'To be good' means the same thing today as it did in Mary's day. . . . Mary is the safest model God has shown to us after Christ for our perfection. . . . Mary has shown us the best method in the world for holiness. Mary lived simply and peacefully in order to more perfectly follow Her Son. The more Marylike we become in our thoughts, words and actions, the closer to Christ we will be drawn." [47] Sister Deborah offers a clear message to women: despite historical and cultural upheaval, Marylike models are timeless and mandatory, but not inimitable.

The periodicals reflect the pressures of social change, often depicting women (and Mary) caught between narrowly circumscribed traditional roles and the desire for "modernized" models of womanhood. This desire opened up possibilities for redefinitions of female power through Marian iconography. Mary's passivity—her "yes" to God—traditionally formed the locus of her strength. However, the images of Mary in this devotional media are explicitly *active*. Later on, I will return to discuss icons of Mary as assembler of armies and musterer of militia, and their implications for American Catholic gender norms. Yet embedded in depictions of Mary as a powerful female force is a Foucauldian disciplinary model of gendered behavior. Mary's panoptic gaze back at the viewer, mindful of sin, and replete with reproach, spurs the internalization of an impossible ideal.[48] At the level of symbol, to be Marylike is a simile (not a metaphor). To *be like* Mary is not to *be* her.

Representations of Marian gender performance in *Immaculata* and the *Miraculous Medal* from the 1950s to the 1970s demonstrate a chronological progression of carefully crafted responses to cultural changes such as the women's movement and the sexual revolution. Contraception, abortion, and pornography become key issues of debate. In high contrast to the perceived laxity of the broader culture, the groups showcase modesty as the central female virtue. Still, this is not a clear-cut case of religious and cultural conservatism. The magazines begin to show the positive aspects of women's more public role within the Catholic Church itself and strive to offer resources for the "modern" Catholic woman. Of course, the religious and cultural revolution of the Second Vatican Council (1962–1965) greatly impacted the organizations' self-presentations, including gendered imagery. Theological movements for Mary as Mediatrix and/or Co-redemptrix also called into question the limits of what was possible for women in the Catholic Church.

Marylike Masculinities

Marylike models of masculinity are primarily relational. A devoted man's relationship to Mary functions as a guide for his place in the world. For men, Mary, the Virgin, becomes the ultimate object of chaste adoration, the handmaiden whose perfect and otherworldly subservience to God makes her the perfect muse for male worldly (but moral) action. Marylike men are responsible husbands, strong fathers, and ethical neighbors. Or they are pious priests, enlisted in Mary's service. In *Miraculous Medal,* Mary leads an ongoing crusade to recruit new priests.

No discussion of Catholic masculinity can fail to acknowledge the role of Jesus. Mary, readers are reminded, though often at center stage, is defined by her connection to Jesus and God. "*To Jesus through Mary*" is an oft-repeated mantra. The repetition of this concept reveals, even in Marian circles, the impact of American Protestant critiques of Catholic "Mary worship." However, in this media, doctrinally compliant gestures toward Jesus do not force Mary to yield her central role for devotees. And the expectation that men imitate the Virgin Mary and her position toward her son complicates the gender norms for Marylike men.

Mary's Army: Militancy, Evangelism, and Egalitarianism

Magazines like *Immaculata* and the *Miraculous Medal* offered prescriptive notions of womanhood and manhood, filtered through Marian theology and practice, that both reaffirmed and challenged traditional gender roles in the Roman Catholic Church and American culture. The Militia of the Immaculata and the Central Association of the Miraculous Medal provided unisex opportunities for devotional participation that in some ways elided gender distinctions. Both women and men are called to serve in "Mary's Army" as Christian warriors by the Militia of the Immaculata. The Association of the Miraculous Medal universally encourages wearing of the "miraculous medal" as a symbol of personal devotion and the mark of Mary's care and protection. The equalizing imagery associated with these devotional practices counters some more traditional gender norms. A militant Mary demands female warriors as well as male ones. As commander, she has power over men in her service. In fact, the Militia of the Immaculata requires both male and female members to become "slaves" to Mary through the practice of "Total Consecration."

Early in the Cold War, members of American Catholic devotional organizations, such as the Militia of the Immaculata, positioned Mary at the forefront of the political, ideological, and religious debate they perceived in the broader culture. Two 1950s images from *Immaculata* stand out as examples of this positioning. On the back cover of the May 1953 issue, a traditional image of Our Lady of the Rosary at Fatima is juxtaposed with a drawing of a Communist soldier with a gun, accompanied by text: "The Commies KNOW who their greatest enemy is. . . . 'The thing that impressed me most, and what I'd like to impress on our people, is that what the Communists hate most is *Mary*.'" The display also cites biblical support for Mary's threat to Communism: "Who is she that cometh forth . . . terrible as an army set in battle array?" (Cant. 6:3 and 9); "I will put enmities between thee and the woman and thy seed and her seed and she shall crush thy head and thou shalt lie in wait for her heel" (Gen. 3:15). The editors do not portray Mary's role as a general in the Cold War as rhetoric or hyperbole but as the fulfillment of gendered biblical prophecy. During this period, they pair direct attacks on Communism involving Mary with more general assertions of Catholic patriotism that invokes her image. The December 1954 front cover of *Immaculata* shows an original drawing entitled "Our Lady of the United States" (see fig. 5.3). A young and beautiful Mary stands against the backdrop of an American flag, arms crossed at her breast and eyes raised heavenward. This Mary, protectress of America, serves as an emblem of American Catholic purity, courage, and national pride. For

FIGURE 5-3 *The Virgin and the Infant.* The Militia Immaculata updated traditional images of the Madonna and Child for modern times, from *Immaculata*, January 1955, front cover.

Courtesy of Militia Immaculata National Center.

Militia of the Immaculata members of this era, Mary is a national heroine ("Our Lady of the Americas"), a prophetess (the voice of warning and reproach at Fatima), a protector (the watchful and consoling mother in fearful times), and, perhaps most striking, a woman warrior (as the Militia of the Immaculata leader and "enemy of Communism").

Headlines heralded catastrophic possibilities if Mary's warnings were not heeded: "Wake Up America! Now . . . Before it is too late!" (May 1950); "It's Mary or Disaster" (June/July 1952). In February 1951, the lead story shows the image of a city skyline and an atomic blast with the headline "We Can Still Change the History of the World." Other articles fuel an atmosphere of suspicion and paranoia: "About Apparitions . . . To be silent in the face of very serious threats against silence after she has asked us to spread her message, seems to us a very great scandal! It is part of the conspiracy of silence against the truth, the fool's game of making believe that everything is all right with the world, when as a matter of fact just the opposite is true" (May 1950).[49] Exposés such as "Mary—Behind the Iron Curtain" (December 1950) strove to keep readers informed about the impact of Communism on religion abroad.

According to the editors of *Immaculata*, the world needed to listen to the Marian message during this time of crisis. But listening was not enough. Militia of the Immaculata members were called to action. In September 1950, the back cover interrogates the reader: "Are you prepared—TO JOIN THE ARMY? The Army making the World Wide Crusade of Prayer and Penance for PEACE?" The Militia of the Immaculata became a "Weapon of the Warrior Queen" (October 1953) and part of Mary's plan for world redemption. The rituals of Total Consecration and Eucharistic adoration were championed as the primary means of religious crusade. Members were also encouraged to "adopt Communists" and to pray for peace and an end to Communism.

Like many of their American Catholic contemporaries in the public sphere, *Immaculata*'s editors were notably self-aware of their role as defenders of the faith. They pose the Catholic Press as an antidote to America's spiritual ills: "Fight the Father of Lies, the Devil of Impurity . . . Mary Means PEACE—for YOU/Your Family, Our Nation, the World/Help Others to Understand. Keep America Spiritually Strong/Our Freedom, Security Depends on it. READ THE BEST!! . . . By Supporting Your Catholic Press."[50] Each year, the magazine widely publicized the national Catholic Press Month and celebrated its participation as an agent of Catholic information. This Catholic press constructed Cold War Marys who became American Catholic media icons, clothed in the discourse of fear, anxiety, patriotism, and pride. These radical representations recruited Catholic men and women to become warriors and evangelists in Mary's name, portraying alternative gender roles that challenged the norms in the wider culture.

Mary the Evangelist, as portrayed in media such as *Immaculata* and the *Miraculous Medal,* serves as a model missionary for these devotional organizations. Mary's primary role as *mother* becomes the central metaphor for all missions, but both men and women are asked to participate in zealous evangelization.[51] The Madonna's knack for capturing public attention through apparitions and prophecies makes her an ideal defender of the faith, despite traditional male models of evangelism in the Catholic tradition. She is the spokeswoman for Catholic universality, "Our Lady of At-One-Ment," who unites all humans who atone for their sins.[52]

The multiple Marys of this devotional media defy our typical assumptions about gender roles and models of and for gendered behavior within American Catholicism during the mid-twentieth century.

Conclusion

For producers of *Immaculata* and the *Miraculous Medal,* being Marylike entailed a broad range of dispositions and practices whose performances differed between the genders. Marylike images functioned as mediated icons for perfected Catholic (gendered) selves, reflected "in the mirror of Mary." Thus, Marylike men and women were not only performing as good Catholics, but as appropriate models of gendered behavior.

My research suggests that Roman Catholic Marian devotional organizations in the United States transformed and disseminated traditional and new representations of the Virgin Mary in service of evangelism, including missions to non-Catholics, "renewal" of lapsed or inactive Catholics, spiritual invigoration of devout Catholics, and the conversion of all people to the Marian message and way of life. Advocating religiously motivated models of gendered identity and behavior is one mode of this evangelistic process. My expanded work offers a close examination of the ways that Mary has been transformed, mediated, and commodified by American

Catholic culture, especially by devotional organizations in the United States since World War I.[53] These groups created new forms of Marian devotion that transgressed old boundaries of ethnicity, class, and culture in surprising ways. Mary became a product of American "mass culture," [54] and devotional organizations promoted and even marketed particular representations of the Madonna. As other studies of religion, media, and commodification have shown, such organizations use media to generate new forms of communal affiliation (national and transnational) centered around particular devotional practices, networks of prayer, and sites of pilgrimage, just as they reconfigure theological and social positions.

For organizations like the Militia of the Immaculata and the Association of the Miraculous Medal, representations of the Madonna serve as missionary, theological, and moral models for both insiders and outsiders. These Marian representations offer important insights into American Catholic participation in public life and particular expressions of ethical and political action based on religious values. Attending thoughtfully to gender issues in Marian devotional practice helps us understand some of the diverse ways that Mary as media icon has shaped American Catholic History.

NOTES

1. For me, the term "representations" includes material images *and* verbal descriptions, including metaphors and doctrine about the role and significance of Mary.

2. Research on devotion to Mary in the United States is especially thin, though scholars like Robert Orsi and Thomas A. Tweed have made invaluable contributions to the field. Still, studies of Marian devotion in America outside the "immigrant church" (both old and new) are greatly needed. In her article "The Marian Revival in American Catholicism: Focal Points and Features of the New Marian Enthusiasm," (in *Being Right: Conservative Catholics in America*, ed. Mary Jo Weaver and R. Scott Appleby, 213–240 [Bloomington: Indiana University Press, 1995]), Sandra Zimdars-Swartz argues that most previous work on Marian devotion was confined to official church pronouncements and the devotion of clergy and religious orders. Less official forms of lay piety, such as Marian devotional organizations in the United States, have typically been neglected.

3. St. Maximilian Kolbe is the patron of the mass media.

4. Ada Locatelli, "Fr. Kolbe Missionaries of the Immaculata," *Immaculata*, March/April/May 2003, 14–15, my emphasis.

5. The Conventual Franciscan Friars, "What Is Marytown?" Marytown, http://www.marytown.com/marytown.html (accessed March 28, 2003).

6. See W.J.T. Mitchell, *Iconology: Image, Text, Ideology* (Chicago: University of Chicago Press, 1986), for an overview of iconology in art historical and literary studies.

7. Jaroslav Jan Pelikan, *Mary through the Centuries: Her Place in the History of Culture* (New Haven: Yale University Press, 1996), 5, my emphasis.

8. David Morgan, *Visual Piety: A History and Theory of Popular Religious Images* (Berkeley: University of California Press, 1998); David Morgan, *The Sacred Gaze: Religious Visual Culture in Theory and Practice* (Berkeley: University of California Press, 2005); David Morgan and Sally Promey, eds., *The Visual Culture of American Religions* (Berkeley: University of California Press, 2001); Colleen McDannell, *Material Christianity* (New Haven: Yale University Press, 1995); Jenna Weissman Joselit, *The Wonders of America: Reinventing Jewish Culture, 1880–1950* (New York: Hill and Wang, 1994).

9. See Pierre Bourdieu, *The Logic of Practice* (Stanford: Stanford University Press, 1980), 112–121, for a discussion of "symbolic capital."

10. See Erika Doss, "Robert Gober's 'Virgin' Installation: Issues of Spirituality in Contemporary American Art," in *The Visual Culture of American Religions*, ed. Morgan and Promey, 129–145; and Mary Ellen O'Donnell, "Apparitions and Interpretations: The Virgin of Guadalupe and American Cultural Catholicism," paper presented to the American Academy of Religion annual meeting, November 22, 2004, San Antonio, TX.

11. Jonathan Z. Smith, ed., *The Harper Collins Dictionary of Religion* (San Francisco: Harper San Francisco, 1995), "Icon," 476.

12. Margaret Miles, *Image as Insight: Visual Understanding in Western Christianity and Secular Culture* (Boston: Beacon Press, 1985), 96–97.

13. Stewart Hoover and Lynn Schofield Clark, eds., *Practicing Religion in the Age of the Media: Explorations in Media, Religion, and Culture* (New York: Columbia University Press, 2002), 4.

14. Ibid., 4.

15. Andrew Tolson, *Mediations: Text and Discourse in Media Studies* (New York: Arnold, 1996), xii.

16. Morgan and Promey, *The Visual Culture of American Religions*, 2–3, with my insertion of their category titles in brackets.

17. Morgan, *The Sacred Gaze*, 222.

18. Catholic Book Publishing Co., "Mariology," in *Dictionary of Mary*, 218.

19. The Dogma of the Immaculate Conception, proclaimed by Pope Pius IX in 1854, and the Dogma of the Assumption proclaimed by Pope Pius XII in 1950.

20. Barbara Corrado Pope, "Immaculate and Powerful: The Marian Revival in the Nineteenth Century," in *Immaculate and Powerful: The Female Sacred Image and Social Reality,* ed. Clarissa W. Atkinson, Constance H. Buchanan, and Margaret R. Miles, 173–200 (Boston: Beacon Press, 1985).

21. See Jenny Franchot, *Roads to Rome: The Antebellum Protestant Encounter with Catholicism* (Berkeley: University of California Press, 1994).

22. A component of Will Herberg's central thesis in his *Protestant, Catholic, Jew: An Essay in American Religious Sociology* (Garden City, NY: Doubleday, 1955).

23. The Militia of the Immaculata, "What Is Consecration?" http://www.consecration.com/learn-more.html (accessed March 28, 2003).

24. Ibid.

25. Ibid.

26. Association of the Miraculous Medal, "The Miraculous Medal Story and Its Meaning," http://www.amm.org/medalp.htm (accessed March 28, 2003).

27. Association of the Miraculous Medal. "The Association of the Miraculous Medal at Saint Mary's of the Barrens," http://www.amm.org/olmiss.htm, (accessed March 28, 2003).

28. Ibid.

29. My translation, from the French.

30. *Immaculata,* June/July 1950, 17–18.

31. In fact, Rev. Joseph A. Skelly, C.M., founded the magazine in 1928 and remained editor until his death in 1963.

32. Noted in first issue, May 1928. This phrase is repeated.

33. Paula Kane, James Kenneally, and Karen Kennelly, C.S.J., eds., *Gender Identities in American Catholicism* (Maryknoll, NY: Orbis Books, 2001), xxii.

34. Distinct from biological sex. Kane's introductory essay traces the scholarly development of this distinction.

35. Ludwig Wittgenstein, *Philosophical Investigations,* trans. G.E.M. Anscombe (Oxford: Blackwell, 1997), §30.

36. *Immaculata* magazine began in 1949 as the primary publication of the Militia of the Immaculata in the United States, run by the Conventual Franciscan Friars and the Franciscan Marytown Press, located originally in Kenosha, WI, and later transplanted to Libertyville, IL. The *Miraculous Medal* magazine, "The National Organ of The Central Association of the Miraculous Medal," began publication much earlier, in 1928, located at the organization's Philadelphia shrine.

37. In *Immaculata* magazine, the term "Marylike" first appears in an October 1953 article/advertisement for women's fashion: "Be Marylike! Buy Marilyke Gowns!" The ad repeats, and the adjective "Marylike" recurs. This phrase was used in many Catholic publications of the time, including a magazine called the *Marylike Crusader* (see Kane, Kenneally, and Kennelly, *Gender Identities in American Catholicism,* 84–88, for a sample of these primary sources).

38. See Clifford Geertz's well-known essay, "Religion as a Cultural System," in his *The Interpretation of Cultures* (New York: Basic Books, 1973).

39. St. Louis Grignon De Montfort, "Our Sanctification, the Will of God, Extract from 'The Secret of Mary,'" *Immaculata,* October 1950, 10.

40. Colleen McDannell, "Catholic Domesticity, 1860–1960," in *American Catholic Women: A Historical Exploration,* ed. Karen Kennelly, C.S.J., 48 (New York: Macmillan, 1989).

41. Ibid., 60–61.

42. "M.I. Roundtable," *Immaculata,* August 1958, 9.

43. Bro. Gabriel, O.F.M.Conv., "These Young Ladies Say: Modesty Is the Best Policy," *Immaculata,* May 1952, 3.

44. Ibid., 3–4.

45. Ibid., 13.

46. *Immaculata,* June/July 1955, 15.

47. Sister M. Deborah, O.P., "From Mother to Child," *Immaculata,* June/July 1955, 15, 20.

48. See Michel Foucault, *Power/Knowledge: Selected Interviews and Other Writings, 1972–1977,* ed. Colin Gordon (New York: Pantheon, 1980), for an overview of Foucault's thought about disciplinary models.

49. *Immaculata,* June/July 1950, 18.

50. *Immaculata,* February 1954, back cover.

51. At the inception of both groups, "mission" is still traditionally defined as the conversion of non-Catholics, usually in foreign lands.

52. The title "Our Lady of At-One-Ment" first appears in *Immaculata* in June/July 1959 and is repeated in later issues.

53. I've chosen World War I as a reference point for several reasons. First, the First World War was a defining event in the early twentieth century that deeply affected both religion and culture on both sides of the Atlantic. Second, the Marian apparition at Fatima, Portugal, with its dire warnings of future destruction, took place during the war, in 1917, even though, as Sandra Zimdars-Swartz notes ("The Marian Revival in American Catholicism," 190), this apparition was not widely known until the 1940s, as the Second World War began. A third reason for choosing this periodization is that the MI and AMM formed around the time of World War I.

54. In *Modernity and Mass Culture* (Bloomington: Indiana University Press, 1991), James Naremore and Patrick Brantlinger define "mass culture": "In general terms, it involves a double inflection, derived from the 'dual revolutions' of the late 18th century: on the one hand it points to the culture of the masses, or the majority of people most of the time; on the other it points to culture mass-produced by industrial techniques. . . . We can only say that meanings of the phrase tend to circulate around the fairly recent processes of democratization and industrialization" (1–2).

6

Cartoon Wars

The Prince of Egypt in Retrospect

ERICA SHEEN

One of the secrets of a blockbuster film's success lies in its ability to be found meaningful among a diverse set of potential audience members. Yet is it possible for a single film to appeal to three vastly different religious and cultural groups? In the case of Stephen Spielberg's film *The Prince of Egypt*, this cross-cultural appeal was certainly an often-stated goal. Drawing upon expertise from leaders within Christian, Jewish, and Muslim groups, the filmmakers projected a desire to contribute to a discourse of unity and universality by ostensibly highlighting points of connection between how these three different traditions view the same story of the prophet Moses. Yet as Erica Sheen argues in this chapter, it is possible that these claims of universality had more to do with "product differentiation" efforts on the part of the film's marketing and promotion departments than with the creation of a universally shared understanding of a common religious story. By offering a comparison with the Cecil B. DeMille classic *The Ten Commandments* and reviewing the various religiously specific tie-ins available for Christian and Jewish filmgoers, Sheen argues that the universalist claims of the film actually mask a nationalist agenda that coincides with U.S. foreign policy as well as U.S. copyright law. This chapter provides a starting point for understanding why it is that some media products, in this case those of *The Prince of Egypt*, can be celebrated as universal in certain Western cultures while banned as exclusivist and offensive in others. Thus, this film can and no doubt has been mobilized to do some of the work of religious lifestyle branding, yet such efforts are seen as consequential in a sphere far beyond that of entertainment and leisure.

When an earlier version of this essay appeared in *Polygraph* in 2000,[1] there had been no critical discussions of representations of Islam on film, and almost no general debate about the political and cultural place of Islam in secular Western society. Today—in the aftermath of September 11, 2001 (9/11), July 7, 2005, and the publication in September 2005 in the Danish newspaper *Jyllands-Posten* of a series of cartoons of the prophet Mohammed—there is almost no discussion of anything else. On February 5, 2006, the London-based *Independent on Sunday* provided the following account of the events in what the world media were by then describing as the "Cartoon Wars":[2]

> The worldwide campaign at street and diplomatic level against European newspapers' publishing cartoons of the prophet Mohamed yesterday assumed ever more serious proportions. In Damascus, thousands of Syrian demonstrators set fire to both the Danish and Norwegian embassies, badly damaging the buildings. In Palestine, dozens of youths attacked the European Union's officer in Gaza, and, in Jordan, the state prosecutor ordered the arrest of the sacked editor of a tabloid weekly who reprinted the cartoons. But, in potentially the most far-reaching consequences of the row, Iran announced it has formed a committee to consider cancelling all trade ties with countries that have published the cartoons, which are deemed to insult the prophet. President Mahmoud Ahmadinejad said the caricatures showed the impudence and rudeness of Western newspapers, and asked commerce minister Masoud Mirkazemi to study stopping economic contracts with countries starting this hateful action. A boycott of Danish goods is already widespread in the Muslim world. Yet, as smaller-scale protests continued in London, among other cities, it is a sobering thought to realise that the whole saga began as the liberal idea of just one well-meaning man.[3]

The one well-meaning man in question was Danish author Kaare Bluitgen. Bluitgen had asked three Danish artists to illustrate a children's book on the prophet Mohammed:

> The intention, since Bluitgen's children attend schools with a majority of Muslim children, was to contribute to integration. "These

children must learn about Danish heroes, and Danish children should learn about Muslim heroes," he said. He asked three artists to illustrate it, but they declined, and word of this reached *Politiken* newspaper, which, on September 12 ran a story asking if, out of fear of reprisals, self-censorship was at work. The papers rival *Jyllands-Posten* then had the idea of asking cartoonists to depict the prophet. A dozen obliged, and crucially, one showed Mohamed with a bomb for a head-piece.[4]

The publication of these cartoons was explosive. In the media carnage that resulted, one thing was immediately obvious: the critical discourse we use for this kind of debate must be counted amongst its casualties. In the coverage provided by the *Independent on Sunday* and the *Observer*—the United Kingdom's two "quality" weekend newspapers—the following terms were used to describe these images, without any attempt to differentiate between the culturally complex modes of intentionality they imply: *cartoon, caricature, depiction, drawing, lampoon, mockery, portrayal, satire, stereotype*. The apparent interchangeability of these terms alerts us to a broader confusion, one that is presented as an opposition between the values of "religious" and "secular" societies, in which the concept of "free speech" is invariably aligned with secularism. Thus, for instance, on February 9 the London *Economist* carried an article on the "Cartoon Wars" that confidently asserted that "free speech should override religious sensitivities." From such a perspective, the elision of the difference between neutral terms like *depiction, drawing*, or *portrayal* and culturally weighted terms like *caricature, lampoon*, or *stereotype* implies that "free" speech is underpinned by privileged terms of political non-accountability. My purpose in re-presenting this discussion of a film that has been all but buried under the debris of this rhetorical fallout is to try to show what the underlying values of this kind of "freedom" really are, whose interests they serve, and whether we really can look to them as the basis of a hope for "integration."

In practice, free speech tends to mean that those societies that endorse it as a "universal" right do not allow it to those they see as threatening their own particular notion of "civilization": hence the U.S. Patriot Act of 2001, or the recent U.K. Terrorism Bill. What legislative measures of this kind make clear is that the rights in question are, at some defining level, territorial.

From this perspective, the questions of representation raised by *The Prince of Egypt* (1998) are an important precursor to the contemporary "Cartoon Wars," not least because the figure of Moses, more obviously so than Mohamed, is cultural common ground for all parties to the conflict. Moses is recognized as a prophet by followers of all three religions of "the Book": Islam, Judaism, and Christianity. Beyond this, his role as liberator and law-giver has given him originary status in the pioneering narratives that underpin the historical rise of American culture, and hence in the founding myths both of contemporary economic globalization and of its dark side, identity politics. The earliest formulations of American codes of law con-sciously affiliated the concept of an emergent "people" with the principles of Mosaic law and the Pentateuch: in Massachusetts in 1636, John Cotton drew up a code known as "Moses, His Judicials," which reemerged in Nathaniel Ward's "Body of Liberties" and became the basis of the influential Law and Liberties of 1648.[5]

It is thus not surprising that Moses was also one of the first heroes of early American film. As William Uricchio and Roberta Pearson have shown, the Moses film helped establish the role of cinema in a political program of Americanization in the first decade of the twentieth century.[6] And in the 1950s, Charlton Heston's still iconic performance helped to position Cecil B. DeMille's 1956 *The Ten Commandments* as the defining film of post-war American globalism. In the prelude preceding the credit sequence, DeMille appears in person to describe the film's significance as a story of individual and collective resistance to totalitarianism, and to present Paramount's new widescreen format VistaVision as the medium for the audience's experience of these transformative values. The idea of widescreen as a "cinema of participation" and a related conception of cinema as a kind of postwar travel agency come together in his suggestion that "those who see this motion picture . . . will make a pilgrimage over the very ground that Moses trod more than three thousand years ago."

It is thus also not surprising that Steven Spielberg, David Geffen, and Jeffrey Katzenberg were drawn to the story of Moses when they launched their new production partnership, DreamWorks SKG, in 1994. But where *The Ten Commandments* unmistakably aligned its political ambitions with Zionism and the Cold War, *The Prince of Egypt* looked toward what Amardeep Singh has described as the "American Perestroika towards the Islamic world,"[7] associated with Bill Clinton's presidency and the Oslo Accord in 1993. The implications of that shift in perspective were made obvious from the outset. Where *The Ten Commandments'* epic credit sequence cites the Holy Scriptures as the basis of its screenplay, *The Prince of Egypt* specifies three textual sources:

1. The Hebrew Bible, Deuteronomy 34:10 ("And there arose not a prophet since in Israel like unto Moses, whom the Lord knew face to face.")
2. The New Testament, Acts 7:35 ("This Moses whom they refused saying, who made thee a ruler and a judge, the same did God send to be a ruler and a deliverer by the hand of the angel which appeared to him in the bush.")
3. The Qur'an, 19:51 ("And make mention in the Scripture of Moses. Lo! He was chosen, and he was a messenger of Allah, a Prophet.")

At the time, this was startling: it seemed to suggest not only that the film was prepared to acknowledge Islam as part of its "inspiration," but also the possibility that Muslims might be included in its audience. From such a perspective, its rationale as a remake of *The Ten Commandments* was precisely to acknowledge the historical and political divisions suppressed by the earlier film and to look beyond them toward reconciliation. Like *The Ten Commandments*, it aligned itself with state-of-the-art technology—here, Cambridge Animations Animo software, which combined 2-D flat animation with computer-generated 3-D objects. But the resulting aesthetic significantly redirected the political force of technological and industrial innovation. Very few animated films show any interest in the philosophical implications of the material absence of a light source from their frames. Indeed, the graphic style that has come to be associated with DreamWorks' competitor, Pixar, has standardized a graphic style based on flat primary contrasts. By comparison, *The Prince of Egypt* developed fully the compositional potential that light offers once it has been released from the constraint of its photographic function within the apparatus. This was one of the film's most studied stylistic features: Jeffrey Katzenberg cited illustrator Gustav Doré and impressionist painter Claude Monet—as well as David Lean's *Lawrence of Arabia*—as the models given to animators who applied for work on the film. The result was a distinctive visual style that resituated the classical cinematographic contrasts between key and fill lighting, monochrome and color, within spatial designs that implied such extreme height and depth of field that they would have been impossible to light on camera. If *The Ten Commandments* offers an equation between the divine fiat, the Hollywood apparatus, and American postwar Zionism, *The Prince of Egypt* brings together the collective labor of multicultural cooperation and the U.S. Middle East peace process.

From such a perspective it is not difficult to find in the background of this production the event Clinton aide George Stephanopoulos has described as "the most inspiring day of his [Clinton's] presidency": the signing of the Oslo Accord in Washington in August 1993. Stephanopoulos recorded the fact that, the night before this historical event, "Clinton rose at three A.M. to read his Bible. . . . He was searching for words as meaningful as the impending moment": "Israeli Prime Minister Yitzhak Rabin and Chairman Yasir Arafat of the PLO were going to shake hands and pledge to return the ancient lands of Judea and Samaria to a time when the land had rest from war (Joshua 11:23)."[8] According to him, the finishing touches to the speech included "an excerpt from the Koran suggested by Prince Bandar of Saudi Arabia."[9] During the ceremony itself, Rabin "accelerated through the seasons of Ecclesiastes to declare that 'the time for peace has come' and closed with a line from the Hebrew prayer book—'May He who brings peace to His universe bring peace to us and to all Israel.'"[10] There is here an intertextuality strikingly similar to that offered by DreamWorks' citation of *The Prince of Egypt*'s three textual sources. The possible significance of an association between the two raises a question that has repeatedly been asked by Edward Said: whether the multicultural values they appear to espouse offer any real hope of reconciliation between Jews and Arabs. Said, of course, was passionately articulate about the need for a "new universality."[11] But he was just as passionately skeptical about the terms for this offered by the Clinton administration. He acknowledged the work done by "protocols, resolutions, conventions, declarations," but nonetheless believed that

> in the Western community of nations presided over by the United States an old, rather than new, nationalist identity has been reinforced, one that . . . has given itself an internationalized and normative identity with authority and hegemony to adjudicate the

relative value of human rights. All the discourse that purports to
speak for civilization, human rights, principle, universality, and
acceptability accrues to it. . . . So completely has the power of the
United States—under which in some measure we all live—invested
even the vocabulary of universality that the search for "new ideological means" to challenge it has become in fact more difficult.[12]

The question, then, that I would seek to direct toward *The Prince of Egypt* is
this: Did it offer a deal which all three signatories to its cinematic accord
would find acceptable?

If we approach the analysis of cinema audiences as at some fundamental level also a question about the occupation of contested territories,
the obvious place to start looking for an answer to this question would be
to consider whether or not readers of the Qur'an could or did watch this
film with the "happiness and satisfaction" it offered to Jewish or Christian
spectators. In fact, *The Prince of Egypt* raised basic questions about audiences in a way that *The Ten Commandments* did not, since its identification
of contrasting sources drew attention to the kind of differences that keep
people of different faiths out of each others cinemas. That said, DreamWorks'
address to an inclusive but divided spectatorship is consistent with the
way Hollywood has begun to acknowledge and address differentiations
within its audience, not only across the years between the two films, but
perhaps even more conspicuously in the years that have followed the
release of *Prince of Egypt*. Widescreen scholarship has pioneered accounts
of the way changes in the cinematic apparatus nuance prevailing models
of audience consensus. Nobody has applied this approach to spectatorship
more successfully than Stephen Spielberg, whose work exploits to the full
the potential a mass-entertainment movie has to address contrasting
interest groups within the same auditorium. Another way of saying this is
that he is outstandingly good at making individual films that behave like a
range of differentiated products, rather than a single product within a differentiated range, the latter being the way individual films typically perform within multiplex-based exhibition programs. From this perspective,
The Prince of Egypt's identification of its three cultural strands has more to
do with product differentiation than with the search for a vocabulary of
universality, and the problems it created for the latter derive in large part

from its overlap with the former. DreamWorks selected the portion of the Exodus story it chose to tell very carefully. By concentrating on the Ten Commandments episode, DeMille focused on the renewal of God's covenant with Abraham. This is common ground for Judaism, Christianity, and Islam, but it is also the point at which the tribes began to be separated by conflict over ownership of the scriptures that have their origin in this defining moment. By concentrating on the *earlier* part of the narrative, DreamWorks appears to have arrested this narrative of historical alienation and to have replaced it with a nostalgic retrospect on a lost brotherhood, thus implying that brotherhood remains a potential within the history of the people subsequently divided by it.

Unfortunately, the film's copyright statement—"DreamWorks SKG is the intellectual property holder of the movie *The Prince of Egypt* and holds copyright over the movie, characters, and storyline"—makes it clear that conflict over ownership of the scriptures rather than brotherhood remains definitive. Copyright on a scriptural storyline has negative implications for a "vocabulary of universality," to say the least—particularly when one member of that lost brotherhood observes an absolute prohibition on any kind of representation of the people and events in question. Although by no means as well reported as current controversies over the Danish cartoons, the release of *The Prince of Egypt* was attended by emphatic protest over the ethics of the appropriation and exploitation of the image of a Muslim prophet. In the words of Ahmed Farooq Mohamed, the vice president of the Supreme Council of Islamic Affairs in the Maldives, "Whether it be Musa [Moses], or any other prophet or messenger, they cannot be animated or portrayed in any form." [13]

In fact—from religious sanction to rights of intellectual property—*all* followers of "the Book" observe related prohibitions. As we shall see, the difference between these positions is not always easy to maintain, and more often than not it has been achieved at the level of conflict rather than political, legal, or critical negotiation. Islam, Judaism, and Christianity have a common origin in the revelation of the Word by God to man; but they have their historical and cultural constitution in war. Only Islam really acknowledges this, and the fact that it does so results in a tendency for Christian and Jewish militarism to naturalize itself as an appropriate civilized response to inappropriate uncivilized aggression. That naturalization derives much of its impetus from the way capitalist systems of production, like Hollywood, rationalize their production of difference at the level of consumption rather than culture, and that can make it hard to see that the process is underpinned by institutional racism. In Georg Lukàcs words, "the decisive progressive role of the bourgeoisie in history is to develop the world market, thanks to which the economy of the whole world becomes an objectively unified system."[14] But this "objectively unified system" is unified above all by its exclusion of institutions that do not operate according to the principles of a world market—like Islamic banking, which observes a prohibition on interest and consequently does not interface with capitalist financial systems. The configuration of *The Prince of Egypt*'s potential audience as world *market* rather than world *culture* could be seen in the way it was represented on the World-Wide Web in terms of tie-ins.[15] An examination of Web sites relating to *The Prince of Egypt* available in April 1999 showed localized patterns of consumption that would confirm suspicions about its "vocabulary of universality." Apart from official Web sites, such as www.spielberg-dreamworks.com and www.prince-of-egypt.com, and special interest sites dedicated to film culture and reviews, Internet marketing associated with this film conspicuously emphasized not just differentiations within its cultural affiliations, but their divisiveness. Jamsline (www.jamsline.com), a Christian music information source, used material from the DreamWorks official Web site and invested it with a distinctly adversarial tone. It described the film "as an epic story, one that combines *universal* themes of faith, heroism and deliverance . . . inspired by the *biblical* story of Moses": "an epic drama that tells the story of two men, one born a prince, the other born a slave, but *only one was born to lead*. A *lie* made them brothers; *the truth* will destroy a kingdom and *forever separate* them: in faith, in heritage, in destiny" (my emphases). What Jamsline had to sell was the three-record sound-track collection—the Original Soundtrack CD, the Inspirational CD, and the Nashville CD—issued by DreamWorks Records in partnership with Provident Music Distribution and made up of "different music genres created in support of a film release . . . [in] an unprecedented collaboration between the arenas of country, R&B, pop and gospel music."

Jewish spectators were similarly well provided for; www.familyhaggadah. com invited its visitors to buy "The Prince of Egypt Passover Haggadah," and "this Passover, experience the Exodus like never before!" It provided sample pages, with "breathtaking illustrations from the movie" and invited purchasers to "buy 5 Haggadahs, get the 6th one free! Use this special Haggadah as a fundraiser in schools and organizations!" Given the issue of copyright, this last injunction is particularly interesting—not least because, even if I could afford to reproduce an illustration here, it would certainly be out of the question to invite *you* to go away and use it to make money. At this point, the possibility that copyright operates as a prohibition rather than a right begins, I think, to present itself—not least in the extent to which it reveals the implicit contradictions of Hollywood's dependence on the relation between copyright and adaptation. As an adaptation of stories held in common between Christians, Jews, and Arabs, *The Prince of Egypt* appears to break free of the limitations of Hollywood's vested interests. As a copyright, it simply extends those interests over the border between Jew and Arab. It goes without saying that there were no Islamic tie-ins. Jeffrey Katzenberg is said to have met with more than five thousand religious leaders in the course of production, including a pontifical council on social reform at the Vatican; and www.prince-of-egypt.com carried a section offering a guide "for the effective religious use of the film for religious leaders, lay leaders, parents and teachers," produced under the auspices of the Islamic Center of Southern California. This described the (copyrighted) storyline as one that "transcends religious differences," even though it went on to enumerate the way the film differs from the version of this story offered by the Qur'an. Arabia. Online Culture Channel carried only news items announcing the fact that the film was banned in Muslim countries. And here we must note what must be one of the most elusive effects of the institutional racism suffered by societies that choose not to participate in the "world market." To the Western reader, they can seem quite simply ill informed, reinforcing that culturally specific association between free speech and "universal" rights that Islam does not endorse. In the article already quoted from the Arabia. Online Culture Channel, we were told that the country has two film theaters seating a few hundred people each, that it has previously banned *The Ten Commandments* "because of Charlton Heston's portrayal of Moses," and (in a footnote) that Charlton Heston is "an American film actor who played the leading male part in some big epic movies." Despite the fact that, within the terms of its representational prohibitions, the connection between these three statements is logical and informative, and that Heston *is* nothing more, or less, than "an American film actor who played the leading male part in some big epic movies," we have to work quite hard to overcome a reflex response that such a society is just out of the loop.

Its portrayal of Moses was not the only problem *The Prince of Egypt* created for Islam. The use of images from the film to illustrate the Passover Haggadah draws our attention to what was seen as one of its most exciting animation effects: its representation of the Ten Plagues. In the Islamic version of the Exodus story, the Ten Plagues is actually Nine Miracles, and the one that is missing is the Slaying of the First Born. This in itself is testimony to the fact that the Jewish story of the Passover is not only not conciliatory, but fundamentally divisive. Its people are separated out by the Passover and remain defined as a people by that separation. In *The Prince of Egypt*, this act of definition is paramount. In fact, it is the importance of this idea more than anything that makes us aware that that third citation—to the Qur'an—has no status at all as a point of entry to the Exodus "experience." *The Prince of Egypt* inserts into its (copyrighted) storyline the reference to a Holocaust that has taken place prior to the events shown in the film. We see Moses preoccupied with the hieroglyphic images of murdered Jewish children that he finds on the walls of the Pharaoh's palace. When he asks his "father" for an explanation, he is told that there had been a famine and "sometimes for the greater good sacrifices have to be made." A flashback implies that this was the reason why Moses' family sent him down the river in a basket. There is thus a Slaughter of the Innocents which typologically precedes the subsequent Death of the First Born, just as the Old Testament Death of the First Born typologically precedes the New Testament Slaughter of the Innocents. This doubling up serves to back-shadow within the film the Holocaust of the 1930s and 1940s—and, in the story of Moses' deliverance and subsequent rediscovery of himself as a Jew, perhaps even to provide a narrative *Durcharbeitung* for the guilt many American Jews who escaped from Germany in the 1930s have acknowledged that they feel because they survived. It also situates the film in a typological relation to Steven Spielberg's *Schindler's List* (1993), so that the Passover film, following the Holocaust film, is itself—particularly as a programmatic statement for the new production company—a kind of Exodus, a coming-out.

Insofar as we can see *The Prince* as in some sense a Spielberg production, it maps a trajectory in the deliverance of the Ark of the Covenant from the secret basement in an American government building to which it was consigned at the end of the Indiana Jones film *Raiders of the Lost Ark* in 1981. Then, the Ark was too powerful but also too arcane to remain in the public eye—a fact that is made very clear in the earlier scene in which Indie and his girlfriend avert their eyes to save themselves from the destruction that lights on their Nazi persecutors. Its emancipation is forcefully presented at the end of *The Prince of Egypt* when the Ark is finally, triumphantly, carried out to Israel and to freedom. In *Raiders of the Lost Ark*, a special effect— whirling streams of light—is reserved for the representation of whatever it is that comes out of the Ark when its lid is removed. In *The Prince of Egypt*, this effect is spectacularly remade in the Passover scene as a climactic revelation of the source of the power invested in this contemporary cinematic apparatus.

All of which means that the fact that, in Islamic tradition, Moses' negotiation of the Exodus is *not* embedded in an endless cycle of killing is less than insignificant. Writing in the opposition newspaper *Al-Wafd*, editor George Fahim described the film as "part of the Jewish-Arab conflict," and the accuracy of this analysis is lost beneath the presupposition that once again this was an inappropriately aggressive response to something that we should be civilized enough to see as just a film for children. Interestingly enough, internal conflicts *within* the world market are presented in positive terms as competition rather than negatively as aggression. Egypt's ban on the film and criticism of its treatment of Egyptian history and culture was treated dismissively in the Western press;[16] Disney's physical assault on a DreamWorks publicity banner in the Virgin Megastore in Orlando in November 1998 received a qualitatively different response:

> The megastore, which is located on Disneyworld property, dismantled the ad on Wednesday after Disney exercised a contractual right to veto any display. "It's part of their lease," DreamWorks Records sales chief Joyce Castagnola told *Variety*. "We have no recourse." Reportedly, the only other item Disney has ever vetoed was a graphic cover of a Marilyn Manson album. Disney says in this case it was protecting its corporate identity and trying to prevent consumer

mix-ups. "It creates confusion about the brand," a Disneyworld spokesperson told Newsweek.com. . . . The bottom line: when it comes to animation, don't mess with Mickey.

Of course, what makes this safe and entertaining is its *cartoon*-like quality. The article from which it is taken, posted on Microsoft's *Newsweek* Web site on November 26, 1998, was titled *"The Prince of Egypt* Exiled from Disney," and its first sentence was "Mickey Mouse is flexing his muscles." From such a position, we might return to Bill Clinton, wakeful in the early hours of that August day in 1993, "searching for words as meaningful as the impending moment." He emerged from what might by any standards have been a dark night of the soul sublimely unscathed. The next morning, he phoned Stephanopoulos: "George, I feel really good about that speech. I've been up since three working on it, and I think I've got it down. I'll be down in ten minutes with the changes." [17] Shortly after, he entered the Oval Office "in an effervescent mood with an iridescent tie—shiny gold horns against a deep blue background, a nod to the trumpet blasts that felled the walls of Jericho. He joked about how he liked Joshua because the only person he left standing in Jericho was Rahab the prostitute." [18] The run-up to the subsequent ceremony was not without its own weighty problems: Arafat's clothing (" 'The Israelis aren't coming if Arafat wears a uniform'; 'Tell him to take the medals off, say its a safari suit, and see if they'll accept that' "); the strategy they should use if the PLO leader tried to kiss Clinton ("If that didn't work, we joked, the president would resort to that time-tested, last best defense against an unwelcome advance—a knee to the groin"); making sure Clinton didn't grin at the wrong moment ("We practiced a closed mouth smile"). Truly, as John Wayne might have said, this was the animated-feature version of global politics.

Notwithstanding, the great moment finally came: "Arafat and Rabin grasped each others hands and pumped them up and down, and the entire lawn exploded—Arab and Jews, Christians and Muslims, Republicans and Democrats, joined for a moment in joy." [19] For Edward Said, this "joy" was a "media-induced euphoria" that, despite "official declarations of happiness and satisfaction, belied the grim actuality that the PLO leadership had simply surrendered to Israel." [20] Now, with the clarity of hindsight, it must be obvious how right Said was. As I write, Western governments—that evidently see democratization of the political process as a justification for the military intervention in Middle Eastern politics—are reeling under the shock of Hamas's electoral victory in Palestine. Their response has been a denunciation of the party as a terrorist organization and a demand to the Palestinian National Authority—an organization established in 1994 following the Oslo Accords and funded by the United States and the European Union—that it should be disarmed before being allowed to participate in negotiations. With his usual unwitting irony, George W. Bush commented, "I don't see how you can be a partner in peace if you advocate the destruction of a country as part of your platform."[21] It has been easy for Said's critics to diminish his distinctive sense of intellectual duty as the petulance of a privileged literary critic, but in doing so they ignore the presence in his work of a Adornian critique of mass media which recent events make increasingly clear should inform our reception of controversies like that surrounding the Danish cartoons.[22] Said was consistently clear that the issues on which he focused throughout his career—the language of universalism, the politics of identity—are, in the final analysis, a "question of land."[23] Like Kaare Bluitgen's idea of a children's book illustrated with pictures of Mohamed, *The Prince of Egypt* could be described as the liberal idea of well-meaning men. Both make clear the extent to which Western secularism masks a religious chauvinism that makes it fundamentally hostile to the political and economic interests of those it seeks to position as partners in peace.

NOTES

1. Erica Sheen, "*The Ten Commandments* and *The Prince of Egypt*: Biblical Adaptation and Global Politics in the 1990s," *Polygraph: An International Journal of Culture and Politics* 12 (2000), 85–100.

2. See, for instance, Daniel McGrory and Dan Sabbagh, "Cartoon Wars and the Clash of Civilisations: the Limits of Free Speech," *The Times*, February 3, 2006; Roy Hanania, "Cartoon Wars," *Dallas Morning News*, February 5, 2006; Anas Altikriti, "This Is Not a Cartoon War," *Guardian*, February 10, 2006.

3. Stephen Castle and David Randall, "The Pen and the Sword," *The Independent on Sunday*, February 5, 2006, 6–7.

4. Ibid.

5. Stephen Botein, "The Legal Profession in Colonial North America," in *Lawyers in Early Modern Europe and America*, ed. W. Prest (London: Croom Helm, 1981), 130.

6. William Uricchio and Roberta E. Pearson, *Reframing Culture: The Case of the Vitagraph Quality Films* (Princeton, NJ: Princeton University Press, 1993).

7. Amardeep Singh, "Preface: World Religions and Media Culture," *Polygraph* 12 (2000): 8.

8. George Stephanopoulos, *All Too Human: A Political Education* (London: Hutchinson, 1999), 189.

9. Ibid., 192.

10. Ibid., 194.

11. Edward Said, "Nationalism, Human Rights, and Interpretation," *Raritan* 12, no. 3 (1993): 44.

12. Ibid., 45.

13. Arabia.Online Culture Channel (http://www.arabia.com, accessed January 1999).

14. Georg Lukàcs, "Realism in the Balance," in *Aesthetics and Politics*, trans. Ronald Taylor (London: Verso, 1980), 31.

15. See James Schamus, "To the Rear of the Back End: The Economics of Independent Cinema," in *Contemporary Hollywood Cinema*, ed. Steve Neale and Murray Smith (London: Routledge, 1998), for an account of the tie-in as the basis of the economic ontology of cinema today.

16. See, for example, Egyptian-American journalist Mona Eltahawy in the *Guardian*, April 1999: "[Egyptian] columnists and expatriates accuse a Jewish-dominated Hollywood of yet again showing bias against Arabs and Muslims. Never mind that ancient Egyptians were not Arabs or Muslims. . . . DreamWorks made it known when the film was released that it had consulted hundreds of experts—scholars of Judaism, Christianity and Islam as well as Egyptologists—to try as far as possible to avoid giving offense. To little avail it seems. *Prince of Egypt* has collided with local pride at the achievements of ancient Egypt and a hatred of Israel that lingers despite the peace treaty signed by Cairo with the neighbouring Jewish state in 1979."

17. Stephanopoulos, *All Too Human*, 191.

18. Ibid., 192.

19. Ibid., 192–193.

20. Edward Said, "Gods That Always Fail," *Raritan* 13, no. 4 (1994): 5.

21. George Bush, White House press conference, January 26, 2006, www.whitehouse.gov/news/releases/2006/01/20060126.html.

22. See, for instance, his interview with Nirmala Lakshman in the *Hindu Magazine* (1996), published as "The Road Less Traveled," in *Power, Politics, and Culture: Interviews with Edward Said*, ed. Gauri Viswanathan (London: Bloomsbury, 2004), 416.

23. See Edward Said, "Interview with Mouin Rabbani," in the *Journal of Palestine Studies*, 1995, republished as "Symbols versus Substance: A Year after the Declaration of Principles," in *Power, Politics, and Culture*, ed. Viswanathan.

PART THREE

∞∞

Representations of the Religious "Other" in Popular Media and in the Marketplace

In the previous section, conflicts between religious groups and their relationships to differing nationalities emerged as an important theme stamped into popular media and into the economic organization of the marketplace. This section builds upon this idea, foregrounding instances in which particular religions, or religious leaders, have been depicted and understood in opposition to a dominant religion within a society. In the first chapter in this section, Phyllis Alsdurf explores how evangelical leaders, emergent in power in the United States in the 1950s, challenged Kennedy's nomination for presidency. Catholicism and its relation to the Vatican were understood in opposition to the hegemony of Protestantism in the United States. In the second chapter in this section, Ferruh Yilmaz considers media coverage and public opinion of immigrants, specifically Muslim immigrants considered "outsiders," within the western European nation of Denmark. The final chapter, by Kwabena Asamoah-Gyadu, looks at how practices of othering can take place within a climate of religious change in western Africa, as Pentecostal frames of reference influence the negative media depictions of traditional prophets and more established Christian denominations in popular fictional films. This section, therefore, opens up questions of which groups seek or are granted the cultural power to define who is an insider or an outsider within a society and how religious identification figures into the prejudices that may support these insider/outsider views.

7

Evangelicalism and the Presidential Election of 1960

The "Catholic Question" in *Christianity Today* Magazine

PHYLLIS E. ALSDURF

Christianity Today is widely viewed as the flagship magazine of contemporary American Protestant evangelicalism. Currently reaching an estimated third of a million people each month, the magazine is widely read by religious leaders and educated members of evangelical and mainstream Protestant congregations. Yet in the 1950s, both this magazine and today's powerful evangelical movement itself were just beginning to emerge on the U.S. cultural landscape. At that point, evangelicalism was still struggling to define itself in opposition to the more hard-line tradition of fundamentalism, with which it shared important historical roots, while also seeking to lay a claim to cultural authority in the way that mainstream Protestant denominations then were assumed to hold. In the pages of *Christianity Today,* as Phyllis Alsdurf demonstrates in this chapter, evangelical leaders found in John F. Kennedy's nomination an issue that could give shape to their concerns and rally supporters around the embrace of an evangelical identity. As Alsdurf notes, writers in *Christianity Today* argued passionately against Kennedy's nomination on the grounds that a Catholic president would change the "American way of life"—which had largely been understood in Protestant terms up until that point in history.

The coalescing of views on Catholicism and John F. Kennedy's 1960 presidential campaign as articulated in the pages of *Christianity Today* magazine marked a defining moment within evangelicalism. These distinctive views of

> "the American nation" and its purpose made it possible for evangelicals to see
> themselves as distinct from other groups and carriers of an important tradition.
> In some ways, as this chapter will demonstrate, even though evangelicals' views
> on Catholicism have since changed, *Christianity Today*'s discussions of "the
> Catholic issue" contributed to what might be considered the "brand" of evan-
> gelicalism as it was constituted at that point in history.

Social movements often achieve their clearest definition by being distinguished from other movements, especially in terms of what one movement
offers that another, perhaps rival, movement does not. Such distinctions
can be forced upon social movements by historical events. For the Protestant evangelical movement in the United States, the 1960 presidential campaign of Catholic John F. Kennedy provided one such historical moment.

Like many other religious movements that preceded it, evangelicalism
achieved distinctiveness, in part, because a small group of influential individuals began to articulate publicly their own sense of urgency and distress
related to social events of the day. As this chapter will discuss, leaders such
as the Rev. Billy Graham, Carl F. H. Henry, and L. Nelson Bell believed that
to some degree the candidacy of John F. Kennedy to the United States' presidency threatened the country's Protestant heritage and the right of religious
freedom.[1] As such, Kennedy's bid for the presidency served as a rallying
point for "New Evangelicals," who, though largely uninvolved in the political
life of the nation, were uncomfortable with the cultural separatism of fundamentalism and believed that biblical teaching "must be applied to every
realm of societal existence."[2] The missives they issued and articles they published in *Christianity Today*, the mouthpiece for the neo-evangelical movement, helped to rally those who, like themselves, felt they must defend the
very foundation of the nation against encroachment by the Vatican and
the "growing power of Romanism."[3] By articulating concerns that others in
the general public shared, evangelical leaders found, in their opposition to a
Kennedy presidency, an emotional charge and purpose that galvanized the
evangelical movement and deepened its "brand" or distinctiveness.

The evangelical movement could not have achieved power and widespread cultural influence without the development of a venue through

which its leaders could communicate dominant evangelical ideology. Noting the importance of a means of communication "in the marketplace of issues, ideas, symbols, and words," Anthony Oberschall states that leaders and activists of a social movement signify that movement to outsiders and the media as well as attract members by "publicizing the justness of their cause through ideological and moral appeals."[4] *Christianity Today* (*CT*) magazine was founded in 1956 by leaders within the National Association of Evangelicals (NAE) as an advocacy publication to give voice to evangelical concerns and help define what it meant to be an evangelical. By articulating evangelical positions in relationship to the wider culture, *CT* helped change people's perception about evangelicals—both within and outside evangelicalism. Through the pages of *CT,* evangelical leaders advocated cooperation and cultural engagement, quite unlike the sectarianism and cultural withdrawal of the traditional fundamentalism with which they had originally been aligned. The magazine soon became the foremost representative of evangelical thought and ideas in the United States and a pathway for evangelicals into majority consciousness.[5]

This chapter will review the writings of three influential evangelical leaders and founders of *CT* on the issue of Kennedy's election to the U.S. presidency in an effort to demonstrate how the movement embraced separation of church and state throughout the mid-1960s in an effort to limit the power of the Roman Catholic Church, even as *CT*—and evangelicalism—began distancing itself from the more strident and intolerant anti-Catholic positions. It will also look at initial coverage of Kennedy's presidency, examining how certain evangelicals came to terms with it, while others did not, and how the expressions of those viewpoints related to a change in evangelicalism more broadly.

A publication is to a large degree an expression of the perspectives and interests of its editorial leadership. Three of the men who gave leadership to *CT* during the 1950s and 1960s were evangelist Billy Graham, whose original vision led to the founding of *CT;* Dr. L. Nelson Bell, *CT*'s executive editor and Graham's father-in-law; and Carl F. H. Henry, *CT*'s first editor. Each represented a distinct voice within evangelicalism, and each had a stake in how evangelical views related to the 1960 presidential campaign and election would be expressed through what quickly became recognized as the main legitimizing vehicle of popular evangelicalism in the United States.

The 1960 Election and "the Religious Issue"

John F. Kennedy's campaign for the U.S. presidency was cause for great alarm among many Americans, the majority of evangelicals included. During Kennedy's campaign, what was known euphemistically as "the religious issue" became a rallying point for theological and political conservatives who feared the encroachment of the authoritarian power of Rome on hard-won American liberties no less so than they feared the spread of a godless communism throughout the world.

Responding to what they perceived as an encroachment on American liberties by an authoritarian Catholic system, a wide range of Protestant groups, including some religious liberals, formed Protestants and Other Americans United for Separation of Church and State (POAU) in 1947. Among the most influential POAU spokespersons was Paul Blanchard, a former State Department official, whose articles and books elucidated the extent to which Catholicism posed a threat to Protestant dominance in the United States. Such anti-Catholic apologists interpreted the Catholic Church as bound by medieval teachings and politically motivated to establish a monolithic rule that would ultimately destroy "the American way of life." Catholics were largely viewed as "foreigners" with alien ideologies that represented a worldview antithetical to that of the true American way of life.[6] The widespread fear of communism within 1950s American culture fostered a hyper-vigilance among political and social conservatives toward any indication of world domination, such as that seen in "Romanism" and the allegiance that the Roman Catholic Church demanded of converts worldwide. Many Protestants—not just fundamentalists and evangelicals—reasoned that the very foundation of Protestant American society was at stake in any accommodation to Catholics because of the "corrupting" power of the Catholic hierarchy in Rome.

Several factors contributed to paranoia among Protestants toward Catholics: reports of persecution of Protestants by Catholics in Latin America and Spain, the numerical growth of the Catholic Church in the United States, an increased influence of Catholics among blacks and in rural areas, and the challenge presented by Catholic leaders to claims that the United States was a Protestant nation.[7] Despite Kennedy's repeatedly stated opposition to both federal aid to parochial schools and the presidential appointment of an ambassador to the Vatican, his Protestant detractors considered a Kennedy presidency a huge inroad for an imagined monolithic "Catholic voice" in government, a perspective that many considered less American than a Protestant outlook.

The religious issue was kept alive during the 1960 campaign despite Kennedy's efforts to put it behind him. In March 1959, for example, Kennedy gave the following assurance in *Look* magazine: "Whatever one's religion in his private life may be for the officeholder, nothing takes precedence over his oath to uphold the Constitution and all its parts—including the First Amendment and the strict separation of church and state."[8]

In April of 1960, Kennedy stated his opposition to federal aid to parochial schools as well as to the appointment of an ambassador to the Vatican at a convention of the American Society of Newspaper Editors (ASNE). "I want no votes solely on account of my religion," he said. "Any voter, Catholic or otherwise, who feels another candidate would be a superior President should support that candidate. I do not want any vote cast for me for such illogical and irrelevant reasons."[9] Speaking to a ministerial association meeting in Houston in September of 1960, he pledged: "I believe in an America where the separation of church and state is absolute—where no Catholic prelate would tell the President, should he be a Catholic, how to act, and no Protestant minister would tell his parishioners for whom to vote."[10]

To a large degree, the Anglo-Protestant worldview of what being American meant was officially unseated with Kennedy's election to the presidency. While Catholics held key political and judicial positions throughout the country at that time, the idea of electing a Catholic president was another matter entirely. There were Catholic justices on the U.S. Supreme Court and numerous Catholic governors and senators, but the possibility of electing a Catholic president seemed to carry unique symbolic significance for Catholics and non-Catholics alike.

CT and Anti-Kennedy Sentiment

Like most conservative Protestant publications of its time, *CT* addressed concerns about Catholicism well in advance of the Kennedy presidential campaign, primarily through items in its news section. In particular, *CT* frequently covered the treatment of Protestant missionaries in countries with high concentrations of Catholics. Sharing a perspective common among Protestants prior to Kennedy's election, *CT* leaders were suspicious that the Vatican intended world dominance, and they indicated grave concerns in letters and memos that the election of a Catholic as U.S. president would open the door for the authoritarian Roman Catholic Church to undermine the country's democratic political system and religious freedoms.

This section analyzes the perspectives and contributions of three important *CT* leaders who represented a range of perspectives in the evangelical response to a Kennedy presidency.

As executive editor of *CT,* father-in-law of evangelist Billy Graham, and a former missionary surgeon in China for many years, Dr. L. Nelson Bell was in a particularly influential position among conservatives. He wrote to a fellow minister after the 1960 election that "the System" of which Kennedy was a part inspired the most fear in Protestants. Bell and others like him were convinced that the Catholic Church, suspect because of its international connections, had launched what he called a "behind-the-scenes campaign to infiltrate our entire American life." [11] In a letter dated September 24, 1960, Bell sums up the crux of his opposition to Kennedy: "I am opposed to Senator Kennedy, not because of his religion, but because of his Church. The Roman Catholic Church is both a secular State and a Church. It is true that it does not have a military force, but it operates through infiltration and intrigue, and has as its purpose the domination of America and the rest of the world. No one could be more opposed to Communism than I am, but it is strange to note that Communism flourishes most vigorously in areas where the Roman Catholic Church has dominated for years." [12] With arguments that were more political than theological in nature, Bell reasoned that opposition to the Catholic Church and communism went hand in hand since both aimed at world domination.

In July 1959, Bell wrote to Henry, who was in Bangkok at the time, about a long talk between Graham and Kennedy's opponent in the presidential race, Vice President Richard Nixon, who "has been attending church regularly and trying to live a consistent Christian life." Nixon "has looked with horror" on any attempt to exploit his personal faith for political reasons, said Bell, but he had agreed to speak at Wheaton College (Graham's alma mater) and write an article for *CT.* [13] That same month Bell wrote to Nixon about his desire "not to in any way make your personal Christian faith a matter of political exploitation"; but he told Nixon that "it is vitally important that Christians in America have a sense of direction when looking to their national leaders." [14] Bell suggested that Nixon write for *CT* on the subject of "Our Christian Heritage and the American Ideal." Noted Bell, "An article by you, reaching the great majority of the Protestant ministers of America, could have a profound effect." [15]

On September 7, 1960, a group of 150 Protestant ministers and laymen, representing thirty-seven denominations, met behind closed doors in Washington, D.C., for the National Conference of Citizens for Religious Freedom. The purpose of the meeting, which Bell helped organize, was a thinly veiled, last-ditch attempt to rally conservative forces against Kennedy's election. The group issued a statement on "the political aspects of Roman Catholicism" that garnered widespread media coverage. Though ostensibly not an endorsement of either candidate, it labeled the religious issue "one of the most significant" of the day and asked if it was reasonable "to assume that a Roman Catholic President would be able to withstand altogether the determined efforts of the hierarchy of his Church to gain further funds and favors for its schools and institutions, and otherwise breach the wall of separation of church and state?" [16]

At the event Bell gave a keynote address that subsequently was printed as a pamphlet and distributed by the thousands through the POAU.[17] The address reveals that Bell and his followers considered a Kennedy defeat to mean the preservation of American political freedoms established by the founding fathers. It chronicled a general loss of concern within the culture "with history and with our Protestant heritage," portraying the American heritage as singularly Protestant. Roman Catholicism, presented in negative imagery built on themes of internationalism, was "ecclesiastically bound," "threatens basic freedoms," was "like an octopus" covering the entire world, and wielded "authority and power over the minds, consciences and wills of men." [18]

Implying that true American history was somehow distinctly Protestant, Bell cautioned against "pseudo-tolerance" toward Catholicism, which would permit the election of a Catholic president because, "once a nation becomes 51% Catholic, the pressure increases and, as the percentage rises in favor of that Church, tolerance recedes and oppression intervenes." The difference between Catholics in America and "their coreligionists elsewhere," said Bell, is evidence of "the effect of Protestant concepts on America as a whole." Thus, Catholics were blamed for undermining the true essence of Americanism because of their "un-American" religious faith, and yet their positive societal contributions were attributed not to their own efforts but to the leavening effect of positive Protestant influence. In conclusion Bell warned, "If the past is forgotten and the present ignored, then the future will be dominated by a System far removed from the faith and freedoms of our fathers." [19]

Bell's opposition to a Catholic president was integrally tied to his concept of nationalism, and he remained firm in his conviction that Kennedy's election would have grave ramifications for the nation's political and moral life. As a late-campaign newspaper ad (endorsed by Bell in a letter) stated, the fight against Kennedy was "a battle to the death between the Roman Catholic church and its double-standard dogma, and Protestantism as we have known and experienced it since the beginning of the freedom of worship in America." [20]

By the late 1950s, Billy Graham had a growing national and international following through the phenomenon of evangelistic crusades that were widely covered in the media. Although Graham did not provide upfront leadership to *CT*, it was his vision for an evangelical counterpoint to the *Christian Century* that led to the launching of the magazine. He had an indisputably important role in the founding and development of *CT*, despite his behind-the-scenes presence. A member of the *CT* board, Graham was instrumental in selecting most of the board members, and his viewpoints, vision, and desires always received careful consideration.

Graham was in Europe at the time of the Citizens for Religious Freedom conference, but he received a visit there from Dr. Norman Vincent Peale, pastor of the prestigious Marble Collegiate Church in New York City and a strong Nixon supporter. [21] Peale's objective was to persuade Graham to speak out on Nixon's behalf, but, as Graham recalled in his 1997 autobiography, he told Peale he "preferred to stay out of the fray." [22] He also noted that from Europe he wrote to both Kennedy and Johnson to inform them of why he would not be voting for them. "It only seemed fair in view of my friendship with the competing candidate." [23]

About the controversial Washington conference, Graham observed that the statement the group drafted contained "no explicit statement about either candidate," but acknowledged that the group's effort "back-fired" and that they were "branded by some as anti-Catholic." [24] Graham claimed to have refused insistent Protestant demands that he declare himself against a Catholic candidate: "While I did not want to appear to endorse Kennedy, neither did I want to seem prejudiced against him on religious grounds. . . . I did not agree with some Catholic teachings and church practices, but warm acquaintance and fellowship with many in that church had long since laid to rest whatever prejudices I might have had." [25]

Pierre Salinger, aide to Kennedy, met with Graham on a train from Cincinnati to Chicago in late April 1960 and requested a statement from him on "the Roman Catholic issue" that Kennedy could use in the West Virginia Democratic primary. Graham refused and later got a phone call from Kennedy himself asking for a statement to the effect that Graham would not hesitate to vote for a Catholic if that person were qualified. Not taking any responsibility for holding an anti-Catholic position himself, Graham diplomatically recalled: "I did not think I saw any serious problem with a Catholic in the White House. Many Protestants, however, did have concerns, including some in my own Southern Baptist denomination. Baptists had a long tradition of stressing the separation of church and state. The idea of having a president who might owe a degree of allegiance to a religious leader who was also head of a foreign political state—Vatican City—concerned some of them greatly." Graham added, "Had I been foolish enough to declare myself, it would have been for Mr. Nixon." [26]

But the following letter from Graham to his friend President Dwight D. Eisenhower, dated August 4, 1960, indicates much more wholehearted sup-port for Nixon and opposition to Kennedy.

Dear Mr. President,

Your speech to the [Republican National] Convention was absolutely superb. This is the kind of fighting speech I hope you will continue to give. I am convinced that the next six months can be the most crucial and decisive of your entire career. You are the one person that the American people will listen to. I hope you will stump the country making this type of speech on behalf of Nixon. Especially would I like to suggest that you give a number of speeches of this caliber in key Southern states. I am sure that even you do not realize with what affection you are held in the South. With the religious issue growing deeper, I believe you could tip the scales in a number of key states from Kentucky to Texas. I believe that Nixon has a fighting chance only if you go all out. I know this would mean two months of hard work, but I believe the reward to the Nation would be as great as when you led the armies at Normandy.

It is also my opinion that you must win the battle in the coming special session of Congress. It seems to me that you could send so many dramatic messages to Congress that you could keep Kennedy and Johnson off-balance and capture the headlines during that period.

In the meantime, be assured that I have never been prouder of you and thanked God for you more than in the last few weeks. You have shown a humility and courage in the face of tremendous obstacles that can only be compared to Abraham Lincoln.

With warmest personal affection,

Billy[27]

This letter indicates the apocalyptic significance Graham assigned to the 1960 election. Implicit in what Graham says is the message that by divine directive it had fallen to Eisenhower to provide spiritual leadership to the nation, as it had to Lincoln during the Civil War and in whose great steps he followed. Eisenhower, by leading the country in a political "battle" just as he once "led the armies at Normandy," could defeat the enemy to true Americanism: (Democratic) Catholicism. While Graham may never have explicitly stated those views within *CT*, his perspective was certainly known to those providing editorial leadership to *CT*, particularly Bell, and reflected in the magazine's content. Publicly, however, Graham consistently distanced himself from the more strident anti-Catholic voices and over time came to represent a moderate brand of evangelicalism that was at least respectful toward ecumenical efforts.

Foremost among the first-generation leaders of neo-evangelicalism and an outspoken champion of its move away from militant fundamentalism was Carl F. H. Henry, *CT*'s first editor. In Henry's writings, a 1986 *CT* article stated, "the theological moorings of contemporary evangelicalism are anchored." [28] His book, *The Uneasy Conscience of Modern Fundamentalism*, published in 1947, became the rallying cry for an "engaged orthodoxy" and signaled a change in the way evangelicals interacted with culture and society. A theologian and seminary professor prior to helping launch *CT*, Henry was a prolific writer with strong journalistic and publishing credentials who distinguished himself as foremost among evangelical intellectuals. [29]

Although stating that he never shared "the extreme view that there is little to choose between Catholicism and Communism," Henry said *CT* constantly contended with "subtle Roman Catholic influences." [30] Nonetheless, he claimed in his 1986 autobiography that during his editorship *CT* "endorsed no candidate, of whatever party," and that, heading into the 1960 political campaign, he told his staff he wanted an "objective presentation and a good conscience in the arena of religion-and-politics. '*CT* is not devoted to the election of a particular presidential candidate; we want to keep the magazine above all parties, programs and personalities' and to 'see the issues squarely in terms of principle.'" [31] Doing so was motivated in part by the fact that *CT*'s legal counsel advised that its tax exempt status could be jeopardized if it published anything that favored one candidate over the other or could be interpreted as "propaganda designed to influence votes." [32] It appears that fear of jeopardizing *CT*'s tax-exempt status made the editors extremely wary of publishing any political pronouncements or articles that implied an endorsement or voting recommendation. Henry claimed that "the *Century* endorsed Kennedy and some feared that if elected Kennedy would void the tax exempt status of *Christianity Today* and other evangelical magazines." [33]

Insight into Henry's early response to the religious issue can be gleaned from a *CT* news article on the "Religion in a Free Society" conference, an event attended by one hundred representatives of Protestantism, Catholicism, Judaism, and non-religious humanism "seeking 'civic unity' in the midst of 'religious pluralism.'" Among attendees were such notable figures as Paul Tillich, Reinhold Niebuhr, Will Herberg, Rabbi Abraham Heschel, and Rev. John Courtney Murray, and theologians from Harvard, Yale, and Princeton. [34] Henry attended as a representative of the evangelical view. *CT*'s report, written under Henry's byline, appears to present a balanced picture of the viewpoints of participants. Regarding a session on Roman Catholic parochial education, the article notes, "Carl F. H. Henry of *Christianity Today* proposed a sustained exchange of thought on Protestant-Catholic anxieties."[35] That suggestion resulted in a three-hour session attended by more than half of the participants, Henry claimed.

Asked for an opening statement at the session, Henry noted that attempts by Catholic scholars to adjust the application of Catholic teachings to the American context was "tacit admission of conflicting interests in the present Roman church-state formula" and that 10 percent of Roman clergy and a larger percentage of laity in the United States "favor the more liberal view." In his closing statement, Henry reported that he identified as the main concern "the authority the Roman church assumes in the political order and its corollary authority over the conscience of its members in socio-political affairs" and that he "noted appreciatively the restatements by contemporary Catholic scholars of the traditional church-state thesis, but pointed out that 'the determination of the hierarchy's official doctrine does not lie with these scholars.'"[36] Henry's news account of the event illustrates the importance of his role as an evangelical spokesman and the firm but conciliatory nature of his approach among scholarly and religious leaders. That Henry was invited to participate in a gathering of national religious figures speaks to the regard with which he was viewed in the wider religious world and perhaps to his ability to enter into dialogue on the issue.

Henry also was one of eighteen Catholic, Jewish, and Protestant representatives asked to participate in a two-day meeting of the Fair Campaign Practices Committee in April 1960 to discuss the role of religion in the campaign. Describing the event in his autobiography, Henry said Catholic participants "were aggressive and had a well-knit and confusing strategy," while Protestants were divided into those who "found the answer to all problems in religious pluralism, those who feared that one who spoke his mind would be considered a maverick, and a fool like myself who said what I believed."[37]

There Henry was challenged about a *CT* article by C. Stanley Lowell, titled "Protestants, Catholics, and Politics," and a *CT* editorial, "Bigotry or Smear?" The latter had been branded "hateful bigotry" by television personality Ed Sullivan in a syndicated column that appeared in more than one hundred newspapers. *CT* staff, in turn, published an open letter to Sullivan from Glenn L. Archer, executive director of POAU, challenging Sullivan's views.[38] Henry told the group that he was willing to print

Sullivan's six-page response to Archer's "Open Letter," if Sullivan would be willing to reciprocate by publishing the *CT* reply in his column. Sullivan ultimately learned of the interchange, and the material was published in both his column and *CT*, Henry reported.[39] After consultation at its meeting, the Fair Campaign Practices Committee issued a statement that "no candidate for public office should be opposed or supported because of his particular religious affiliations," but "a candidate may be properly questioned about issues relevant to the office he seeks and about the bearing of his religious faith and conscience on them," according to the *CT* news report.[40]

In April 1960 Henry was invited to Capitol Hill for a conversation with Vice President Nixon, who "was impressed with the scope of our circulation to the Protestant leadership," Henry wrote in notes on the meeting. When Nixon asserted that religion "will tool us most effectively for opposition to Communism," Henry "shocked him" by stating that "you cannot use religion that way, if it is worth anything." Henry said Nixon was "too nebulous" in the area of religion, and he stressed to Nixon that he could "get much more definite in speaking about God before there is any danger of antagonizing either a Jew, Catholic or Protestant." When Nixon mentioned the desperate need for a sense of national purpose and moral leadership, Henry countered that "evangelical dynamisms" reinforce the political tradition. "The state and church under God, I said, means we must not hesitate to speak of 'the will of God'—a vocabulary plain enough to be understood at grass roots." The key to social problems, he told Nixon, is found not in legislative action but rather "in personal conscience and decision." Nixon agreed and said he disapproved the trend of expecting the government to do everything.[41]

Henry states in his autobiography that Nixon "clearly hoped that *Christianity Today* would endorse his candidacy, to offset the *Century*'s endorsement of Kennedy." In a memo written after the meeting, Henry recalled, "If the great principles are held in the forefront, I said, the American people in general will respond to them, and evangelical forces will help wage the battle. . . . We cannot commit *Christianity Today* to a party or candidate, I said, . . . but we are going to hold forth the principles, and the candidate who rises to them is the man who is going to reap its influence."[42]

Though not a spokesperson in the anti-Kennedy effort, Henry appears from correspondence and memos to have offered little resistance to Bell's commitment to use resources at his disposal to fight Kennedy's election. Bell was heavily involved in the anti-Kennedy propaganda campaign and articulated in his speeches and writings some of the central arguments used against Kennedy by evangelicals and fundamentalists. For example, despite Henry's stated commitment to "objective coverage" in *CT*, there is no indication that he opposed Bell's decision, made while he was at conferences in Latin America and Switzerland, to run a politically sensitive essay by a former Roman Catholic priest entitled "A Catholic for President?" Bell, Henry notes, maintained political contacts in Washington on behalf of *CT* and also knew the most about the board's desires. After lawyers warned that publishing the essay could endanger *CT*'s tax status, it was not used.[43]

It must be acknowledged, however, that a growing division between Henry and Bell led, in part, to Henry's unhappy departure from the magazine in 1968. Memos and correspondence reveal growing conflict between the two men and between Henry and *CT* board members over issues of Henry's editorial freedom as editor-in-chief and Bell's particularly close relationship with board members Billy Graham, Harold Ockenga, and J. Howard Pew. A resignation by Henry in 1961, for instance, was narrowly averted after Graham played the role of peacemaker. But Henry continued to chaff under the pressure of Pew's reactionary social and political views, often communicated via Bell, on the magazine's editorial content and direction.[44] After finally leaving *CT* in 1968, Henry cited his unwillingness to accommodate "forces" on *CT*'s board that wanted a "more aggressive denunciation of ecumenical perspectives."[45] One could infer that Henry's failure to more clearly address the bigotry of anti-Kennedy, anti-Catholic efforts was influenced to some degree by concern over the impact such a challenge would have on the future of the magazine.

CT Coverage of "the Religious Issue"

Concern over the perceived threat that Catholicism posed can be found in internal memos as well as *CT* articles, news items, editorials, and some advertising. While the editors avoided making any direct political endorsement— Bell, in particular, was extremely cautious about printing anything overtly political that might jeopardize the magazine's pending tax-exempt status with the IRS—they did address "the religious issue" prior to the election.

As early as January 1957, C. Stanley Lowell of the POAU cautioned readers that activities of the Catholic Church worldwide soon could be duplicated in the United States and outlined how the Roman Catholic Church "intimidates Congress, censors and silences opposition, collects vast sums from the public treasury and drives toward official recognition and establishment."[46] And he warned, "If the Protestants do not unite in determined opposition to this drive, another decade will see the end of Church-State separation here. We shall have, to all practical effect, a religious establishment in a country whose Constitution forbids it."[47]

An increase in news items related to Catholicism can be noted in *CT* between 1957 and 1958, with fourteen published in 1958 compared to two in 1957. Many of these related to continuing Catholic-Protestant tensions in Spain and Columbia; others dealt with various aspects of Catholicism and church-state relations in the United States, particularly federal aid to parochial schools, strongly endorsed by Catholics and opposed by Protestants. The total number of articles, news items, editorials, and letters related to Catholicism went from ten in 1957 to twenty-two in 1958. By 1959 that number climbed to thirty and in 1960 reached a high of thirty-three.

The religious issue was first directly addressed in a 1958 news report about a national television program with an inter-faith panel responding to "what it would mean to have a Roman Catholic occupying the White House."[48] It quoted a lengthy interchange from the debate to illustrate the moderator's bias against Glenn Archer, executive director of POAU, and ended by editorializing: "Participants reportedly had been admonished beforehand not to insult Catholics in whatever remarks they made. No one seemed to be worried about insulting Protestants."[49]

Articles in *CT* that year also laid an important foundation for the coverage that followed after Kennedy received the Democratic Party nomination. Another article by Lowell, "If the U.S. Becomes 51% Catholic," posed the question, "Will the United States ever become a Roman Catholic nation?" The first step by which the Roman hierarchy would gain ascendancy, he predicted, would be elimination of all restrictions on the use of tax funds to support parochial schools, followed by state stipends to priests, stepped-up grants to Catholic welfare activities, full tax support of Catholic schools, censorship of the media, and carefully restricted worship services for Protestants, including the banning of Protestant conversions once

Catholics reached a majority. A dismal prophecy followed: "Protestants would be treated with snide amusement and official contempt. They would be reduced to second-class citizens and treated as damned souls. Their young would be cajoled and bribed to leave their traditional faith. They would be steadily, systematically whittled away. They would be left at length a devout but inconsequential minority, just as Protestants are in Spain today." The article ends with a cryptic note: "After 51 per cent—*that!*" [50]

An editorial in 1959 titled "Should Americans Elect a Roman Catholic President?" never directly answered the question but documented Catholic commitment to papal infallibility, an issue that raised problems for a Catholic presidential candidate, the writer concluded: "Many observers believe that election of a Roman Catholic to the presidency of the United States sooner or later would be a threat to our freedoms and the American way of life." [51] While never mentioning or endorsing Nixon outright, this editorial makes clear the position of *CT* leaders that a Catholic should never be elected president until sections of Catholic canon law had been repudiated.

In 1959, yet another article by Lowell was published, this one addressing "the Catholic genius for politics." Lowell concludes with a caricature of Catholics designed to reinforce anti-Catholic sentiment among *CT* readers: "It is an immature concept of public function which Protestants fear in a Catholic President. They fear, too, a daily circus of priests and nuns parading in full regalia in and out of the White House to the accompaniment of endless photos on the front pages, the back pages, and the middle pages. Many of these matters involve no exercise of presidential prerogatives at all. They are matters of taste, matters of restraint on the part of the Roman Catholic church and it press agents. This is a large area in which Catholics, both lay and clerical, have much to learn." [52]

Among the "collateral results" of electing a Catholic president would be the need to balance all future political races with a Catholic on every ticket, Lowell warned, and "a sympathetic explosion of public displays of the Roman Catholic faith." Lowell stated: "Most Catholic politicians do not seem to understand the subtleties of a system like ours. They dote on public demonstrations of their denominational symbols and observances. . . . Catholics frequently show insensitivity to the religious sensibilities of those who do not share their faith. They may flaunt their religious practices and virtually force them on the entire community. They have an astonishing faculty for never suspecting that the symbol or observance which inspires them may be shocking and abhorrent to persons of another faith."[53] The way of life Lowell sought to protect—the "system like ours"—was not in any sense inclusive and assumed that Protestantism was the standard against which all other systems were to be judged.

Fourteen news articles in 1960, three major articles, and eight editorials emphasized Catholicism, Kennedy or the religious issue, and the presidential election. As expected, issues related to Catholicism received increasing emphasis during the election year, particularly in *CT* editorial columns and letters to the editor, the latter used for interchanges between POAU leaders and their detractors, as well as a lengthy letter to Kennedy from Charles Clayton Morrison, founding editor of *Christian Century* and honorary POAU chairman.

As mentioned earlier, the editorial "Bigotry or Smear?" questioned whether it was "bigotry to oppose the election of a Roman Catholic for president" and cited examples of Protestant persecution at the hands of Catholics in Colombia and Spain. Claiming that the Vatican "does all in its power to control the governments of nations," the editorial concluded that opposition to a Catholic president was not bigotry and that to suggest so was "a smear campaign."[54] As part of the coverage resulting from that editorial, Archer's "Open Letter to Ed Sullivan" in a subsequent issue of *CT*, took Sullivan to task for his criticism of *CT* in his nationally syndicated column, "Little Old New York." Archer noted the "honest reservations" of many citizens about a Catholic candidate for president and questioned why the pope, as reported in the *New York Times*, could threaten excommunication of Catholics who didn't vote as the Vatican advised without being labeled a bigot.[55]

Later, Sullivan responded with a three-column letter to the editor, "The Only Irrelevancy," published in the April 25 issue of *CT*, calling *CT*'s original editorial "an expression of bigotry designed to split Americans apart, at the exact moment when our nation is face to face with a gigantic communist conspiracy to overthrow it." "The only thing that is irrelevant" in the presidential campaign, Sullivan charged, "is the religion of Richard Nixon or the religion of John Kennedy. Let us vote for or against candidates on the basis of their proven loyalty to our form of government, and on their ability to discharge the duties of the office they seek."[56]

"The Big Debate: A Catholic President?" provided *CT*'s coverage of the West Virginia primary as well as Kennedy's address to the American Society of Newspaper Editors, where he "began to speak freely of the religious issue even while discrediting its importance," the article said. It claimed that Kennedy "scolded the press so severely that not a single editor of the 400 present took up his offer to answer questions." The final two paragraphs of the news report provide an interesting window into the effort by the *CT* reporter to get further clarification from Kennedy on the religious issue:

> Questioned privately on how he would define his primary allegiance, Kennedy initially described it to a *Christianity Today* reporter in terms of the "public interest," then indicated that it would be better expressed as a "composite" which includes "conscience."
>
> Did he feel that only a bigot would cite religious grounds for opposing a presidential candidate? No, but he said he found it hard to understand what intellectual anxiety there would be when one has answered in the negative (as Kennedy has) the all-important question: Would you be responsive to ecclesiastical pressures or obligations that might influence you in conduct in the affairs of office in the national interest?[57]

An "Open Letter to Sen. Kennedy" by Charles Clayton Morrison was published as a three-page "Letter to the Editor" in *CT* after it was rejected for publication in the *Century*. Bell was eager to publish something by this "elder statesman of religious journalists" and sought legal counsel on whether or not *CT* should do so. Morrison posed several questions to Kennedy that he claimed had been "systematically ignored" in political discussions: concern over Kennedy's understanding of the meaning of church-state separation, U.S. relations with the Vatican, the suppression of personal freedom by the Catholic Church, and federal aid to parochial schools.[58] Morrison said his questions arose not from "anti-Catholicism" but from a belief that the authoritarian nature of the Catholic Church "puts it outside of and inimical to a democratic structure of society."[59] An editor's note at the end of the letter indicated that *CT* had offered its pages to Kennedy for a reply which the magazine never received.

"Pre-Election Review of the 'Religious Issue,'" in the October 24 news section, focused on persisting Protestant "anxieties," in the face of a "lack of authoritative answers," that led to the meeting of more than 150 clergy and lay leaders from thirty-seven denominations for the National Conference of Citizens for Religious Freedom. It acknowledged that the meeting generated controversy and actually had a "suppressing effect" upon discussion of the issue, claiming: "Objectivity and impartial interpretation was hard to find in press reports of the conference, which was often pictured as Republican-oriented, fundamentalist bigotry." The article acknowledged that misunderstandings "were not entirely attributable to press bias" and noted that reporters had been barred from the proceedings, except for two who "'contrived' to hear some of the proceedings, but not all. Their piecing together was not wholly accurate." No mention was made in the coverage of Bell's role in the event or of his keynote address.[60]

Calling the religious issue "a victim of modern news media methods," one that did not lend itself "to brief summaries and 'headlinese,'" the article stated: "With a few notable exceptions, major newspapers and newsmagazines presented only the mediating and liberal views of American Protestants on the Church-State issue. The traditional Protestant position was often ignored or made to appear irrational." The report acknowledged a hate-literature campaign and "irresponsible and exaggerated charges" from extremist elements, but claimed that "many Protestants still have misgivings about a Roman Catholic in the White House" because of the silence of the Catholic hierarchy to questions raised.[61]

Defining Evangelicalism in Response to a Catholic Presidency

Central concerns in *CT* content about the religious issue—the Catholic doctrine of papal infallibility, reports of Catholic persecution of Protestants, and the Catholic position on church-state relations—were similar to those expressed on the pages of other publications, including the more politically liberal *Christian Century*. Both publications cited the poor human rights record of the Catholic Church in such countries as Colombia. Both questioned the failure of the Roman Catholic Church hierarchy to clarify its positions on papal infallibility and church-state relations. Both noted that Kennedy's attempts to distance himself from official church doctrine were of little comfort when the Vatican demanded ultimate loyalty from its members.

A lack of social and economic analysis of positions held by either political party or candidate distinguished *CT* from the *Century,* however, along with *CT*'s failure to move the campaign discussion beyond concern over Catholic doctrine. Despite Bell's strong personal devotion to Nixon, *CT* offered virtually no editorial coverage of Nixon's positions or Republican Party platforms. Furthermore, *CT* leaders repeatedly published the reactionary views of C. Stanley Lowell, amounting to five articles and one lengthy book review between 1957 and 1960. Together these present an apocalyptic vision of the disastrous effects that accommodation to Catholic pressures would bring. Writing in an oppositional style that assumed an us-them stance between Protestants and Catholics, Lowell used emotionally charged language to paint a portrait of Catholics as less committed to American values and as outsiders determined to destroy all that "true" Americans held dear. Lowell's fear-mongering, no doubt convincing to *CT* readers, leaves the impression that *CT*'s campaign coverage was primarily reactionary and bigoted, although, in fact, Lowell's writing stands alone in this regard.

CT content once Kennedy had won the election also indicates a slightly more open attitude toward the president-elect. An editorial in the November 21, 1960, issue said Kennedy needed "the good will of all citizens, a place in the prayers of God's people, and firm support for every policy that promotes the best interest of the land." During the campaign, *CT* had been concerned "with principle rather than party and personality," the editorial said, and had focused on such issues as inflation, spending, church-state relations, and expansion of the federal government. Noting that Kennedy had "courageously declared himself on the side of American rather than Vatican tradition," the editorial questioned whether his "election-year idealism will blossom into post-election realism" and added that a "hostile press" had been "lured into a shrewd campaign to label all criticism of Roman Catholicism as bigotry."[62] It presented a more dispassionate perspective on Kennedy's election than the predictions of doom to American democracy and inevitable persecution of Protestants found in Bell's correspondence.

Two months later, an editorial published just after Kennedy's inauguration stated that the event had carried with it "more the mood of destiny than in the past" and focused on Eisenhower as a man of prayer, despite his "theologically flaccid" farewell prayer that "simmer[ed] down to little more than 'faith in faith.'" The editorial writer, however, interpreted that generic prayer as appropriate in light of the principle of separation of church and state, which necessitated that "a leader whose private convictions are Christological should formulate only theistic pronouncements in his public life." The picture of a humble, God-fearing Eisenhower was contrasted to Kennedy, whose inaugural guests included "Sinatra and the Hollywood assortment of characters around him." The editorial indicated a slight but significant shift in assumptions about the place of religion in the life of the nation now that the "state religion" was no longer a generic form of Protestantism.[63] Increased religious diversification would necessitate building a higher wall between church and state and sequestering religious expression to a private sphere.

In Kennedy's first year as president, *CT*'s coverage of Catholicism continued to note Vatican pronouncements and instances of Catholic persecution of Protestants; however, its primary focus was on pending legislation that would give federal aid to parochial schools. Opposing it was a coalition of such unlikely allies as members of the National Association of Evangelicals, National Council of Churches, Southern Baptists, Seventh-Day Adventists, and POAU, according to a *CT* editorial. Serving as a test case of whether Kennedy would fulfill his campaign promise on church-state relations regardless of pressure from the Catholic hierarchy, aid for parochial schools was "no mere Protestant versus Roman Catholic squabble," the editorial stated.[64] Rather, Roman Catholic pressures were criticized as hostile to American constitutionality and to sound public policy.

Such statements indicated that evangelicals were discovering the strength of constitutional arguments for putting limitation upon the encroachment of religion—Catholicism, in this case—into the public sphere. An editorial after Kennedy's assassination said that his stance on church-state relations won him begrudging admiration from conservative Protestants because he had "kept his promise to the nation and had held the line on the church-state issue."[65]

In the June 5, 1961, issue of *CT*, Edward L. R. Elson, pastor of National Presbyterian Church in Washington, D.C., of which Eisenhower was a member, asked, "Has America Lapsed into a 'Post-Protestant' Era?" He called for "a better expression of the Protestant way of life," concluding: "Protestantism in America is neither dead nor dying. . . . Jesus said to his disciples on a mountain side, 'Ye are the salt of the earth.' That is what Protestants have been to America. They have given the taste, the tang, and meaning to American life."[66]

Elson referred to Protestantism not as the essence of American life, but as the "tang" or spice of that life. Subtle though that distinction is, it signaled a shift in how Protestantism was being constructed by evangelical spokesmen. Protestantism, Elson seemed to acknowledge, was now one of many ingredients within the melting pot of American religion. That shift was augmented by new developments within Catholicism as plans for Vatican II began to unfold.

Once Kennedy's adherence to his campaign promise had been established, evangelicals began to construct a modified image of their place in American society, a place whose security depended upon a firmly established wall of separation between church and state. Perhaps more than any other church-state issue, that of federal aid to parochial (i.e., Catholic) schools served as a litmus test for wary Protestants of how effectively the experiment with a Catholic president was working. Forced into forfeiting their image of America as a Protestant land, evangelicals endorsed, more strongly than they ever may have imagined, a separate sphere for religion as a means of ensuring no Catholic encroachment into areas of the state's purview.

Religion, considered at the start of the 1960 campaign as passé by many political analysts, proved a volatile and hotly debated campaign topic in the secular and religious press of the day. Because it marked the end of an Anglo-Saxon Protestant monopoly on American cultural identity as had no other event, Kennedy's presidency carried great symbolic significance. And at *CT,* the election of Kennedy signaled a weakening of power for such prophets of doom as Bell and an undermining of the conspiratorial worldview they promulgated.

Conservative Protestant arguments against electing a Catholic president were tied more to fear that a Catholic president would change forever "the American way of life" than to theological concerns. Convinced that American heritage was essentially Protestant, evangelicals opposed tolerance of a diversity that threatened to impinge on the dominant political

power structure. Repeated reference in speeches, articles, and correspondence to the American way of life implied an idea with which everyone
agreed. This way of life was linked to the founding fathers as an "imagined
community" of Protestant conservatives.[67] Implicit within such references
was a perception of Catholics as external enemies with an alien ideology
who were bringing conflict to an otherwise harmonious society.

The construction of evangelicalism through *CT*'s content and by its
leadership has been, to paraphrase Stuart Hall, negotiated and renegoti-
ated over time in relationship to changing social, political, or theological
influences.[68] By reinforcing certain values and ideas, *CT* leaders have shaped
evangelicals' understanding of themselves and their place in the world and
have attempted to articulate an evangelical worldview or ideology. Analyzing
what *CT* leaders defined as evangelicalism in response to the election of a
Catholic U.S. president—an event some would call a defining moment in
American religious history—reveals how evangelical ideology has been
constructed over time and how modern evangelicalism was shaped at
a defining moment in American religious history. Because *CT* leaders
saw a great need to define evangelicalism and their purposes in the face of
John F. Kennedy's potential election, this presidential campaign soon after
CT's founding provided an event that crystallized a clearer construction of
evangelicalism than at perhaps any other time. Ultimately, Kennedy's election led to increased emphasis by Protestant evangelicals on the separation of church and state in order to limit the power of the Roman Catholic
Church and prevent its encroachment into matters of the state. Today, that
perspective seems especially ironic in light of efforts by evangelicals since
the early 1990s to break down walls of separation and give religion—or, at
least, evangelicalism—its rightful place in the public square.

NOTES

1. See Mark G. Toulouse, "Christianity Today and American Public Life: A Case
    Study," *Journal of Church and State* 35, no. 2 (spring 1993): 241–284.

2. From a 1957 news release issued by another influential evangelical leader, the
    Rev. Harold J. Ockenga, senior pastor of Park Street Church in Boston as well
    as president of Fuller Theological Seminary in Pasadena, California, and of the
    National Association of Evangelicals. Ockenga coined the term "New Evangelicals"
    or "neo-evangelicalism" to describe those who accepted the basic doctrinal
    premises of fundamentalism but rejected its cultural obscurantism. In that

same press release he stated: "Fundamentalism abdicated leadership and responsibility in the societal realm and thus became impotent to change society or to solve social problems. The New Evangelicalism adheres to all the orthodox teachings of Fundamentalism but has evolved a social philosophy. The New Evangelicalism has changed its strategy from one of separation to one of infiltration. . . . The New Evangelical is willing to face the intellectual problems and meet them in the framework of modern learning. . . . The evangelical attempts to apply Christian truth to every phase of life." Ockenga continued by noting that the *Christian Century* had expressed "fear that this movement may challenge the religious scene and change the religious climate in this nation." Harold J. Ockenga, "News Release," December 8, 1957, quoted by James Laden Hedstrom in "Evangelical Program in the United States, 1945–1980: The Morphology of Establishment, Progressive, and Radical Platforms" (PhD diss., Vanderbilt University, 1982), 174–175.

3. Editorial, "Government Service as a Christian Vocation," *Christianity Today,* June 24, 1957, 22.

4. Anthony Oberschall, *Social Movements: Ideologies, Interests, and Identities* (London: Transaction Publishers, 1993), 21–22.

5. Founded as a counterbalance to the theologically and politically liberal *Christianity and Crisis* and *Christian Century,* CT (*Christianity Today*) had within eight months surpassed the *Century*'s circulation, Henry stated in a Report to the Board, May 28, 1957. Thanks to a $400,000 start-up grant from J. Howard Pew, chairman of the board of the Sun Oil Company and a political and theological conservative, *CT* was sent free of charge to Protestant clergy and seminary students and faculty for the first year. By 1957 it was reporting paid subscriptions of 43,000 and a controlled circulation of 120,000 to 130,000. By September 1958, Henry reported that *CT* was not just responding to issues of the day, but steering the course of the debate, citing as examples a series on eschatology and *CT*'s coverage of the British involvement in the fundamentalist-modernist debate (Henry, Report to the Board, September 9, 1958).

6. David Noble, *The End of American History* (Minneapolis: University of Minnesota Press, 1989), 64.

7. Theodore H. White, in his book *The Making of the President, 1960* (Atheneum Publishers, 1961), noted that between 1928 (the year Catholic candidate Alfred E. Smith ran for president) and 1957, the percentage of Catholics in the United States had grown from 13 percent to 26 percent and that from 1950 to 1959, due to "the Catholic birth rate," the Catholic population had increased by 35.8 percent. Meanwhile, the general population increased by 16.6 percent, giving the Catholic sector 41 percent of the population growth in the country, he concluded.

8. Fletcher Knebel, "Democratic Forecast: A Catholic in 1960," *Look,* March 3, 1959, 41.

9. "Texts of Speeches by Kennedy, Symington, and Humphrey at Editors' Convention," *New York Times,* April 22, 1960, 16.

10. "Transcript of Kennedy Talk to Ministers," *New York Times,* September 13, 1960, 22.

11. Letter from Bell to Rev. Dr. Lee Ralph Phipps, Townsville, Pennsylvania, November 14, 1960, Billy Graham Center Archives, Wheaton College, Wheaton, Illinois.

12. Letter from Bell to Thomas W. Ferguson of River Plain Farms, Ferguson, North Carolina, September 24, 1960, Billy Graham Center Archives.

13. Letter from Bell to Henry, July 9, 1959, Billy Graham Center Archives.

14. Letter from Bell to Vice President Richard Nixon, July 6, 1959, Billy Graham Center Archives. There is no indication that such an article for *CT* was ever written by Nixon.

15. Letter from Bell to Vice President Richard Nixon, July 6, 1959, Billy Graham Center Archives.

16. "Latest on 'The Religious Issue,'" *U.S. News and World Report,* September 19, 1960, 97.

17. L. Nelson Bell, "Protestant Distinctives and the American Crisis," an address given in Montreat, N.C., on August 21, 1960, and in Washington, D.C., on September 7, 1960. This address was later published in brochure form by the Presbyterian Journal Book Room, Weaverville, N.C. As one admirer wrote to Bell, "I doubt if Tom Paine ever wrote a better pamphlet than yours!" Letter to Bell from Mrs. Lillie Mae Wheeling, Birmingham, Alabama, November 15, 1960, Billy Graham Center Archives.

18. Bell, "Protestant Distinctives and the American Crisis."

19. Ibid.

20. "Facts the Voters Should Know," advertisement in "a local paper" sent to Bell by W. B. Rouse, New Bern, N.C.; and letter from Bell to Rouse, November 8, 1960, Billy Graham Center Archives.

21. Billy Graham, *Just As I Am* (San Francisco: HarperCollins, 1997), 391–392.

22. Ibid., 391.

23. Ibid., 392.

24. Ibid., 332.

25. Ibid., 390.

26. Ibid.

27. From the Billy Graham Center Archives.

28. "*CT* at Thirty," *Christianity Today,* November 18, 1986, 20.

29. A weekly newspaper editor on Long Island and stringer for the *New York Times,* the *New York Herald-Tribune,* and the *Chicago Tribune,* Henry became a Christian in his twenties and then went to Wheaton College in the late 1930s. There he met Graham and other future evangelical leaders. After earning a ThD from Northern Baptist Theological Seminary and a PhD from Boston University, he taught for almost ten years at Fuller Theological Seminary in Pasadena,

California, before leaving in 1956 to help launch *CT*. Throughout his lifetime Henry wrote thirty-eight books and edited another eleven.

30. Graham, quoted in Carl F. H. Henry, *Confessions of a Theologian: An Autobiography* (Waco, TX: Word Books, 1976), 196.

31. Ibid., 193.

32. Letter to the *CT* Board of Directors from Bell, August 4, 1960, Billy Graham Center Archives.

33. Henry, *Confessions*, 195.

34. Carl F. H. Henry, "Religion in a Free Society," *Christianity Today,* May 26, 1958, 30.

35. Ibid., 34.

36. Ibid.

37. Henry, *Confessions*, 194.

38. Glenn L. Archer, "Open Letter to Ed Sullivan," *Christianity Today,* March 14, 1960, 23.

39. Ed Sullivan, "The Only Irrelevancy," in "Eutychus and His Kin," *Christianity Today,* April 25, 1960, 17–18.

40. "What's Fair in Politics?" *Christianity Today,* April 25, 1960, 27.

41. Written summary of Henry's half-hour conversation with Nixon at the Capitol on April 14, 1960, Billy Graham Center Archives.

42. Henry, *Confessions*, 196.

43. Ibid.

44. Ibid., 254–266.

45. Ibid., 290.

46. Henry quoted in C. Stanley Lowell, "Rising Tempo of Rome's Demands," *Christianity Today,* January 7, 1957, 11.

47. Ibid., 13. Two years later *CT* reported that this article had "reached a million people," no doubt through the literature distribution of the POAU. See C. Stanley Lowell, "Protestants, Catholics, and Politics," *Christianity Today,* July 20, 1959, 5.

48. "Religion and the Presidency," in "News," *Christianity Today,* June 23, 1958, 30.

49. Ibid., 31.

50. C. Stanley Lowell, "If the U.S. Becomes 51% Catholic," *Christianity Today,* October 27, 1958, 8.

51. "Should Americans Elect a Roman Catholic President?" *Christianity Today,* October 26, 1959, 23.

52. Lowell, "Protestants, Catholics," 8.

53. Ibid.

54. "Bigotry or Smear?" *Christianity Today,* February 1, 1960, 4, 20. See Glenn L. Archer, "Open Letter to Ed Sullivan," March 14, 1960, 23; and Ed Sullivan, "The Only Irrelevancy," April 25, 1960, 17, in *Christianity Today.*

55. Archer, "Open Letter," 23.

56. Sullivan, "Irrelevancy," 17.

57. "The Big Debate: A Catholic President?" *Christianity Today,* May 9, 1960, 33.

58. Charles Clayton Morrison, "Open Letter to Sen. Kennedy," *Christianity Today,* September 12, 1960, 18, 32–33.

59. Ibid., 33.

60. "Pre-Election Review of the 'Religious Issue,'" *Christianity Today,* October 24, 1960, 25.

61. Ibid., 31.

62. "Another Era Underway in the American Venture," *Christianity Today,* November 21, 1960, 21.

63. "Transition in Washington and the Need of Prayer," *Christianity Today,* January 30, 1961, 24.

64. "Public Funds for Public Schools," *Christianity Today,* April 10, 1961, 20.

65. "The Assassination of the President," *Christianity Today,* December 6, 1963, 24.

66. Edward L. Elson, "Has America Lapsed into a 'Post-Protestant' Era?" *Christianity Today,* June 5, 1961, 5.

67. See Benedict Anderson, *Imagined Communities* (New York: Verso, 1983).

68. Stuart Hall, "Encoding/decoding," in *Culture, Media, Language: Working Papers in Cultural Studies, 1972–1979* (London: Routledge, 1992), 138–138. First published in 1980 by the Academic Division of Unwin Hyman Publishers Ltd.

8

Religion as Rhetorical Resource

The Muslim Immigrant in (Danish) Public Discourse

FERRUH YILMAZ

In the Western world, Muslims have long been depicted as the "Other" in public discourse, an idea brought home with the 2006 controversy and worldwide
protests surrounding the publication of the Mohammed cartoons in the Danish
periodical *Jyllands-Posten*. This controversy brings to the fore an important
question in the realm of religion's representation in the media and in the marketplace: How is it that such stereotypical practices persist (perhaps especially)
in Western countries where multiculturalism is often celebrated and where
rational understanding is seen as a logical outcome of journalism and its role in
creating an informed public? In this chapter, Ferruh Yilmaz addresses this question through an analysis of the political discourse about immigration in Denmark
and through a close examination of how individuals in Denmark negotiate the
issue of immigration in the context of interpersonal interviews. Long considered
to be a tolerant and antiracist society, Denmark has been touted as an exemplar
of northern European progressivism. Yilmaz traces the ways in which this self-
perception contributed the success of anti-immigration campaigns that influenced Denmark's elections at the turn of the millennium.

When Seinfeld (an actor and the main character in the once-popular
American sitcom of his name) blames society for all the problems his friend
George has, it is meant as a joke. We have become suspicious of statements
such as "society does this" or "society does that"; we know that society as an
abstract category with independent agency does not make much sense.

When it comes to religion or culture, these reservations are put aside and sweeping generalizations are made without hesitation. We talk about religion, particularly Islam, as if it is a well-defined totality governed by a rigid set of rules and as if its totality determines every single act of its "members." I suggest taking a Seinfeldian approach to religion: we cannot talk about religion as if it has independent agency. The basic premise for this chapter is straightforward: Islam does not exist. It is impossible to locate it as a unified or homogenous set of practices, ideas, or beliefs. It has no central representational system through which anyone is authorized to speak. Yet, we speak of Islam as Seinfeld speaks of society, only without the attached sarcasm, with consequences all too real and at times lethal for people who are designated as Muslims. If Islam does not exist as a unity, why do we talk about it as if it does? More importantly, what does such talk do? It is the goal of this chapter to explore this question.

When Jean-Marie Le Pen of the National Front eliminated Socialist Prime Minister Lionel Jospin in the first round of France's presidential election in 2002, it became an embarrassment for established social democratic regimes throughout Europe. Le Pen's success was not a sudden development but was the result of a decades-long transformation of French public discourse. The cultural framing of the immigration debate as we know it today gained its taken-for-granted status during the 1980s, although its current articulation is only one among many ways that immigration had been understood in the 1960s and 1970s. Le Pen's National Front had successfully articulated immigration (as well as the European Union) as a threat to the French nation and had linked immigration with the European Union threat, with regionalist movements, with the maintenance of the social welfare state, and with increasing unemployment.[1]

Far Right populist movements with similar anti-immigrant views have been gaining ground all over Europe, from Italy and Austria to Belgium and Holland. Nowhere is the contrast between the old political discourse and the new more dramatic than in Denmark, however. As the title of an article in the *New York Times*, "Denmark Is Unlikely Front in Islam-West Culture War" (January 8, 2006), suggests, Denmark is an "unlikely" location for such unrest, at least in relation to the general image of Denmark as an "icon of northern European welfare-state progressivism, and the erstwhile poster child of liberal immigration policy."[2] A basic premise for this chapter is that there can be no culture war between Islam and the West since they are not given, clearly definable entities with independent agencies.

Before moving into a more detailed discussion, I first review the theory of Orientalism and hegemony so as to set up a framework for studying the construction of the West-versus-Islam dichotomy and its consequences. Next, I analyze Danish public discourse on immigration to show how the dichotomy between Danishness and Islam has moved into the center of social life. I then analyze interviews conducted with native Danes to examine how popular discourse orients itself toward the hegemonic articulation. My main goal is to illustrate how flexible ideas about immigrants, religion, and culture are "fixed" into hegemonic articulations through rhetorical tools such as explanatory links and opinion polls.

Orientalism, the West, and Islam

On July 28, 2002, Robert A. Kittle, an editor, published a page-long article in the *San Diego Union-Tribune* on Islamic awakening, after having returned from a three-week study tour of the Islamic world. The article began thus:

> Flanking sun-drenched Sultanahmet Square, overlooking the Bosphorus in the heart of the old city, stand two of the finest architectural achievements in the world: the magnificent Aya Sofya, or Church of Holy Wisdom, and the imposing Blue Mosque. Completed under the Byzantine emperor Justinian in 536 A.D., the soaring Aya Sofya, with its ethereal mosaics of Christ, John the Baptist and the Virgin Mary, is a powerful testament to Christendom and Western civilization in general. In contrast, the stunningly beautiful Blue Mosque, erected 1,100 years later during the Ottoman era to upstage the Aya Sofya, is an equally potent tribute to Islam. The two nearby monuments symbolize the age-old rivalry between two cultures: the largely democratic and secularized West, built on the Enlightenment ideals of reason and individual liberty spawned in 18th century Europe and America; and the largely authoritarian and theocratic societies of the Muslim world, shaped over the past 14 centuries by the unchanging orthodoxy of the Holy Koran.

Eager to describe the culture clash between Western civilization and Islam (which in turn was not defined as a civilization), Kittle collapses the wide variety of Muslim religious and political traditions and practices into one single category of "unchanging orthodoxy" that, he seems to claim, has had no interaction with modernity, secularization, or rationality. His language is deceptive: although he seems to be speaking of two rival cultures, Christianity is not understood as a culture in the same sense as Islam. Whereas the spirit of Christianity cannot be comprehended through the Holy Bible, Islam, in his interpretation, is reduced to the Koran because as a holy book it does not change.

It is easy to find similar descriptions of Islam in vernacular writings and academic research. This process of collapsing Islam into a singular idea that is opposed to the Christian West is foundational to Edward Said's argument in *Orientalism*.[3] He defined Orientalism as an academic discipline with a style of thought and a corporate institution that has been based "upon on ontological and epistemological distinction made between 'the Orient' and 'the Occident.'"[4] An Orientalist style of thought constructs "the Orient" as a clear, distinct, and identifiable entity out of a shapeless mass of impressions from a vide variety of geographies, cultures, or practices. The Orient has to be produced as a totalized entity out of many and vastly different societies and traditions by treating the differences as parts of the same essence. This is what Ernesto Laclau and Chantal Mouffe called hegemonic articulation—different elements that have no necessary relationship with one another are articulated together in an equivalential chain.[5] The Orient is thus a Western invention; it is a product of Orientalist inscription that signifies not a cultural or geographical entity but the distinction between the Orient and the West. The Orient does not have an essence because the true essence of the Orient always escapes predication and can only be represented in opposition to another totality ("the West"). But as Said reminds us in *Covering Islam,* the relationship between these totalities is not symmetrical: "We must immediately note that it is always the West, not Christianity, that seems pitted against Islam. Why? Because the assumption is that whereas 'the West' is greater than and has surpassed the stage of Christianity, its principal religion, the world of Islam— its varied societies, histories, and languages notwithstanding—is still mired in religion, primitivity and backwardness."[6]

In other words, Islam helps to produce the West as—as Kittle puts it in the earlier quote—"democratic and secularized, built on the Enlightenment ideals of reason and individual liberty." If this narrative—that the Western civilization, having transcended religion, evolved into reason and modernity—is to make sense, it is necessary to push the Other back in time. This is a hegemonic operation that produces a relationship of domination between the West and the Islamic Orient.

The first step is to delimit the object of examination—the Islamic Orient. Certain ideas, beliefs, and practices have to be emphasized as the essence of the object. It means that the Orient is not a given that awaits examination by the experts; it has to be produced discursively (through emphases and omissions). As Michel Foucault reminded us, discourses produce not only the object of inquiry but also the subject position from which the inquirer speaks. Producing knowledge about a group means producing power over that group. The examiner "knows" more about the object of study—the Islamic Orient—than the Orientals can ever know. This knowledge produces the moral and scientific authority of the examiner and others who share the knowledge/authority (Western intellectuals, politicians, journalists, institutions, and corporations). In other words, a discourse about the Orient and Islam not only produces them as examinable categories but constructs the very identity of the West as the examiner. As the locus of the examiner, the West becomes something greater than religion; it is a scientific center of inquiry based on reason. If Christianity (rather than the West) was compared to Islam, they would just be two different but equal religions among other religions and symbolic systems; there would be nothing antagonistic between them. In this case, Islam would not be constitutive of the West.

This is why Kittle can make the church, John the Baptist, and the Virgin Mary stand for enlightenment ideals rather than religion. Islam is no longer the symbol for just another religion with specific content but religion per se. It is, to borrow from structuralist anthropology and Lacanian psychoanalysis,[7] an "empty signifier" of no symbolic value in itself. The struggle for hegemony is the struggle to fill this empty space with specific meaning. In Orientalist discourse, Islam is filled with characteristics such as backwardness, authoritarianism, and dogmatism. For fundamentalist Islamists, the West stands for corruption, fakeness, and oppression, whereas Islam signifies truth, purity, and anti-imperialist struggle. In this sense, both the Orientalist discourse and Islamic fundamentalism articulate their identities around the same frontier between the West and Islam.

Islam versus Danish Culture: The New Ontology of the Social

In Denmark, during the 1980s, the extreme Right seized the popular discourse by creating an antagonism between Danish "people" and the cosmopolitan political and cultural elite. In this vision, these leaders were to blame for the problems of immigration because they permitted immigration from Muslim countries, thus allowing these immigrants to become what the Far Right claims is a threat to Danish national identity and culture. Thus these newcomers to Denmark came to be signified mainly by the category "the Muslim immigrant." [8] In this articulation, Danishness has been connoted with rationality, freedom, individualism, progress, and efficiency; the capacity to negotiate and reach consensus; the nation-state' democracy; and Christianity as well as secularism. Immigrant (Muslim) culture is constructed as the opposite: irrational, prejudiced, emotional, intolerant, criminal, alien, one-sided, ineffective, backward, culturally and traditionally bound, and despotic. This articulation draws on the new hegemonic order of the world: Danishness is equated with the West, while the immigrant stands for the Middle East, or more precisely the new "enemy" that is Islam. Islam, therefore, is a category that signifies the antagonism between religious fanaticism and enlightened individualism.[9]

Most articles, books, and research reports on immigration in Denmark begin with the mantra that the problems with immigration in Denmark reflect huge demographic changes.[10] For instance, two prominent Danish political scientists begin their influential book on Danes' attitudes toward immigrants with the much-repeated wisdom that "the Scandinavian countries have long had some of the most uniform—or homogenous—populations in the world. . . . It is hardly wrong to describe post-war Scandinavian countries as relatively free of ethnic dividing lines." [11]

The problem with this narrative is not so much whether Denmark was really ethnically homogenous in the past but its understanding of the past through the perspective of the contemporary discourse. Everybody would agree that ethnic homogeneity was not a great concern prior to the 1980s, but there is a fundamental difference with regard to how one might explain the focus on ethnicity in current discourse. Some, whose viewpoints could be characterized as "positivist," see the preoccupation with ethnic homogeneity as the result of immigration from culturally alien countries. In this perspective, homogeneity would not be a concern in a homogenous society; only an external intrusion would bring it to the forefront. Yet for others who take what might be called a "constructivist" view of history, ethnicity (Danishness) is a political construct that has "the status of the ontology of the social." [12] It means that we come to understand our social selves (social divisions) in terms of ethnicity today, but we project this understanding back into the past as if ethnicity was the main dividing line then. In other words, immigrants from other societies could as well have been conceived in terms other than ethnic/cultural. Previously, social struggles were articulated as struggles between the working class and capitalists, feminists and the male power, or gays and homophobic social structures. Since the mid-1980s, the topic of immigration has been reconfigured away from these struggles and has moved into the center of public discourse as the defining source of social identifications. The main struggle is no longer conceived as being between the working class and capitalists but between ethnic Danes as a cohesive society and the Muslim intruders who threaten cohesion and the existence of the welfare state (welfare state is now understood as a result of a cohesive—homogenous—Danish society rather than the outcome of class struggles).

The point is this: if there is a relationship between demography and ethnicity, it is a hermeneutic relationship based on a hegemonic articulation of an ethnic antagonism. It means that there is no necessary relationship between demographic change itself and conceptualization of it in ethnic-cultural terms. In fact, even in anthropology, the notion of ethnicity did not come into widespread use until the 1960s. [13]

A quick look at how immigration was debated in earlier periods illustrates this argument. Bent Jensen's overview of the media coverage of immigration in the Danish media since the 1870s demonstrates that the debate on immigration throughout history shows similarities and differences. [14] In the second half of the nineteenth century, the immigration debate was about the Swedish workers. The actual debate was characterized by themes such as criminality, cultural differences, economic burden, and social problems. The working class (which at that point was in the making politically and organizationally) simultaneously opposed immigration and supported immigrants. The workers opposed immigration because Swedish workers were used to break strikes and suppress wage increases. But at the same time, working-class organizations were inherently internationalist (I mean internationalists, not international in scope), which meant that the working-class identity was in the center regardless of national background. Thus, the criticism against Swedish workers was subdued as long as they were organized in labor unions. For the right-wing political organizations, immigrants were just another source for increasing production and profit. Immigration was thus an element introduced to the discursive (social) relations, and the struggle was about how to configure that element within the framework of the main social division (workers versus capitalists).

If one insists on the positivist interpretations of the history, objections may be made that Swedish workers were not culturally different from Danish workers. Yet, Jensen's overview of the latest phase of immigration from Muslim countries in the 1960s and 1970s shows similar patterns. Immigrants were mainly discussed in terms of their contribution to and burden on the welfare system. Working-class organizations were again ambiguous in their attitude: they accepted the import of a foreign workforce as long as those workers were organized and hired on the basis of labor agreements (so that they did not split the working-class movement but were made part of it). Also in this period, concerns about wage suppression, working conditions, criminality, and social problems dominated the debate.

This contrasts with the contemporary immigration debate, where the focus is entirely on immigrants' culture. There is a general consensus among researchers that the change dates back to the mid-1980s, when the focus shifted from immigrants' social problems to their problematic culture, which is mainly expressed in terms of the "Muslim threat." At the beginning of the 1980s, the focus was on "respectful integration of immigrants" and "immigrants' rights"; in the second half, Danes discussed "making demands of immigrants," "refugees of convenience," and "the Muslim threat." [15] There was a remarkable jump in the polls of Danes' views on "whether immigrants constitute a threat to our national character": 23 percent declared agreement with the statement in 1985 while around 40 percent agreed after 1987. The media coverage, too, was extremely concerned with the "Muslim threat." [16]

Since then the Muslim threat has been the dominant theme in Danish public discourse on immigration. But merely illustrating the discursive change does not necessarily indicate the hegemonic status of the immigration discourse. My argument is that the discursive change is not limited to the way immigrants are discussed: the discourse on immigration has moved into the center of public discourse, and immigrants have come to signify the social antagonisms within society.

The clearest articulation of the antagonism is a controversial book published by the anti-immigrant Danish People's Party (DPP) in 2001: *Denmark's Future: Your Country—Your Choice* . . . has on the cover a picture of a fierce-looking, bearded Muslim immigrant wielding a gun in a demonstration on the main square of Copenhagen (the picture had been previously published in the liberal daily *Politiken*).[17] The book is organized in two parts. The first section contains a brief history of immigration, statistics on immigration, cases of immigrant's criminality, problems with immigrants in Germany, international conventions, and the relationship between religion, culture, and democracy. The second part is called "Denmark's Future" and contains a discussion of DPP's proposals to keep Denmark as a cohesive country. The first part draws a picture of a Denmark ridden with problems because of immigrants and their culture (one of the chapters is called "The Impossible Combination of Islam and Democracy"); the second part creates an image of an idyllic Denmark that will be restored to its original state through the DPP's proposals.

The visual organization of the book gives the text a very specific meaning and impact. The first part contains many photographs of immigrants in everyday situations, but the combination of photos, illustrations of the Danish flag, and the text about changing demographics relays an image of a Denmark that is being invaded by alien intruders (including women with headscarves). This image is contrasted by the visual organization of the second part. The second part, titled "Denmark's Future," features a photo of an idyllic, flower-covered Danish meadow under a clear blue sky, echoing the tradition of landscape paintings that have been an important part of the Danish nation-making process.[18] Accompanying explanations of the

Danish People's Party's policies in this section are idyllic pictures of pristine lakes, deep green woods, colorful cottages, white swans, peaceful Danes in everyday activities, and beautiful, smiling children—almost all of whom are blond. In short, the nationalist-racist antagonism between the Danish nation and the Muslim-alien threat is represented by these two sections: one describes the grim realities of Denmark; the other describes the desire for a cohesive Danish nation.

If the antagonistic picture painted by the DPP was limited only to the rhetoric of the extreme Right, this would not constitute what I call a racist hegemony. What makes it hegemonic is that this characterization is echoed in mainstream discourse, in communication by institutions, and in legal provisions. The liberal daily newspaper *Politiken*, for example, had a number of articles on immigration in August 2001. The logo of the theme was a picture of three young immigrant women with headscarves walking by a shop window that featured three almost naked mannequins wearing lingerie and decorated with Danish flags. In the summer of 2001, *Politiken* and right-wing *Jyllands-Posten* had a fierce debate on feminism and Muslim women, and the debate pages were full of contrasting images of women in burkas or with headscarves and blond Danish women who were in Western clothes or half-clothed (they are actually naked). The photos were chosen to illustrate the claims of feminists who described Muslim culture as oppressive and sexist. There is much to say about the way the debate was covered, but my point here is that both liberal and conservative newspapers chose to illustrate immigration stories pictures connoting an antagonism between Danishness and immigrant (Muslim) culture.

Another striking example of the change since the mid-1980s is illustrated in how the queen of Denmark has been involved in the debate. In her annual New Year's speech on December 31, 1985, Queen Margrethe intervened in the debate on immigration and scolded Danes for their negative attitudes toward immigrants, calling their utterances "dumb-smart." The tone was clearly humanitarian, and she promoted tolerance toward the new "guests," who, she noted, may have problems adjusting to Danish society. Two decades later, the queen stated that she was "crazily naïve" when she called Danes "dumb-smart," for she now realizes that Islam constitutes a great challenge for Danes.

Populist Ideas Move to the Center of Political Discourse

Despite this gradual shift in the immigration debate, it came as a surprise for the rest of the world when the immigration debate took center stage during an inflammatory election campaign in November 2001. The DPP's landslide victory attracted world-wide attention. Yet this was an election in which every major party in Denmark competed to appear tough on immigration. The opposition (the Liberals, the Conservatives, and the DPP) managed to capitalize on this climate of fears, moral panics, and enemy images and ousted the Social Democratic–Radical Party coalition despite the fact that traditional economic indicators looked good and unemployment rates were at record-low levels. The Liberal Party adopted a rhetoric similar to that of the DPP and had the Muslim threat as the focus of its campaign with the election slogan, "Time for change." The election poster carried a well-known photo of Muslim immigrant youths leaving the court after having been convicted of the "gang rape" of a white Danish girl. They created the expectation that not only could they put a virtual stop to any further inflows of undesirable aliens, but they could also reinstate Denmark to its former status as a peaceful, ethnically homogeneous, and politically sovereign welfare state.[19] Immigration has since been at the center of the policies within the Liberal/ Conservative government and was in part the reason for that government's repeated the electoral success in February 2005.

According to the latest integration law proposal (December 2005), all immigrants seeking work and residence permits in Denmark will have to sign a declaration that sets up detailed but elusive criteria for earning the right to stay in Denmark. The declaration makes explicit all of the points that I have been making about the articulation of an incommensurable dichotomy between two fundamentally different cultures: civilized and reflexive, on the one hand, and barbaric and primitive, on the other. According to the proposal, a foreigner seeking a residency permit has to declare allegiance to Danish laws and democratic principles; must become self-providing, pay taxes, and respect gender equality and sexual orientation; must not discriminate on the basis of gender or skin color; must not participate in terrorist activities; and, if a male, must promise not to beat up his wife or children. The penalty for not fulfilling the declaration ranges from a reduction in welfare payments (if one receives any) to losing a residency permit altogether.

Many of the provisions in the declaration are not revolutionary: immigrants have long been deported if they commit crimes, restricted in their geographical mobility, and denied the right to bring family members from other countries. What is new is the clear expression of perceived cultural/ethnic difference that echoes Orientalist binaries: Muslim immigrants hail from primitive cultures and thus embrace the opposite of the modern, emancipated, democratic values of Denmark.

The transformation of the Liberal Party (in coalition with the Conservative Party) is particularly interesting as it is intimately connected to the central role that immigration has come to play in creating visions for the future of Denmark. The leader of the party, Prime Minister Anders Fogh Rasmussen, in his book *From Social State to Minimal State,* argued that inequality was a motivating force for society and that it was the individual that was at the center of focus. A decade later, "cultural struggle" has moved into the center, and he declared: "It is the result of the cultural struggle that determines Denmark's future, not the economic policy. If you want to steer a society in a different direction, you have to take on the debate on values" (interview in *Weekendavisen,* January 17, 2003). In his speech in the parliament on February 24, 2005, he formulated his vision for the future as "a Danish society with a strong competitive ability and with a strong cohesive force—a society without great social and economic inequalities." The obstacle for that vision is "an aggressive practice of Islam [that provides] the greatest challenge to the cohesive force in Danish society." The source of the problem is "some isolated groups of immigrants who challenge the democratic values" (*Jyllands-Posten,* November 28, 2005).

As this shift in vision illustrates, cultural antagonism has moved into the center of social ontology. It is not that the representatives of the racist populist movement have come to power (although they have gained considerable influence in parliamentary politics). Rather, their vision for society as ethnically homogenous and thus a cohesive community has been adopted by the mainstream political establishment.

Immigrants as a Topic in Interaction

The dichotomous framework of Muslims and Danes is also prevalent in everyday talk among ordinary Danes. In a previous interview-based research project among ethnic Danes in 1996, I found that immigrants, culture, and

Islam are often described by ethnic Danes as the greatest problems facing Denmark.[20] In the current project, I analyzed twenty qualitative interviews conducted in 2001 with ordinary ethnic Danes. This time, the questions were not confined to "views" on immigrants; ethnic Danes were also asked to describe Danish culture. To avoid cueing the participants into a given dichotomy (immigrants versus Danes), the interviewers were instructed to begin their interviews with general questions about Denmark and its place in the wider world. A quick overview of the interviews shows that when the talk moves to the topic of immigration, the range of "explanatory frameworks" that people use becomes limited to this cultural and religious dichotomy.[21]

At first sight, three themes emerged in these conversations: (1) the construction of a framework of dichotomy that contrasts the "freedom" of Danish society with the "faith" of immigrants; (2) the belief that faith is directly related to and results in social problems; and (3) the equation of immigrants with criminal activities. These themes reflected people's orientation toward political concerns rather than merely their mindset about Muslim immigrants, an idea I will return to at a later point.

When asked about immigrants, one respondent immediately articulated the dichotomy of the purported freedom of Danish society in contrast to the faith of immigrants: "It is difficult to integrate them in Danish [culture] that is so free because they have such a strong faith" (Louise). Another respondent similarly relied on the dichotomy of religious similarities and differences: "Previous immigrants have been Jewish and Christian. They were similar to us, so it has been easy to integrate them. I don't think Muslims will be integrated. It hasn't been the case" (Klaus). Similarly singling out Muslim immigrants as more problematic than other groups, another respondent said: "Immigrants are Arabs and Somalis. There are also many Chinese but they fit into the street image. At least, they don't wear the scarf" (Trine). Another noted, "I would admit that it may be my prejudice, but in my thought most of them [immigrants] are Muslims" (Ulla).

According to the statistics, only half of the total number of immigrants (about 4.2 percent are Muslims, compared to a total of 8.2 percent who are immigrants) are from countries normally associated with the term "third world" (including non-Muslim countries such as Sri Lanka or Vietnam), but the interesting point here is not whether or not these utterances actually reflect reality. Rather they reflect the focus on Muslims in immigration discourse as the source of contemporary problems, as Trine's statement about Chinese immigrants illustrates. Trine is clearly aware of the existence of other immigrants, but as a general category immigrants are signified by their headscarves because people with headscarves are excluded from the repeated vision of how Denmark has been and should be. Klaus may or may not actually think that Jewish and Christian immigrants were similar to "us." As my brief summary of the earlier debates showed, cultural differences and social problems were also themes in the debate even in the case of Swedish immigrants who can understand and speak with Danes.[22] Furthermore, Jewish immigrants' own accounts show that Jewish immigration was far from painless and they were discriminated against. Thus, Klaus's statement is not an actual assessment of the problems with earlier immigration; rather it has a rhetorical function in this interactional context: to exclude the Muslim immigrants through a particular narrative of the past from the perspective of today's hegemonic discourse. He employs circular logic to support his claim that Muslim immigrants cannot be integrated: "They cannot be integrated because it has not been the case." If he were to judge the success of integration by the same criteria—assuming that Jews are integrated in the way he talks about Muslim immigrants—he would have to wait a few centuries.

That the particularities of Islam are very much related to problems of immigration was clear in other respondents' comments. In response to the question, "What is the biggest concern in relation to immigrants?" one woman replied, "I think of criminality and mass rapes. It originates in their weird, precarious view on their own women and Danish women" (Inger). Another similarly noted, "It is scary [to think] that they maybe have a completely different way of thinking than us. What you mostly hear from Muslim countries are things like oppression of women and dictatorship and holy war and such things" (Trine). This difference between "their" culture and "ours" means that, as one respondent noted, "My set of values tell me that you don't kick down an old lady" (Birgitte), and that "They have to learn that you do not steal and you do not rape young women" (Dorthe). Another woman noted, "Here we don't kill [people]. We don't do such things in Denmark. It is illegal, and it is punishable" (Emma).

Muslim immigrants, thus, were frequently equated with crime and criminals in these conversations, something that was explained as an outgrowth of their very different culture. However, it is the antagonistic framework that makes possible the explanatory links between criminality and Islam rather than their view of what Islamic culture really is. In the flow of conversation, the respondents were often not questioned about the details of their utterances, but in a few cases, when they were asked to reflect about what they had said, they felt the need to make qualifications. None of the respondents insisted that Islam tells its followers to "commit crime and gang rapes," "kick down an old lady," "steal and rape young woman," or "kill people." They were not able to sustain the view that Muslims rape because they lack sexual emancipation when asked to explain Danish rapists, who are presumably raised in a culture of sexual emancipation. When forced to reflect, respondents acknowledged that in Muslim countries stealing, murder, rape, or violence are not legal nor would Muslim immigrants expect such acts to be unpunishable in Denmark.[23] My sample is full of utterances such as, "I am not saying that all Danes are angels. There have always been rapists, but examples of rape by a group [of men] are difficult to find among pure Danes. I don't know if it has anything to do with the lack of sexual emancipation" (Anne-Sofie). These kinds of rebuttals often have their own rhetorical purposes but nevertheless show the difficulty of sustaining a consistent description of Islam or Muslim immigrants as criminals. Rather, these utterances are used to exclude the Muslim immigrant from the "imagined community." The utterances also show that the explanatory links are made arbitrarily and haphazardly rather than on the basis of firm beliefs about the essence of immigrants' Muslim culture. Yet these rhetorical constructions have material consequences for Muslim immigrants who are discriminated against with reference to their culture in their everyday encounters with Danes (e.g., when a Muslim immigrant is refused a job because "he does not respect female leaders") and in terms of their legal rights (Denmark has the toughest anti-immigration rules in Europe, including a rule preventing immigrants age twenty-four or younger from bringing in spouses from outside Denmark).[24]

The point here is that immigrants (or Muslims or Islam) are, in a sense, empty categories whose status is defined not so much by any actual features but by the place they are assigned in an antagonistic relationship to the category of Danes whose features also are defined in this process. The category of immigrants, and with it Islam, then, signifies that which is excluded from Danish identity. This point becomes clearer with these statements from native Danes about Danish culture.

In their statements, Danes stressed the importance of "equality" and anti-elitism in their culture, noting their "independence" from traditional sources of power and authority. This sense of egalitarianism is often described as the backbone of Danish culture. "Danes are more recumbent and easygoing . . . [and] they do not care so much about money and status" (Trine). As one respondent noted, "It is like a Danish mentality that we think we are all equal in Denmark, and that there isn't anybody who has more advantages than others, and that we all have a right to be treated in the health system, and then that everybody has free schooling" (Dorthe). These values are also directly related to a specific religious tradition: "The Christian value base: It is things like you have to take care of the weak. You have to be good with each other. And also we do not punish with capital punishment . . . in Denmark and Europe" (Trine). Even though they are different from those of other European cultures, Danes acknowledge a shared religious and political heritage with Europeans, as the same respondent notes, "We have a common European cultural background with Americans and Australians" (Trine). Another respondent also commented on what this shared heritage has meant in Denmark: "I think it is very clear that language is one of the greatest identity makers . . . because it is what we think with, what we see with . . . [B]ut it is not the grammar that makes us so rationally minded as we are . . . [I]t is a shared history . . . Americans must also be able to find their sources in Greece or in the New Testament" (Niels).

Yet Danes, other respondents noted, are not overly religious, and this freedom from religion is also something to be prized and is a reason for the culture's egalitarianism, according to one respondent: "I think our religiosity has been watered down very much, maybe because we are doing so well, because we have also achieved so much equality, whereas immigrants or those with an Islamic culture are so deeply rooted in it. They don't understand that you have a free will, that you can break loose from it" (Inger). The free will of Christianity has contributed to an egalitarian society, according to this respondent, whereas the lack of independence from

Islamic traditions has contributed to the sense that people cannot break free from religion. In this statement, of course, the respondent fails to recognize either that the breaking free of Christianity would unmoor Danes, or that such breaking is actually impossible due to history.

What we saw in Kittle's article from *San Diego Union Tribune*—that a church with its mosaics of Christ, John the Baptist, and the Virgin Mary stands for Enlightenment ideals—is also evident in these statements. As Niels clearly stated, the sources for the rationally minded Europeans—and Americans—can be found in the New Testament as well as in Greece. When immigrants are the issue, the Danish identity becomes adjusted to mean Western civilization, conceptualized as the most advanced phase in a universal developmental path whose distinctiveness is defined by its modernity as opposed to immigrants' boundedness in cultural traditions represented by Islam. However, the category of Danishness as Western civilization can only be sustained when opposed to Islam.

There are substantial variations and contradictions within and across these interviews. While tracing the roots of Western civilization to Greece at one moment, Niels could not see much in common between Greeks and Danes, the latter of whom have more in common with Americans. The concept of Western civilization with a positive content is also very difficult to sustain across interviews: If one of the important aspects of Christian modernity is the removal of capital punishment ("we do not punish with capital punishment in Denmark and in Europe" [Trine]), how is it possible to talk about a common cultural background between Europeans and Americans? But the interesting point is that these utterances still work as plausible explanations despite these inconsistencies that show that Danishness is a loosely held totality. They work as plausible explanations because they are tuned to the rhetorical demands of the immediate situation and make sense in the micro-contexts of the interaction.

Interestingly, while the cultural antagonism that characterizes the DPP's viewpoints is often reproduced, most of the participants also expressed antiracist and tolerant sentiments and clearly distanced themselves from the DDP (some of them vote for parties that are left of the Social Democratic Party). There was also evidence that some became aware of the racist implications of their utterances within the context of the interview and dealt with it in different ways. At the end of one interview, for example, one participant reflected on what she had been saying and observed that she sounded very much like Pia Kjærsgaard, the leader of the DDP. She then said that she could not stand hearing herself say those things—a statement that helped her distance herself from racism of the DPP. Many of those interviewed blamed the media for their own "prejudices" and expressed a genuine wish to get to know immigrants personally rather than repeating what they had heard through the media.

These slippages in category constructions and inconsistencies in opinion expressions indicate that we have an analytical problem here. If the participants cannot sustain category descriptions throughout the interview, and if there are substantial variations across the interviews, is it then useful to take the obvious similarities across utterances as an expression of patterns in discourse?

Analyzing Hegemony

As I noted earlier, most of the participants in the interviews display tolerant, egalitarian, and sometimes antiracist sentiments despite the fact that they reproduce the racist dichotomy within which categories are constructed and filled with content. An analytical procedure of sifting good accounts from bad accounts, ignoring their functions in the interaction, is, therefore, inappropriate for an ideological analysis. We need to find ways of critically analyzing the rhetorical purposes, alive to the way versions are constructed and stabilized as factual (independent of the speaker).[25] First, rather than identifying ideological statements, categories, or ideas in an account, the focus must be shifted to the ideological function of the account (i.e., how accounts justify exclusion rather than what kind of ideas are deployed in accounts). Secondly, an identification of what *counts* as factual and plausible may give us a clue as to the limitations in the use of the interpretative resources available to account for the world. Why, for instance, is it that one kind of factual statement rather than another has been assumed to work as an adequate justification for the specific argument in the interview context?[26]

My specific argument is that the hegemonic effect is produced by the *responsive* nature of discourse. As we have seen, although participants' descriptions of Danishness may vary contextually, their repertoire immediately becomes limited when they are cued to think of Danish identity in relation to immigrants. This is the result of the interview situation, which produces an abstract and theoretical discourse, because people engage in the business of opinion expression in a way that is highly responsive to how the issue is discussed in public discourse, rather than to the contingencies of actual situations. In this sense, interviews function in the same way as opinion polls that ask for opinions on controversial issues. Controversies are already defined by the pollsters, who take their cues from hegemonic interventions in discourse. If opinion polls create opinions, interviews invoke specific responses that are organized as opinion expressions, too. Particular articulations become hegemonic through discursive interventions in public debate that define what the controversy is *about*, limiting the range of responses that can be given to those definitions and fixing the meaning through articulatory chains that are opposed to each other. This is where the DPP and their forerunners have succeeded in fixing the meaning of immigration in public discourse: they succeeded in defining the basic terms on which the questions could be formulated and responses could be given. This is how people can simultaneously express egalitarian and antiracist sentiments and reproduce the racist dichotomy of the West versus Muslims.

Hegemony, therefore, should no longer be understood as an ideological project that binds people's heads together or as an aggregate of opinions and attitudes. Rather, it is a *political* project that is accomplished through rhetorical strategies of repeated linkages and with the help of opinion-making techniques. I will now briefly discuss two instances of the hegemonic project: explanatory frameworks that repeat links between the social formations and particular actions,[27] and opinion-making techniques that fix and translate everyday talk into policy proposals that in turn institutionalize and stabilize the hegemonic articulations.

Explanatory Linkages

I use the term "explanatory framework" to refer to the repeated linking of certain social groups (Muslims immigrants) with certain actions (crime). The cumulative effect of the explanatory frameworks is an exclusion of the group both in everyday contexts and by laws and other provisions. They are informed by the hegemonic articulations of social identities and feed into the hegemonic articulations. They are major articulatory moments of hegemonic discourse. "Immigrant criminality" is a good example of these linkages.

In 1998, the then general director of the Danish Public Broadcasting Corporation (DR) Christian Nissen responded to public criticism that the media portrayed immigrants in a negative light by focusing too much on the criminal action by immigrants. He described the situation as a dilemma because, on the one hand, DR, as a public service station, is obliged to reflect the reality objectively and cannot, therefore, embellish (beautify) reality by toning down the negative actions by immigrants; and, on the other hand, it has to continually reflect on the effects of its broadcasting and its own role in creating animosity. He asked, "Are we building bridges between social and cultural groups, or are we widening the gap even further?" His own answer was that news is by nature oriented toward conflicts, and DR objectively told about "four young immigrants who beat up two Danes in a dark street" and then tried to repair the possible damage through other types of programs that involved debate and commentaries. He added: "The fight in the dark street is newsworthy, whereas thousands of well-functioning immigrants are never covered in a news broadcast. Are we, then, going to adjust news criteria? Are we going to aim at broadcasting positive images of immigrants every time we have images of violence?" [28]

I could devote a whole section to an analysis of Nissen's argumentation, but due to space constraints, I will only discuss the "news criteria" and "newsworthiness" that he invokes as justification of covering immigrant violence. My argument is that it is only on the basis of the antagonism between Danes and immigrants that his argument makes sense. A simple question in this context would reveal this: "What makes violence by four immigrants against two Danes in a dark street newsworthy?" A fight between two Danish youth groups would—regardless of the illumination of the street—never make the news. Fights between immigrant youths are often not considered newsworthy. It is the identities of the perpetrators and victims that renders the incident newsworthy, or rather, the fact that it is immigrant youth who are behind the violent act. So, newsworthiness is not determined by violence per se, but by who resorts to violence.

If a Dane or group of Danes resorts to violence, this is covered as an individual act of deviance from the social/cultural norms. If an immigrant or group of immigrants resort to violence, however, it is a cultural act that threatens the social peace that is believed to be sustained through the "Danish" norms: norms that the immigrants, it is believed, subvert. Immigrant violence is thus a direct challenge to Danishness. This is why violence by young immigrants gains the status of social conflict and becomes newsworthy. It is only in this context that statements such as "they have to learn not to commit crime" and "my culture does not tell me to kick down an old lady" make sense. Only in a discourse where immigrants are represented as a cultural threat does the government find it justifiable to form an integration contract and force immigrants to promise that they will not commit crimes or resort to violence. Through repetition, the explanatory framework (or the link) has achieved the status of truth and has made itself into the commonsensical, taken-for-granted reflection of reality.

This premise is never explicated in Nissen's argument; if it were, it would immediately be subject to debate. Nissen's argument is that the DR has to cover objectively the issues that pertain to "conflict." This argument can only function if what constitutes conflict is treated as a taken-for-granted wisdom. When presented this way, it demands tremendous intellectual capacity to explicate the argumentative links and intervene at the level of the assumption/premise. Its rhetorical force does not come from its logical connections but from repetition that renders it commonsensical. It is not important whether he actually believes that immigrants pose a danger to Danish culture. What is important here is that this assumption provides a powerful rhetorical resource for his actual argument that the DR has to cover conflict.

The special character of the link between the "immigrant" and "violence" is conditioned upon the culturalized categories of Danes and immigrants and justifies the media's focus on "immigrant crime" as a phenomenon of particular significance. The media's focus feeds back into the discursive environment and strengthens the frontier between Danishness and Muslim culture.[29]

The media's response to hegemonic interventions is similar to responses by the pollsters and the political establishment. They all respond (and contribute) to controversies and thus create access for those who have rhetorical resources to create controversy. After a while, the repeated connections between, say, criminality and immigrants' culture become naturalized.

Journalists deploy this framework in their stories, either without reflection or because this connection is what is expected and rewarded. So, a rational debate on immigration as a public concern becomes only possible as a dialogue among the limited range of positions that can be taken within the framework of the hegemonic articulation. If the basic principles for the debate are not accepted, communication and thus any debate will be impossible. The role of the media in defining the parameters for a public debate is thus crucial.

Conclusion

In this chapter I have tried to develop the argument that religion—Islam in this case—should primarily be understood as an empty category, the content of which is filled associatively in the course of discursive articulation. It is an "empty signifier" with no determinate meaning, but it gains a specific meaning through its rhetorical function as the signifier of a fundamental antagonism between the traditional culture of Islam (seen as backwardness) and Western societies (seen as modernity). This empty signifier is "ideology at its purest, i.e. the direct embodiment of the ideological function of providing a neutral all-emcompassing space [Danishness or the West] in which social antagonisms are obliterated, in which all members of society can recognize themselves."[30] The struggle for hegemony is the struggle for how the empty signifier should be "overdetermined," that is, colored by a particular signification. It means, to return to the dichotomy in Kittle's article, that we need to understand Islam as "unchanging orthodoxy" in relation to its function in constructing the West as a civilization "built on the Enlightenment ideals of reason and individual liberty." As historians and scholars of Middle East continually affirm, the very equation of an entire world of Islamic cultures with the "unchanging orthodoxy of the Holy Koran" is nonsensical. Holy books consist of orthodoxies—be it the Old or New Testament or the Koran—and the word "orthodoxy" implies resistance to change. The strategic rhetorical movement here is to equate Islam to the Holy Koran whereas Christianity is defined more generally as a culture that has evolved and surpassed the dogmas of the book. Like in the West, the Islamic world consists of many different beliefs, practices, and branches. This variation in itself is testimony to change (if the Koran was the sole source, we would have a uniform religious practice that is reproduced universally). Moreover, the history of Islam, as Said's examination of Orientalism clearly shows, can never be clearly distinguished from that of colonialism and modernity.

The second part of my argument is that hegemonic articulations are the result of discursive interventions that set up specific antagonisms according to which identity categories are made meaningful and have an explanatory power for the social world. In modern times, repeated linkages between actions and identity categories, and between news reports and opinion polls, play a great role in fixing, however temporarily, the meaning of categories. They also direct the media's response to some interventions in discourse rather than others because of their institutional and daily routines, their professional ideologies, and their embeddedness in the ideological environment within which public debate is conducted.

Hegemony about racial, ethnic, and religious prejudices should not, then, be understood as coherent expressions of an ideology that has pervaded popular discourse. It is not that people, without any reflection, reproduce prejudicial views that have become common sense. Almost on the contrary, people often express their dislike for the kind of implications their utterances have, as noted earlier. But, as Colin Leys has elegantly stated, for an idea to become hegemonic, it is not necessary that it be loved. It is merely necessary that it have no serious rival for explaining the world.[31]

NOTES

1. Rod Benson, "Shaping the Public Sphere: Journalistic Fields and Immigration Debates in the United States and France, 1973–1994" (PhD diss., University of California Berkeley, 2002).

2. Sasha Polakow-Suransky, "Fortress Denmark?" *American Prospect* 6, no. 3 (2002): 21–24.

3. Edward W. Said, *Orientalism* (Harmondsworth: Penguin, 1978).

4. Ibid., 2–3.

5. E. Laclau and C. Mouffe, *Hegemony and Socialist Strategy: Towards a Radical Democratic Politics,* 2nd ed. (London, New York: Verso, 2001).

6. Edward W. Said, *Covering Islam: How the Media and the Experts Determine How We See the Rest of the World* (New York: Pantheon, 1981).

7. S. Žižek, "The Matrix; or, The Two Sides of Perversion," paper presented at Inside the Matrix—International Symposium at the Center for Art and Media, held in Karlsruhe, Germany, October 18, 1999.

8. The elite's sin was to allow the destruction of the Danish nation; although immigration became the center of focus, the "Eurocrats" of the European Union and other cosmopolitan elites were also targeted as a part of this threat. The problem is that Eurocrats do not have the same *cultural* significance as Muslims—Eurocrats allow the destruction of Danish culture.

9. For further discussion, see T. B. Dyrberg, "Racisme som en nationalistisk og populistisk reaktion på elitedemokrati," in *Diskursteorien på arbejde*, by T. B. Dyrberg, A. D. Hansen, and J. Torfing (Copenhagen: Roskilde Universitetsforlag, 2000), 221–246; T. B. Dyrberg, "Racist, Nationalist, and Populist Trends in Recent Danish Politics," *Research Papers from the Department of Social Sciences*, Research Paper no. 19/01 (Roskilde: Roskilde University, 2001); Ferruh Yilmaz, "De har sejret ad helvede til!" (Their triumph is complete!), in *Fra Racisme til det stuerene—Myndighedernes respons og ansvar* (From racism to the drawing-room—the authorities' response and responsibility), ed. E. Tinor-Centi (Copenhagen: Documentation and Counseling Centre on Racial Discrimination in Denmark, 2000).

10. Ø. Gaasholt and L. Togeby, *I Syv Sind. Danskernes holdninger til flygtninge og indvandrere* (Aarhus: Forlaget Politica, 1995); P. Hervik, *Mediernes muslimer. En antropologisk undersøgelse af mediernes dækning af religioner i Danmark* (Copenhagen: Nævnet for Etnisk Ligestilling, 2002); Ü. Necef, "Indvandring, den nationale stat og velfærdsstaten," in *Ubekvemme udfordringer*, ed. P. Seeberg (Odense: Odense Universitetsforlag, 2001), 31–64.

11. Gaasholt and Togeby, *I Syv Sind*, 9 (my translation).

12. Laclau and Mouffe, *Hegemony and Socialist Strategy*, xiv.

13. R. Jenkins, *Rethinking Ethnicity: Arguments and Explorations* (London: Sage, 1997).

14. Bent Jensen, *De Fremmede i Dansk Avisdebat—fra 1970'erne til 1990'erne* (Copenhagen: Spektrum, 2000).

15. Gaasholt and Togeby, *I Syv Sind*, 162.

16. J. G. Madsen, *Mediernes konstruktion af flygtninge—og indvandrerspørgsmålet* (Aarhus: Magtudredningen and Aarhus University, 2000), 87.

17. Kristian Thulesen Dahl, Soren Espersen, and Anders Skjodt, *Denmark's Future: Your Country—Your Choice* . . . (Copenhagen: Danish People's Party, 2001). The Danish People's Party (DPP) is the Far Right anti-immigrant party that gained 13 percent of the votes in the latest election in February 2005. The party's support is vital for the right-wing Liberal/Conservative coalition that does not have parliamentary majority.

18. Dahl, Espersen, and Skjodt,, *Denmark' Future*. K. Hvenegård-Lassen, *Grænseland. Minoriteter, rettigheder og den nationale idé* (Copenhagen: Danish Center for Human Rights, 1996).

19. Ulf Hedetoft, "'Cultural Transformation': How Denmark Faces Immigration," *Open Democracy*, October 30, 2003, www.opendemocracy.org.

20. Ferruh Yilmaz, "Medieforbrugernes opfattelse af den etniske virkelighed," in *Medierne, minoriterne, og majoriteten: en undersøgelse af nyhedsmedier og den folkelige diskurs i Danmark*, ed. M. Hussain, F. Yilmaz, and T. O'Connor (Copenhagen: Board for Ethnic Equality, 1997).

21. I use the term for the lack of a better concept. There are many concepts that describe similar ideas: "interpretative repertoires," "explanatory packages," "frame," and so on. Except for the notion of "interpretative repertoires," the other designations all refer to some kind of cognitive structures that help "understand," "sort out," "interpret," and "act" on the world. These cognitive structures, schemes, templates, or whatever the respective approach calls them shape the world prior to the actual context of the interaction/pronunciation. My use of the term "explanatory framework" has no such cognitive association: it is loosely connected clusters of discursive resources that are repeatedly used to explain different kinds of phenomena under one umbrella term (such as "immigrant criminality" or "honor killings"). Their meaning can only be fixed through their name (hence the notion of empty signifiers). They are thus rhetorical tools for social action. "Honor killings," for instance, once it enters discourse, is used to describe various kinds of murders in different kinds of settings for a variety of rhetorical ends.

22. Swedish, Norwegian, and Danish languages are extremely close. Only historical coincidences separated them into three distinct languages.

23. These views nevertheless justify the official treatment of immigrants as expressed in the integration contract's appendix.

24. The law was sharply criticized by EU Commissioner for Human Rights Alvaro Gil-Robles in 2004, but the criticism was dismissed, like all other critiques by international institutions, by the then Integration Minister Bertel Haarder, who called the law "women progressive"—because it was an effective tool against arranged marriages—and accused Gil-Robles for not understanding cultural differences because Gil-Robles himself was a Spaniard who had a similar culture of arranged marriages (*Politiken*, March 1, 2005).

25. See J. Potter, "Wittgenstein and Austin." in *Discourse, Theory, and Practice: A Reader*, ed. M. Wetherell, S. Taylor, and S. J. Yates (London, Sage, 2001), 39–46.

26. M. Wetherell, "Positioning and Interpretative Repertoires: Conversation Analysis and Post-structuralism in Dialogue," *Discourse and Society* 9, no. 3 (1998): 387–412.

27. Žižek, "The Matrix; or, The Two Sides of Perversion."

28. Christian Nissen, in *Nyhedsbrev om Denmarks Udlændinge* (Newsletter about Denmark's foreigners), no. 76, February 1998, published by Udlændingestyrelsen.

29. Here are just a few examples: In the spring of 2003, the Danish minister of finance suggested that parents of minors who committed crimes should participate in mandatory courses in parental responsibility. The initiative was especially aimed at foreign-born parents. In September 2003, during negotiations about the Danish finances for 2004, the Danish Peoples Party (a right-wing

party that is part of the parliamentary base for the present government) demanded that young criminals with a foreign background be placed in a special "ethnic" facility designated for them alone, due to their unwillingness/inability to adjust to life in a normal prison. According to the government's new proposal for restriction on immigration (November 2005), immigrants are going to sign a document where they have to promise not to commit crimes.

30. Žižek, "The Matrix; or, The Two Sides of Perversion."

31. Colin Leys, "Still a Question of Hegemony," *New Left Review* (1990): 125.

9

∽∽

"Blowing the Cover"

Imaging Religious Functionaries
in Ghanaian/Nigerian Films

KWABENA ASAMOAH-GYADU

Instances of religious lifestyle branding now can be found in every corner of the globe, in part because religious leaders and their adherents are constantly in the process of rearticulating their faith commitments as a means by which to remain relevant and attractive to the cultures in which they find themselves. Across the large continent of Africa, this rearticulation has taken different forms over the years in response to Christian missionary work and, more recently, in response to the growth of Islam.

When missionaries first arrived in Africa in the early to the middle part of the nineteenth century, they brought a brand of denominationally affiliated religion that, for some, came to be seen as too staid for a population steeped in traditional practices of healing, amulets, rituals, and prophets, a population concerned with what they perceived as the realities of supernatural evil. By the end of the century, a movement to re-Africanize the population had taken hold, with prophet-healing churches emerging to address the concerns local Christians had regarding witchcraft, healing, and potions. This movement has been cast as "demonic" by the now-emergent Pentecostal/charismatic churches, which began to gain a stronghold in African life in the 1970s and continue to gain influence today. The Pentecostal/charismatic groups have strongly promoted their "brand" of religion, seeking to differentiate themselves from both the staid missionary traditions and the personality cults of the prophet-healing churches.

The Pentecostal/charismatic efforts at differentiation have entered the popular imagination, often appearing in popular Ghanaian and Nigerian films that feature corrupt prophets, ineffectual or evil-influenced leaders of former missionary churches, or both. The extent to which these popular representations have gained acceptance among populations in Africa is an indication of the ways in which the Pentecostal/charismatic churches have been successful in gaining the cultural authority to define what (or who) is evil and which are the appropriate ways to address evil. But the success of these films is also indicative of the ways in which media that seek to identify and in some cases pillory religious "Others" can meet the commercial concerns of the emergent East African film industries, even as they undermine religious understanding (or promote religious intolerance and stereotypes) in significant ways.

The production of video films, one of the most lucrative economic activities in sub-Saharan Africa today, has become an important medium for the expression and sustenance of African religio-cultural worldviews within public space. In African contexts generally, the sacred and secular dimensions of everyday life, to a very large extent, remain inseparably linked.[1] Religion is a survival strategy, and so when in crisis or seeking to understand and improve destinies, people resort to the religious realm for interpretation and intervention. African traditional worldviews of mystical causality have survived the Christian advance and are sustained, particularly within the independent, indigenous Pentecostal/charismatic streams of the faith. These traditional worldviews are constantly played out in African video films and explain their popularity both on TV and in the markets. Jonathan Haynes, in the book *Nigerian Video Films*, refers to the routine appearance of the supernatural in the daily affairs of Nigerians and how this is reflected in local films: "witchcraft as a weapon in domestic or neighborly antagonisms, mysterious fates that can only be elucidated by a diviner, selling one's soul to dark occult power for the sake of wealth—all are stock elements in these videos."[2] In keeping with African fascinations with the impingement of the supernatural on everyday life, video films have become a popular area within which beliefs in mystical causality and the various dynamics of religious mediation are articulated.

The reference Jonathan Haynes makes to the role of the "diviner" as the elucidator of mysterious fates in African video films is critical to the focus of this essay. The mediation of power, healing, protection, and general prosperity by religious specialists, whether belonging to the Christian, Muslim, or African traditional religions, is central to the practice of religion in Africa. The diviner or traditional priest, in the worldview of the Akan of Ghana, is the religious mediator par excellence, as David Ekem explains:

> Akomfo function as intermediaries between their communities and deities into whose service they have been called. In a typical priestly capacity, they present the community's needs to the deities and interpret the deities' wishes to the community. Their close contact with the spirit world places them in an extraordinary position, their very persons being regarded as sacred. . . . It is not uncommon to find groups or individuals flocking to various Akan shrines on festive, calamitous and ordinary occasions to approach the deities for help.[3]

Like the *okomfo* (singular), the task of a Yoruba diviner, called *babalawo* (father of secrets), is to reveal the destinies of clients and show them how to improve upon their lot in life. With specific reference to a Ghanaian/Nigerian video film, *The Last Prophet,* released in 2002 by Coruma International Ltd., and examples drawn from other audio-visual sources, this essay scrutinizes the character, nature, and understanding of religious mediation as sustained in the media, especially in home video films. Closely tied to the prominence of religious specialists as persons of sacred power is a widespread notion that religious mediation is at the same time open to abuse and charlatanry, and certain Christian pastors resort to the occult in order to enhance their supernatural powers. The Ghana/Nigeria home video films *End-Time* (Volumes 1 and 2) and *Church Business* (Volumes 1 and 2), now also available on DVD, are both dedicated to exposing pastors who, driven by material gain, resort to all kinds of occult forces as the power base of their ministries.

The host of a radio program in Ghana therefore voiced a common suspicion on the part of the Ghanaian population: that pastors can call on occult powers for help with their work. On the afternoon of Friday, April 11, 2003, the popular drive-time phone-in program on Joy FM sought public responses to the following hypothetical scenario: "The pastor of your church is a renowned miracle worker; after benefiting from his healing ministry during a life-threatening condition, you soon discovered that the source of the pastor's miraculous power is the 'occult.' The matter raises concern in the church and you are invited to testify: Will you 'blow the cover'?"[4] In both Ghana and Nigeria, video films and other audio-visual programs are the media "not just for isolated religious messages and meanings," but also for what Asonzeh Ukah describes as "a forest of religious symbols and values."[5] Birgit Meyer articulates the relationship between the storylines of African video films, on the one hand, and daily life, on the other, more succinctly:

> [It] would be inadequate to approach video-films as artistic products to be viewed in their own right, from the perspective of the distant spectator. Rather it has to be taken as a point of departure that these films impinge on everyday life as much as they claim to represent it. In the video-film industry, . . . the cinema and TV screens do not function as windows through which spectators look at the world from a distance. In the same way, those who make the film perceive what happens in front of the camera as to be fully entangled with real life, rather than occurring in a virtual space, within the safe confines of artistic production. Ghanaian popular cinema, with regard to production as well as consumption, blurs the boundary between everyday life and its representation.[6]

Although produced essentially for commercial gain, what is visualized of religious mediation in TV theater and video films may sometimes be exaggerated, but they are neither made up nor contrived. Some of the stories forming the subjects of these video films and TV drama are woven around everyday experiences at the courts of religious specialists. The fall-outs from public experiences with religious specialists are openly discussed and regularly carried as news in the print and broadcast media. Subsequently, the stories find their way onto the screen for wider public consumption. In both Ghana and Nigeria some Pentecostal/charismatic churches have taken advantage of the popularity of this form of Christianity to produce video films as an evangelical tool. These efforts by African churches to produce their own video films amount to "religious communication," a phenomenon well discussed by Ukah, based on a study in Nigeria.[7] This essay pursues a different trajectory as one in "communication about religion" because the programs and videos discussed are not meant to advance the doctrinal idiosyncrasies of particular religious confessions. The production of material popular culture through the video films discussed here is informed not by missionary/evangelical considerations (although that should not be completely ruled out), but essentially by commercial interests. Whether we are talking about Ghana or Nigeria, the fact of the matter is that the new African video films sell because the supernatural ideas propounded in them resonate with African religio-cultural worldviews of the power of supernatural evil and the roles of religious functionaries as mediums of both intervention and deception.

Religious Specialists/Functionaries

Religious specialists or functionaries are persons who, on account of their perceived closeness to supernatural realities, possession of mystical powers of intuition, and knowledge of the workings of mysterious religious formulae and objects, occupy center stage in religion as mouthpieces of transcendent beings and powers. Close proximity to the sacred may be acquired on the basis of profound subjective encounters with "the holy."[8] It is the access one claims, or is perceived to have, to the feared but revered supernatural realm that gives the religious functionary, to quote I. M. Lewis, "a unique claim to direct experiential knowledge of the divine and, where this is acknowledged by others, the authority to act as a privileged channel of communication between man and the supernatural."[9] Of particular importance to the followers of the religious specialists in African traditional cultures, such as those of Ghana and Nigeria, are the medicines they supply for healing, prosperity, and protection against evil. Yet as Lewis notes elsewhere, the "mystical gifts" of prophecy, clairvoyance, and the ability to see into the supernatural realm in order to retrieve communication from there have naturally attracted the attention not only of the devout, but also of skeptics.[10] The elements of skepticism and devotion to religious specialists mentioned by Lewis are both present in African religion, and the new video films provide a popular context in which both the negative and positive sides of religious mediation are dramatized.

Types of Churches and Religious Functionaries

Although not stated explicitly, the question put to the public by the Joy FM radio host cited above was posed from a Pentecostal/charismatic viewpoint. Pentecostal/charismatic Christianity is a form of Christian expression that values, affirms, and encourages an experiential presence of the Holy Spirit in the church as part of normal Christian expression. Its emphasis on the "power of the Holy Spirit" means it has a strong interventionist theology, particularly in the promise of healing from diseases and deliverance from the demonic. Since the late 1970s, this form of Christianity has become the most visible and palpable evidence of the shift in the center of gravity of the Christian faith from the northern to the southern continents, particularly Africa. Central to their theology is the belief that God wants all believers to prosper materially. Rituals of prayer for healing and deliverance have therefore been instituted to take care of the shortfalls in the prosperity message.

Pentecostal/charismatic pastors, in keeping with the African worldview of mystical causality, are respected as people who possess "the anointing of God" and who can offer powerful prayers that terminate the afflictions visited on people through demonic possession, witchcraft, and other occult sources of affliction. It is also not lost on the public, as depicted in the video film *Church Business,* that not all power may be from God.

Prior to the rise of the Pentecostal/charismatic churches in the 1970s and, indeed, since the turn of the twentieth century, African independent or prophet-healing churches led by indigenous prophets had been working in Africa. Prophet-healing churches, known in Ghana as "Spiritual" and in Nigeria as "Aladura" (praying people) churches, emerged spontaneously in response to the staid, silent, and "orderly" forms of worship associated with the historic mission denominations of the mid-nineteenth century. The pastoral strategy of the prophet-healing churches, or AICs, was to move away from the cerebral nature of historic mission Christianity and "re-Africanize" local Christians by presenting them with more relevant, effective, and indigenous Christian alternatives to the purely traditional beliefs and practices of traditional priest-healers. The prophets leading these movements produced syncretistic rites for healing and deliverance from the harmful effects of witchcraft, curses, and other supernatural evils. As the Christian equivalent of traditional priests, these prophets also became

the source of potions for love, success at school, business, and employment and encouraged forms of prayer, fasting, and other disciplines meant
to sustain the function of religion as a means of explanation, prediction,
and control.

In African Christian discourse, generally, African traditional religions
and rituals are demonized as belonging to the realm of the devil, as forcefully discussed by Birgit Meyer in her seminal work *Translating the Devil*.[11]
The Pentecostal/charismatic forms of Christian expression have therefore
been very critical of the AICs by demonizing them as groups whose practices are too close to those of traditional priest-healers. The Pentecostal/
charismatic emphasis on the personal experiences of power following receipt
of the Holy Spirit means they feel able to deal with the problems of evil
without recourse to those traditional remedies that the AIC prophets
have infused with Christian significance. Pentecostal/charismatic pastors,
on the one hand, constantly vilify the historic mission churches for
their formalism, intellectualism, and powerlessness and, on the other
hand, vehemently castigate the AIC prophets as being in league with the
forces of traditional religion. As new religious movements, Pentecostal/
charismatic churches, and their pastors, make extensive use of the media.
The media in Ghana and Nigeria also exploit the popularity of this
new type of Christianity by giving a lot of room to Pentecostal preachers
and their supernaturalistic hermeneutics. There is a great deal of Pentecostal discourse on TV and radio, and African "popular video movies," as
Meyer notes, "take up typically Pentecostal concerns."[12] We turn now to a
film that dramatizes the tensions felt as independent indigenous leaders
came to be viewed, from a Pentecostal perspective, as trafficking in the
occult.

The Last Prophet

The film *The Last Prophet* typifies the conception of older African independent prophets as obtaining their powers from dubious and occult
sources. As a result, the belief is that their clients are put in further danger
rather than helped to overcome their troubles. The main character in this
Ghanaian version of a Nigerian movie is Prophet Desmond Amuma. In the

opening scene, we encounter a half-naked woman being bathed or baptized in a river, with the hands of the prophet all over her. This suggests immediately to the viewer that we are about to encounter a religious functionary with dubious credentials and morality. The title "prophet" is the preferred designation of the leaders of the older independent churches because of their principal role as "seers" into and "revealers" of information from the spiritual realm of existence. The appearance of the prophet as imaged in the film is a primary and important indicator of the sort of religious specialist that the producer intended to portray.

Prophet Amuma is styled as a Spiritual/Aladura church prophet, an image that is determined by his accoutrements, paraphernalia, and modus operandi. There is a cross embossed onto the front of Prophet Amuma's robe. He wears another oversized metallic cross over his white or sometimes red cassock with a girdle and, on occasion, is shown wearing a beret. This appearance is carefully crafted to distinguish the prophet from his modern Pentecostal/charismatic counterparts. The latter usually put on Western-styled tuxedo suits or traditional three-piece *agbada* as indices of the prosperity gospel that has become the trademark of this new stream of African-initiated churches.

The Aladura prophet, unlike the modern Pentecostal/Charismatic pastor whose main instrument in ministry is the Bible, also carries a prophetic staff that is supposed to be reminiscent of Moses' staff. The African prophets' methods of healing include the use of holy water, blessed olive oils, and other sacramentals meant to serve as "faith extensions" for clients. Quite frequently, prophets operate from beaches, riverbanks, mountaintops, and other sacred spaces like the Garden of the Church of Twelve Apostles in Ghana. Water is considered an important substance for ritual cleansing in these prophet-healing churches, and so there is always some on hand either in large stagnant forms or in handy containers. The staff, a symbol of the prophetic office, is supposed to be imbued with supernatural power, and together with the other substances it is used as an instrument for healing. Riverbanks are where baptism and other cleansing rituals to get rid of supernatural evil and sin often take place.

These African prophets are always the center of their movements, and people consult them in the same way that traditional priests may be consulted in times of crisis. In *Prophetism in Ghana* Christian Baëta gives the following profile of the late Prophet Nkansah of the African Faith Tabernacle and his church:

> Prayers are held every day at 5 am and 7 am. The prophet then spends his time receiving visitors and holding special sessions of prayer for divine healing. . . . When patients under his treatment see him coming, they must kneel on the ground and bow their heads. He places his right hand on them and blesses them. . . . [T]hey came not only to be healed but also to obtain accessions of strength or power (Akan: tumi) for themselves personally, as well as for their farms and other undertakings. They bring such liberal presents that the prophet now owns considerable property.[13]

In the film, Prophet Amuma, in keeping with this tradition of a personality cult, is imaged as being so revered that his followers and clients lay prostrate anytime he appears. Prophecy in African Christianity is mainly diagnostic, and there is a correlation between the following of a prophet and how accurate his revelation of causative factors in crises is. That the prophet deserved such reverence was seen in his ability to read life histories, amounting to some sort of fortune-telling. For most of the problems diagnosed by Prophet Amuma, there was a single cause—supernatural evil, perpetuated by witches, wizards, demons, or personal enemies, particularly envious mothers-in-law. Prophet Amuma literally conjures money for the poor and supplies handkerchiefs and other symbolic ritual elements for protection against enemies. In addition to the large number of adult women who visit him, there is another group of people—the rich, famous, and powerful politicians—who all troop to the church of the prophet to seek protection, increase their wealth, or even acquire the property of others whom they covet.

We are shown scenes of people driving very powerful cars, mainly huge Mercedes Benz cars heading toward the church's meeting grounds. Women who want to boost market sales also come to seek assistance from the prophet. The traders happily go away with blessed holy water to sprinkle on their wares. The African independent church prophets, as may be gathered from Baëta's observations above, often have a large number of floating members whose only interest is to have their problems solved.

Once their problems are dealt with, people may just stop seeing the prophet, or else move on from prophet to prophet until they secure that for which they are looking. This perception of independent prophetic ministries as sustained by such floating members who bring luxurious gifts in gratitude is also evident in the film. Prophet Amuma became the beneficiary of a four-wheel-drive vehicle donated by a politician seeking his intervention to win elections.

These stories, as I have tried to illustrate, are not far-fetched. Indeed, among the gifts donated to Prophet Nkansah and reported by Baëta was a "touring car" donated to him by a chief; and many cocoa farmers, seeking his intervention, gave cocoa pods in lieu of other presents to the prophet.[14] More recently, in the 2000 parliamentary elections in Ghana, two candidates, a former diplomat and a retired army officer belonging to the same party, traded accusations in both the electronic and print media about how the other had used medicines or juju to improve his fortune in the elections. The army officer, Captain Sowu, was peeved that the retired diplomat, Victor Gbeho, had stood against him as an independent candidate and won although they both belonged to the then ruling party, the National Democratic Congress. This situation is common in African politics and is the subject of a study by Rosalind Shaw on Temne diviners in Sierra Leone. Shaw concludes from the study that "the 'eating' and incorporation of medicines prepared by diviners is central to the constitution of power, both within and outside the arena of state politics."[15] In the African search for power, people fulfill such needs not only from the diviners, but also in the churches of powerful prophets widely acknowledged as sources of powerful substances for achieving success.

In one of the scenes of *The Last Prophet*, a pastor who wanted to increase the membership of his church consulted Amuma for help. Prophet Amuma prescribed a ritual in which the consulting pastor was expected, as part of the ritual for an increased following, to bury a live cow on the church premises: "as many maggots as will visit the carcass of the cow," the client was told, "so shall the following of your church be." Prophet Amuma is at points shown performing occult rituals in order to sustain his powers. The insight provided through the camera is so that the audience may be warned against judging the credibility of religious functionaries on the basis of signs and wonders. As usual, testimonies formed an important part of Prophet Amuma's church services and were the main source of his following. The issues in the film are resolved when Prophet Amuma is eventually exposed as a fraud dependent on evil powers under the veneer of the Bible. The end comes when God's Spirit exposes the prophet and his life ends in disgrace. In the end, the evil powers of the prophet turn not only on him, but also on those who benefited from his occult powers, with one man who had gone for riches going insane.

Translating Reality onto Screen

In Africa the traditional priest-healer, we have observed, is the religious specialist par excellence. Healing, exorcism, divination, diagnosis, and the restoration of ill or disturbed persons to health are crucial functions of the traditional priest. Within the context of the multiplicity of religions, these therapeutic functions of traditional priest-healers are shared with Muslim clerics, or "Mallams," and the indigenous Christian prophets we have mentioned. The healing function renders the independent Pentecostal churches, in particular, culturally and religiously amenable to the masses of people who find in them a congeniality and familiarity absent from the worship and liturgy of Africa's historic mission churches whose theologies are considered non-interventionist. Whereas the traditional priest-healers, AIC prophets, and Pentecostal/charismatic pastors may be generally portrayed in African video films as potential sources of power, mainline church pastors, with their bookish theology, are often imaged as weak and unable to intervene in crisis. That some sources of power could be questionable and dangerous is what determines the differences among the various categories of religious functionaries or specialists.

Stories of connivance between people desirous of becoming rich or seeking protection for their wealth and religious specialists who provide ritual contexts that affirm traditional worldviews of mystical causality for such services predominate as themes in these African video films. The issues raised are common occurrences about which people talk and gossip. In the Thursday, May 8, 2003, issue of the *Ghanaian Times,* for example, it was reported that a teacher had found himself in the grips of the law for an incestuous relationship with his own daughter. He had allegedly defiled his thirteen-year-old girl on the instructions of a traditional priest as part of the ritual process for obtaining *sikaduro* (medicine money). Riches, it is widely believed, may be ritually obtained from traditional shrines and Muslim clerics through human sacrifices or through the exchange of vital human organs. So if a man is very rich and unable to make babies, for example, he may easily be suspected of exchanging his manhood for money at a shrine. Through video films and screen drama, producers attempt to "blow the cover" of such religious specialists prescribing immoral rituals and confirm growing negative public perceptions of these religious operatives as exploiting their supernatural connections for private gain.

The study by Shaw on Temne diviners, referred to earlier, for example, talks about diviners as specialists who healed and prepared medicines for their clients. The diviners affirmed that they prepared medicines to create or sustain the power of important people and that the ingredients of such medicines were revealed either by patron spirits or through divination and dreams.[16] Since bare skill may not be considered sufficient for success in life, the assistance of the supernatural is sought in the process toward the realization and sustenance of any endeavor: winning in sports, politics, acquisition and protection of riches, academic laurels, promotion or success at the workplace, and other endeavors that bring honor to people or families. It is commonplace, as evident in *The Last Prophet,* for African politicians, rich people, sportsmen, women, and even some pastors in their search for power (by their own later confessions) to rely on medicines for protection, to perform miracles, or to sustain their wealth and influence. Medicines obtained from diviners for these purposes "may be applied by eating or drinking them, by washing with them, by boiling them and inhaling the steam, by dropping them in the eyes, by wearing an underskirt soaked in them, by sowing them inside a belt tied around the waist, or by enclosing them in amulets hung around the neck."[17]

Many such medicines require the periodic performance of prescribed rituals in order to sustain their efficacy. It is not uncommon for African films to center their stories on beneficiaries of medicines who forgot aspects of the required ritual to sustain the efficacy of medicines or who took such rituals for granted after getting what they wanted. The formulae attached to the medicines then failed, and the clients were exposed as people whose endeavors were sustained by recourse to medicines. That is what happened to Mr. Hammond, a contractor in another Ghanaian/Nigerian film, *Asimo.* He had won contracts through Asimo's help and had gone on to become rich. Unfortunately, he was unable to obey a simple rule pertaining to his periodic rituals, and thus he went insane.

Films and theater arts also frequently capture the "true stories" of people who go for *sikaduro* (juju/medicine money) and then get carried away in licentious living and, in the process, slip into abject poverty or even go mad because they forget to sustain the wealth through prescribed rituals. Thus, Shaw refers to a general image of an unholy alliance between people of power and influence and traditional religious functionaries in Africa. She talks about how popular critiques of the "corrupt wealth" and dominance of politicians, in particular, link them to evil medicines prepared by diviners or to compacts with malefic spirits.[18] Some prophet-healers, as well as traditional priests and Mallams, are portrayed in the media as being in league with harmful supernatural forces whose powers of beneficence may offer only temporary relief.

The main sources of trouble for Prophet Amuma are money and women. Christian pastors, as Oha demonstrates from the Nigerian film *The Great Mistake*, are also constantly exposed in the media for living scandalous lives and, particularly, for their involvement in sexual immorality.[19] A disproportionate number of scandals appearing in the news on the prophet-healing churches relate to money and women. So, as usual, women are the chief clients of Prophet Amuma. Women are, in keeping with public opinion, portrayed as vulnerable and easy prey for the dubious machinations of such prophets. In popular Ghanaian discourse, prophets of the independent churches are called by all kinds of epithets that reflect their inclination toward the abuse of women. These include the Akan phrases *ka mo to ho* (push me down) and *dum kanea* (put off the light). These are offensive phrases suggesting that Spiritual church prophets take sexual advantage of women either by pushing them onto their beds when the women least suspect or putting off the light in the prayer rooms so they can abuse them.

In line with this popular thinking, the opening scene of *The Last Prophet* was a way of confirming public opinion on independent church prophets as dubious and untrustworthy. Incidentally, I was watching this film with two young women who, on seeing the Prophet Amuma's hands fondling his female client, remarked: "O women! We are too vulnerable. If you have not seen 'the light,' such false prophets simply take advantage of you." "That's all they [the prophets] do," the women volunteered, thus affirming the veracity of the film's story as confirming real-life experiences. Reference to "the light" here has to do with the realization of the deception of such prophets and the leaving of their company to join a "Bible-believing" church, as the new Pentecostal/charismatic churches are also called.

Thus, Africa's new video movies, as Meyer observes, concern themselves with articulating what "resonates with the structures of feeling of their audiences."[20] The phone-in program on Joy FM, referred to earlier, therefore, only sought to open up for public discussion through radio something that is normally part of popular discourse regarding the operations of religious functionaries. This is the emphasis that the radio program sought to draw attention to: that the sources of miracles could be dubious and demonic. The question on the program, I have noted, was posed from a Pentecostal/charismatic viewpoint. Pentecostal/charismatic Christians are aware that functionaries of Islam and those of indigenous religions serve as alternative or complementary sources of healing and protection for many people, including Christians. Pentecostal/charismatic Christianity, in particular, frowns upon this resort to non-Christian resources of supernatural succor, which are considered devilish. That is why the prophet-healing churches, on account of their reliance on syncretistic rites and incorporation of African traditional symbolism into their methods of healing, are classed together with traditional shrine specialists and consigned to the realm of the devil. Pentecostal/charismatic enthusiastic forms of Christianity, therefore, claim to offer more Christian and sanitized ritual contexts within which alternatives to traditional and Islamic sources of healing may be offered.

Traditional Western mission Christianity, as a child of the Enlightenment, generally plays down the supernatural; and, therefore, radical spiritual experiences do not feature prominently in its activities. So, in these films, pastors of historic mission churches would usually be portrayed as powerless in the face of demonic affliction and satanic onslaughts on lives. This is only an affirmation of general public opinion, which also explains why people drift from mission churches into Pentecost/charismatic ones. The result of mission church's powerlessness is that their agents, pastors, and church elders often clandestinely visit traditional shrines to fortify themselves, as in the African film *Break with the Past*. As compared to the mission churches, independent African initiatives in Christianity undoubtedly make a strong case for a viable faith that demonstrates the power of Christ through the ability of his spirit to intervene in crises.

That the images of rich and powerful people visiting shrines or prophets whose powers are obtained from the spiritual underworld are not figments of the imagination of producers is evident in conversion testimonies at Pentecostal/charismatic meetings. The Full Gospel Businessmen's Fellowship International (FGBMFI) is one of the most high profile Pentecostal/ Charismatic Para-church groups in Ghana today. The high points of FGBMFI meetings are the opportunities for converted patrons of non-Christian religious functionaries to reveal how in their "previous life" they remained "churchgoers" (though not real Christians) by practicing the "a little bit of Jesus, a little bit of medicine" philosophy that is so much a part of African religious life. Most of these testifiers claim a background in one of the historic mission churches. Their stories are narrated to reflect the subdued nature of the non-rational aspects of religion in these former mission churches. At FGBMFI meetings, stark revelations are made by the powerful in society regarding how they consulted traditional priests, Mallams, and Spiritual/Aladura church prophets who took them through diabolical rituals from which Jesus has now delivered them. The media only articulates and returns to the public for further consumption and discussion what the public knows all along: first, that people consult mediums to succeed in life, second, that even pastors are not exempt from using juju to win followings, and, third, that the sources of such medicines could be dangerous from what Pentecostals/charismatics define as a genuine Christian point of view.

African Video Films and Fascination with Evil

The fascination with supernatural evil and the availability of supernatural power through religious specialists to counteract its effects is what attracts many Africans to religion. This explains why film producers find irresistible subjects dealing with supernatural power and the interaction between its agents and clients. The ways of the supernatural are mysterious, and where the mysteries are played out in home video films, they keep people yearning to see, discuss, wonder, and understand more because these films speak to their situations. The search for religious and theological solutions from churches and shrines has become a collective paranoia in sub-Saharan African religions. In a recent newspaper publication, a retired Ghanaian civil servant, diplomat, and minister of state, K. B. Asante, regretted the Ghanaian penchant for resorting to shrines and "juju men" in order to succeed in life. Writing under the caption "Have You Ever Heard of Mami Water?" in the Ghanaian weekly *Chronicle on Saturday*,[21] Asante considered the persistent resort to supernaturalistic interpretation of events the bane of progress in Ghana:

> Many visit fetish shrines and consult juju men. They seek protection from Malams with powerful talismans and their prayers and incantations to put the Devil at bay to confound their enemies. They flock to priests who invoke the blessings of the good Lord in mysterious ways. Television drama supports the view that many are obsessed with the power of the supernatural. Shouts that disturb our peace from strange churches confirm that many expect favorable intervention from above. They do not believe that they can do much for themselves and their community. As life becomes difficult they blame the government and seek divine or occult intervention. Our development plans are unlikely to yield the desired result if many maintain this mindset.[22]

The African media carry to the public the general belief that the search for solutions from traditional shrines, Mallams, and independent church prophets could lead to the sexual abuse of women and the demonization of politicians and businesspeople who come to riches, fame, and power through the help of such dubious religious functionaries. In the process of imaging religious functionaries, African films and TV drama have become means of moralization. Through these media, the public is counseled against the unbridled pursuit of "signs and wonders." The phenomenon of religious mediation enabled by supernatural contact, as we have seen, is one that virtually dominates media coverage on religion, including TV theater, local sitcoms, and the ever-popular new African video movies. In the Ghanaian local sitcom *Effiewura* (Landlord), for example, the image of "the man of God" used is that of the indigenous prophet-healer. The prophet is always drunk and seduces women. He promises to "fast and pray" for clients and collects money for the purpose, but only spends it sleeping in hotels with gullible married women looking for solutions to their problems.

In an observation that there is a correlation between the African worldview of spiritual causation and the rise of prophet-healing churches, a former surgeon general of Ghana, Dr. Emmanuel Evans-Anfom, submitted that "the springing up and growth of the present day Spiritual churches and emergence of a certain type of spiritual healer, many of whom are nothing but charlatans, is an extension of the idea of evil spirits, or demons being active in the causation of disease."[23] As Meyer demonstrates from the Ghanaian film *Nkrabea,* based on a true story, "destiny," rumors, and stories about the involvement of powerful people with occult forces have been taken up by the film industry.[24] The films in question "celebrate Christian morality but thrive on revealing occult practices that exist on the dark side of modernity."[25] The point of the film *The Last Prophet* was, first, to expose the prophet as a charlatan and, secondly, to warn those who follow signs and wonders about the occult and dangerous sources from which such prophets are believed to obtain their powers. Help obtained from such sources, popular Christian opinion suggests, does not last. For, eventually, all the gains are lost, and conditions could become worse than they were before such help was obtained.

Conclusion: "Blowing the Cover"

In recent years, the search for solutions to life's debilitating problems has been moved into the arena of the electronic media, with the personal charismatic accomplishments of religious functionaries featuring prominently in this popular discourse. In African films, confrontations between evil and the power of God almost always portray the Pentecostal/charismatic pastor as the agent of God, a person of power with the ability or the anointment to confront evil in the powerful "name of Jesus." Pentecostal religion has generally been received in Africa as a powerful religion capable of dealing with the effects of evil medicines that are used as means of achieving political success and power. Pentecostalism, in the minds and experiences of the public, appears to be able to contain the occult much better than established mission churches. The older mission churches prefer not to talk about the powers of darkness in public and even regard them as superstitious figments of popular imagination.

Pentecostal/charismatic churches, however, take seriously the threat of sorcery and claim that dependence on the power of God enables the unmasking of the occult or demonic side of modern religion and has the ability to deliver victims of possession and oppression.

The preaching of the prosperity message that suggests that those who have God's favor upon them must succeed in life has not helped the phenomenon of perennial searches for solutions in African religious life. Mystical causality is real, but in modern African Christianity it has been overstretched in order to make up for the shortfalls in the message of prosperity. With the employment of spiritual causality as the main cause of the world's woes also comes the instillation of fear into people who move from prophet to prophet in search of solutions to their problems. The church, according to the New Testament, is supposed to be made up of people who, having been rescued from the hands of their enemies, are enabled to serve God "without fear in holiness and righteousness" (Luke I: 74–75). Building the theology of the church entirely around persons of sacred power distorts its ecclesiology and engenders abuse and exploitation. The media will continue to serve as an instrument for blowing the cover of culprits and sensitizing the public against overdependence on other people's charismatic abilities.

NOTES

A lengthier version of this essay was originally published in the *Legon Journal of the Humanities: University of Ghana Faculty of Arts Journal* 14 (2003): 1–20.

1. "Africa" in this essay refers essentially to Africa south of the Sahara. I am aware of concern that the use of "Africa" in context-specific studies could be misleading. Nevertheless, I am certain that wherever "Africa" is used in this essay, the issue raised is quite representative. This principle is similar to that of categorizing certain things as "European" or "Western" even when they relate to particular geographical contexts.

2. Jonathan Haynes, *Nigerian Video Films* (Athens: Ohio University Press, 2000), 3.

3. J. D. K. Ekem, *Priesthood in Context: A Study of Akan Traditional Priesthood in Dialogical Relation to the Priest-Christology of the Epistle to the Hebrews, and Its Implications for*

a Relevant Functional Priesthood in Selected Churches among the Akan of Ghana (Hamburg: Verlag and der Lottbek, 1994).

4. Joy FM was established in Accra ten years ago when the Ghanaian airways were liberalized following the adoption of a democratic system of government after almost twenty years of military dictatorship in Ghana. It advertises itself as a Christian station with its slogan, "taking you closer to heaven." After ten years Joy FM and its affiliate stations now cover more than half the country.

5. Asonzeh Frank-Kennedy Ukah, "Advertising God: Nigerian Christian Video-Films and the Power of Consumer Culture," *Journal of Religion in Africa* 33, no. 2 (2003): 203–231, 205.

6. Birgit Meyer, "Occult Forces on Screen: Representation and the Danger of Mimesis in Popular Ghanaian Films," *Etnofoor* 15, no. 2 (2002).

7. Ukah, "Advertising God," 203–231.

8. Rudolf Otto, *The Idea of the Holy: An Inquiry into the Non-Rational Factor in the Idea of the Divine and Its Relation to the Rational,* trans. John W. Harvey (1923; repr., Oxford: Oxford University Press, 1950), 158.

9. I. M. Lewis, *Ecstatic Religion: A Study of Shamanism and Spirit Possession,* 2nd ed. (London and New York: Routledge, 1989), 15.

10. Ibid.

11. Birgit Meyer, *Translating the Devil: Religion and Modernity among the Ewe in Ghana* (Edinburgh: Edinburgh University Press, 1999).

12. Birgit Meyer, "Popular Ghanaian Cinema and 'African Heritage,'" *Africa Today* 46, no. 2 (1999): 94–113, 105; see also Ukah, "Advertising God," 204; Obodimma Oha, "The Rhetoric of Nigerian Christian Videos: The War Paradigm of the 'The Great Mistake,'" in *Nigerian Video Films,* ed. Jonathan Haynes (Athens: Ohio University Press, 2000), 192–199.

13. Christian G. Baëta, *Prophetism in Ghana: A Study of Some "Spiritual" Churches* (London: SCM, 1962), 114.

14. Ibid.

15. Rosalind Shaw, "The Politician and the Diviner: Divination and the Consumption of Power in Sierra Leone," *Journal of Religion in Africa* 26 (1996): 36.

16. Ibid., 40.

17. Ibid., 38–39.

18. Ibid., 30.

19. Oha, "Rhetoric of Nigerian Christian Videos," 194.

20. Birgit Meyer, "Pentecostalism, Prosperity, and Popular Cinema in Ghana," *Culture and Religion* 3, no. 1 (2002): 71.

21. K. B. Asante, "Have You Ever Heard of Mami Water?" *Chronicle on Saturday,* April 12, 2003, 3.

22. Ibid.

23. Emmanuel Evans-Anfom, *Traditional Medicine in Ghana: Practice, Problems, and Prospects* (Accra: Ghana Academy of Arts and Sciences, 1986).

24. *Nkrabea,* Amahilbee Productions, Ghana, 1992.

25. Birgit Meyer, "The Power of Money: Politics, Occult Forces, and Pentecostalism in Ghana," *African Studies Review* 41, no. 3 (1998): 19.

PART FOUR

◇◇

Media Courted, Media Resisted

Popular Rituals and Artifacts in the Crafting of New Public Religious Practices

Why is it that some formerly important religious events and holidays seem to fade away over time, while other new events emerge on the public scene? How do these events capture the energy of a cultural, religiously inflected "happening" among a diverse population and become transformed into a media spectacle? In this final section, two such new, or newly reconstructed and mediated, events are considered: the Burning Man festival in Black Rock City, Nevada, and the Day of the Dead festivities that are gaining popularity throughout Latin America and in the United States. In each case, event organizers sought specific agendas in relation to these public events. Also in each case, organizers of these events grappled with the tensions of desiring the media attention so as to promote the event, while also at some point recognizing that the event's increasingly spectacular and commercial elements risked undermining and changing the event's original goals and purposes. Thus, these two chapters consider how it is that religious practices that accomplish political work in a society undergo change in relation to the mediated and commercial realm, and how practitioners at those events interpret and even incorporate changes into the public rituals themselves in response.

In the first chapter of this section, Lee Gilmore reflects on the ways in which Burning Man event organizers sought to manage what might be termed the Burning Man "brand" by both encouraging free artistic expression and carefully overseeing all media portrayals of the event. In the final chapter, Regina Marchi considers how Day of the Dead events risk commodifying and to some extent homogenizing Latin American identities, even as these events accomplish cultural work left undone by the commercial mandates of an increasingly youth-oriented culture in the United States.

10

"Media Mecca"

Tensions, Tropes, and Techno-Pagans at the Burning Man Festival

LEE GILMORE

As one of the most recent ongoing religio-cultural "happenings" in U.S. history, the Burning Man festival provides festival-goers with opportunities for radical self-expression and an alternative to the consumer lifestyle of contemporary American society. In this chapter, Lee Gilmore traces the ways in which event organizers and participants have come to understand the event in a self-reflexive process involving its emergence as, at once, a countercultural, spiritual, counter-consumerist, and yet deeply mediated spectacle. A former volunteer member of the event's Media Team, Gilmore offers insights into how the event organizers interacted with media professionals in these professionals' ongoing interest in covering this colorful and offbeat event. She notes the ways in which the organizers intentionally sought to challenge the objective stance that journalists often assume in relation to such events, encouraging instead a "new journalism": an ethnographically oriented approach to coverage, much more suited to the norms of the event itself. She also traces the ways in which coverage of the event was made to fit certain norms, or "frames," of news storytelling, particularly in relation to the popular frames of the "sex, drugs, and rock and roll" storyline and the "techno-pagan" and "spiritual" characterization of the event and its participants. In addition to these frames, however, Gilmore argues that other interpretations of the event, usually much more personal in nature, appear regularly in the realm of cyberspace as participants find one another and extend their self-expressions into the realm of new media.

Every year since the mid-1990s, thousands of individuals have converged upon an otherwise obscure corner of northwestern Nevada during the last week of August to participate in the Burning Man festival—a colorful and eclectic celebration of art, fire, and community. Given its many visually and narratively compelling elements, combined with a rapidly growing attendance, Burning Man has been the subject of a prodigious amount of different kinds of media attention. The event has been covered by a number of large mainstream commercial organizations, such as CNN, the Associated Press, and the BBC, as well as local news stations and newspapers, along with dozens of other international outlets. Burning Man has also been visited by hundreds of aspiring documentary film makers, resulting in a dozen or so completed films about the festival, of differing length and quality. Furthermore, the event has also been featured on thousands of both commercial and personal Web sites, many of which have an interactive or community-oriented aspect.

Following a brief summary of the festival's history and a review of relevant literature, this essay examines Burning Man's complex relationship with the media by illustrating how media portrayals have helped to shape both public understandings and private experiences of this event, and how Burning Man's organizers have learned over time to influence coverage. I also analyze the production and reproduction of contemporary cultural notions of premodernity, modernity, postmodernity, and spirituality by interrogating the mass media's deployment of specific "ethnographic" or "techno-pagan tropes" in framing this event. This in turn includes analyses of the ritualistic and "spiritual" elements of Burning Man that have contributed to the public construction of "techno-paganism" as a dominant media narrative for this event. Finally, I also look to the significance of interactive Internet media and its role in shaping both the experience and construction of "community" at Burning Man.

Black Rock City, U.S.A.

Burning Man began in 1986 as a celebration by a man named Larry Harvey and a handful of his closest friends who, for no particular or premeditated reason, decided to build an eight-foot-tall wooden effigy and burn it on a San Francisco beach at the summer solstice. When onlookers from all up and down the beach converged as the figure went up in flames, Harvey later described the experience as one of "impulsive merger and collective union" and soon decided to repeat the event the following year.[1] The event rapidly gained a large local following with each subsequent year, until by 1990 the crowd in attendance had grown to over 800 rowdy revelers—and "the Man," as the figure itself was by now known, had grown to forty feet. When local park police were called to the scene to prohibit its burning, it became clear that this event had outgrown its original setting. Harvey and his companions subsequently decided to relocate "the Burn" to Nevada's Black Rock Desert on the following Labor Day weekend, where it has continued to grow and evolve into an international festival that now draws tens of thousands of participants. The dominant feature of Black Rock Desert, located one hundred miles north of Reno, is a four-hundred-square-mile, utterly flat, bone dry, hardpan alkali plain known as "the playa," where temperatures can range from below 40 degrees to well over 100 degrees and fierce dust storms can rage with winds exceeding seventy-five miles per hour. This harsh, dramatic, and almost alien environment presents numerous challenges. Less than a hundred intrepid adventurers made the trek in 1990, but attendance roughly doubled with each subsequent iteration, until the event drew around 8,000 participants in 1996. The growth rate is no longer exponential, but has continued to rise each year such that it was populated by just over 35,500 individuals—who have come to be known as "Burners"—from around the globe in 2005. Billing itself as a venue of "radical self-expression," this week-long event appeals to those who seek a temporary alternative to the consumer lifestyle dominated by corporate culture.

The Burning Man festival now manifests as a temporary metropolis called Black Rock City, laid out in an arch of concentric semicircular streets surrounding an open central area. Featuring dozens of participant-created art installations, the central point of Black Rock City is marked by "the Burning Man" itself—a towering effigy, made of latticed wood and outlined with neon-tubing, that is ceremonially (and spectacularly) torched at the event's conclusion. Black Rock City also features basic civic amenities such as a central café, several daily newspapers, dozens of pirate radio stations, professional medical and emergency services, an internal volunteer peace-keeping force called the Rangers, and hundreds of regularly serviced chemical

FIGURE 10-1 A Burning Man installation: *The Medium Is the Religion,* by Irie Takeshi.

Photo by author, by permission of the artist.

toilets. In contrast to many other festivals and in keeping with this community's anti-commodification ethos, vending is strictly prohibited at Burning Man. The café, which sells only coffee and chai (tea), functions as a core community hub and, along with an ice concession, is the only place where money is exchanged within Black Rock City limits. Organizers instead promote the ideal of a *gift economy*, in which participants are encouraged to freely share their resources and creativity, while also promoting *radical self-reliance*, requiring attendees to bring all of their own supplies, including food, shelter, and a minimum of a gallon and a half of water per person per day. Furthermore, many participants not only bring everything they need to survive for one week in a very difficult desert setting, but also go to considerable expense and effort to transport the materials needed to create monumental art, imaginative performances, and eclectic "theme camps," which are temporary constructions dedicated to a particular concept or activity, each functioning both as an interactive entertainment venue for the city populace and as a hub for its own extended community (for example *Motel 666*, the *Temple of Atonement*, and *Flight to Mars*). Some of these artworks and camps have been inspired by one of a series of annual themes—such as "The Inferno," "The Wheel of Time," "The Floating World," "Beyond Belief," and "The Vault of Heaven"—that have been devised for each iteration of the event since 1996. While never encompassing the totality of creative expression at Burning Man, these themes provide a starting point that teases out various mythological and other symbolic threads that are embedded in global cultures.

Along with such concepts as *gifting, radical self-reliance,* and *radical self-expression,* the core principle underlying this event is the injunction to *participate* in some way, with the corollary that there should be *no spectators.* Simply put, this means all attendees are expected to make some kind of positive contribution to the collective experience, in whatever self-expressive way individuals so choose. The natural desert environment necessitates another of the event's primary mandates—*leave no trace.* This entails scrupulously cleansing the playa surface of all physical traces of the festival at its conclusion, down to the last pistachio shell, boa feather, and burn scar. This requirement is enforced by the Bureau of Land Management (BLM)—the federal agency which manages the Black Rock Desert and thus has the authority to issue or withhold event permits—and means that Black Rock City must be built from scratch each year, disappearing like Brigadoon at the festival's conclusion.

The festival is organized by a year-round staff of about two dozen individuals, assisted by over three thousand volunteers, and is legally held by the Black Rock City Limited Liability Corporation (LLC), consisting of the six most senior staff members, with Harvey as its executive director. In keeping with the event's anti-commodification ethos, this organization consistently refuses all offers of corporate sponsorship, such that it is funded almost exclusively by ticket sales, ranging in price from $185 to $280 each (depending on time of purchase) in 2006.[2] These funds are used to build the considerable infrastructure of Black Rock City, to cover insurance and miscellaneous administrative costs, and to sponsor theme art. Additionally, the Burning Man organization pays over $500,000 annually to the BLM, based on a usage fee charged per person per day.

I have engaged as a participant-observer in this festival since 1996. The Burning Man community's distinct emphasis on participation has made this an especially interesting and challenging endeavor and has required an ongoing evaluation of my own insider/outsider status in this community.

In following the injunction to participate, I chose to volunteer with the Burning Man organization. From 1998 to 2001, I was an active member of the Media Team, which is the volunteer group responsible for managing all press and media relations for the festival, both on-site at the event as well as throughout the year.[3] This work served as an invaluable aspect of my ethnographic research, gave me close access to core event organizers, and provided me with a special understanding of the media's unique relationship to this festival.

Theorizing Media and Ethnography

The mass media are increasingly complex and multifaceted phenomena that exert significant influence on the ongoing construction of human cultures, constituting critical spaces for cultural production and negotiation. Yet the media are not simply some amorphous or anonymous forces imposing a particular cultural hegemony upon the masses. Rather, the media are institutions and organizations operated by men and women who are embedded in particular cultural contexts and thereby subject to the same sets of cultural forces and references as are other individuals. Furthermore, the so-called new media of the Internet affords an increasingly visible interactivity, making it clearer than ever that the media's role in the construction of culture is not a simple one-way transmission. Thus, mass media can be conceived as reflexive mechanisms that serve to shape cultural consciousness and are, in turn, simultaneously shaped by a wide range of cultural influences.

James Carey has notably argued that communications theorists would be well served to shift from a "transmission" view of communication to a "ritual" view. Rooting his understanding of the term "communication" in its sense of both "participation" and "community" (as well as in the ideas of both Clifford Geertz and Emile Durkheim), he states that "a ritual view of communication is directed not toward the extension of messages in space but toward the maintenance of society in time; not the act of imparting information but the representation of shared beliefs."[4] This perspective has influenced much recent scholarship on the media, resulting in a shift toward cultural- and practice-oriented approaches to media analysis, as well as a significant upsurge in interest in the spaces of overlap and connection between the realms of "media," "ritual," and "religion."

Some have gone so far as to notice ways in which the media constructs
social rituals of a kind in response to significant national or international
events, such as the royal wedding of Charles and Diana, the funeral of
John F. Kennedy, or presidential debates. This concept of "media event"
as ritual was first articulated by Daniel Dayan and Elihu Katz, who applied
the theories of Victor Turner to their argument that these events engender
a sense of *communitas* amongst very large audiences.[5] These events serve
to cast public figures in mythic roles, confer legitimacy, reaffirm social values, redefine social boundaries, and define memory and history, among
other attributes. Dayan and Katz were careful to differentiate between
"ceremonial" media events—which they categorized as contests, conquests,
and coronations—and "news" media events that might also enthrall national
or international audiences, noting, for example, that they were "interested
here in the Kennedy funeral—a great ceremonial event—and not the Kennedy
assassination—a great news event."[6]

The recognition that there is an aspect of ritualization to media representations—particularly given the ritualistic nature of the Burning Man
festival itself—provides an intriguing framework in which to understand
the media's role in constructing and representing culture and can be illus-
trative for understanding some aspects of the relationship between Burning Man and the media. Of course, mediated portrayals of Burning Man
have yet to reach the scope or significance of the events with which Dayan
and Katz were chiefly concerned. One clear illustration of this difference in
both the character and reach of representation took place in 1998 when
major media outlets such as CNN shelved their planned reports on Burning Man (for which they had sent a small crew to Black Rock City) in favor
of ubiquitously covering the death of Princess Diana, which occurred
within the same week as the festival. Given this significant difference in
scope, the concept of a ritualized "media event" as Dayan and Katz proposed
it remains perhaps only tangentially relevant to the present study. Ronald
Grimes also offered this caution: "The equating strategy (media = ritual) has
limited utility. It turns heads, it attracts attention, but the shock value is
short-lived. . . . If in the long run there is nothing more to say than 'Media
activity is ritual activity,' each idea loses its capacity to provoke interesting
perspectives on the other, because there is insufficient tension between
them."[7] Grimes does not completely discount the power of the metaphorical

linkage between the two concepts, but instead argues for a more nuanced treatment of the notion of ritual. "Scholars need to ask not just whether some aspect of media is ritual, but in what respect it is ritual. Do we treat something as ritualistic because it is formulaic? Because it is repetitive? Because it is religious? In short, what definition of ritual do we imply by our claim?" [8]

In defining and locating what he meant in ascribing some ritualistic quality to "the news," Richard Schechner did in fact locate this feature in its repetitiveness, stating: "The ritual is in the format, in the programming, not in the content as such. The format insures that certain contents, certain classes of events, will be repeated; and repetition is a main quality of ritual. . . . Each facticity is part of a sequence of similar events: this fire is followed by the next and the next; this international crisis by the next and the next." [9] This assessment of the theatrical characteristics of the media points not only to the machinations by which certain classes of *events* are privileged over others, but also to the ways in which certain kinds of culturally constructed *ideas* are lifted up for consideration above others. These ideas can be rendered as a set of *tropes* which the media tends to return to time and time again, relying on these discourses to frame the ways in which the news becomes communicated and understood.

This is related to the concept of "framing" the news, as initially articulated by Todd Gitlin, who was in turn drawing on Erving Goffman's theory of frame analysis. [10] Gitlin defined media frames as "little tacit theories about what exists, what happens, and what matters." [11] In this practice of framing, the individuals who constitute the media make specific choices about both which facts *and* perspectives get selected for coverage and which are left out, in any given story. These cumulative choices rely upon pre-existing cultural constructs and, thereby, come to constitute sets of rhetorical tropes to which the media turn in framing their representations of events.

While scholars should remain cautious about injudiciously stretching Carey's initial insights on the link between media and ritual, his ideas have engendered a number of evocative applications of anthropological and sociological theories of ritual to studies of the media. One effective response has been voiced by Nick Couldry, who called for a "post-Durkheimian" approach to understanding the ritualized power of the media, an approach that recognizes all claims of the socially integrative functions of the media as precisely that: *claims*. In this way, he intended to sidestep the problems of totalizing and functionalist frameworks, while recognizing that the media does in fact *claim* to wield socially unifying and centralizing authority, whether or not it actually possesses such powers. These authorizing claims in turn grant legitimacy to media tropes, which also in turn reestablish and reify the media's totalizing claims of social unification. Couldry went on to argue that "it is impossible to see Durkheim's image of 'primitive' social experience—a temporary gathering in the desert!—as anything more than a starting point for understanding the vast, dispersed complexity of contemporary societies, and how, if at all, they cohere." [12] While it is certainly beyond the scope of this chapter to analyze the "vast, dispersed complexity" of contemporary societies and their relations with the media, it is, of course, another sort of "temporary gathering in the desert" that is the subject of analysis here. This ironic parallel is significant. Burning Man participants enact a freeform cultural bricolage by appropriating a plethora of non-Western cultural elements in creating artworks and costumes for the event. Thus, it does not require a great leap of imagination to see Burning Man as a pastiche of the "primitive" or "premodern" that is unfolding in a distinctively "postmodern" context. As Couldry went on to observe, "Look around any [social gathering, such as an annual music festival], and you will quickly find in people's clothes, bodily style, language and so on, traces of countless other spaces and histories, all quite independent from that gathering and not specifically intended to be expressed there." [13] Although Burning Man is not a "music festival" per se, the parallels in this statement seem apparent in the multiplicity of cultural styles and traces that can be observed there. Burning Man participants draw upon innumerable cultural sources in creating, negotiating, and *mediating* their experiences of this event, sources which are reflexively located in and represented by the mass media. Yet Couldry concluded that "there is no contemporary parallel for the Durkheimian totemic ritual in the desert where all society's central meanings and values are at stake." [14] While the negotiations of values and meanings that take place at Burning Man may not serve to mediate those concepts for our *entire* society, it is nevertheless the case that any given social meaning, value, or symbol may (in theory) be called forth for expression and representation in this context.

As participants are inspired by their quests for "authenticity" or "otherness" to enlist these icons and concepts in constructing their experiences and expressions of the event, the media likewise often turn to what I am calling *ethnographic tropes* in framing their representations of the event. These tropes entail the practice of a kind of "exoticizing" or "othering" gaze that can be observed in some media depictions of Burning Man and that may be related to actual approaches to gathering information at the event.

The discipline of ethnography itself is traditionally rooted in the practice of participant observation, in which the ethnographer becomes at once a participant in the cultural life of her/his subjects while maintaining a critical ideological distance. In the past few decades this discipline has undergone a significant shift toward increasingly reflexive strategies, which strive to more holistically situate both observer and observed within their discreet and overlapping cultural contexts and, in turn, away from historical tendencies to stereotype ethnographic subjects as primitive, backward, and exotic objects. In general, however, the mass media have not quite absorbed or noticed the potential relevance of these postmodern insights for their own discipline and can be seen to still cling to modern popular constructs, falling back on well-worn and well-known tropes when it comes to describing a phenomenon such as Burning Man. This is not necessarily the result of "bad" journalism; these are simply the categories to which members of Western cultures most typically have ready access when attempting to represent or describe a phenomenon such as Burning Man. These constructs are what I am calling "ethnographic tropes"—that is, common narratives about cultures that understand them with recourse to various qualities that could be called premodern, modern, or postmodern. Illustrations of this dynamic will be given below, following a description of the Burning Man organization's media relations processes.

Press Here

Media coverage of Burning Man has naturally increased as the event itself has grown, a phenomenon that festival organizers have successfully learned to negotiate over the years. Beginning in 1998, Burning Man's "Mistress of Communications," Marian Goodell, who joined the LLC in 1997, formed a new team of volunteers to assist her with all matters pertaining to media relations. She staffed this brand new Media Team largely with individuals who also worked professionally in press relations outside of the event, as well as others trained and employed as journalists, photographers, and, occasionally, ethnographers.[15] This Media Team now works year-round and has instituted an increasingly thorough and discerning mechanism for dealing with the large number of media groups that want to cover the event.

Because of the concrete ramifications—both locally and globally—of the ways in which the event is portrayed and perceived, organizers have become increasingly savvy in their relations with the media, as well as increasingly selective—as far as is both possible and prudent—of the media groups that will be allowed to cover the event. One reason for this selectivity is that organizers seek to minimize the intrusion of cameras and to protect participants and the event in general from commercial exploitation. Several attempts have been made to exploit the visually stunning imagery and edgy Burning Man "brand" in advertisements, music videos, and pornography, each of which has been resisted and defeated in turn, thanks to the LLC's trademark on the words "Burning Man." Images of the event and its artworks are also protected as intellectual property and cannot be used for commercial purposes without written permission of organizers. A semi-pro-bono attorney is retained to defend these rights.

In order to effect these policies, all commercial or professional media outlets are now required to pre-register via a Web-based form that collects information about the kind of story and use intended.[16] Another central aspect of the media registration process rests in the organization's requirement that *all* participants who are intent on shooting any moving images—whether for professional or private use—must sign a use agreement form. The vast majority of these are from Burners who simply want to shoot "home movies" in order to record their experience and, perhaps, show it to their friends back home. These participants are simply asked to sign a "personal use agreement" confirming that there is no commercial or public intent with their footage and that, should their intention change, they must first contact the Burning Man organization in order to negotiate rights from that point forward.[17] Those who do have professional intentions must pre-register with the Media Team and sign a commercial use agreement (the requirements of which vary from outlet to outlet) that generally prohibits the filmmakers from showing participants nude or using drugs (in order to protect individuals' privacy), delimits the venue(s) in which the finished product is intended to be shown (in order to prevent the footage from being sold to undesirable or unauthorized outlets), requests that appropriate credit be given to the artists whose work may be shown, and occasionally stipulates that some portion (usually 10 percent) of any proceeds be shared with the Burning Man organization.

Aside from these commercial agreements, broadcast and print news outlets are not limited by the Burning Man organization in large measure because it wants to nurture healthy relations with the press in order to more positively mediate the event's public image. Additionally, the organization doesn't want to be perceived as attempting to limit or regulate the freedom of the press, which has the right to cover events held on public land, and so they encourage legitimate news media outlets to attend. However, select entertainment-oriented media organizations are not welcome, chief among these being MTV, as Burning Man organizers do not want the event to be portrayed or perceived as a "spring break-esque" party, nor are they inclined to publicize the event to the stereotypical MTV demographic.

While there are numerous print and broadcast journalism outlets which cover the event each year, a significant majority of these applications come from aspiring documentary film makers. This phenomenon has been nurtured in part by the increasing affordability of high-quality digital video cameras, and it is this category of media that receives the most stringent scrutiny and is the most restricted form of coverage. This is done in large measure in order to prevent the potentially intrusive atmosphere that could be induced by too many camera crews, and also to simply limit the number of potentially repetitive documentary films that reach the public to those that propose to tell a unique story and are the most likely to be professionally carried out. For example, many of these applications propose to follow and film a first-time Burner in order to capture his or her wide-eyed "rite of passage." But this angle has been proposed so many times that it has become something of a joke among the members of the Media Team, and very few of these kinds of proposals are approved.

The Burning Man organization will on occasion work very closely with select film crews whose expertise and sensitivity to the nature of the event are expected to result in widely screened and sympathetic portrayals, such as the producers of *Confessions of a Burning Man* (2003), which did, in fact, record the adventures of a diverse group of four first-time attendees, as well as the producers of *Beyond Burning Man* (2004), which focused on a behind-the-scenes look at the orchestration of the event. While larger film crews such as these do sometimes receive special access and interviews, the organization will also lend extra support to one-person efforts where the "angle" seems especially interesting or unique, such as Renee Roberts's *Gifting It* (2002), which looked at the idea of Burning Man's "gift economy" and received significant publicity from the organization around its release.[18]

Some participants complain that the organization's media relations process is overly controlling and bureaucratic. However, the organization has learned several important and sometimes difficult lessons about the need to control the dispersal of images from the festival, as well as attempts to profit from these images. Perhaps the most significant media intrusion on the event was the production and release of two videos by a company called Voyeur Video, in which nude or partially nude female participants were intrusively filmed without their knowledge or consent. The Burning Man organization successfully took Voyeur Video to court to halt the sale of these videos.

Organizers encourage and often work closely with journalists, as they recognize the extent to which outside perceptions impact this unconventional event's ability to survive in the political climate of Nevada year after year. As one important example, in 1997 ABC's *Nightline* produced a one-hour special on Burning Man that portrayed the event in a very positive light and also reported on some of the ways in which the festival was being financially squeezed by local bureaucrats. This in turn attracted the attention of politicians at the state level and ultimately helped to ensure that the event was allowed to continue in subsequent years. Another example of the media's direct impact on the event in a more negative vein occurred in 1999 when the Associated Press issued a story with the headline "Drug Problem Surfaces at Burning Man," which claimed that between eighty and ninety people daily had required treatment for drug-related medical issues.[19] In actuality, these numbers reflected the *total* number of daily medical incidents, the majority of which involved dehydration and miscellaneous cuts and scrapes and were not, in fact, drug related. The clinical director of the Reno-based Regional Emergency Medical Services Authority (REMSA), which is hired each year to provide medical and emergency services on-site, later publicly clarified that the reporter had misinterpreted the information he had been given.[20]

However, the misrepresentation of the facts notwithstanding, this article was picked up by numerous outlets across the country and had a direct negative impact on the event, as the local authorities, who felt they could not afford to look "soft on drugs" in the eyes of their constituents, dramatically increased police presence at the event the following year. This not only resulted in increased arrests, but also contributed to a restless and potentially dangerous atmosphere brought on by participants' feelings that there were under siege. Because of this incident, Burning Man organizers are now much more careful to correctly contextualize such information for reporters and assiduously downplay the incidence of recreational drug use at the event. Instead, the media is pushed to explore other storylines away from the obvious "sex, drugs, and rock-and-roll" angle, onto more subtle (and perhaps more interesting) stories such as the event's interactions with and re-definitions of art, ritual, and culture.

Burning Man organizers' increased skill in media management was aptly demonstrated following the 2003 event, in which both print and broadcast coverage was dominated by reports of an extremely unfortunate accident in which a young woman lost her footing attempting to step off of a slow moving "art car"—a highly modified vehicle that had been transformed into a mobile interactive sculpture—and was tragically killed when she fell beneath the vehicle's wheels. The Burning Man organization's mastery of both media spin and political process was now notable in the aftermath, for while in the past media coverage might have tended to harshly portray such an accident in terms of irresponsibility or some inherent danger in the event, reports instead stressed the entirely accidental nature of this tragedy, emphasizing that "event organizers work closely with local and federal safety officials to prevent accidents," and went on to quote Goodell as saying, " 'It is unfortunate that, despite these precautions, this unusual accident' occurred." [21]

In addition to instituting the registration, selection, and "spin" process outlined above, organizers have also attempted to creatively invite the press to step outside of some of their usual reporting habits by calling upon the event's participatory ethos and encouraging the media in attendance at Burning Man to be fully *participants*, not *spectators*, thus invoking a more reflexive practice of participant observation and potentially reorienting the traditional ethnographic or journalistic gaze.

Going Native

Despite the extent to which organizers have learned to become allies with the media, many participants have traditionally resisted the media, perceiving it as fundamentally tied to corporate culture and as responsible for reducing Burning Man to a commodified spectacle. The media have been viewed, to some extent correctly, as spectators at an event where participation is upheld as a key value and "no spectators" prevails as a long-standing motto. In a unique attempt to change this problematic dynamic, in 1998 the new Media Team decided to involve the press in attendance at the event in a rite of passage. Upon arrival to check in at "Media Mecca"—as the media tent was now officially dubbed—reporters were asked to don one of the few dozen costumes which Media Team volunteers had collected for this purpose and to have their photograph taken with a Polaroid camera; their photo was then put on display at Media Mecca for the duration of the festival.[22] The intention was to encourage members of the media to "go native," or at least to adopt "native" dress, as well as to have the lens of camera turned back on them for a change. This practice was not continued in subsequent years, having been determined to be a bit too cumbersome and perhaps confrontational when what was really needed for the media check-in process was both expediency and a welcoming attitude. However, another tradition begun that year that continues as of 2005 was the distribution of a "press pass" with the tag line, "This pass entitles you to nothing in particular!"

The intention with these activities was to help media members better integrate into the event and become full-fledged participants rather than distanced observers. As a member of the Media Team during that period, I can attest to seeing more than one reporter initially show up in khaki safari gear—resembling a stereotypical anthropologist or *National Geographic* reporter—only to come back two days later wearing nothing but a sarong and some body glitter. Prior to 1998, many working media would come to the event only for a day, or stay in the hotel in nearby Gerlach. But from this point forward, they not only were encouraged to come and camp within the festival itself for as long as possible, but were furthermore required to do so if they wanted to secure key interviews with organizers such as Larry Harvey. The Media Team even adopted a motto which was displayed prominently on the cover of the press kit in 1999—"The best coverage of Burning Man always has been and always will be that which is profoundly personal. Immerse yourself."

The Media Team's attempts to reflexively situate members of the media who come to cover the event not only invite comparison to the ethnographic endeavor of participant observation, but are similarly rooted in broad sets of tensions around notions of objectivity in journalism. Michael Schudson has traced the "ideal of objectivity" in the media to the origin of the Associated Press in 1848, but he noted that this did not immediately become journalism's standard expectation. It wasn't until after World War I that journalists began to question the nature of vested interests, propaganda, and their own potential collusion with these forces, such that they began to strive for "objectivity." Schudson defined this term as meaning that "a person's statements about the world can be trusted if they are submitted to established rules deemed legitimate by a professional community. Facts here are not aspects of the world, but consensually validated statements about it." [23]

By the 1960s, the notion of "objectivity" came to be seriously questioned and was now thought to reproduce "a vision of social reality which refused to examine the basic structures of power and privilege," a perspective prompted and nurtured by the larger social tensions and problems of the day.[24] The "news" also came more and more to be understood as a commodity and, therefore, as subject to the whims and pressures of the market, a critique which the Burning Man community continues to launch against the media. Schudson identified a number of critiques of the ideal of objectivity in journalism which emerged from this era, including "the argument that the process of news gathering itself constructs an image of reality which reinforces official viewpoints. . . . [Objectivity] is a practice rather than a belief. It is a 'strategic ritual,' as sociologist Gaye Tuchman puts it, which journalists use to defend themselves against mistakes and criticism." [25] In this regard, the notion of objectivity itself can be understood as a *frame* though which the media perceives and represents events.

One response to these observations and tensions in the late 1960s was the development of what was hailed as the "new journalism," described by journalist Nat Hentoff as " 'powered by feeling as well as intellect,' the kind of journalism which 'can help break the glass between the reader and the world he lives in.' " [26] Schudson noted that "while 'new journalism' did not have much direct impact on news-writing in daily papers, it did have indirect effects. It fed the imaginations of daily reporters—*Rolling Stone*, for instance, came to be read in newsrooms across the country."[27] The tradition and sentiments of new journalism live on today as I have encountered at least one young journalist who declared in his Media Team registration that he planned to write a new journalism piece. Thus, in addition to pushing, and to some extent attempting to subvert, the boundaries between participant and observer (or native and outsider), the Burning Man Media Team also tapped into a larger set of questions and tensions within the media itself when they encouraged the press in attendance to abandon the pretenses of objectivity by immersing themselves and becoming engaged participants.

Although members of the media have often been seen as outsiders at the event, some of the earliest media coverage of this festival was actually generated by "native" Burners who were also professional journalists and who were motivated to share what they understood to be a remarkable story with their readers. In particular, there was a series of early online *Wired* articles in 1995, setting the stage for both a big cover story in *Wired* magazine in 1996 and a coffee-table collection of photographs, from HardWired's short-lived foray into book publishing, which was also produced by Burners/Wired employees.[28] The point here is that the boundary between participant and spectator, or native and outsider, has always been vague at Burning Man, often intentionally so.

By blurring and contesting the borders between native/outsider or participant/spectator perspectives, Burning Man organizers have encouraged members of the media to *participate* in reflexively negotiating the markers between self/other and self/culture alongside other participants, as explored in previous chapters. American studies scholar Jeremy Hockett has gone so far as to argue that the Burning Man festival can be, for all attendees, "understood as occasioning an 'ethnographic ritual' that invites participant observation, as individuals are encouraged to reflect on their own culture and their own roles in constructing that culture."[29] My own research likewise indicates that this festival does seem to foster some impulse to explore the frontiers of self/other/culture for many participants. Many participants likewise seem compelled to write down their stories and share them with the world—thus enacting the "graphy" component of "ethnography"—through posting their Burning Man stories to various e-mail lists, online bulletin boards, or their own Web sites.

Furthermore, as organizers hoped, some of the most thought-provoking media coverage of the event—what we might think of as "thick description," to continue invoking the ethnographic parallels—does in fact come from those reporters who reflexively immerse themselves in the festival, allowing themselves to go native, rather than remaining at an artificial and self-imposed distance.[30] Yet reflexive impulses notwithstanding, many mass-media-generated stories about Burning Man have tended to deploy ethnographic tropes by framing the event in terms of the *techno-pagan*, who is at once "primitive" or "tribal" (pre-modern) and technologically sophisticated (postmodern), while another common theme emerges in stories that frame the event by comparison to "religion" or "spirituality."

Tropes and Techno-Pagans

Although some of the vignettes shared earlier demonstrate the extent to which oversimplifications and unfavorable press have been reduced as organizers improved their relationships with the media and their skills in media spin, many mass-media depictions of Burning Man have nevertheless tended to exoticize and sensationalize the event. This slant is in keeping with the media's propensity to focus primarily on *bad news*, such that in order to *be* news, all news must be bad news. As Michael Schudson observed, "news tends to emphasize conflict, dissention, and battle; out of a journalistic convention that there are two sides to any story, news heightens the appearance of conflict even in instances of relative calm."[31] Thus, even among some of most well-meaning reporters, who may even be dedicated Burners themselves or who have otherwise gone native, the trend has been to capitalize on the more shocking and titillating aspects of the event, in general keeping with the truism that stories eliciting shock and fear will sell more newspapers and air time. By focusing on the shocking, different, or weird happenings of Burning Man, the media distance the event and its participants from what is held to be normative.

One illustration of the tension between organizers' public relations efforts and journalists' interest in telling both compelling and truthful stories can be observed in the proclivity of many media representations to focus on the "sex, drugs, and rock-and-roll" angle at the expense of other, less scandalous but perhaps equally provocative aspects of Burning Man. This is not to say that sex, drugs, and rock and roll (or, perhaps more properly in this context, "rave") are not to be found at Burning Man, but rather that the media's sometimes too-singular focus on these aspects is the result of quick surface impressions, rather than more substantive examinations. This has certainly not escaped the notice of festival organizers, and in 1999 Scott Sonner of the Associated Press reported, "Organizers say they've gotten a bad rap in recent years from the media, which tends to focus on the nudity, pagan rituals, and hallucinogenic drugs that make the rounds." [32] Yet, of course, even in attempting to turn the media's attention away from the ever-reliable shock value of "nudity, pagan rituals, and hallucinogenic drugs," this Burning Man spokesperson nevertheless drew the reporter's attention right to it. Another instance of organizers' simultaneous resistance and capitulation to exoticizing stereotypes can be seen on a Web page on the burningman.com site that is specifically directed to the media, upon which the image selected to accompany an essay debunking the "top media myths" is of an individual who has painted his skin dark black, is wearing a brightly colored sarong, and is standing next to a cauldron of fire—giving the impression of a non-indigenous man who has "gone tribal." [33] This correspondence may be entirely unintentional, but it could also perhaps be understood as a bit of self-satire that, in its way, comments upon (and perhaps contributes to) the dynamics of the media's deployment of ethnographic tropes.

Below are a number of examples that illustrate these "othering" language strategies in operation, highlighting the ways in which the event has been repeatedly painted with reference to some kind of regressive paganism or primitive tribalism, while also declaring the event to be somehow the ultimate technological or postmodern happening:

The *primitive survivalist aspects* of the festival may seem to contrast with *the digital world of its inhabitants*, but Burning Man has become *a pastiche of various parts of our culture and history*. It has the spontaneous-gathering feel of Woodstock, the *spirituality and temporary community* of the Rainbow Gathering, the campiness, outrageousness and identity-transformation of the drag-queen scene, the edginess and danger of a Harley-Davidson convention and *the burning and worship of, well, the ancient Druids.*[34]

It is fair to say that Burning Man is the influential *tribal-techno-feral-pagan-digital event*, happening, rave or whatever in the world. Out there in the desert, *witches, warlocks and wired sorcerers* use technology as if it were some *electronic crystal ball*. It is a living *post-postmodernist* Hieronymous Bosch painting with just a touch of Fellini.[35]

It is a curious waltz between *the beginning of the millennium and its end.* There is *a pre-Christian paganism* that befits this ancient rock: *the pilgrimage*, the boulevard leading to The Man and his incineration, during which people dance and whoop in the smoke. . . . It is also about *cyberspace*—an assembly organised entirely through the Internet. Most campers are *cybergeeks*; *Wired* magazine called the festival "the holiday of choice for the Digerati." [36]

As these examples each demonstrate, the media's proclivity to sensationalize Burning Man actually often pulls the event in two directions simultaneously—toward the primitive and the high-tech, the premodern and postmodern. The following selection in particular demonstrates a number of elements that operate in the deployment of this trope, from the journalists' collective struggle to "fix a label on" (and thereby frame) the event through recourse to earlier media explications to Harvey's own clear awareness of the event's paradoxical "techno-pagan" elements:

Furrowed brows outside the press trailer: my colleagues in the media and I are finding it hard to *fix a label on all this.* Is it guerrilla performance art or a pyromaniacs' ball? "Mad Max" or "Priscilla, Queen of the Desert?" Is it, as previous journalists have suggested, "an atavistic, avant-garde, neo-pagan flame-back," "a post-modern carnival of the absurd," or a "post-hippie proto-apocalyptic art ritual?"

The founder of the Burning Man, an elegantly ravaged San Francisco artist and landscape gardener named Larry Harvey, can discourse for hours on the meaning of the festival. Sitting on a deckchair in a dark suit and black hat, smoking cigarette after cigarette, he spins and weaves his theories, explaining the Burning Man in terms of *post-Freudian identity crises, the demise of primitive mythocentric religions, and the sterility of the corporate-controlled consumerism* which passes for culture in America these days. "These are post-modern times," he says at one point. *"Everything that's ever happened before is happening now*, in one form or another, but none of it really compels us, and transforms us. We can access unimaginable quantities of information and images through the Internet, we can communicate with everyone in the world, but so what? The Burning Man Festival celebrates *technology as a potential tool for freedom*, but it also reverts back to something *primordial, prehistoric, proverbial*. Throughout our evolution, in all corners of the planet, human beings have come together and gathered around fire, and this ritual still invokes *a very basic, primal response*." [37]

In this vignette, the journalists' collective search to "fix a label" on this event can on one level be understood as evincing the shared quest to understand and describe the *meaning* of this event, an exercise that all participants likely enact on some level, even (and perhaps especially) Harvey, although in this case the effort becomes to circumscribe the event within some simplistic but catchy sound bite. Because this particular conversation was conveyed into the public sphere, it thereby contributed to the persistence of the techno-pagan trope in media descriptions of the event, perhaps generating other "buzz phrases" that future journalists would turn to when working to write up their versions. The Burning Man organization itself has parodied this pursuit to boil the event down to some pithy adage with a feature called "The Burning Man Phrase Generator ©" that appears at the bottom of the aforementioned "media myths" page. My own random test of this system provided such phrases as "retro-tribal-futuristic-orgy," "nerdo-druidic-underground-conspiracy," and "crypto-hipster-dada-hoedown."

It should be noted, of course, that not all media representations of Burning Man necessarily partake of these particular tropes, as witnessed by some of the examples given earlier in this essay, such as documentaries like *Gifting It* and the ABC *Nightline* episode. Furthermore, and particularly in the light of Harvey's own contribution to the framing discourse, it should be noted that my analysis of the recurrent techno-pagan theme as a particular trope or frame does not mean that there are not numerous observable aspects of Burning Man that readily lend themselves to these narratives. Many participants themselves often adopt dress (or lack thereof) that embraces what has come to be called the "modern primitive style," replete with tattoos, body piercing, and body painting based on a variety of global indigenous motifs and practices. Indeed, these motifs are entirely in keeping with the high degree of cultural appropriation and bricolage which are fundamental aspects of this event. But while these may be among the more visually stunning elements, they are not the only qualities of the event. The persistent exoticizing, othering, and distancing strategies of ethnographic tropes remain commonly deployed frames that may limit other ways of perceiving and portraying the event.

"Pagans" and "Spirituality"

Another common theme in media representations, as also highlighted in many of the examples given above, is to frame the event through recourse to its apparent religious or spiritual dispositions. For example: "The burning seems symbolic of many things. It could be taken as *a purging, cleansing ceremony in your basic spiritual kind of way*. A sort of group re-birthing if you like, but without the artsy fartsy, hippy trippy, New Agey stuff. Like its famous ancestor, Woodstock, Burning Man is also a celebration of change, but it takes it a lot further. It is about the *pulling down of old belief systems and structures, and replacing them, if only temporarily, with a new autonomous zone*." [38] The media's interest in the potential spiritual resonance or significance of this event was perhaps most noticeable in 2003, when several reporters picked up on that year's stated theme—"Beyond Belief"—and explored these correspondences. One reporter called my own institution, the Graduate Theological Union (GTU), for quotes and spoke with President James Donahue, who speculated: "This can be anything from a kind of playfulness, to narcissism, to a more serious spiritual quest. . . . It is what you make of it. People bring their own interests and desires to it." [39] The article also quoted a professor of sociology from the GTU, Jerome Baggett, who stated, "The people who are going to Burning Man—Boomers and Xers—are the most educated generations in history. They're trained to question." [40] Finally, the same article quoted Sarah Pike from the California State University at Chico, who stated: "It can be a religious experience, but there's no particular dogma that's adhered to. . . . This is moving for people who don't feel comfortable with organized religion."[41] Aside from the delightful irony that Baggett and Pike both served on my dissertation committee, these perspectives in their turn contribute to the public positioning of Burning Man as an alternative to traditional "religions" by reverberating this discourse into the public sphere of the media.

Yet while these learned voices might provide more socially contextualized frames for the event that speak in terms of "questing," "questioning," and the absence of "dogma," the repeated turn in the media remains to "paganism" as the religious type that seems most clearly reflected at Burning Man, or that most strongly surfaces in the ritualistic elements that give the event spiritual resonance. For example, the writer of this article employed descriptors such as "bizarre rites," "bacchanalia," and "ancient ceremonies and symbolic sacrifices that barely echo today in modern mainstream Western religions" and quoted two participants who stated, "Burning Man touches something primal—it doesn't have words," and "I'm a pagan and this is a chance for me to dress in a bizarre way, but also to flaunt my paganism."[42]

Pagan scholar Michael York has argued that paganism may be understood as a "root religion" that to some extent underlies all global religions, saying that, "historically, all other religions are offshoots and/or counterdevelopments of the root religion. . . . [I]f we wish to understand any religion, we must also understand paganism as the root from which the tree of all religions grow."[43] From this perspective, while Burning Man lacks any avowed theology and, furthermore, remains officially and ideologically distanced from the category of "religion," it nevertheless does display a number of ritualistic elements and motifs that echo this underlying global, cultural paganism in the "basic, primal response" (as Harvey termed it) that it can generate in participants' experiences. As York went on to say, "inasmuch as paganism is the root of religion, it confronts the earliest, the most immediate, and the least processed apprehensions of the sacred. This is the experiential level on which paganism in both its indigenous and contemporary forms wishes to concentrate."[44] Something like this "experiential level" appears to unfold in many participants' experiences, and that thereby contributes to the prevalence of "paganism" as a trope by which to delimit or label this event.

Cybergeeks and Online Communities

Having illustrated and contextualized some of the apparently pagan elements of the Burning Man festival, I should finally like to look more closely
at the "techno" half of the techno-pagan trope. This aspect emerges in part
from the tremendous impact that media representations can have on the
perceptions of attendees, thus influencing individual expectations and
serving to attract certain demographic populations. Perhaps the clearest
incidence of this was by way of the November 1996 *Wired* magazine cover
story, in which science-fiction writer Bruce Sterling proclaimed Burning
Man to be the "New American Holiday" for the so-called "digerati." [45] Less
important, perhaps, than the substance of this piece was its venue, as the
article drew numerous new participants to the event, hailing largely from
the San Francisco Bay Area and Silicon Valley "techie" communities, many
of whom were awash in large amounts of disposable income during the
"dot.com" heyday. This contributed significantly to the course the event
would take in those years, as demonstrated by an increase in large-scale,
technologically complex, and expensively produced artwork. In addition,
several high-profile, high-tech individuals are known to have attended
during that era, including Jeff Bezos, CEO of Amazon.com, and Google
founders Larry Page and Sergey Brin, among others. [46]

Indeed, a lot of media coverage in those years focused upon the significant influence of the dot.com boom and culture upon the event, featuring
headlines such as "Bonfire of the Techies: Hordes of Playful Digerati
Assemble for a Hallowed Annual Rite" [47] and "Geeks at Burning Man: Or
How I Spent My Summer Vacation on the Playa." [48] Of course, by the time
the dot.com bubble burst in 2001, these headlines shifted to "Burning
Man's Dotcom Hangover" [49] and "Dot-com Fallout Hits Burning Man:
Decline in Attendance Tied to Economic Downturn." [50] This perception
and portrayal of Burning Man as a playground for computer geeks leads to
a consideration of the online dimensions of the event as the media zone
where the line between participant and observer may be most noticeably
obscured. Indeed, Burning Man has even been compared to the Internet
itself, as an open and seemingly limitless space populated by individual
nodes for creativity and community, be they theme camps or Web
sites. [51]

The Internet serves as an essential organizing and communications tool for both the Burning Man organization and the larger Burning Man community who have turned to the Internet as a space in which to continue to radically express themselves, sharing their experiences of the event with the world through this medium and building community with one another year-round. In addition to the organization's own Web site (www.burningman.com), numerous commercial media sites have produced features on Burning Man, and thousands of participants have created their own Web sites and Web pages to showcase their photos, share their stories, and organize their theme camps. Furthermore, Burners all over the world stay connected year-round through numerous regional and global e-mail discussion lists as well as bulletin boards such as the "e-playa" hosted on burningman.com.

In addition to the official e-playa bulletin board, other online community spaces for Burning Man include several social-networking Web sites, such as myspace.com, tribe.net, and livejournal.com, in which participants developed Burning Man–related content and communities within the sites' provided structures. Other social-networking sites, such as sixdegreeburn.com and netplaya.com, were created by Burning Man participants specifically for the Burning Man community. Participants in at least two "3-D worlds"— secondlife.com and there.com—have created Burning Man–themed spaces within their virtual realms. Finally, there are several subscription-based e-mail discussion lists which also serve as popular vehicles for year-round conversations about the event and as explicit spaces for community building, including the burnman-list@dioxine.net (founded and hosted by Burner Eric Pouyoul since 1994 and once the "official" e-mail list for the event) as well as several regional discussion lists hosted or supported by the organization, such as newyork-list@burningman.com, burningman-list@burnaustin.org, and playadust@euroburners.org, to name just a few, and it is very probable that there are countless other online venues for Burning Man.

Given the fact that the explosion of online communities is a relatively recent occurrence, scholars are only beginning to analyze the social significance of the phenomena and are sometimes struggling to keep up with the rapid changes in technology and the Internet industry. For example, Sherry Turkle's groundbreaking *Life on the Screen* (1995) deals primarily with nodes of online interactivity known as MUDs (Multi-User Domains or

"Dungeons") that are no longer the most popular meeting points for online community, which is now more frequently dominated by arenas such Web-based bulletin boards, e-mail lists, live chat rooms, "blogs," and "massively multi-player online games." Nevertheless, her explorations remain relevant and important keys to framing the experiences and constructions of identity in online spaces. Her study concerned the ways in which MUDs could be "places where the self is multiple and constructed by language, they are places where people and machines are in a new relation to each other, indeed can be mistaken for each other. In such ways, MUDs are evocative objects for thinking about human identity and more generally, about a set of ideas that have come to be known as 'postmodernism.'" [52] An interesting parallel to Burning Man can be readily observed here, as many participants utilize the festival as a space in which to negotiate and reformulate both individual and collective identities, experiencing various forms and degrees of personal transformation through the experience. Many Burners adopt a nickname, or "playa-name," for use at the festival; this often then becomes an identity (or an aspect of identity) that follows them home into their daily lives. Furthermore, these monikers are also sometimes employed as online identities, as e-mail addresses and other online "handles."

A more recent sociological investigation of online communities was conducted by Mary Chayko, who described Internet-based relationships as "sociomental," stating: "They are a manifestation of an absolutely genuine and often deeply felt sense that despite physical separation, a closeness among people, a nearness, exists; that while the physical distance separating people may be great, the social distance between them may be very small indeed. They represent an experience of communion with another person, one that does not depend on face-to-face meetings to be initiated or maintained. Sociomental bonds [are] bonds between people who cannot or do not meet face-to-face." [53] This concept is helpful in understanding and emphasizing the potential depth and significance of Internet-based relationships. However, it remains somewhat limited in its applicability to the significance of online communities in relation to an event like Burning Man, which, of course, also exists as an actual "embodied" community. Many Burners who participate in Internet-based communities related to the festival endeavor to meet their online companions face-to-face, as is a common occurrence among such communities and friendships, but in this instance there are numerous physical community mechanisms available to them through regional events and parties as well as, of course, the event itself.

It is tempting to compare the sense of "genuine closeness" and "experience of communion" that Chayko found to be experienced by some online communities with Victor Turner's notion of communitas, as Dayan and Katz did in their study of media events.[54] While it is impossible to ascertain the emanation of communitas stemming from online contexts with any rigor without a more in-depth study than is feasible in the present project, I suspect that something like this does occur in many such situations. My observations in this regard are largely limited and unstructured, but there certainly does seem to be a degree to which the experience of "surfing the Web" in its various forms can be extremely consciousness-absorbing. In the immersive quality these spaces can foment there may be some sense of the liminoid—of being somehow disembodied and in between worlds—that resonates to at least some degree with Turner's notions. The spatial metaphors of liminality also surface here, as noticeable in the frequency with which the Internet is termed as a "space," when in actuality the Internet exists only as a series of electrical impulses, translated first into computer codes and then into human interfaces.

Online media is further distinct from other forms of media in its interactivity, its reciprocity, and its (theoretically, at least) unrestricted access to any and all comers with the necessary technology. This ability to "talk back" to the mass media, and, indeed, the potentiality for anyone to establish her/his own "media" site, renders another similarity between the Internet and Burning Man, as both may be potential zones for "radical inclusivity" and "radical self expression." The extent to which all members of a society participate in discourses and tropes that shape and frame constructions and experiences of culture becomes ever more apparent through this visibly and viscerally reflexive medium.

As with all other social and cultural contexts, the notion of online community is a construction and, furthermore, is multiply constructed and inherently polyvocal. This is certainly apparent in the case with Burning Man's online communities, where a lively diversity of discourses proliferates. For example, the e-playa and tribe.net are both infamous as spaces in which to complain about or critique the event. Thus, the Internet for Burners is simultaneously a place where genuine human ties and communities are forged as well as a space for multiple contested and competing voices.

While I remain cautious about stretching this concept too far, the potential sense of communitas in online communities leads us back to where we began this chapter by noticing the parallels between ritual and the media. Burning Man's relationship to the Internet is fundamental to its community-building mission, both on- and off-line. Through the various online media described above, participants are able stay connected to other Burners well beyond the physical and temporal limitations of the event itself, such that the Burning Man community has a truly global scope. The Internet serves to represent the event both internally and externally, as participants use online media to share and build upon the experience with one another and to share these experiences with the rest of the world. Thus, as with the pagan thematics and impulses discussed above, there is, indeed, a great deal about this event that lends itself to the perception and/or construction of the techno half of the techno-pagan trope.

Conclusion

Burning Man's relationship with print, broadcast, film, and online media is multifaceted. Burning Man organizers for their part have exerted much effort on building relationships with members of the media in order to foster more sensitive portrayals of the event and thus protect it from the potentially destructive consequences of bad press. These efforts, in turn, shape how the event is both framed and experienced. It may seem ironic that the Burning Man organization seeks to transgress many social norms while also not wanting to be publicly portrayed as too transgressive, or as transgressive in the wrong ways. Yet fundamentally, I believe this stems from the organizers' learned political savvy and should be understood as a response to some incumbent political realities that must be capitulated to, or at least treaded cautiously around. Such tensions should not be surprising given that the event is paradoxically attempting to institutionalize a "temporary autonomous zone." [55] By using the media to convey their unconventional social vision to a much larger audience, organizers seek not only to manage the event's public image, but, ultimately, to use the media to influence mainstream culture. In the course of the event's explosive growth in the mid-1990s, Harvey consciously decided that he wanted as many people as possible to experience Burning Man, despite the logistical difficulties imposed by the growth. And in this, he recognized that the media were a key to spreading the message.

While participants themselves often construct the event and their experience of it in terms of a kind of neo-tribalism, these cultural constructs are, in turn, fed by the media, creating causal and reflexive loops between individuals and media, participants and spectators, self and society, and normative and other. The techno-pagan trope indicates some of the basic concepts and constructions that our culture has recourse to when seeking to create social and experiential alternatives to traditional or normative religions, such as Burning Man can be for many participants. Even our concepts of premodernity, postmodernity, or just plain modernity are all themselves constructs which serve to define, delimit, and also thereby constrict categories of human experience. While Burning Man can perhaps be understood as a postmodern reaction to modernity in the guise of the premodern, it might also be said that Burning Man expresses a simultaneity of multiple modernities, in the sense of our current contemporary constructions of and categories for experience.

While the concept of mass media *as* social ritual should be cautiously employed, it is useful by way of shedding light on the ritualistic patterns and tendencies both within media representations *and* on the part of those who constitute them. Taking this as a starting point for understanding and contextualizing some of the particular themes which the media repeatedly deploy in constructing their centralizing and authorizing claims, the media's habits regarding their representations of Burning Man can be viewed as commonly utilized *tropes* that result from the media's framing practices. These tropes can be compared to ethnographic narratives that highlight and play off of the tensions between notions of premodernity and postmodernity in which the event is situated and through which the media and Burning Man participants alike partake of the collective public construction of meanings, spiritualities, and cultures. Through repetition and adroit manipulation of cultural symbols, the media, like ritual, can help to create perceptions of unity in the ways in which social events are experienced by providing pervasive and prescriptive frameworks for understanding.

NOTES

1. Larry Harvey, quoted in Brian Doherty, *This Is Burning Man* (New York: Little, Brown and Company, 2004), 31.

2. See http://afterburn.burningman.com (accessed December 23, 2005) for more on the organization's finances. Also, for an analysis of Burning Man's general relationship to "the market," see Robert V. Kozinets and John Sherry, "Welcome to the Black Rock Café," in *AfterBurn: Reflections on Burning Man*, ed. Lee Gilmore and Mark Van Proyen (Albuquerque: University of New Mexico Press, 2005).

3. My need to pursue more formalized research necessitated a retreat from most of these volunteer responsibilities in order to have more time to pursue other angles of research during the event itself. I remained minimally involved for a couple years as the academic liaison, meaning that I responded to e-mailed queries from other academics.

4. James Carey, *Communication as Culture: Essays on Media and Society* (Boston: Unwin Hyman, 1989), 18.

5. See Daniel Dayan and Elihu Katz, *Media Events: The Live Broadcasting of History* (Cambridge: Harvard University Press, 1994).

6. Ibid., 9.

7. Ronald L. Grimes, "Ritual and the Media," in *Practicing Religion in the Age of the Media: Explorations in Media, Religion, and Culture*, ed. Stewart M. Hoover and Lynn Schofield Clark (New York: Columbia University Press, 2002), 226.

8. Ibid., 227.

9. Richard Schechner, *Between Theater and Anthropology* (Philadelphia: University of Pennsylvania Press, 1985), 315.

10. See Erving Goffman, *Frame Analysis: An Essay on the Organization of Experience* (New York: Harper and Row, 1974).

11. Todd Gitlin, *The Whole World Is Watching: Mass Media in the Making and Unmaking of the New Left* (Berkeley: University of California Press, 1980), 6–7.

12. Nick Couldry, *Media Rituals: A Critical Approach* (London: Routledge, 2003), 8.

13. Ibid., 8–9.

14. Ibid., 9.

15. I was not the only individual with ethnographic training who joined the Media Team. Others included Katherine Chen, who was at the time completing her sociology doctorate at Harvard by conducting a study of volunteerism at Burning Man, and Karie Henderson, who did a visual anthropology senior thesis on Burning Man at the University of California, Santa Cruz.

16. For more information on Burning Man's media relations policies, see the "Press Here" section of their Web site: http://www.burningman.com/press (accessed December 23, 2005).

17. It does not actually matter that some participants will inevitably capture moving images without signing any personal or other use agreement, as the fact that the organization has consistently articulated this policy renders it legally binding.

18. For more information on these films, see, respectively: http://www.burning-manconfessions.com/; http://www.goneoffdeep.com/; and http://www.giftingit. com/ (all accessed December 23, 2005).

19. Martin Griffith, "Drug Problem Surfaces at Burning Man Festival," Associated Press, September 4, 1999.

20. See Lessley Anderson, "Burning Spin: Organizers of the Burning Man Festival Pull Out All the Stops to Control the Press—and It's a Good Thing They Do," *San Francisco Weekly*, August 28, 2002.

21. Linda Goldston, "Burning Man Death Was a First at Festival," *San Jose Mercury News*, September 2, 2003.

22. The "Media Mecca" moniker for the media registration tent, which continues to be used as of 2005, was selected for its evocation of the idea that all members of the media should go there at least once during their visit to Black Rock City.

23. Michael Schudson, *Discovering the News: A Social History of American Newspapers* (New York: Basic Books, 1978), 7.

24. Ibid., 160.

25. Ibid., 185–186.

26. Nat Hentoff, "Behold the New Journalism—It's Coming after You!" in *The Reporter as Artist: A Look at the New Journalism Controversy*, ed. Ronald Weber (New York: Hastings House, 1974), 52; quoted in Schudson, *Discovering the News*, 187.

27. Schudson, *Discovering the News*, 188.

28. See Janelle Brown, "Quest for Fire: Playing with Matches at the Burning Man Festival," *HotWired*, September 8, 1995, available from http://hotwired.wired. com/road/95/36/index5a.html (accessed January 30, 2005); and Brad Weiners and John Plunkett, eds., *Burning Man* (San Francisco: HardWired, 1997).

29. Jeremy Hockett, "Burning Man as Ethnographic Experience: Participant Observation and the Study of Self," in *AfterBurn: Reflections on Burning Man*, ed. Lee Gilmore and Mark Van Proyen (Albuquerque: University of New Mexico Press, 2005).

30. For background on the term "thick description," see Clifford Geertz, "Thick Description: Toward an Interpretive Theory of Culture," in *The Interpretation of Cultures* (New York: Basic Books, 1973), 3–30.

31. Michael Schudson, *The Sociology of News* (New York: W. W. Norton and Company, 2003), 50.

32. Scott Sonner, "Burning Man Drawing 20,000 to Nevada's Black Rock Desert," *Las Vegas Sun*, September 1, 1999.

33. See Larry Harvey, "Media Myths: Setting the Record Straight on Burning Man Myths (and a few new ideas)," at http://www.burningman.com/press/myths.html (accessed December 23, 2005).

34. Michael Colton, "America's Hottest Festival; An Eclectic Arts Event Draws 15,000 to the Nevada Desert in August. Call It 'Weirdstock,'" *Washington Post*, August 27, 1997, D01, emphasis mine.

35. Alex Priedite, "Where High-Tech Meets Low Life and Many a Wood Man Has Met His Match," *Australian Financial Review*, October 4, 1997, 4, emphasis mine.

36. Ed Vulliamy, "Anarchy rules at wildest party on Earth; Ed Vulliamy in Black Rock Desert, Nevada, joins the pyro-fetishists, cybergeeks and guys just nuts about guns at the Burning Man festival," *Observer*, September 6, 1998, 8, emphasis mine.

37. Richard Grant, "Ten Thousand Go Mad in Nevada; Once a year, Californians head for the desert for four days of art, sex, guns and primal ritual. Richard Grant goes feral at the Burning Man Festival, while a 40ft effigy (and much else) goes up in smoke," *Independent* (London), November 17, 1996, 10.

38. Priedite, "Where High-tech Meets Low Life."

39. Don Thompson, "Burning Man Festival a Focus for Parties, Religious Yearning," *San Francisco Chronicle*, August 29, 2003.

40. Ibid.

41. Ibid.

42. Ibid.

43. Michael York, *Pagan Theology: Paganism as a World Religion* (New York: New York University Press, 2003), 167.

44. Ibid., 167.

45. Bruce Sterling, "Greetings from Burning Man," *Wired* 4, no. 11 (November 1996): 196–206, 274; also available from http://www.wired.com/wired/archive/4.11/burningman.html (accessed January 30, 2005).

46. Google first began incorporating various seasonal themes into its logo when Page, Brin, and other early Google employees made their own pilgrimage to the event in 1999. See http://www.npr.org/templates/story/story.php? storyId=1521761; and http://www.google.com/intl/en/holidaylogos99.html (both accessed December 23, 2005).

47. Kevin Kelly, "Bonfire of the Techies: Hordes of Playful Digerati Assemble for a Hallowed Annual Rite," *Time Magazine*, August 25, 1997.

48. Joyce Slaton, "Geeks at Burning Man: Or how I spent my summer vacation on the playa," *SFGate*, September 8, 1999; available from http://www.sfgate.com/cgi-bin/article.cgi?file=/g/a/1999/09/08/burningman.DTL (accessed December 23, 2005).

49. Bill Werde, "Burning Man's Dotcom Hangover," *Village Voice*, September 12–18, 2001.

50. James Sullivan, "Dot-com Fallout Hits Burning Man: Decline in Attendance Tied to Economic Downturn," *San Francisco Chronicle*, August 27, 2001.

51. One source for this analogy can be found in the transcript of Larry Harvey's speech at the "9th Annual Be-In," January 1997; see http://www.burningman.com/whatisburningman/people/cyber.html (accessed December 23, 2005). This concept has also been expressed in personal communications with Ron Meiners, Bruce Damer, and Mark Pesce, among others. I am especially indebted to numerous conversations with my husband, Ron Meiners, an online community professional, for my understandings of Burning Man's relationships with the Internet.

52. Sherry Turkle, *Life on the Screen: Identity in the Age of the Internet* (New York: Simon & Schuster, 1995), 17.

53. Mary Chayko, *Connecting: How We Form Social Bonds and Communities in the Internet Age* (Albany: State University of New York, 2002), 1–2.

54. See, among others, Victor Turner, *The Ritual Process: Structure and Anti-Structure* (Ithaca, NY: Cornell University Press, 1969).

55. See Hakim Bey, *T.A.Z.: The Temporary Autonomous Zone, Ontological Anarchy, Poetic Terrorism* (New York: Autonomedia, 1985).

11

Day of the Dead as a
New U.S. Holiday

Ritual, Media, and Material Culture
in the Quest for Connection

REGINA M. MARCHI

The final chapter in this section, and, indeed, in this volume, brings us full circle in the exploration of religion as a global, commercial, ideological, lived, and ever-changing phenomenon. Originally a family ritual celebrated in cemeteries in Mexico and other communities in Latin America and the American Southwest, Day of the Dead became a new U.S. holiday when Chicano activists saw in it a way to celebrate Latino culture and, thus, circulated its practices in art galleries, community centers, and other locations where Latinos lived and congregated. It has gained popularity beyond the Latino community in part, Regina Marchi argues, because there are few such opportunities in Western culture in which individuals can publicly contemplate death and commemorate those who have come and gone before us.

Because of Chicano activists' desire to create a politically and ethnically positive communal event, most Day of the Dead organizers welcomed media coverage and the further expansion of celebration activities into schools, cultural centers, and other activist locations. Media publicity spurred an increased interest in the celebration, fueling heightened production of Day of the Dead–related products and a commodification of the tradition in ways that could not have been anticipated. Subsequently, participation in Day of the Dead activities has, for some, become a chic activity that may be a way to participate in a form of religious or cultural lifestyle branding. For others, however, participation grows out of a deep desire to honor deceased family and friends. Day of the Dead, as a public, mediated, and aesthetically rich event, makes both responses possible. Its resonance, Marchi argues, rests in the fact that reflecting on death and celebrating the lives of deceased loved ones offers a fundamental contradiction to several consumerist messages. Rituals commemorating the dead suggest that, unlike products, people who are gone cannot easily be replaced; that buying things cannot always provide happiness and fulfillment; and that a full life, rather than the mere transience of youth, is beautiful and to be celebrated.

This chapter, therefore, brings us to a few concluding ideas. Having explored religious lifestyle branding in the consumerist United States from early to contemporary forms, having considered the ways in which religious practices may be mobilized for nationalist and political ends through media and commercial artifacts, having considered, finally, the way that media and the commercial marketplace fundamentally reshape and construct opportunities for new cultural and religious events, this chapter helps us to consider how religious rituals and market imperatives sometimes have distinct but mutually beneficial objectives that can illuminate human needs and promulgate new grassroots cultural practices.

Those who regularly read the "Metro" or "Culture" sections of newspapers have probably noticed that public Day of the Dead celebrations and exhibits have grown enormously popular in the United States over the past thirty years. Since the early 1970s when these Mexican-inspired events were first organized by Chicano activists in California, the holiday has become an emblem of autumn for many community-based agencies, schools, museums, galleries, universities, and public libraries. And Latinos aren't the only ones celebrating. Each year, increasing numbers of non-Latinos from various racial and ethnic backgrounds construct Day of the Dead altars, view exhibits, attend memorial vigils, and participate in processions as a way to contemplate death. This contemplation can involve remembering a friend or relative who is gone, viewing tributes created by others for their loved ones, or taking time to reflect on the impermanence of life. For many, these rituals offer a model of ongoing connection with the departed in a society reluctant to confront mortality.

FIGURE 11-1 Day of the Dead items fill the display window of a major California museum's gift shop (fall 2003).

Photo by author.

This chapter examines how the Chicano-initiated celebration of Day of the Dead, a ritual largely unheard of in the United States thirty years ago, has become popular among Latinos and non-Latinos alike, impacting mainstream attitudes regarding death. It considers reasons why this holiday has gained popularity among the general public and examines the role of the mass media in promoting Day of the Dead and the commodities associated with it as a new U.S. tradition.

Background on Day of the Dead

In Mexico and other Latin American countries, the "Days of the Dead" are officially observed on November 1 and 2, the dates of the Roman Catholic celebration of All Saints' Day and All Souls' Day.[1] A syncretic mix of Catholic beliefs and indigenous practices of honoring the departed, the two days are considered as one holiday throughout Latin America. Rituals are celebrated in diverse ways from country to country and from region to region *within* countries. Key practices of the holiday include such activities as preparing special foods and/or drinks for the spirits traditionally believed to visit earth on these dates, refurbishing and decorating family gravesites, creating home altars in honor of the departed, holding picnics and/or candlelight vigils in cemeteries, and attending mass. In indigenous communities such as the Mayan highlands of Guatemala, the Mixtec areas of Mexico, and the Aymara communities of Bolivia, altars for the dead are laden with ceremonial items and offerings, including special meals, breads, flowers, fruits, soft drinks, alcoholic beverages, cigars, cigarettes, candy, cacao beans, chocolate, and other commodities that the deceased enjoyed in life.

While ritual remembrance of the dead has ancient roots in indigenous communities throughout Latin America, integral concepts of Latin American indigenous spirituality, such as a veneration for ancestors, an acceptance of the natural cycle of life and death, and an ongoing communication between the living and the dead, are common to many non-Western religions, particularly those found in Asian, African, and Native American cultures. This commonality may partially explain the appeal of Day of the Dead to many non-Latinos in the United States. As one Japanese American explained: "Day of the Dead is actually similar to the practices of a lot of other cultures and religions. My Mom is Buddhist, so I grew up going to Obone. It's pretty much exactly the same celebration—a night where the spirits come to earth to visit and to play and eat and drink. . . . Different cultures, no matter what continent they're on, can relate to the fact that there are different parts of death. The body. The mind. The spirit."[2]

The earliest documented Mexican All Saints' Day and All Souls' Day observances in the United States occurred in areas of South Texas and the American Southwest, where, for generations, members of the Mexican American community faithfully visited local cemeteries on November 1 and 2 to clean and decorate family gravesites.[3] Like Day of the Dead celebrations in Latin America, these observances were family centered, with certain communal activities practiced at the cemetery. Carried out because of the religious beliefs of practitioners, they were not performed for a public audience and attracted no media attention or outside participation beyond the immediate community. While visiting cemeteries, attending mass, having a special family meal, or lighting candles for the departed at small home shrines were practices familiar to many Mexican American Catholics, these acts resembled All Souls' Day practices of Italian, Polish, Irish, and other Catholic ethnic groups living in the United States. They did not entail overtly indigenous customs, such as constructing elaborate, harvest-laden altars, using skull imagery, consuming *pan de muerto* (bread for the dead), or other southern Mexican traditions introduced to the United States by Chicano artists in the 1970s. While decorating family graves and picnicking in the cemeteries on November 1 and 2 were practiced in some Southwestern U.S. areas, these activities were virtually unknown to large, urban Mexican American communities in the mid-twentieth century.[4]

From Folk Practice to Urban Celebration

In the context of the civil rights movement of the 1960s and 1970s and the Chicano movement's struggles for economic equity, political power, and cultural respect in a society that had denigrated and exploited Mexican Americans for generations, Chicano artists, inspired by the spirituality and beauty of Mexico's Dia de los Muertos celebrations, began to organize public Day of the Dead events in California as a way to celebrate Mexican American identity. As they reached back to their ancestral past for resources with which to contest an oppressive mainstream culture, they found that the deep spirituality of Day of the Dead made it an attractive icon for adoption by the Chicano movement. Spirituality was a vital unifying component of Chicano identity and iconography, offering U.S. Latinos new perspectives on the metaphysical, apart from what many considered to be the restrictive scriptures of a historically oppressive Catholic Church.[5]

From their beginning, California Day of the Dead events reflected the hybrid nature of Chicano spirituality, incorporating the multiple sacred influences impacting Chicano identity, such as Catholic iconography, Mayan and Aztec symbols, Native American spiritual practices, and Afro-Caribbean religions. This hybrid assemblage of diverse religious influences was woven together by Chicano artists for the purpose of creating a feeling of cultural unity that could assist in struggles for political justice. As Tere Romo explains, "Chicano spirituality evolved from multiple sources by way of Spanish Catholicism, Moorish mysticism, African beliefs and a Mesoamerican indigenous worldview—all filtered through an American-lived experience."[6]

The first recorded Day of the Dead events in California were organized in 1972 by artists at two art galleries: Self Help Graphics, in Los Angeles, and La Galería de la Raza, in San Francisco.[7] Artists at Self-Help Graphics, the first community-based, Latino visual arts center in Los Angeles, organized a Day of the Dead procession in which people dressed as skeletons and walked to a nearby cemetery. This evolved into an annual Day of the Dead procession and art exhibit. In the same year, La Galería de la Raza, a Chicano art gallery in the predominantly Latino Mission District of San Francisco, held the city's first altar exhibit, organizing an annual Day of the Dead procession in later years. Because education about Mexican culture was a fundamental goal for Day of the Dead organizers, both agencies worked with local media and schools to educate the public about the history and meaning of the ritual. Workshops on how to make altars, sugar skulls, pan de muerto, and other Day of the Dead crafts were held in schools and community organizations, attracting growing numbers of children and families each year.

California Day of the Dead celebrations are distinct from celebrations of the same name occurring in Latin America. Whereas the primary goal of Latin American observances is to honor deceased family members, the primary goal of U.S. celebrations is to honor Latino culture.[8] Day of the Dead traditions practiced in Latin America occur within the context of Catholicism, while most Day of the Dead celebrations in California and elsewhere in the United States occur within the secular spaces of community centers, art galleries, museums, and public schools. Based on a conceptual framework of Latin American observances, U.S. activities include traditional Mesoamerican components, such as the construction of ornate altars or *ofrendas* (in which individuals or groups create intricate visual tributes to the departed), the performance of cemetery rituals (where participants decorate graves, hold vigils, pray, sing, or dance in honor of the dead), and participation in candlelight processions (in which participants walk through town carrying candles and/or photos of the deceased).[9]

California Day of the Dead art and altar installations combined Catholic iconography such as crucifixes, devotional candles, pictures of Jesus, Mary, or various saints together with indigenous symbols such as images of Aztec or Mayan deities, copal incense,[10] offerings of food, drink, and marigolds, used in Mesoamerica to honor the dead. While religious material goods typically signify membership in a particular community, they are also used by artists to communicate meanings other than their overtly religious ones as artists encourage the public to think about the relationship between art, religion, and politics. Drawing on the Mexican tradition of altar-making and the artistic tradition of eclectic assemblage, Chicano artists created Day of the Dead altars with religious objects arranged in colorful, textured, humorous, and provocative ways. Thus, they used Latin American material culture as a resource through which to express the spiritual, social, and historical connections Mexican Americans felt toward Mexico. Religious items were commonly juxtaposed with nonreligious objects from Mexican popular culture, including boxes of powdered cocoa, bars of chocolate, decks of playing cards, alcoholic beverages, the children's game *lotería*, stuffed animals, and other items reminiscent of the lives of the deceased. Expressing the important role material objects serve as mediators in relationships among humans and between them and their physical world, these items, arranged as art, symbolically represented Latino identity to a wider U.S. public.

U.S. Day of the Dead events have evolved to include many nontraditional components, such as educational workshops, performance art, and spoken-word events where participants read poems or tell stories about the departed. They include public lectures on the history of Day of the Dead or lectures that use the seasonal theme to discuss existential topics related to death. They feature movie screenings ranging from documentaries about Day of the Dead (such as Lourdes Portillo's *La Ofrenda: Days of the Dead* or Victoria Llamas's *La Muerte Viva, The Day of the Dead: A Living Tradition*) to videos about Mexican crafts and traditions (such as Judith Bronowski and Robert Grant's film *Pedro Linares: Folk Artist*) to classic Mexican films with themes revolving around Day of the Dead (such as Roberto Gavaldon's *Macario* and Ismael Rodriguez's *Animas Trujano*). Altars have become "altar installations" comprised of mixed media such as sculpture, oil paints, silkscreen, mobiles, collage, computers, televisions, sound systems, video footage, and Web sites.

California's vast cultural diversity has provided opportunities for close physical proximity and cultural exchange between Chicanos and numerous other ethnic and racial groups, resulting in Day of the Dead altars that also incorporate spiritual symbols from non-Latino cultures. The impact of diverse cultures on Chicano artists, together with the fact that Day of the Dead was soon adopted by many people beyond the Chicano community, resulted in increasingly hybrid altars that reflect diverse Latin American, Asian, African, Middle Eastern, Native American, and other spiritual influences.

Day of the Dead and the Media

Unlike Day of the Dead practitioners in Latin America, where ritual activities such as altar-making, visiting the cemetery, or preparing special foods for the holiday are part of the quotidian fabric of community life, passed down from generation to generation, many people in the United States, whether Latino or non-Latino, learn about Day of the Dead activities via the mass media.[11] During the weeks preceding November 1 and 2, in major U.S. cities and small towns, daily and weekly newspapers announce Day of the Dead events, explaining the "who," "what," "where," "when," and "why" of the celebratory activities. Posters promoting the festivities are typically hung in windows of stores, community organizations, and schools, while banners and billboards are placed in commercial centers, parks, and university campuses. Early each fall, community centers, art galleries, and museums mail thousands of postcards to their constituents announcing the dates of Day of the Dead exhibits, workshops, and related events. Entertainment magazines and the "Calendar," "Arts," or "Events" sections of newspapers include Day of the Dead listings each week from late September through November. Most sponsoring galleries, museums, universities, stores, cafes, and community centers now post schedules of their Day of the Dead activities on their Internet Web pages.

The following are only a few of the events listed during the two weeks prior to November 1 in the weekly *San Diego Reader*.[12] I have found similar events listed in newspapers from cities across California and, in fact, across the United States:

Art for the Dead: This celebration at the Chicano Park Gazebo on Friday November 1. Expect to find altar building, spoken word, music and a marketplace to celebrate Days of the Dead. A special offering will be built to commemorate the second cycle of mourning for the twin towers victims.

Dia de los Muertos is being celebrated all over town this week. Bazaar del Mundo has activities planned from Saturday, October 26 through Sunday, November 2, with traditional decorations, activities and artists' demonstrations. Hours 10:00 am to 9:00 pm. . . . Admission is free.

Bring Mementos, Photographs and Objects that remind you of deceased loved ones to the Dia de los Muertos Celebration planned for Wednesday, October 30 at San Diego State University. The event begins with a slide-illustrated lecture . . . and ends with a community altar-making ceremony. The altar will be on view in Love Library through Friday November 22. Free.

The Day of the Dead Festivities at Casa Familiar Civic and Recreational Center take place on Friday, November 1. There's altar making all day, with the observance getting underway at 6:00 pm and a *velación* [communal time to remember the dead] . . . from 8:00 pm to midnight.

Noche de Muertos, head to Voz Alta Cultural Center to celebrate life and death with a poetry reading honoring those who have passed away. . . . The event starts at 8:00 pm on Friday, Nov. 1.

This small sampling of media announcements illustrates how, from a primarily family-oriented religious observance in Latin America, focusing on the ritual preparation of homes and graves in honor of departed relatives, Day of the Dead is transformed in the United States into an advertised cultural "happening," primarily celebrated in community centers, schools, libraries, museums, and parks. The period of celebration—usually lasting a few days in Latin America—extends up to two months in the United States, with exhibits and activities often starting in late September or early October and continuing until late November or early December.[13] Aided by media coverage and the implementation of multicultural school curricula over the past thirty years, Day of the Dead has gone from being viewed by the mainstream as a "strange" fringe practice of Latino artists to becoming a commonly known seasonal event, adopted and promoted by growing numbers of Latino and non-Latino Americans as encompassing a healthier attitude toward death.

Because U.S. celebrations are predominantly public, rather than private family events, art gallery spaces and the mass media have been key vehicles for communicating and publicizing these re-invented rituals. Early Day of the Dead events at Chicano arts organizations were publicized mainly within the Latino community via hand-typed flyers and word of mouth. However, the vibrant Latin American aesthetic and indigenous metaphysical philosophy soon attracted the interest of major museums that, in turn, attracted increasing media attention from local newspapers and television stations. Chicana artist and educator Yolanda Garfias Woo, affectionately known in San Francisco circles as "la madrina de Los Muertos" (the godmother of Day of the Dead) for her pioneering workshops on Day of the Dead in California schools in the 1960s, was invited to do an altar exhibit at the prestigious De Young Museum in San Francisco in 1975. All three major TV networks covered the opening of the exhibit, and Garfias Woo notes, "It was the first time a major museum was interested in Dia de los Muertos, something so ethnically *outlandish*. . . . We got invited to do a lot of TV programs. . . . This was a real turning point for the community, as well as for me, in terms of being public." [14]

The media of gallery exhibits, museum catalogs, promotional posters (themselves spectacular works of art by Chicano artists), and T-shirts advertising Day of the Dead events served to educate many Latinos and non-Latinos about this emerging ritual celebration. This promotion was greatly enhanced by news media coverage of Day of the Dead exhibits and processions throughout the 1980s and 1990s. Recognizing the power of the media to educate the general public about Mexican and Chicano culture and impact public perceptions of this unconventional and sometimes controversial celebration—perceptions that, in turn, could affect the receptivity of future community and institutional support—most event organizers encouraged the press to attend exhibits and events.[15] They routinely sent out press releases and information packets and spent time conducting interviews with reporters. Broadcast journalists were welcome to film or record Day of the Dead processions, exhibits, and other activities, as were members of the general public. Unlike Day of the Dead activities in Latin America, where cameras are often considered to be obtrusive, California's activities were and are an anticipated part of the proceedings.[16]

Over the past thirty years, Day of the Dead has received a substantial amount of attention from mainstream media institutions ranging from the Associated Press and National Public Radio to local TV news stations and newspapers, independent documentary filmmakers, and myriad smaller news outlets. These media outlets produce stories on Day of the Dead

FIGURE 11-2 Day of the Dead T-shirts, candles, skeletons, and picture frames at a tourist shop in San Diego's Old Town State Park (fall 2004).

Photo by author.

activities not only in cosmopolitan cities such as Los Angeles, New York, San Francisco, Chicago, and the District of Columbia, where Latino communities have lived for many years, but also in areas of the country with historically little or no Latino presence, such as Omaha, Nebraska; Columbus, Ohio; Kansas City, Kansas; Milwaukee, Wisconsin; Oklahoma City, Oklahoma; and Seattle, Washington, all of which have experienced large migrations of Latinos over the past twenty years. In recent years, there have been Day of the Dead episodes on primetime U.S. television shows such as PBS's *American Family* and HBO's highly popular series *Six Feet Under* and *Carnivale*. National magazines such as AAA's travel magazines *Horizons* and *Westways* and *Better Homes and Gardens*, *Ladies' Home Journal*, and *Holiday Celebrations* feature articles on how to celebrate Day of the Dead. National news publications such as *U.S. News and World Report* and the *New York Times* include stories on Day of the Dead. In addition, the celebration is the subject of thousands of English-language commercial, nonprofit, and personal Web sites geared toward a U.S. audience.

The Internet has become an important tool for both organizing and advertising Day of the Dead festivities. Enter the term "Day of the Dead" in the Google.com search engine and over 3,650,000 entrees appear.[17] The majority of Internet sites provide a history of the holiday, replete with vivid photographs and information on upcoming events. Many sites are created and maintained by educators who freely share their Day of the Dead curricula with the public. Others are designed by art galleries, community centers, or universities (usually Spanish Language or Latin American Studies departments) to promote or display their Day of the Dead exhibits. Still others are sponsored by online catalogs, stores, and museums that sell Day of the Dead products ranging from educational curricula and books to Day of the Dead sugar skulls, toys, decorations, art, T-shirts, cups, tequila glasses, and much more. A large number of the sites provide information on how to make Day of the Dead altars, decorations, and traditional holiday foods such as *pan de muerto* or *mole*.

Beyond the Chicano Community

Over the past two decades, neoliberal economic restructuring has intensified inequality and unemployment in Latin America, greatly escalating migratory pressures. In the biggest migration flow in the history of the continent, Latin Americans are in the midst of an unprecedented exodus to the United States.[18] Manuel Castells describes this as a new globalized immigration system dominated by large numbers of people from the "South" moving to wealthier centers in the "North" in search of work.[19] Since 1980, so many immigrants from Mexico, Central America, South America, and the Caribbean have migrated to the United States that there are now more Latinos than African Americans attending U.S. schools.[20] As record numbers of Latino immigrants travel both to and within the United States, following job opportunities located far beyond the traditional geographic locations of U.S. Latino communities, Day of the Dead events are becoming the norm rather than the exception in cities across the country. Today,

Guatemalans, Salvadorans, Nicaraguans, Colombians, Ecuadorians, and other Latin American immigrant groups participate in Day of the Dead celebrations in the United States, interweaving the Chicano ritual with their regional traditions in what folklorist Olivia Cadavál has called "a pan-Latino American Day of the Dead model." [21]

While Day of the Dead celebrations have appealed to a diverse group of Latinos who share a religious and cultural heritage of honoring the dead on November 1 and 2, the ritual has also been enthusiastically adopted by many non-Latinos. During the past six years of my research in California, I have met people of Asian (Chinese, Japanese, Korean, Indonesian, Filipino), African (Somali, Ugandan, Ethiopian, South African), African American, Italian American, Polish American, Irish American, Jewish, Palestinian, Iranian, and other heritages participating in Day of the Dead altar exhibits and processions. Participants may be devout or lapsed Catholics, Protestants, Jews, Buddhists, Muslims, neo-pagans, followers of indigenous spirituality, or atheists. They may be upper class, working class, or undocumented. They may identify as black, Asian, white, Latino, Mestizo, or indigenous. They may be politically conservative, liberal, radical, or apathetic. But a common "faith" that unites them is their belief that the act of remembering the dead in public ways, whether through poignant visual tributes, solemn candlelight vigils, or colorful processions, is powerful and healing.

The American Way of Death

In mainstream U.S. culture, death is a topic to be feared and avoided—a kind of obscenity not to be uttered in public. We say someone "passed on" or "slipped away." We put sick pets "to sleep." We outlaw the practice of euthanasia, so that accepting death as a release from life's physical pain and suffering becomes a crime worthy of imprisonment. Unlike in Latin America, where poverty causes a large majority of the population to face death on a frequent basis, the relative affluence and technological advancements of the United States create a sense of invulnerability among the general population. It is not unusual for individuals in the United States to live for twenty or more years without experiencing the death of a family member, and this sense of invulnerability fosters a reluctance to confront mortality.[22] Even when terminal illness strikes, the "fiction of probable recovery" is often maintained until the last moments of life, rather than acknowledging death as a natural part of the life cycle.[23]

Illustrating how Americans avoid the topic of death, the majority of senior citizens do not prepare wills or discuss their wishes with family members regarding final medical care procedures or funeral arrangements.[24] Peter Metcalf and Richard Huntington contend that in societies with difficult living conditions and little social mobility, people hold more accepting attitudes toward death and play active roles in death proceedings (i.e., preparing bodies for burial, planning funerals, engaging in mourning and remembrance rituals). However, in the United States, with its strong cultural emphasis on individualism and upward mobility, most people view death in negative terms and play only passive roles in death rituals. Further distancing U.S. society from death is the fact that most Americans now die in hospitals, where family members are frequently absent in the final moments. Revealing a collective cultural discomfort with death, families very seldom ask to see the body of a relative before its removal from hospital to funeral home.[25]

In a consumer culture that emphasizes the new and improved version of everything, physical degeneration and fatality are contrary to dominant ideologies of competition and rugged individualism. Some critical cultural scholars have argued that the prosperity of U.S. consumer society has depended on the continuous promotion of youthful values. Since the turn of the twentieth century, they note, U.S. corporations broke with older cultural traditions of reverence for the elders in order to increase mass production: "The endurance required by monotonous factory work had laid a severe economic and psychological burden on the lives of working people. Youth had provided an idiom for the transformation in production, and the elevation of the youth value within the culture had provided an ideological weapon against the traditional realms of indigenous authority as it had been exercised in the family and community in the periods before mass production."[26] In an economic system dependent on ever-expanding production, corporate marketers and media producers enhanced their selling power by promoting "youth values," such as impulsiveness, immediate gratification, and contempt for authority, over "adult values," such as respect for tradition, reverence for authority, and a willingness to sacrifice.[27]

American society is obsessed with looking and acting young, and being youthful has become almost synonymous with being *alive*. We are socialized to believe that with the right diet, exercise, grooming products, and cosmetic surgery we can be young forever. Within this mindset, thoughts of death are rigorously resisted. In contrast to many traditional societies where elders are revered, many elderly and infirm in the United States are discarded by society like outdated appliances, left to die alone and in poverty. Unlike most Latin Americans, who are socialized to consider *la muerte* as another stage of life, many people in the United States feel so removed from death that they lack positive ways to relate to the deceased. For many people (especially young Americans) their earliest notions of death come from the ghoulish images of commercial haunted houses and Hollywood slasher films.

With the rise of the funeral industry in the twentieth century, Americans became physically separated from their dead. Bodies were no longer cleaned and dressed by family members. Wakes were no longer held at home. Professional morticians transported corpses to funeral parlors for institutionalized viewing and, for the majority of people, active community rituals of leave-taking, mourning, and remembering were lost. Today, most burials are not conducted in front of the public, who are led out of the cemetery by funeral professionals before the coffin is lowered into the ground. An underlying reason for this practice is economic expediency, since more funerals can be processed per day when families vacate the cemetery premises as quickly as possible.

At a recent funeral I attended in Boston, the family was prevented not only from watching the burial, but also from viewing the grave. On arrival at the cemetery, mourners were led to a generic "chapel" where, after ten minutes of hurried prayer led by an unknown chaplain, people were dismissed. Those who asked to lay flowers by the tomb were told by the funeral home staff that there was no time to visit the gravesite because another funeral party was scheduled to arrive in ten minutes, and mourners needed to move their cars to make way for the incoming group. Death has become big business in the United States, and families today have fewer opportunities than ever to adequately process the loss of loved ones.

This was not always the case. Until the early twentieth century, death was widely contemplated in the United States and occupied an important place in mass culture, where mourners readily found sources of community support. In the mid-nineteenth century, American religious movements "sought to promote a homely, even domestic view of the world to come." [28] Cemeteries were considered to be "schools of moral philosophy and catalysts of civic virtue" where the living regularly engaged in meditative promenades to contemplate the shortness of life and learn from the exemplary lives of the interred; walking, reading, and picnicking in cemeteries were actively promoted by moral leaders as being "healthful, agreeable and refreshing" activities that would inspire visitors to work hard and do good in life.[29]

So widespread was the desire to stimulate retrospection and reverence regarding life and death that magazines, newspapers, and advice books of the 1800s encouraged American families to take Sunday walks in cemeteries to cultivate "a cheerful association with death." Visiting the United States in 1847, English writer Harriet Martineau observed that thoughts of death "filled a large space in peoples' mind." [30] As recently as the early twentieth century, the American public still viewed death as an expected part of life. Senior citizens born in the early 1910s and 1920s note that in Catholic schools students were taught to begin each day by praying for "a happy death." [31] Parents routinely purchased life insurance policies for their infants, cognizant of the reality that many children would be stricken by commonplace childhood illness and not reach adulthood. Over time, however, these commonplace reflections on death became all *but* common.

North America's commercialized version of All Souls' Day—Halloween—is bereft of any serious commemoration of the departed, while Memorial Day, the official U.S. holiday for visiting cemeteries, began as a day to honor Civil War dead and continues to focus primarily on the honoring of military dead. As with Flag Day and Independence Day, the American flag is a major symbol of Memorial Day, along with military parades and veterans' ceremonies. Rather than highlighting the *lives* of the deceased, the day focuses on their *deaths* as a way to commemorate patriotism and, implicitly, U.S. capitalism and the foreign policy that supports it. The somber tone of contemporary Memorial Day observances, where buildings and graves are often draped in black, stands in stark contrast to the vivid ambiance of Day of the Dead, where altars typically brim with flowers, fruits, cornstalks, gourds, candles, and other symbols of vitality, reflecting the coexistence of harvest and winter, life and death, as balanced parts of the life cycle.[32] With its focus on war dead (as opposed to "the dead" in general), Memorial Day has become irrelevant for the majority of Americans who do not have deceased veterans in the immediate family and for whom the holiday is just another long weekend of cookouts and shopping sales.

A Desire for Public Remembrance

However, growing numbers of Americans feel dissatisfied with the mainstream culture's mode of handling death. A collective desire for public ways to remember the dead is visible in phenomena such as the enormous public response to the Vietnam War Memorial in D.C., the spontaneous creation of a public shrine at the site of the 1995 Oklahoma City bombing, and the ubiquitous appearance of outdoor altars in New York City after the tragedy of September 11, 2001. Filled with mementos of the dead, these public spaces represent opportunities for the public to remember and mourn communally. As is done with Day of the Dead altars, families of Vietnam veterans place objects (such as uniforms, hats, boots, photos, candles) along the memorial wall, converting it into a public shrine for those killed. After the Oklahoma City bombing, residents and visitors attached items (such as stuffed animals, baby shoes, hair ribbons, and poems) to a hurricane fence surrounding the bombed area, transforming a bleak wire barrier into a public shrine.[33] More recently in New York, hundreds of makeshift altars consisting of photos, flowers, letters, candles, and other mementos appeared along sidewalks, parks, schools, government buildings, storefronts, subways, and fire stations as a tribute to those killed in the World Trade Center explosion.

Such public acts are efforts not only to honor the dead, but also to communally grieve and heal. The rising popularity of public shrine-making in the United States over the past twenty years indicates a shift in practice from conventional "Anglo" or "non-ethnic" forms of remembrance considered appropriate during most of the twentieth century and may shed light on why mainstream Americans are embracing Day of the Dead in growing numbers. Given the dearth of opportunities in U.S. society to publicly honor departed friends and family in a celebratory way, Day of the Dead offers participants an opportunity to reconnect with recessed memories, symbolically keeping deceased loved ones alive.

Mainstream Appeal

The annual Day of the Dead procession in San Francisco, first organized by La Galería de la Raza in 1981, when a few dozen people walked around the block holding candles and photos of their dead, now attracts upwards of twenty thousand participants annually. At least half of the procession participants are non-Latino. During her ethnographic field work on Day of the Dead in San Francisco in the 1980s and 1990s, Suzanne Shumate Morrison noted that non-Latinos of various racial backgrounds enthusiastically participated in both the creation and viewing of altars at the Mission Cultural Center and, in fact, comprised the majority of annual procession participants. She wrote: "Non-Latinos initially approached the November 2 procession through the barrio as 'semi-tourists' but are now full-fledged and enthusiastic participants. In fact, every year that I have been present [1984–87 and 1990–91], Anglos have constituted the majority of the processants."[34] This was still the case when I attended the Mission procession during the years 2001–2003. When I asked what attracted her to Day of the Dead, one Anglo-American woman involved in organizing the Mission Day of the Dead procession replied:

> During Day of the Dead, there's no negative energy, but an incredible solidarity. A completeness of people coming together to celebrate their loved ones and their own emotions, which rarely happens here. It's a time to acknowledge that we're all human and are dealing with some pretty heavy emotions that we're all here to support. Just by being in the park or in the procession, you're supporting somebody's process of healing. What makes Day of the Dead unusual is that you're literally walking in the street with hundreds of people, thousands of people who you don't know, but there's a feeling of community. . . . You see strangers hugging each other . . . [and] crying together. It meets a human need for affiliation, on a really elemental level.[35]

In Sacramento, California, Day of the Dead events had become so popular with non-Latinos that a round-table discussion was held in November 2000 at Sacramento State University to discuss the reasons why. One participant in the discussion explained: "Each year, more non-Latinos have participated. . . . I think everyone's consensus is that there is no venue in American tradition which lets us honor and celebrate our dead. Once people have died, their memory becomes a private matter for the family . . . [and] there is no public remembrance past the funeral. It's as if they were swept under the carpet and we move on to the next thing. With Dia de los Muertos, the entire community is involved . . . [and] there is that public acknowledgment of the dead." [36]

The popularity of Day of the Dead among non-Latinos in California was confirmed in my interviews with staff from more than a half a dozen museum shops and folk art stores where Day of the Dead merchandise is sold. In every conversation, respondents informed me that Day of the Dead is their most lucrative time of year and that at least half (and frequently more than half) of the clientele who buy Day of the Dead products are non-Latinos. I was informed that the best-selling Day of the Dead products were sugar skulls, miniature skeleton figurines, *papel picado*,[37] and other items used to decorate altars, suggesting that many people are adopting the practice of altar-making. The owners of a popular San Diego gallery and folk art store that distributes Day of the Dead merchandise wholesale to retailers across the United States noted, "Day of the Dead is our busiest time of the year . . . [and] about 65 percent of out clients are non-Latinos." [38] Similarly, the owner of a folk craft store in San Francisco said: "October is our big season. . . . You would be *amazed* at how many sugar skulls we sell here. I sell over a thousand. For a small store, that's a *lot*. . . . I think that everyone I know, at this point, is making altars at home now. It's sort of like decorating the Christmas tree, an annual ritual. Schools have altars. Museums have altars. Companies have altars. I get invited to all kinds of city events. Supervisor Ammiano lost his partner to AIDS awhile back, so he does an altar every year in his office in City Hall. I would say my clients are about 50 percent Latino and 50 percent non-Latino." [39]

Staff at bakeries I visited in Latino communities in San Francisco, Los Angeles, and San Diego also reported that Day of the Dead was their busiest time of the year. Some reported that their pan de muerto sales in October and early November annually exceed the amount of money earned during all other months of the year combined. Bakers reported that a large number of clients purchasing pan de muerto were non-Latinos, particularly teachers who bought it for their students' Day of the Dead celebrations. Florists in

Latino neighborhoods also report a rising business in the sale of marigolds,[40] popularly used to decorate altars and graves during Day of the Dead.

Non-Latinos are not only attending Latino-organized Day of the Dead activities in growing numbers, but also adopting the custom and creating their own rituals. For example, each year the Solana Beach, California, congregation of the Unitarian Universalist Fellowship holds a Day of the Dead community altar ceremony. Worshipers and the general public are invited (via word of mouth, church bulletins, and listings in local newspapers) to bring photos, stories, and favorite mementos of departed loved ones to share at a communal altar. When I attended this event in November 2001, the attendees consisted of approximately 150 white, upper-middle-class people. One by one, individuals placed items (such as candles, photos, books, jewelry, or alcoholic beverages) on the Latin American–styled altar (adorned with fruits, tamales, Mexican chocolate, marigolds, pan de muerto, papel picado, and mementos from other Latin American countries, such as Guatemalan woven tapestries and Salvadoran *pirografía* crosses), then took the microphone to speak about someone they had lost. The atmosphere was both happy and emotional, as people related jokes and stories about loved ones. Numerous participants mentioned that it was the first time they had talked publicly about the deceased since his or her death, which, in many cases, had occurred years ago.

In my interviews with non-Latino Day of the Dead participants, all discussed what they felt was a dearth of opportunity for honoring the dead in mainstream U.S. culture. A Korean American from Los Angeles said, "Americans tend to be morbid and depressed about death, while the Latino culture honors their ancestors and celebrates their life through their death." [41] An Irish American from Boston who recently lost her father and created an altar for him said, "I think it's a much healthier version of dealing with death and dying. Making the altar is very healing. It makes a connection with the people who have gone before us and affirms what they did in life." [42] Many other respondents stated that participating in Day of the Dead helped them to process the loss of family members. For example, a native of Kentucky who participated for four consecutive years in Day of the Dead celebrations held in San Francisco said:

> I loved the diversity of it. Aztec dancers, crowds of skeletons, yuppie
> couples, Latino moms with kids in strollers. I loved the somber yet

celebratory tone of the marchers. I took the time to reflect on the loss of a favorite aunt who died unexpectedly that year. I hadn't been able to go to her funeral. My experience that night gave me some much-needed closure on her death. It was wonderful to reminisce about her in such a supportive atmosphere. My traditional Catholic upbringing has left me extremely unfulfilled when it comes to dealing with death. In the past few years, I've found myself actively pursuing other culture's rituals and practices around death in an effort to unravel my own feelings.[43]

The cathartic aspect of Day of the Dead rituals is similarly noted by a Polish American respondent who participated in a Day of the Dead procession in Chicago: "One thing I thought was neat at a procession at the local cemetery was almost a roll call, where people could call out the name of a dead family member or friend and the entire group would answer 'Presente,' acknowledging their presence among us. It was amazingly soothing for me, as I had just lost my mom and found that many people were just too uncomfortable with death to even talk about it."[44]

All of the respondents referred to a dichotomy between U.S. cultural death practices, which they considered "unfulfilling" or "depressing," and the personalized, communal rituals of remembrance common in Latin America, which they called "celebratory," "supportive," and "healing."

Tere Romo, who has curated Day of the Dead exhibits in California and elsewhere for over thirty years, notes, "The audiences who come are very diverse. It's one of the few exhibits that you can walk into a gallery and see a crowd that is totally diverse, . . . African Americans, Asians, Latinos, whites, all ages, moms with their kids, schoolchildren, old people, and every age in between. It has an attraction across generations and ethnic groups."[45] According to Barbara Henry, the educational curator at the Oakland Museum of California, some twenty thousand people attend the Day of the Dead exhibit during a six-week period each year. Henry explains the popularity of the exhibit, now in its thirteenth year, in the following way:

A number of people have said that they don't have anything from their culture that helps them deal with death. One woman sent me a letter about three months after the exhibit closed, telling me how it helped her deal with the death of her mother. We've had a number of grief counselors and people from the health profession who have come here and used this exhibit with their clients to help them process death. There was one group of terminally ill patients. We've gotten written comments from many people telling us about how coming to this exhibit has become an annual tradition for their family.[46]

Another employee at the Oakland Museum notes that the museum's annual Day of the Dead exhibit is a "healing tool" for many people: "We've received lots of letters from people thanking us and saying that it's helped them reflect, or telling us how they've adopted the tradition. Not just Latino people. One of the great things we have here is a wall of reflection, where you can write messages to people who have passed on. I've seen families crying, hugging each other. So there's something we can offer people who are in pain, to help them heal."[47]

In Oceanside, California, several thousand people attend the Day of the Dead celebrations that have been organized annually since 2001 by the local business community in conjunction with the city's Mixtec indigenous residents, who have migrated to California from Oaxaca, Mexico. I was at the first opening celebration on the night of November 1, 2001, where nearly one thousand people attended a bilingual Day of the Dead mass held at St. Mary's Star of the Sea Church in downtown Oceanside and later participated in a candlelight procession through the streets of this "all-American" city, as Oceanside is referred to on the city's official Web page.

Nearly half of the participants appeared to be Anglos, for whom this was their first exposure to Day of the Dead. Many I spoke with called the event "interesting," "beautiful," and "different." The rest of the public was comprised of a mix of recent Oaxacan immigrants and U.S.-born Latinos from Oceanside and the surrounding towns in San Diego's North County region, many of whom had learned about the event in the *San Diego Reader*, the *North County Times*, or the *San Diego Union Tribune*.[48] Artist David Avalos, who created an altar dedicated to his father at the 2002 Oceanside celebration, noted: "It was a mixed crowd. There were Oaxacans mixed with the kind of folks you'd expect to see at the Del Mar Fair."[49] An art professor at the California State University at San Marcos, Avalos observed: "I teach a class called Chicano Art in the Border Region. And what I find is that people respond to Day of the Dead because it gives them an opportunity they don't have otherwise. . . . [F]or students who aren't of Mexican ancestry, and even those who are of Mexican ancestry and don't practice the tradition, it gives them an opportunity to connect with their own personal history, and that's a spiritual resource that we're often denied. . . . It's a spiritual resource to be able to look back on your family history. When you find out more about dead relatives, you find out more about yourself." [50]

How do Chicanos and other Latinos feel about the fact that so many non-Latinos are getting involved in Day of the Dead celebrations? The vast majority of people I interviewed expressed positive feelings. Rene Yañez, who together with Ralph Maradiaga organized San Francisco's first Day of the Dead exhibit at La Galería de La Raza and has been curating highly acclaimed and provocative exhibits ever since, offers the following perspective:

> Death doesn't discriminate. As a Chicano Latino curator, we started Day of the Dead to create alliances of Chicano culture and work together with other people. I've worked with people from China-town. I've worked with black groups in Oakland. I've worked with mainstream groups. This allowed me to learn, as a Chicano curator, about how other cultures think and feel and where we fit in the scheme of things. Because if you're going to be a Chicano curator and not learn from other cultures, then you're very isolated and not being relevant to your own culture. . . . Irish, Korean, Japanese, African people all bring something to the table. Other Latinos bring something to the table. It's a chain reaction. [51]

A few respondents expressed some concern that the celebration may be in danger of straying too far from its roots. One Bay Area Latina noted about the Mission's Day of the Dead procession: "People come from all over the Bay Area, which is a good thing, but . . . perhaps unintentionally when people like something, they . . . begin to change the very essence of what it is. Something becomes very popular and very hip, but there is a way we can appreciate the essence without changing it." [52] Another Chicana artist explained, "The only thing that worries me is when I think that the person doing the installation actually misunderstands what Muertos is.

It concerns me only because I don't want the tradition to get lost. It was so hard to find it, to get it in the first place." [53]

Reflecting on Day of the Dead's popularity with both Latinos and non-Latinos in the United States, Avalos notes that American culture has always been a conglomeration of diverse cultural practices that are transformed as people adopt them:

> People go to the ballpark and drink beer and eat hotdogs because of Germans coming over here in the mid-nineteenth century with the idea that having a beer and a sausage was the good life. If all of the immigrants . . . that came to the U.S. didn't bring something of their culture, we'd all be running around with those funny hats and buckles on our shoes, like the Puritans. The United States has an interesting cultural dynamic where, on one hand, this is a place where you can come and shed your past for the purpose of creating a new future, unlike anything that you knew in your past. It takes a generation or two for people to realize, "Hey, in the process we've lost something. Now we have to go back and restore or reproduce it." [54]

Conclusion

It appears that many twenty-first-century Americans long to recapture the mutual support and sharing of a way of life and death abandoned in the early twentieth century. What was lost with the professionalization of death by the medical and mortuary industries was the collective time and space to tell stories about departed loved ones. U.S. Day of the Dead rituals, inspired by Mesoamerican traditions, adopted and transformed by Chicanos and other Latinos in the United States, and promoted by the media, offer mainstream American society an important custom from the premodern past: storytelling about those we have lost. Incorporating photos, favorite foods, and other personal items, Day of the Dead exhibits are, essentially, stories about people.

In a capitalist, commodity-oriented society such as the United States, it is not surprising that people signal their participation in and adoption of the Day of the Dead tradition by acquiring and arranging commodities on their altars. Displaying the material culture of Day of the Dead via objects such as pan de muerto, sugar skulls, papel picado, devotional candles, skeletal figurines, religious statues, flowers, and other commercially produced items allows both Latinos and non-Latinos to publicly connect with the Chicano/Latino community and the metaphysical philosophies of Latin America while literally demarcating a public space (in homes, schools, parks, community centers, galleries, offices, and wherever else altars are created) for honoring personal and collective memories of the dead.

Assembling an altar, walking in a community procession, or participating in related rituals gives participants an opportunity to symbolically and verbally discuss the deceased, sharing buried memories that facilitate healing while keeping departed loved ones "alive" in spirit. The growing popularity of Day of the Dead in the United States indicates an increasing disenchantment with mainstream values of eternal youth and extreme individualism that, respectively, eschew the topic of human mortality and privatize mourning. As an emergent new U.S. holiday, Day of the Dead offers mainstream America an opportunity not only to process the loss of loved ones, but to respond to the loss of community that has become the hallmark of contemporary American society.

NOTES

1. Throughout Latin America, November 1 and November 2 are described by a variety of names, including but not limited to Todos Santos (All Saints'), Dia de los Muertos (Day of the Dead), Dia de los Difuntos (Day of the Departed), Dia de los Fieles Difuntos (Day of the Faithful Departed), and Dia de las Animas Benditas (Day of the Blessed Souls).

2. Personal interview, San Francisco, California, June 5, 2003.

3. John O. West, *Mexican American Folklore* (Little Rock: Little Rock Publishers, 1989); Lynn Gosnell and Suzanne Gott, "San Fernando Cemetery: Decorations of Love and Loss in a Mexican American Community," in *Cemeteries and Gravemarkers: Voices of American Culture*, ed. Richard E. Meyer (Ann Arbor: UMI Research Press, 1989); K. Turner and P. Jasper, "Day of the Dead: The Tex-Mex Tradition," in *Halloween and Other Festivals of Death and Life*, ed. Jack Santino (Knoxville: University of Tennessee Press, 1994).

4. When large numbers of indigenous Oaxacans immigrated to California in the late 1980s and 1990s, numbering over sixty thousand today, they began to construct elaborate Day of the Dead altars in their homes. This is a relatively recent practice and does not negate the fact that prior to the 1970s, indigenous-style Day of the Dead altars were not part of Mexican American collective culture. For more on the construction of indigenous altars in private family settings among

Oaxacan immigrants in California, see Bonnie Bade, "The Dead Are Coming: Mixtec Day of the Dead and the Cultivation of Community," in *Proceedings of the 1995 and 1996 Latin American Symposium: "Death, Burial, and Afterlife," "Landscapes and Mindscapes of the Ancient Mayas,"* ed. Alana Cordy-Collins and Grace Johnson (San Diego: Museum of Man, 1997), 7–20.

5. Tere Romo, *Chicanos en Mictlán* (San Francisco: Mexican Museum of San Francisco, 2000).

6. Ibid., 30–31.

7. Suzanne Shumate Morrison, "Mexico's Day of the Dead in San Francisco, California" (PhD diss., Theology Department, UC Berkeley, 1992); Romo, *Chicanos en Mictlán*; and personal interviews.

8. Morrison, "Mexico's Day of the Dead"; Romo, *Chicanos en Mictlán*; Olivia Cadavál, "'The Taking of the Renwick': The Celebration of the Day of the Dead and the Latino Community in Washington, DC," *Journal of Folklore Research* 22, no. 2–3 (1985); Lara Medina and Gilbert R. Cadena, "Dias de Muertos: Public Ritual, Community Renewal, and Popular Religion in Los Angeles," in *Horizons of the Sacred: Mexican Traditions in U.S. Catholicism,* ed. Timothy Matovina and Gary Riebe-Estrella (Ithaca, NY: Cornell University Press, 2002).

9. Music is often a part of the procession and participants may wear skeletal costumes and masks or carry props such as banners, signs, cardboard coffins, or giant skeletal puppets, as occurs at Day of the Dead processions in San Francisco, Chicago, and Los Angeles.

10. Ceremonial incense made of pine resin, used by Mesoamericans in religious rituals since pre-Columbian times.

11. While many participants learn about Day of the Dead from their personal involvement in community agencies or arts organizations, from educational curricula in schools, or from word of mouth, a large number of people attending the exhibits, processions, and workshops report that they read about the festivities in the newspaper. This is based on personal interviews and conversations with people not involved with a particular community agency or school.

12. Taken from the *San Diego Reader* during weeks of October 24, 2003, in which there were six different Day of the Dead events advertised, and October 31, 2003, in which there were eight different Day of the Dead events advertised. There were additional announcements of these and other events in the *San Diego Union Tribune,* the *North County Times,* and many smaller community newspapers.

13. For example, during the years 2002–2005, exhibits at El Centro Cultural de La Raza (San Diego) went from late September to mid November, while exhibits at Self Help Graphics (Los Angeles) and the Peabody Museum of Harvard University (Cambridge) went from late October until the first week of December.

14. Personal interview, June 6, 2003, San Francisco, California.

15. Some people unfamiliar with the meaning of Day of the Dead accused event organizers of engaging in death cult activities. One early organizer noted, "The

Captain of the Mission Police Station refused to give me a permit to hold the Day of the Dead procession. He called me a devil, saying, 'Over my dead body.' People thought we were a death cult. They made references to Charles Manson." Personal interview, June 3, 2002.

16. In my research of six years, I encountered only one nonprofit organization whose staff would not speak with me about its annual Day of the Dead celebrations and did not welcome media coverage. While such attitudes may exist among some organizations that prefer to limit their celebration to immediate constituents, the majority of California organizations sponsoring public Day of the Dead events/activities are receptive to media attention. Given the fact that early Day of the Dead events were held in a context in which racism and prejudice against Mexican Americans, as well as fears around Mexican immigration, had long been in operation in mainstream society, most organizers considered news coverage of the celebration a useful way to educate the public about Mexican culture.

17. As of June 21, 2005.

18. Marcelo M. Suarez-Orozco, "Mexican Immigration and the Latinization of the United States," *ReVista, Harvard Review of Latin America* (fall 2001): 40.

19. Manuel Castells, *The Rise of the Network Society* (Malden, MA: Blackwell Publishers, 1996).

20. Suarez-Orozco, "Mexican Immigration and the Latinization of the United States."

21. Cadaval, "The Taking of the Renwick," 181.

22. Charles Jackson, *Passing: The Vision of Death in America.* (Westport, CT: Greenwood Press, 1977).

23. Peter Metcalf and Richard Huntington, *Celebrations of Death: The Anthropology of Mortuary Ritual* (Cambridge: Cambridge University Press, 1991).

24. *60 Minutes II*, June 23, 2004, 8:00 PM, ABC.

25. Metcalf and Huntington, *Celebrations of Death.*

26. Stuart Ewen, *Captains of Consciousness: Advertising and the Social Roots of the Consumer Culture* (San Francisco: McGraw-Hill, 1976), 142.

27. William Leach, *Land of Desire: Merchants, Power, and the Rise of a New American Culture* (New York: Vintage, 1993); Thomas Frank, *The Conquest of Cool: Business, Culture, and Counterculture and the Rise of Hip Consumerism* (Chicago: University of Chicago Press, 1997).

28. Metcalf and Huntington, *Celebrations of Death*, 208.

29. Richard E. Meyer, *Cemeteries and Gravemarkers: Voices of American Culture* (Ann Arbor, UMI Research Press, 1989), 295.

30. Quoted in ibid., 298.

31. Personal interviews with senior citizens at the Anna DeFronzo Senior Center, Boston, Massachusetts, July 1999.

32. For a discussion of the symbolism of harvest imagery in pre-Christian death rituals, see Jack Santino's books *The Hallowed Eve: Dimensions of Culture in a Calendar Festival in Northern Ireland* (Lexington: University Press of Kentucky, 1998) and *Halloween and Other Festivals of Death and Life* (Knoxville: University of Tennessee Press, 1994).

33. So enormous was the outpouring of offerings to this unplanned commemoration that the Oklahoma City Memorial Museum was opened in April 2000 to house them all.

34. Morrison, "Mexico's Day of the Dead," 2.

35. Personal interview, San Francisco, June 5, 2003.

36. Personal correspondence, April 21, 2001.

37. Colorful and ornate tissue paper cutouts used to decorate altars and graves during Day of the Dead and used to decorate churches, schools, and homes during other important holidays in Mexico and Central America.

38. Personal interview with Claudio and Maribel DeLucca, owners of Back from Tombstone, San Diego, California, April 24, 2003.

39. Personal interview with Nancy Chárraga, owner of Casa Banampak, San Francisco, California, June 5, 2003.

40. Marigolds are known in Mexico as *cempasuchil* and in Central America as *flor de muerto* or *flor de cempa*.

41. Personal interview, April 17, 2001.

42. Personal interview, May 4, 2001.

43. Personal correspondence, April 21, 2001.

44. Personal interview, April 10, 2001.

45. Personal interview with Tere Romo, June 2, 2003.

46. Personal interview with Barbara Henry, Oakland Museum of California, June 3, 2003.

47. Personal interview, Oakland, California, June 3, 2003.

48. Personal conversations with parish priest and event participants, Oceanside, November 2, 2001.

49. Personal interview with David Avalos, San Marcos, California, July 29, 2003. The Del Mar Fair is a traditional all-American fair held each year in San Diego County.

50. Personal interview with David Avalos, Cal State, San Marcos, July 29, 2003.

51. Personal interview with Rene Yañez, San Francisco, June 3, 2003.

52. Personal interview, June 5, 2003, San Francisco, California.

53. Personal interview, June 6, 2003, San Francisco, California.

54. Personal interview with David Avalos, Cal State, San Marcos, June 3, 2003.

Afterword

STEWART M. HOOVER

Religion has always existed in relation to the marketplace. There is nothing new about this. What is new, and amply demonstrated by the contributions here, is the extent of religion's confrontation with the market and the evolving and expanding array of ways that the marketplace—particularly the media marketplace—is coming to determine and define the aspirations and possibilities for religion in late modernity. This confrontation has a history, and, as is shown here, this history is not one defined by sudden breaks and fissures so much as by gradual accommodation.

Conversations about religion and the marketplace usually begin with a set of received ideas about the seeming contradictions and potentials of further entanglement of the two. The preface and introduction detailed some of the most important of these, but there are a range of them. Some worry about the authenticity of religious practices or artifacts in the commodity marketplace. Others are concerned that religious ideas and symbols are necessarily diminished or limited by such mediation. As the introduction emphasized, many of these concerns are rooted in implicit hierarchies of cultural taste which see mediated and commodified representations as necessarily lesser forms. At the root of these reservations are worries about what might happen to religion, in both its universal and particular forms, when it submits itself to a media sphere—that religion might be permanently changed as a result.

This set of concerns constitutes the first of three general areas addressed by these chapters. Implicit in each of them is an address of the questions of authenticity, of the nature of religion as it adapts and is adapted to new forms and contexts of articulation. It is increasingly common among a subset of those who study contemporary religion to suggest that its commodification and mediation in late modernity should be seen as natural things—an evolutionary process that has actually been underway from the very beginning of human symbolization and human religiosity. But this is far from the commonplace view in wider discourse, and the contributions we have seen here try to implicitly or explicitly locate the ways in which particular phenomena might be undermining received ideas about what religion is, what the media are, what the marketplace is, and how they should be kept separate.

As these authors ably point out, they are not separate; they are coming together. But, it is no longer adequate to simply point out that religion is increasingly subject to the media marketplace. What is needed, and what scholarship can provide, is an explanation of two further areas ably addressed here: (1) precisely how these processes are taking place and (2) potential and realized implications. This book thus represents an important turn in analysis and interpretation. Instead of merely describing a set of trends, these chapters probe deeply into the question of how religion is expressed and represented in the marketplace, and the question of how religion—and the market—might be changing as a result.

The first of these is in some ways the least understood. The implicit moralism that reflexively criticizes marketplace religion tends to ignore the vital and fundamental question of how it, in fact, makes sense for religion, religious ideas, and religious actors to behave in the ways they do. As religion is reflexively practiced in late modernity, the received skepticism becomes a serious challenge to be overcome as the various social actors involved are for the most part *aware* that religion and the marketplace are not *supposed* to mix. So, how is it that they come to do so? The tacit assumption of the notion that authentic religion is somehow beyond the market and that the market might even be a profanation of religion resides as a subtext of much we see here.

And yet there is ample evidence in these pages of how religion moves *toward* the market. In the accounts we see here, *mediation* is a central factor. The religions and religious impulses described here are keenly connected with questions of communication. Whether in a mode of proclamation (religious broadcasts, Bible and tract publishing, etc.) or solidarity and group maintenance (identity-oriented programs, publications, and films), the phenomena we see here are fundamentally concerned with the conveyance of symbols and artifacts. The larger question of whether all of religion is essentially communication must await another day and another context, but what we see here is suggestive of that, too. A larger communicational context is also implied: the fact that, in the contemporary world, religious and spiritual ideas and resources must exist in the public, mediated context if they are to exist at all. And, as is demonstrated in these pages, there are sources and centers of production of religious and spiritual symbols and ideas that exist well *outside* the boundaries of formal religion.

The context of the media and the media marketplace is definitive today, and, as we know from the work here, religion has been adapting to this reality (with greater and lesser success) for some time now. The form and nature of these adaptations is fascinating and is—as I have said—one of the major contributions of this book. We see the issue of authenticity expressed in differing ways as presumably authentic forms and expressions confront the realities of the market. In some cases, the transition to the market has been easy and straightforward. Early Bible distributors, for example, responded to market incentives that have become commonly accepted. The market can come to be determinative, as we see here, because it provides economic benefits. Aligning with the market provides income to go on. The market also provides legitimacy. Religiously oriented publications or programs can be conferred a certain status by their presence in "secular" or "crossover" contexts. But there are also costs. Particularity can be lost as the market incentive is to universalize the message to achieve greater and greater market share. Thus the answer to the question—Does the market inevitably secularize?—seems to be the affirmative, but at the same time there are examples of particularisms that endure. Jewish identity and Evangelical identity are the goals of some very successful marketplace efforts.

In general, it seems that as religion moves into the media marketplace a number of incentives, factors, and implications come into play. There is a need to communicate, both with "insiders" and with "outsiders." The media marketplace is the most important context of publication and public discourse, providing both the channels and the means and tools through which communication takes place today. Marketplace logics begin to come into play as things progress: a given program, publication, or practice must begin to succeed both religiously/spiritually *and* commercially. Perhaps most importantly and interestingly, once particular religious expressions enter the media marketplace, they begin to encounter religious ideas and expressions from other sources and locations, including entirely secular ones, both domestic and international. And, as we see here, these secular sources have long been part of the mix as well.

As religious ideas and expressions move out, as it were, we can begin to see fascinating questions and implications in their encounter with the media marketplace and, through it, with wider contexts of cultural interaction and discourse. The whole question of *taste*, raised by a number of these scholars, is one example of this. Taste, as a social and cultural dimension of location, value, and identity, is a fundamental dimension of media expression and experience. To what extent are the tastes represented in these various contexts religious tastes—and thus rooted in particular questions of religious meaning and identity—and to what extent are they class tastes, and thus integrated into larger contexts and discourses? This dimension interacts, of course, with questions of secularization and universals. The answer, from these studies, is nuanced and complex, as it is clear that class taste and religious taste are, in fact, interrelated, sharing cultural, historical, and practical roots. It is possible, for example, for the elastic and fungible particularisms described here to accommodate themselves to secular tastes and values in order to further their reach, and it is clear that purely secular (and thus presumably more universal) sources easily traffic in the particularly religious. This elasticity is one of the wonders of the commodity marketplace (and, of course, of late modern cultural practice), and the resulting complexity is a challenge to scholarship.

The works in this book address these questions and others and help provide the basis for further and deeper consideration of the question of how religion comes to interact with the marketplace in the first place. But they also provide some intriguing insights into the third analytical area I laid out at the beginning—the whole question of the implications and outcomes of these trends. Authenticity is at the core of much that we see here, so the question of what happens to "authentic" religious symbols and expressions when they encounter the marketplace is a fundamental one. The picture here is complex and nuanced as well. The consensus view here would probably look at the issue from the perspective of what is *achieved* rather than what is *ascribed*. That is, rather than looking at what happens to pure and particular symbols and practices when they interact with the market, the authors here call our attention to outcomes. In what contexts are these symbols alive and meaningful? Has the ability of individuals and groups to know and use them in making sense of their worlds been enhanced or harmed by their interaction with the media marketplace? Is there more or less knowledge of these resources, symbols, and values than there might have been without mediation?

The question of secularization must also be addressed as an outcome. It is clear from all of these studies that the particular gives way to the universal when religion encounters the media marketplace. Even those practices that seek to secure a traditional identity in late modernity find themselves adapting to the nomenclatures of the day. Economic incentives drive the move toward wider and wider distribution, and the resulting competition with other sources and resources in the public marketplace may drive increasing participation (as the rational-choice theorists would have us believe). Further, exposure in the marketplace places particular and traditional religious sources in a context where religious symbolism from non-religious or secular sources is increasingly part of the mix. The contributions to this volume also raise an intriguing question—analogous to the question of taste I raised earlier—of whether it is, in fact, secularization or modernity that is confronted in the media sphere. If the former, it would mean that the whole legitimacy of religion is somehow under assault through its encounter with the media marketplace. If the latter, it might mean that the seeming challenge is not from secularism per se, but from modes of communication and expression that are the consequence of late modernity's integration of capitalism and the market.

There is some evidence available to address this question, and it is also present in these pages. Were secularism to somehow be undermining religion, we would expect to see consequent declines in religious practice. Instead, what we are seeing is a transformation of religious expression and practice. Religious interest remains high. Even in the most secularized settings of Europe and the West generally, religious and spiritual interest, seeking, and questing persist. Powerful evidence of this is available in these chapters. But the evidence also points to the fact that the nature of religion and spirituality is changing in large and important ways. In late modernity, religion and spirituality are increasingly found outside the formal contexts and in the wider cultural, media, and commodity marketplaces.

What happens to the particular and authentic—and to religions in general—as a result? Once again, the scholars represented here would seem to want us to look at what is *achieved*. Aspects of particularism may be lost, but wider exposure of religious symbols and ideas may be gained. The elasticity and fungibility of cultural practice in the media marketplace again is a factor. Engaged and reflexive audiences can and do work through the various means and modes of articulation to find meaningful resources and identities. In the media age and in late modernity, this is also a transnational phenomenon. These complex mediated articulations transcend time and space—physically and culturally—and bring religious diversity to global and local contexts.

There is one very clear implication for religion, however, and that is the challenge that all of this poses to traditional religious institutions and religious authorities. They are losing—and to a great degree already have lost—the ability to control their own symbols and the means by which those symbols are expressed and communicated. We see in these pages three sources of this challenge. First, there is the fact of the many accommodations even formally religious interests must make as they encounter the media marketplace. These chapters detail—and I've highlighted here—the question of the means and methods whereby particular symbols and expressions are communicated and, in the main, become more universal and less particular as a result. But the challenge goes beyond the various ways that this happens to the overall question of authority. Through these, formal religion is surrendering its authority over some its most important resources. In the main, though, the lure of the marketplace is great, and this process continues.

The second source of the challenge to religious authority here is more structural. Many of the phenomena we see here involve the activities of what sociologists call "para-church" organizations. That is, while the symbols are formal and traditional, they are entering media discourse through the efforts of organizations that exist alongside the formal institutions. To the extent they are successful, the interactions, expressions, and connections that result have the potential to move to the center of contemporary understandings of what these various religious and spiritual claims mean. These voices can, in time, become authorities of their own, existing along-side the traditional ones. Add to this that a range of such "para-institutional" organizations are now active globally, and the globalizing capacities of the media marketplace bring more and more of those resources to local and particular contexts. Traditional authorities thus face challenges not only from non-formal sources in their own contexts, but from such sources from other contexts.

Finally, as shown in these pages in various ways, there is the challenge from so-called secular sources of religious symbols and ideas. Internationally, the entertainment media increasingly convey religious and spiritual resources (though—as we see here—this is by no means a new phenomenon). Some of these even constitute direct challenges to particular religions and traditions. Others more generally provide resources that in their form and content provide attractive alternatives. As we've seen here, the marketplace is a factor precisely because it defines success in late modernity. Increasingly, then, religious institutions and religious authorities face the challenge of universalist, secular voices that wish to compete directly with them in a context which favors its own ways of making and articulating culture.

Whether or not these portents come to pass for institutional religion, the range of questions addressed in these pages provides a substantive review of important trends in the worlds of media and religion. They lead the way for scholarly research that looks in more depth at questions that have been raised but not yet fully addressed. From them, we not only learn that the marketplace is of increasing significance to religion and spirituality in late modernity, but also learn the ways that that is happening. They also point toward some fascinating and compelling questions regarding the ongoing form and shape of religion. Religion certainly exists outside the media and outside the marketplace and will continue to do so. However, in these pages we learn that it is being changed in important and permanent ways by its encounters there.

CONTRIBUTORS

PHYLLIS E. ALSDURF is an assistant professor of English at Bethel University in St. Paul. She completed her PhD in journalism and mass communication at the University of Minnesota. A practicing journalist, Alsdurf is author or coauthor of scholarly articles as well as a number of books for the general public, including *Battered into Submission: The Tragedy of Wife Abuse in the Christian Home* (1989).

KWABENA ASAMOAH-GYADU is a dean and lecturer at Trinity Theological Seminary in Ghana and a former fellow at the Center for the Study of World Religions at Harvard Divinity School. He completed his PhD in theological studies at the University of Birmingham, U.K. He is currently researching the appropriation of modern media technologies by Pentecostal/charismatic movements in West Africa.

ANNE L. BORDEN is a visiting assistant professor at Kennesaw State University in Tennessee. She completed her PhD in sociology at Emory University in Atlanta. Her research interests include the sociology of religion and the sociology of organizations.

LYNN SCHOFIELD CLARK is an assistant professor and the director of the Estlow International Center for Journalism and New Media at the University of Denver's School of Communication. She is author of *From Angels to Aliens: Teenagers, the Media, and the Supernatural* (2003), which received the National Communication Association's Best Scholarly Book Award of 2003 from the Ethnography Division. She is also coauthor of *Media, Home, and Family* (2004) and coeditor of *Practicing Religion in the Age of the Media* (2002) and is currently writing a book on young people, new media, and challenges to traditional sources of authority.

MARYELLEN DAVIS is an assistant professor of theology in Catholic Studies at Lewis University in Romeoville, Illinois. Her research interests include U.S. Catholic history, religion, and culture, and the philosophy of religion.

LEE GILMORE is a lecturer in religious studies, arts, and humanities at Chabot College in California. She completed her PhD at the Graduate Theological Union in Berkeley, California. She is coeditor with Mark Van Proyen of *AfterBurn: Reflections on the Burning Man Festival* (2005). Her research interests include the cultural and historical studies of religions.

STEWART M. HOOVER is a professor of media studies, professor adjoint of religious studies, and the director of the Center for Media, Religion, and Culture at the University of Colorado. He is author of *The Religion of the Media Age* (2006), *Religion in the News* (2001), and *Mass Media Religion* (1998) and coauthor of *Media, Home, and Family* (2004) as well as editor or coeditor of numerous other books.

REGINA M. MARCHI is an assistant professor of communication at Rutgers University. She completed her PhD in the Department of Communication at the University of California, San Diego. Her research interests include culture and politics, social movements and the media, and the commercialization of culture.

DAVID NORD is a professor in the School of Journalism at Indiana University. He is the author of *Faith in Reading: Religious Publishing and the Birth of Mass Media in America* (2004), *Communities of Journalism: A History of American Newspapers and Their Readers* (2001), and *Newspapers and New Politics: Midwestern Municipal Reform, 1890–1900* (1981). He is a three-time recipient of the Catherine Covert Award for the best article of the year in mass communication history (1984, 1990, and 2003).

ERICA SHEEN is a lecturer in the School of English at Sheffield University, U.K. She is author of *The Best in This Kind: Shakespeare and the Institution of Theatre* (forthcoming), coauthor of *The Cinema of David Lynch: American Dreams, Nightmare Visions* (2004), and coeditor of *Literature, Politics, and Law in Renaissance England* (2005) and *The Classic Novel: From Page to Screen* (2000).

GAURI VISWANATHAN is Class of 1933 Professor in the Humanities and the director of the Southern Asian Institute at Columbia University. She is author of *Outside the Fold: Conversion, Modernity, and Belief* (1998) and *Masks of Conquest: Literary Study and British Rule in India* (1998).

HILLARY WARREN is an assistant professor in communication at Otterbein College, Ohio. She is author of *There's Never Been a Show like Veggie Tales: Sacred Messages in a Secular Market* (2005). Her research considers how religious families maintain distinctive cultures within a mediated society. Her earlier work on religious media, child-rearing, and markets has been published in the *Journal of Media and Religion, Religion and Popular Culture: Studies on the Interaction of Worldviews* (2000) and in several encyclopedias. She has also served as head of the Religion and Media Interest Group of the Association for Education in Journalism and Mass Communication and as consulting editor on the *Encyclopedia of Religion, Communication and Media*.

FERRUH YILMAZ is a PhD candidate in communication at the University of California, San Diego. His research interests focus on popular discourses concerning ethnicity, migration, immigration policies, nationality, and culture.

Index